S
T
U
D
Y

T
E
X
T

CIM

PROFESSIONAL DIPLOMA IN MARKETING

PAPER 7

MARKETING COMMUNICATIONS

In this July 2008 edition

- A **user-friendly format** for easy navigation

- Regular **fast forward** summaries emphasising the key points in each chapter

- Recent examples of marketing practice

- Fully revised for recent exams and developments

- A full further reading list, key concept list and **index**

FOR EXAMS IN DECEMBER 2008 AND JUNE 2009

BPP
LEARNING MEDIA

Seventh edition July 2008

ISBN 9780 7517 4868 0 (previous edition 0 7517 4173 5)

British Library Cataloguing-in-Publication Data
A catalogue record for this book
is available from the British Library

Published by

BPP Learning Media
BPP House, Aldine Place
London W12 8AA

www.bpp.com/learningmedia

Printed in Great Britain

We are grateful to the Chartered Institute of Marketing
for permission to reproduce in this text the syllabus,
tutor's guidance notes and past examination
questions.

Your learning materials, published by BPP Learning
Media Ltd, are printed on paper sourced from
sustainable, managed forests.

Contents

The BPP Study Text

Aims of this Study Text

> To provide you with the knowledge and understanding, skills and application techniques that you need if you are to be successful in your exams

This Study Text has been written around the **Marketing Communications** syllabus.

- It is **comprehensive**. It covers the syllabus content. No more, no less.

- It is targeted to the **exam**. We have taken account of **the pilot paper**, guidance the examiner has given and the assessment methodology.

> To allow you to study in the way that best suits your learning style and the time you have available, by following your personal Study Plan (see below)

You may be studying at home on your own until the date of the exam, or you may be attending a full-time course. You may like to (and have time to) read every word, or you may prefer to (or only have time to) skim-read and devote the remainder of your time to question practice. Wherever you fall in the spectrum, you will find the BPP Study Text meets your needs in designing and following your personal Study Plan.

> To tie in with the other components of the BPP Effective Study Package to ensure you have the best possible chance of passing the exam

Recommended period of use	Elements of the BPP Effective Study Package
3-12 months before exam	**Study Text** Acquisition of knowledge, understanding, skills and applied techniques
1-6 months before exam	**Practice & Revision Kit (9/2008)** Tutorial questions and helpful checklists of the key points lead you into each area. There are then numerous Examination questions to try, graded by topic area, along with realistic suggested solutions prepared by marketing professionals in the light of the Examiner's Reports.
From three month before the exam until the last minute	**Passcards** Work through these short memorable notes which are focused on what is most likely to come up in the exam you will be sitting.

Settling down to study

By this stage in your career you may be a very experienced learner and taker of exams. But have you ever thought about *how* you learn? Let's have a quick look at the key elements required for effective learning. You can then identify your learning style and go on to design your own approach to how you are going to study this text – your personal Study Plan.

Key element of learning	Using the BPP Study Text
Motivation	You can rely on the comprehensiveness and technical quality of BPP. You've chosen the right Study Text – so you're in pole position to pass your exam!
Clear objectives and standards	Do you want to be a prizewinner or simply achieve a moderate pass? Decide.
Feedback	Follow through the examples in this text and do the Action Programme and the Quick Quizzes. Evaluate your efforts critically – how are you doing?
Study Plan	You need to be honest about your progress to yourself – don't be over-confident, but don't be negative either. Make your Study Plan (see below) and try to stick to it. Focus on the short-term objectives – completing two chapters a night, say – but beware of losing sight of your study objectives.
Practice	Use the Quick Quizzes and Chapter Roundups to refresh your memory regularly after you have completed your initial study of each chapter.

These introductory pages let you see exactly what you are up against. However you study, you should:

- **Read through the syllabus** – this will help you to identify areas you have already covered, perhaps at a lower level of detail, and areas that are totally new to you

- **Study the examination paper section**, where we show you the format of the exam (how many and what kind of questions and so on)

Key study steps

The following steps are, in our experience, the ideal way to study for professional exams. You can of course adapt it for your particular learning style (see below).

Tackle the chapters in the order you find them in the Study Text. Taking into account your individual learning style, follow these key study steps for each chapter.

Key study steps	Activity
Step 1 **Chapter Topic list**	Study the list. Each numbered topic denotes a **numbered section** in the chapter.
Step 2 **Introduction**	Read it through. It is designed to show you **why the topics in the chapter need to be studied** – how they lead on from previous topics, and how they lead into subsequent ones.
Step 3 **Explanations**	Proceed **methodically** through the chapter, reading each section thoroughly and making sure you understand.
Step 4 **Key Concepts**	**Key concepts** can often earn you **easy marks** if you state them clearly and correctly in an appropriate exam.
Step 5 **Exam Tips**	These give you a good idea of how the examiner tends to examine certain topics – pinpointing **easy marks** and highlighting **pitfalls**.
Step 6 **Note taking**	Take **brief notes** if you wish, avoiding the temptation to copy out too much.
Step 7 **Marketing at Work**	Study each one, and try if you can to add flesh to them from your **own experience** – they are designed to show how the topics you are studying come alive (and often come unstuck) in the **real world**. You can also update yourself on these companies by going on to the World Wide Web.
Step 8 **Action Programme**	Make a very good attempt at each one in each chapter. These are designed to put your **knowledge into practice** in much the same way as you will be required to do in the exam. Check the answer at the end of the chapter in the **Action Programme review**, and make sure you understand the reasons why yours may be different.
Step 9 **Chapter Roundup**	Check through it very carefully, to make sure you have grasped the **major points** it is highlighting
Step 10 **Quick Quiz**	When you are happy that you have covered the chapter, use the **Quick Quiz** to check your recall of the topics covered. The answers are in the paragraphs in the chapter that we refer you to.
Step 11 **Illustrative question(s)**	Either at this point, or later when you are thinking about revising, make a full attempt at the **illustrative questions**. You can find these at the end of the Study Text, along with the **Answers** so you can see how you did.

Developing your personal study plan

Preparing a study plan (and sticking closely to it) is one of the key elements in learning success.

First you need to be aware of your style of learning. There are four typical learning styles. Consider yourself in the light of the following descriptions. and work out which you fit most closely. You can then plan to follow the key study steps in the sequence suggested.

Learning styles	Characteristics	Sequence of key study steps in the BPP Study Text
Theorist	Seeks to understand principles before applying them in practice	1, 2, 3, 7, 4, 5, 8, 9, 10, 11 (6 continuous)
Reflector	Seeks to observe phenomena, thinks about them and then chooses to act	
Activist	Prefers to deal with practical, active problems; does not have much patience with theory	1, 2, 8 (read through), 7, 4, 5, 9, 3, 8 (full attempt), 10, 11 (6 continuous)
Pragmatist	Prefers to study only if a direct link to practical problems can be seen; not interested in theory for its own sake	8 (read through), 2, 4, 5, 7, 9, 1, 3, 8 (full attempt), 10, 11 (6 continuous)

Next you should complete the following checklist.

Am I motivated? (a) [   ]

Do I have an objective and a standard that I want to achieve? (b) [   ]

Am I a theorist, a reflector, an activist or a pragmatist? (c) [   ]

How much time do I have available per week, given: (d) [   ]

- The standard I have set myself

- The time I need to set aside later for work on the Practice and Revision Kit

- The other exam(s) I am sitting, and (of course)

- Practical matters such as work, travel, exercise, sleep and social life?

Now:

- Take the time you have available per week for this Study Text (d), and multiply it by the number of weeks available to give (e)   (e) [   ]

- Divide (e) by the number of chapters to give (f)   (f) [   ]

- Set about studying each chapter in the time represented by (f), following the key study steps in the order suggested by your particular learning style

This is your personal **study plan**.

Short of time?

Whatever your objectives, standards or style, you may find you simply do not have the time available to follow all the key study steps for each chapter, however you adapt them for your particular learning style. If this is the case, follow the skim study technique below (the icons in the Study Text will help you to do this).

Skim study technique

Study the chapters in the order you find them in the Study Text. For each chapter, follow the key study steps 1–2, and then skim-read through step 3. Jump to step 9, and then go back to steps 4–5. Follow through step 7, and prepare outline Answers to the Action Programme (step 8). Try the Quick Quiz (step 10), following up any items you can't answer, then do a plan for the illustrative question (step 11), comparing it against our answers. You should probably still follow step 6 (note-taking).

Moving on...

However you study, when you are ready to embark on the practice and revision phase of the BPP Effective Study Package, you should still refer back to this Study Text:

- As a source of **reference** (you should find the list of key concepts and the index particularly helpful for this)

- As a **refresher** (the Chapter Roundups and Quick Quizzes help you here)

A note on pronouns

On occasions in this Study Text, 'he' is used for 'he or she', 'him' for 'him or her' and so forth. While we try to avoid this practice it is sometimes necessary for reasons of style. No prejudice or stereotyping according to sex is intended or assumed.

Syllabus

Aims

The **Marketing Communications** module develops the skills and knowledge that enable marketers to manage marketing communications and brand support activities within organisations. It provides participants with an understanding of the concepts and practice of promotional activity at an operational level. Although reference is made to relevant strategic issues in order to provide a relevant context for learning, the focus is primarily on creating applied coordinated promotional activities, campaign development and the management of relationships with a variety of stakeholders, particularly customers and members of marketing channels.

Learning outcomes

Participants will be able to:

- Explain the role of marketing communications and advise how personal influences might be used to develop promotional effectiveness.

- Explain how the tools of the promotional mix can be coordinated in order to communicate effectively with customers and a range of stakeholders.

- Devise a basic media plan based on specific campaign requirements using both offline and online media.

- Develop marketing communication and brand support activities based on an understanding of the salient characteristics of the target audience.

- Explain the main elements, activities and linkages associated with the formulation and implementation of a marketing communications plan.

- Recommend a suitable marketing communications budget.

- Explain the importance of developing long term relationships with customers, channel members, agencies and other stakeholders and transfer such knowledge to the development of marketing communication activities.

- Suggest suitable methods to influence the relationships an organisation has with its customers, any marketing channel partners and other stakeholders, using marketing communications.

- Use the vocabulary of the marketing communications industry and be able to communicate effectively with other marketing practitioners.

Knowledge and skill requirements

Element 1: Understanding customer dynamics (20%)		Covered in chapter(s)
1.1	Explain how individuals can influence the effectiveness of marketing communications through word-of-mouth communications, as opinion leaders, as opinion formers or in multi-step models.	1
1.2	Describe the main concepts associated with buyer information processing and explain how marketing communications might be used to change or reinforce attitudes, alter perceptions and develop knowledge and understanding about a brand.	1
1.3	Describe the main concepts associated with the purchase decision process, including source credibility, involvement, perceived risk, and how they influence marketing communications.	1
1.4	Assess the principal differences between consumer and organisational markets and consider how they impact on marketing communications.	2
1.5	Summarise the importance for organisations of ethics and corporate responsibility, and their impact on brand reputation.	2

Element 2: Coordinated marketing communications (45%)		
2.1	Define and explain the roles of marketing communications to differentiate, remind or reassure, inform and persuade (DRIP).	1
2.2	Evaluate the effectiveness of each of the promotional tools using appropriate criteria such as cost, communication effectiveness, credibility, and control.	4
2.3	Explain the meaning of the terms above-, through- and below-the-line.	4
2.4	Explain the role of each of the promotional tools within a coordinated marketing communications mix.	4
2.5	Evaluate the effectiveness of co-ordinated campaigns.	8
2.6	Identify primary and secondary media (online and offline) and contrast their main characteristics.	6
2.7	Explain key media concepts (reach, frequency, duplication, GRPs, flighting) and describe the principal approaches used to measure media effectiveness.	6
2.8	Compare information and emotional based advertising messages and explain the concept of likeability.	6
2.9	Outline the key characteristics associated with push, pull and profile strategies.	5
2.10	Describe the main characteristics of key accounts and explain the stages and issues associated with key account management.	5, 11
2.11	Describe how co-ordinated marketing communications can be used to develop key account relationships.	5, 11
2.12	Explain how marketing communications can be used to launch new products, support brands, maintain market share, develop retention levels, encourage customer loyalty, and support internal marketing within the organisation.	5, 11

		Covered in chapter(s)
2.13	Draw and describe the main parts of a marketing communications planning framework and explain the principal linkages between the various elements.	3
2.14	Explain the main methods used to determine a marketing communications budget.	3
2.15	Discuss the main issues concerning the use of marketing communications in an international and global context, such as media availability, culture, religion, education and literacy.	7
2.16	Evaluate the effectiveness of marketing communications activities, tools, media and campaigns.	8

Element 3: Marketing channels (20%)		
3.1	Identify and explain how the promotional mix can be suitably configured for use in a range of marketing channels and business-to-business situations.	9
3.2	Explain, in terms of the impact on marketing communications within a relationship context, the structural concepts: interdependence, independence, disintermediation and reintermediation.	9
3.3	Explain the role of trust, commitment and satisfaction when developing marketing communication activities for use in the marketing channel and business-to-business contexts.	9
3.4	Identify the causes of conflict in trade channels and explain how marketing communications can be used to resolve such disagreements.	9
3.5	Explain how Internet- and digital-based technologies can be used to enhance marketing communications and relationships within channels and between business-to-business partners.	10

Element 4: Relationship management (15%)		
4.1	Compare the principles of transaction and relationship marketing.	11
4.2	Explain the characteristics of relationship marketing including the features, types, levels, development and implementation steps and communication issues.	11
4.3	Describe how marketing communications can be used to develop relationships with a range of stakeholders, based on an understanding of source credibility, trust and commitment.	11
4.4	Explain in broad terms the nature, structure, ownership and any key issues facing the marketing communications industry in any single country or region.	12
4.5	Describe how agencies manage their operations in order to meet client needs: pitching, briefing, structure, review, the role of account planners and managers, relationship management.	12
4.6	Explain how advertising agencies and marketing communication agencies use resources to meet the needs of clients with international and global requirements.	12
4.7	Describe in broad terms the regulatory and voluntary arrangements that are used to manage relationships between the public, customers, clients and agencies.	12

Related skills for marketers

There is only so much that a syllabus can include. The syllabus itself is designed to cover the knowledge and skills highlighted by research as core to professional marketers in organisations. However, marketing is performed in an organisational context so there are other broader business and organisational skills that marketing professionals should also posses. The 'key skills for marketers' are therefore an essential part of armoury of the 'complete marketer' in today's organisations. They have been identified from research carried out in organisations where marketers are working.

'Key skills for marketers' are areas of knowledge and competency common to business professionals. They fall outside the CIM's syllabus, providing underpinning knowledge and skills. As such they will be treated as systemic to all marketing activities, rather than subjects treated independently in their turn. While it is not intended that the key skills are formally taught as part of programmes, it is expected that tutors will encourage participants to demonstrate the application of relevant key skills through activities, assignments and discussions during learning.

Using ICT and the Internet

Planning and using different sources to search for and select information; explore, develop and exchange information and derive new information; and present information including text, numbers and images.

Using financial information and metrics

Planning and interpreting information from different sources; carrying out calculations; and presenting and justifying findings.

Presenting information

Contributing to discussions; making a presentation; reading and synthesising information and writing different types of document.

Improving own learning and performance

Agreeing targets and planning how these will be met; using plans to meet targets; and reviewing progress.

Working with others

Planning work and agreeing objectives, responsibilities and working arrangements; seeking to establish and maintain co-operative working relationships; and reviewing work and agreeing ways of future collaborative work.

Problem solving

Exploring problems, comparing different ways of solving them and selecting options; planning and implementing options; and applying agreed methods for checking problems have been solved.

Applying business law

Identifying, applying and checking compliance with relevant law when undertaking marketing activities.

Assessment

CIM will normally offer two forms of assessment for this module from which centres or participants may choose: written examination and continuous assessment. CIM may also recognise, or make joint awards for, modules at an equivalent level undertaken with other professional marketing bodies and educational institutions.

Marketing journals

In addition to reading core and supplementary textbooks participants will be expected to acquire a knowledge and understanding of developments in contemporary marketing theory, practice and issues. The most appropriate sources of information for this include specialist magazines eg *Marketing*, *Marketing Week*, *Campaign and Revolution*; dedicated CIM publications eg *Marketing Business*; and business magazines and newspapers eg *The Economist*, *Management Today*, *Business Week*, *The Financial Times*, and the business pages and supplements of the quality press. A flavour of developments in academic marketing can be derived from the key marketing journals including:

Admap

European Journal of Marketing

Journal of the Academy of Marketing Science

Journal of Consumer Behaviour: An International Research Review

Journal of Consumer Research

Marketing Intelligence and Planning

Journal of Marketing

Journal of Marketing Management

Websites

The Chartered Institute of Marketing

www.cim.co.uk	CIM website with information and access to learning support for participants.
www.cim.co.uk/learningzone	Direct access to information and support materials for all levels of CIM qualification
www.cim.co.uk/tutors	Access for Tutors
www.shapetheagenda.com	Quarterly agenda paper from CIM

Publications online

www.ft.com	Extensive research resources across all industry sectors, with links to more specialist reports. (Charges may apply)
www.thetimes.co.uk	One of the best online versions of a quality newspaper.
www.economist.com	Useful links, and easily-searched archives of articles from back issues of the magazine.
www.mad.co.uk	Marketing Week magazine online.
www.brandrepublic.com	Marketing magazine online.
www.westburn.co.uk	Journal of Marketing Management online, the official Journal of the Academy of Marketing and Marketing Review.
http://smr.mit.edu/smr/	Free abstracts from Sloan Management Review articles
www.hbsp.harvard.edu	Free abstracts from Harvard Business Review articles
www.ecommercetimes.com	Daily enews on the latest ebusiness developments
www.cim.co.uk/knowledgehub	3000 full text journals titles are available to members via the Knowledge Hub – includes the range of titles above - embargoes may apply.
www.cim.co.uk/cuttingedge	Weekly round up of marketing news (available to CIM members) plus list of awards and forthcoming marketing events.

Sources of useful information

www.1to1.com	The Peppers and Rogers One-to-One Marketing site which contains useful information about the tools and techniques of relationship marketing
www.balancetime.com	The Productivity Institute provides free articles, a time management email newsletter, and other resources to improve personal productivity
www.bbc.co.uk	The Learning Zone at BBC Education contains extensive educational resources, including the video, CD Rom, ability to watch TV programmes such as the News online, at your convenience, after they have been screened
www.busreslab.com	Useful specimen online questionnaires to measure customer satisfaction levels and tips on effective Internet marketing research
www.lifelonglearning.co.uk	Encourages and promotes Lifelong Learning through press releases, free articles, useful links and progress reports on the development of the University for Industry (UFI)
www.marketresearch.org.uk	The Market Research Society. Contains useful material on the nature of research, choosing an agency, ethical standards and codes of conduct for research practice
www.nielsen-netratings.com	Details the current levels of banner advertising activity, including the creative content of the ten most popular banners each week (within Top Rankings area)
www.open.ac.uk	Some good Open University videos available for a broad range of subjects
www.direct.gov.uk	Gateway to a wide range of UK government information

www.srg.co.uk	The Self Renewal Group – provides useful tips on managing your time, leading others, managing human resources, motivating others etc
www.statistics.gov.uk	Detailed information on a variety of consumer demographics from the Government Statistics Office
www.durlacher.com	The latest research on business use of the Internet, often with extensive free reports
www.cyberatlas.com	Regular updates on the latest Internet developments from a business perspective
http://ecommerce.vanderbilt.edu	eLab is a corporate sponsored research centre at the Owen Graduate School of Management, Vanderbilt University
www.kpmg.co.uk www.ey.com/uk	The major consultancy company websites contain useful research reports, often free of charge
www.pwcglobal.com	Pricewaterhouse Coopers
http://web.mit.edu	Massachusetts Institute of Technology site has extensive research resources
www.adassoc.org.uk	Advertising Association
www.dma.org.uk	The Direct Marketing Association
www.theidm.co.uk	Institute of Direct Marketing
www.export.org.uk	Institute of Export
www.bl.uk	The British Library, with one of the most extensive book collections in the world
www.managers.org.uk	Chartered Management Institute
www.cipd.co.uk	Chartered Institute of Personnel and Development
www.emerald-library.com	Article abstracts on a range of business topics (fees apply)
www.w3.org	An organisation responsible for defining worldwide standards for the Internet

Case studies

www.1800flowers.com	Flower and gift delivery service that allows customers to specify key dates when they request the firm to send them a reminder, together with an invitation to send a gift
www.amazon.co.uk	Classic example of how Internet technology can be harnessed to provide innovative customer service
www.broadvision.com	Broadvision specialises in customer 'personalisation' software. The site contains many useful case studies showing how communicating through the Internet allow you to find out more about your customers
www.doubleclick.net	DoubleClick offers advertisers the ability to target their advertisements on the web through sourcing of specific interest groups, ad display only at certain times of the day, or at particular geographic locations, or on certain types of hardware
www.facetime.com	Good example of a site that overcomes the impersonal nature of the Internet by allowing the establishment of real time links with a customer service representative
www.hotcoupons.com	Site visitors can key in their postcode to receive local promotions, and advertisers can post their offers on the site using a specially designed software package
www.superbrands.org	Access to case studies on international brands

The CIM's Magic Formula

In recent years the CIM have introduced a framework called the Magic Formula. The Magic Formula is a very useful tool to ensure that learners are tested to the correct level. They use this magic formula to help then write assignments and set exam questions and so it is highly relevant for you to understand it in order to make sure that you are writing to the correct level of depth and analysis.

Four parts have been used to build the Magic Formula and each has a weighting in terms of the marks available within the assessment marking scheme, these are

1. Format and Presentation = 10%
2. Concept = 30%
3. Application = 30%
4. Evaluation. = 30%

The percentage weightings vary for each level of CIM qualification. The Introductory Certificate for example has a higher weighting for concepts and the Professional Postgraduate level has the highest proportion of marks for evaluation. You should familiarise yourself with exam and assignment papers and try to work out how the marks have been divided according to the elements of the Magic Formula. The final section of this study text will break down an exam question with reference to the Magic Formula. You will also find some additional demonstrations of the Magic Formula on our website within the CIM learning materials pages. Go to www.bpp.com/learningmedia.

The Exam Paper

Format of the paper

		Number of marks
Section A:	Compulsory question, probably in more than one part	50
Section B:	Choice of two questions from four (25 marks each)	50
		100

Analysis of past papers

December 2007

Part A (compulsory question worth 50 marks)

1   Case study: a medium-sized premium ice cream producer seeking to differentiate its brand and develop a franchise network.

    (a)   Different uses of marketing communications to support national/local brands
    (b)   Relationship issues for franchisees, and how managed by communications
    (c)   How understanding buyer behaviour influences marketing communications
    (d)   How online and digital communications may be used

Part B (answer two questions, 25 marks each)

2   Large public service organisation (PSO): use of PR to counter negative publicity; use of rational/emotional messages in promotion; importance of source credibility.

3   Luxury watchmaker changing advertising agency: *report* on sequence of events and criteria for agency appointment; role/content of client briefs; tasks of account manager, creative team, media planner; ways of developing client/agency relationship.

4   Railway operating company: *report* on characteristics of broadcast/outdoor media, recommending one; use of interactive media; recommendations for media mix.

5   B2B financial services: *notes for meeting* on characteristics of marketing mix and tasks of marketing; design and use of website; role of key account management.

What the examiner said

Candidates still exhibit insufficiently broad and deep knowledge of concepts, theories and frameworks. 'This is not a pure training course: candidates need to understand some of the underlying principles.'

'Better marks were earned by candidates who wrote reasonably fluently, who did not rely on a succession of tables and bullet points, who demonstrated wide reading … and contextualised their answers within the scenario presented in the stem of the question. Their work often demonstrated a good depth of knowledge, an ability to interlink topics and relate them to the question or use examples as necessary.'

June 2007

Part A (compulsory question worth 50 marks)

1   Case study: a local council is undertaking a campaign to encourage people to claim the benefits to which they are entitled.

   (a)   Marketing communications tools and media to support the campaign
   (b)   How to change attitudes towards claiming benefits
   (c)   Use of marketing messages to encourage people to apply

Part B (answer two questions, 25 marks each)

2   Electronics manufacturing company: *report* to Production Department on personal selling v advertising effectiveness; personal selling messages to support organisation purchase decision process; three tasks of key account manager.

3   B2B financial services: influence of website on marketing communications; re-establishing trust with channel partners (by-passed by direct marketing); CSR issues influencing marketing communications.

4   Animal protection charity: *report* on radio and consumer magazines as media; recommendations for media mix; three ways of measuring the effectiveness of a media plan.

5   Manufacturer of industrial oils: *notes for meeting* on use of CRM systems; potential communications problems implementing CRM; characteristics of transactional v relationship marketing.

What the examiner said

The examiner affirms the increasing use of the 4Cs framework, and the decreasing use of grids and tables in favour of genuine comparative answers.

Candidates need to pay more attention to media and media concepts: 'Candidates must be able to understand, integrate and apply offline and online media in a variety of profit, not-for-profit and other situations.' Another poorly-understood topic was Corporate Social Responsibility (CSR): this is now a key area in which marketing communications has a role.

Key skills which require improvement included: contextualising answers; applying theory to practice; answering evaluatively (not just descriptively) where required; and using examples to illustrate points.

December 2006

Part A (compulsory question worth 50 marks)

1   Case study: a plant baker selling a range of products under the family name brand to grocery retailers.

   (a)   Developing 'source credibility' and 'likeability' in advertising messages
   (b)   Using marketing communication to generate call-to-action
   (c)   Theory of channel conflict and conflict management
   (d)   Recommendations to develop online marketing communications

Part B (answer two questions, 25 marks each)

2   Briefly document: sales promo v advertising; communication mix through product life cycle; trust in relationship with ad agency.

3   Leading soft drink brand: different communications mix for distributor and customers (why and how); use of ICT to enhance channel/B2B relationships.

4   Ferry operator: advantages/disadvantages of outdoor and print media; adopting relationship marketing; use of sponsorship.

5   Advantages/disadvantages of change from local to global communications strategy; impact of change on communications agency; issues in marketing communications industry.

What the examiner said

The examiner was pleased with the level of knowledge on specific issues, but disappointed by lack of 'depth' of knowledge, ability to link topics together, and therefore ability to 'follow through with justification, reason, recommendation or application'. In particular, students need to improve their skills in:

(a)   Contextualising answers and applying theory in practice
(b)   Answering evaluatively – not merely descriptively – where asked
(c)   Using examples to illustrate points and theory
(d)   Focusing on the specific requirements of each question and context.

Attention must also be given to answer structure and presentation

Candidates are advised to *number* sections/paragraphs in reports, to support a clearer structure: those who *plan* their answers do notably better than those who don't. Many students lose marks giving brief notes, bullet point list or grids to answer *discursive* questions, which require explanation and elaboration of points (comparisons, evaluations, justified recommendations and so on).

June 2006

Part A (compulsory question worth 50 marks)

1   Case study: Procter & Gamble, global manufacturer and marketer of a wide range of consumer products, is about to launch a new shampoo brand.

(a)   Communications mix to support brand launch.
(b)   Methods to measure effectiveness of mix/tools recommended.
(c)   Key aspects of B2B marketing communications; impact on P&G.
(d)   Why adopt corporate social responsibility?

Part B (answer two questions, 25 marks each)

2   Notes for meeting with chocolate brand manager: characteristics of rational/emotional messages; methods of evaluating campaign effectiveness; use of word-of-mouth in offline OR online campaigns.

3   Advertising agency report: advertising v direct marketing and personal selling; methods of agency remuneration; structure/issues of marketing communications industry.

4   City council litter awareness campaign: advantages/disadvantages of cinema and print media; reach, frequency, OTS; media mix recommendations.

5   Notes for meeting: B2B MC mix; use of new/digital media to assist personal selling; use of key account management to assist customer relationship development.

What the examiner said

Candidates need to develop:

(a)   The depth of answers, using relevant detail, examples and discursive elements requested (comparison/contrast, explanation, etc).

(b)   Depth of knowledge about the strengths and limitations of different media – both digital and traditional.

(c)   The ability 'to understand, integrate and apply offline and online media in a variety of profit, not-for-profit and other situations'.

(d)   Better examination technique: contextualisation; time management; answer planning, structure and layout.

December 2005

Part A (compulsory question worth 50 marks)

1   The case study concerned a company that managed a network of dealers as well as its own sales force.

      (a)   Relationship marketing in the channel
      (b)   Channel conflict
      (c)   CRM systems
      (d)   Online marketing communications

Part B (answer two questions, 25 marks each)

2   PR and direct marketing, source credibility; rational and emotional messages

3   Developing the marketing communications budget, agency remuneration; effectiveness of advertising campaigns

4   International marketing communications; car manufacturers; corporate social responsibility

5   New media and traditional broadcast media; measuring off-line media effectiveness.

June 2005

Part A (compulsory question worth 50 marks)

1   The case study was about a furniture company seeking to communicate its product in an increasingly competitive market, and to reverse its downmarket image.

      (a)   Appointment of new marketing communication agency
      (b)   Client brief and key roles
      (c)   Above the line activities
      (d)   The client/agency relationship

Part B (answer two questions, 25 marks each)

2   CRM systems; new media and digital technologies

3   Configuring the promotional mix; marketing channel relationships

4   Promotional tools; B2B sales promotions

5   Broadcast and outdoor media; media costs and planning

December 2004

Part A (compulsory question worth 50 marks)

1 The case study scenario revolves around a charity that supports people suffering from life threatening health problems. A report is required.

  (a) The role of marketing communications in the organisation. The limitations of trying to stimulate demand at this organisation.

  (b) The significance of ethics and corporate responsibility when developing a brand.

  (c) Ways in which marketing communications might be used to influence levels of trust, commitment and satisfaction.

  (d) Development of relationships through attitudes and credibility.

Part B (answer two questions, 25 marks each)

2 A knitwear company intends to move towards a direct marketing strategy using the internet

  (a) Comparison between the two distribution channel concepts of interdependence and dependence.

  (b) Impact on marketing communications mix.

  (c) Impact on end user customers.

3 (a) Conflicts in marketing channels and the use of communications in conflict resolution.
  (b) Key account management.
  (c) CRM systems. Transactions marketing.

4 (a) Personal selling versus advertising.
  (b) The purchasing decision process; messages delivered through personal selling.
  (c) Sales force tasks.

5 (a) Ways of developing a communications budget
  (b) Methods of rewarding an agency
  (c) Regulatory and voluntary arrangements vis-à-vis ethics and corporate responsibility.

June 2004

Part A (compulsory question worth 50 marks)

A vehicle recovery service is facing increasing competition and environmental changes. Marketing communications messengers are based on branding. There is a strong new entrant.

1 (a) Types of message
  (b) Marrcomms and attitude change
  (c) Magazines
  (d) Direct mail

Part B (two questions from four, 25 marks each)

2 Business-to-business communications: new technologies and key accounts

3 Switch from above-to below-the-line communication

4 Public relations and stakeholder conflict

5 Move from local to global communications structure

December 2003

Part A (compulsory question worth 50 marks)

1   Profile of the marketing communications strategy of L'Oréal, one of the world's leading cosmetics and fragrances companies.

    (a)   Evaluate the content and approach of the brand support messages
    (b)   Use of source credibility
    (c)   Influence of international marketing strategy on marketing communications
    (d)   Influencing relationships with intermediaries

Part B (answer two questions, 25 marks each)

2   Objectives of promotional activity (brand development versus encouragement of purchase)

    (a)   Direct marketing and advertising
    (b)   *Evaluating* the promotional mix
    (c)   *Word-of-mouth* communications

3   (a)   Outdoor and print media
    (b)   Sales promotion techniques
    (c)   Relationships marketing vs transition marketing

4   (a)   Issues facing the marketing communications industry
    (b)   Regulatory arrangements
    (c)   *Ethics* and corporate responsibility

5   Appointing an advertising agency and *evaluating* advertising effectiveness.

Pilot Paper

Part A (compulsory question worth 50 marks)

1   Established company making medium quality kitchen furniture, seeking to modernise and attract new customers.

    (a)   Evaluate current and future roles of marketing communications for the company
    (b)   importance of perceived risk, and how marketing communications could overcome it
    (c)   Use of Internet and digital based technologies
    (d)   Recommend and justify a suitable co-ordinated marketing communications mix

Part B (answer two questions, 25 marks each)

2   Promotional tools, sales promotion and public relations

3   Media concepts, opportunities and choice

4   Marketing channels: independence/interdependence, conflicts, international issues

5   Advertising agency: account management, client brief, relationship marketing

The Pilot Paper and BPP's suggested answer plans are reproduced at the back of this Study Text.

Guide to the assignment route

- Aims and objectives of this guide
- Introduction
- Assignment route, structure and process
- Preparing for assignments: general guide
- Presentation
- Time management
- Tips for writing assignments
- Writing reports
- Resources to support assignment-based assessment

Aims and objectives of this guide to the assignment route

- To understand the scope and structure of the route process
- To consider the benefits of learning through the assignment route
- To assist students in preparation of their assignments
- To consider the range of communication options available to students
- To look at the range of potential assignment areas that assignments may challenge
- To examine the purpose and benefits of reflective practice
- To assist with time-management within the assignment process

Introduction

At time of writing, there are over 80 CIM Approved Study Centres that offer the assignment route option as an alternative to examinations. This change in direction and flexibility in assessment was externally driven by industry, students and tutors alike, all of whom wanted a test of practical skills as well as a knowledge-based approach to learning.

At Stage 1, all modules are available via this assignment route. The assignment route is however optional, and examinations are still available. This will of course depend upon the nature of delivery within your chosen Study Centre.

Clearly, all of the Stage 1 subject areas lend themselves to assignment-based learning, due to their practical nature. The assignments that you will undertake provide you with an opportunity to be **creative in approach and in presentation.** They enable you to give a true demonstration of your marketing ability in a way that perhaps might be inhibited in a traditional examination situation.

The assignment route offers you considerable scope to produce work that provides existing and future **employers** with **evidence** of your **ability.** It offers you a **portfolio** of evidence which demonstrates your abilities and your willingness to develop continually your knowledge and skills. It will also, ultimately, help you frame your continuing professional development in the future.

It does not matter what type of organisation you are from, large or small, as you will find substantial benefit in this approach to learning. In some cases, students have made their own organisation central to their assessment and produced work to support their organisation's activities, resulting in subsequent recognition and promotion: a success story for this approach.

So, using your own organisation can be beneficial (especially if your employer sponsors you). However, it is equally valid to use a different organisation, as long as you are familiar enough with it to base your assignments on it. This is particularly useful if you are between jobs, taking time out, returning to employment or studying at university or college.

To take the assignment route option, you are required to register with a CIM Accredited Study Centre (ie a college, university, or distance learning provider). **Currently you would be unable to take the assignment route option as an independent learner.** If in doubt you should contact the CIM Education Division, the awarding body, who will provide you with a list of local Accredited Centres offering the Assignment Route.

Structure and process

The **assignments** that you will undertake during your studies are normally set **by CIM centrally** and not usually by the study centre. All assignments are validated to ensure a structured, consistent, approach. This standardised approach to assessment enables external organisations to interpret the results on a consistent basis.

Each module at Stage 1 has one assignment, with four separate elements within it. This is broken down as follows.

- The **Core Section** is compulsory and worth 40% of your total mark.

- The **Elective Section** has four options, from which you must complete **two**. Each of these options is worth 25% of your total mark. Please note here that it is likely that in some Study Centres the option may be chosen for you. This is common practice and is done in order to maximise resources and support provided to students.

- The **Reflective Statement** is also compulsory. It is worth 10%. It should reflect what you feel about your learning experience during the module and how that learning has helped you in your career both now and in the future.

The purpose of each assignment is to enable you to demonstrate your ability to research, analyse and problem-solve in a range of different situations. You will be expected to approach your assignment work from a professional marketer's perspective, addressing the assignment brief directly, and undertaking the tasks required. Each assignment will relate directly to the syllabus module and will be applied against the content of the syllabus.

All of the assignments clearly indicate the links with the syllabus and the assignment weighting (ie the contribution each assignment makes to your overall marks).

Once your assignments have been completed, they will be marked by your accredited centre, and then **moderated** by a CIM External Moderator. When all the assignments have been marked, they are sent to CIM for further moderation. After this, all marks are forwarded to you by CIM (not your centre) in the form of an examination result. Your **centre** will be able to you provide you with some written feedback on overall performance, but **will not** provide you with any detailed mark breakdown.

Preparing for assignments: general guide

The whole purpose of this guide is to assist you in presenting your assessment professionally, both in terms of presentation skills and overall content. In many of the assignments, marks are awarded for presentation and coherence. It might therefore be helpful to consider how best to present your assignment. Here you should consider issues of detail, protocol and the range of communications that could be called upon within the assignment.

Presentation of the assignment

You should always ensure that you prepare two copies of your assignment, keeping a soft copy on disc. On occasions assignments go missing, or second copies are required by CIM.

- Each assignment should be clearly marked up with your name, your study centre, your CIM Student registration number and ultimately at the end of the assignment a word count. The assignment should also be word-processed.

- The assignment presentation format should directly meet the requirements of the assignment brief, (ie reports and presentations are the most called for communication formats). You **must** ensure that you assignment does not appear to be an extended essay. If it does, you will lose marks.

- The word limit will be included in the assignment brief. These are specified by CIM and must be adhered to.

- Appendices should clearly link to the assignment and can be attached as supporting documentation at the end of the report. However failure to reference them by number (eg Appendix 1) within the report and also marked up on the Appendix itself will lose you marks. Only use an Appendix if it is essential and clearly adds value to the overall assignment. The Appendix is not a waste bin for all the materials you have come across in your research, or a way of making your assignment seem somewhat heavier and more impressive than it is.

Time management for assignments

One of the biggest challenges we all seem to face day-to-day is that of managing time. When studying, that challenge seems to grow increasingly difficult, requiring a balance between work, home, family, social life and study life. It is therefore of pivotal importance to your own success for you to plan wisely the limited amount of time you have available.

Step 1   **Find out how much time you have**

Ensure that you are fully aware of how long your module lasts, and the final deadline. If you are studying a module from September to December, it is likely that you will have only 10-12 weeks in which to complete your assignments. This means that you will be preparing assignment work continuously throughout the course.

Step 2   **Plan your time**

Essentially you need to **work backwards** from the final deadline, submission date, and schedule your work around the possible time lines. Clearly if you have only 10-12 weeks available to complete three assignments, you will need to allocate a block of hours in the final stages of the module to ensure that all of your assignments are in on time. This will be critical as all assignments will be sent to CIM by a set day. Late submissions will not be accepted and no extensions will be awarded. Students who do not submit will be treated as a 'no show' and will have to resubmit for the next period and undertake an alternative assignment.

Step 3   **Set priorities**

You should set priorities on a daily and weekly basis (not just for study, but for your life). There is no doubt that this mode of study needs commitment (and some sacrifices in the short term). When your achievements are recognised by colleagues, peers, friends and family, it will all feel worthwhile.

Step 4   **Analyse activities and allocate time to them**

Consider the **range** of activities that you will need to undertake in order to complete the assignment and the **time** each might take. Remember, too, there will be a delay in asking for information and receiving it.

Preparing terms of reference for the assignment, to include the following.

1   A short title

2   A brief outline of the assignment purpose and outcome

3   Methodology – what methods you intend to use to carry out the required tasks

4   Indication of any difficulties that have arisen in the duration of the assignment

5   Time schedule

6   Confidentiality – if the assignment includes confidential information ensure that this is clearly marked up and indicated on the assignment

7   Literature and desk research undertaken

This should be achieved in one side of A4 paper.

- A literature search in order to undertake the necessary background reading and underpinning information that might support your assignment

- Writing letters and memos asking for information either internally or externally

- Designing questionnaires

- Undertaking surveys

- Analysis of data from questionnaires

- Secondary data search

- Preparation of first draft report

Always build in time to spare, to deal with the unexpected. This may reduce the pressure that you are faced with in meeting significant deadlines.

Warning!

The same principles apply to a student with 30 weeks to do the work. However, a word of warning is needed. Do not fall into the trap of leaving all of your work to the last minute. If you miss out important information or fail to reflect upon your work adequately or successfully you will be penalised for both. Therefore, time management is important whatever the duration of the course.

Tips for writing assignments

Everybody has a personal style, flair and tone when it comes to writing. However, no matter what your approach, you must ensure your assignment meets the **requirements of the brief** and so is comprehensible, coherent and cohesive in approach.

Think of preparing an assignment as preparing for an examination. Ultimately, the work you are undertaking results in an examination grade. Successful achievement of all four modules in a level results in a qualification.

There are a number of positive steps that you can undertake in order to ensure that you make the best of your assignment presentation in order to maximise the marks available.

Step 1   Work to the brief

Ensure that you identify exactly what the assignment asks you to do.

- If it asks you to be a marketing manager, then immediately assume that role.

- If it asks you to prepare a report, then present a report, not an essay or a letter.

- Furthermore, if it asks for 2,500 words, then do not present 1,000 or 4,000 unless it is clearly justified, agreed with your tutor and a valid piece of work.

Identify whether the report should be **formal or informal**; who it should be **addressed to**; its **overall purpose** and its **potential use** and outcome. Understanding this will ensure that your assignment meets fully the requirements of the brief and addresses the key issues included within it.

Step 2   **Addressing the tasks**

It is of pivotal importance that you address **each** of the tasks within the assignment. **Many students fail to do this** and often overlook one of the tasks or indeed part of the tasks.

Many of the assignments will have two or three tasks, some will have even more. You should establish quite early on, which of the tasks:

- Require you to collect information
- Provides you with the framework of the assignment, i.e. the communication method.

Possible tasks will include the following.

- *Compare and contrast.* Take two different organisations and compare them side by side and consider the differences ie the **contrasts** between the two.

- *Carry out primary or secondary research.* Collect information to support your assignment and your subsequent decisions

- *Prepare a plan.* Some assignments will ask you to prepare a plan for an event or for a marketing activity – if so provide a step-by-step approach, a rationale, a time-line, make sure it is measurable and achievable. Make sure your actions are very specific and clearly explained. (Make sure your plan is SMART.)

- *Analyse a situation.* This will require you to collect information, consider its content and present an overall understanding of the situation as it exists. This might include looking at internal and external factors and how the current situation evolved.

- *Make recommendations.* The more advanced your get in your studies, the more likely it is that you will be required to make recommendations. Firstly **considering and evaluating your options** and then making justifiable **recommendations**, based on them.

- *Justify decisions.* You may be required to justify your decision or recommendations. This will require you to explain fully how you have arrived at as a result and to show why, supported by relevant information. In other words, you should not make decisions in a vacuum; as a marketer your decisions should always be informed by context.

- *Prepare a presentation.* This speaks for itself. If you are required to prepare a presentation, ensure that you do so, preparing clearly defined PowerPoint or overhead slides that are not too crowded and that clearly express the points you are required to make.

- *Evaluate performance.* It is very likely that you will be asked to evaluate a campaign, a plan or even an event. You will therefore need to consider its strengths and weaknesses, why it succeeded or failed, the issues that have affected it, what can you learn from it and, importantly, how can you improve performance or sustain it in the future.

All of these points are likely requests included within a task. Ensure that you identify them clearly and address them as required.

Step 3   **Information search**

Many students fail to realise the importance of collecting information to **support** and **underpin** their assignment work. However, it is vital that you demonstrate to your centre and to the CIM your ability to **establish information needs**, obtain **relevant information** and **utilise it sensibly** in order to arrive at appropriate decisions.

You should establish the nature of the information required, follow up possible sources, time involved in obtaining the information, gaps in information and the need for information.

Consider these factors very carefully. CIM are very keen that students are **seen** to collect information, **expand** their mind and consider the **breadth** and **depth** of the situation. In your *Personal Development Portfolio*, you have the opportunity to complete a **Resource Log**, to illustrate how you have expanded your knowledge to aid your personal development. You can record your additional reading and research in that log, and show how it has helped you with your portfolio and assignment work.

Step 4   **Develop an assignment plan**

Your **assignment** needs to be structured and coherent, addressing the brief and presenting the facts as required by the tasks. The only way you can successfully achieve this is by **planning the structure** of your assignment in advance.

Earlier on in this unit, we looked at identifying your tasks and, working backwards from the release date, in order to manage time successfully. The structure and coherence of your assignment needs to be planned with similar signs.

In planning out the assignment, you should plan to include **all the relevant information as requested** and also you should plan for the use of models, diagrams and appendices where necessary.

Your plan should cover your:

- Introduction
- Content
- Main body of the assignment
- Summary
- Conclusions and recommendations where appropriate

Step 5   **Prepare draft assignment**

It is good practice to always produce a **first draft** of a report. You should use it to ensure that you have met the aims and objectives, assignment brief and tasks related to the actual assignment. A draft document provides you with scope for improvements, and enables you to check for accuracy, spelling, punctuation and use of English.

Step 6   **Prepare final document**

In the section headed 'Presentation of the Assignment' in this unit, there are a number of components that should always be in place at the beginning of the assignment documentation, including **labelling** of the assignment, **word counts**, **appendices** numbering and presentation method. Ensure that you **adhere to the guidelines presented**, or alternatively those suggested by your Study Centre.

Writing reports

Students often ask 'what do they mean by a report?' or 'what should the report format include?'.

There are a number of approaches to reports, formal or informal: some report formats are company specific and designed for internal use, rather than external reporting.

For continuous assessment process, you should stay with traditional formats.

Below is a suggested layout of a Management Report Document that might assist you when presenting your assignments.

- *A Title page* includes the title of the report, the author of the report and the receiver of the report

- *Acknowledgements* – this should highlight any help, support, or external information received and any extraordinary co-operation of individuals or organisations

- *Contents page* provides a clearly structured pathway of the contents of the report – page by page.

- *Executive summary* – a brief insight into purpose, nature and outcome of the report, in order that the outcome of the report can be quickly established

- *Main body of the report divided into sections, which are clearly labelled.* Suggested labelling would be on a numbered basis eg:
    - 1.0   Introduction
    - 1.1   Situation Analysis
    - 1.1.1 External Analysis
    - 1.1.2 Internal Analysis

- *Conclusions* – draw the report to a conclusion, highlighting key points of importance, that will impact upon any recommendations that might be made

- *Recommendations* – clearly outline potential options and then recommendations. Where appropriate justify recommendations in order to substantiate your decision

- *Appendices* – ensure that you only use appendices that add value to the report. Ensure that they are numbered and referenced on a numbered basis within the text. If you are not going to reference it within the text, then it should not be there

- *Bibliography* – while in a business environment a bibliography might not be necessary, for an **assignment-based report it is vital**. It provides an indication of the level of research, reading and collecting of relevant information that has taken place in order to fulfil the requirements of the assignment task. Where possible, and where relevant, you could provide academic references within the text, which should of course then provide the basis of your bibliography. References should realistically be listed alphabetically and in the following sequence
    - Author's name and edition of the text
    - Date of publication
    - Title and sub-title (where relevant)
    - Edition 1st, 2nd etc
    - Place of publication
    - Publisher
    - Series and individual volume number where appropriate.

Resources to support assignment-based assessment

The aim of this guidance is to present you with a range of questions and issues that you should consider, based upon the assignment themes. The detail to support the questions can be found within your BPP Study Text and the 'Core Reading' recommended by CIM.

Additionally you will find useful support information within the CIM Student website www.cim.co.uk -: www.cimvirtualinstitute.com, where you can access a wide range of marketing information and case studies. You can also build your own workspace within the website so that you can quickly and easily access information specific to your professional study requirements. Other websites you might find useful for some of your assignment work include www.wnim.com – (What's New in Marketing) and also www.connectedinmarketing.com – another CIM website.

Other websites include:

www.mad.com	– Marketing Week
www.ft.com	– Financial Times
www.thetimes.com	– The Times newspaper
www.theeconomist.com	– The Economist magazine
www.marketing.haynet.com	– Marketing magazine
www.ecommercetimes.com	– Daily news on e-business developments
www.open.gov.uk	– Gateway to a wide range of UK government information
www.adassoc.org.uk	– The Advertising Association
www.marketresearch.org.uk	– The Marketing Research Society
www.amazon.com	– Online Book Shop
www.1800flowers.com	– Flower and delivery gift service
www.childreninneed.com	– Charitable organisation
www.comicrelief.com	– Charitable organisation
www.samaritans.org.uk	– Charitable organisation

Part A
Understanding customer dynamics

Influencing customer decisions

Syllabus content – knowledge and skill requirements

- How individuals can influence the effectiveness of marketing communications through word of mouth communications, as opinion leaders, as opinion formers or in multi-step models (1.1)
- The main concepts associated with buyer information processing and how marketing communications might be used to change or reinforce attitudes, alter perceptions and develop knowledge and understanding about a brand (1.2)
- The main concepts associated with the purchase decision process, including source credibility, involvement, perceived risk, and how they influence marketing communications (1.3)
- The roles of marketing communications to differentiate, remind or reassure, inform and persuade (DRIP) (2.1)

Introduction

Most organisations, whether they operate in the private, public, not-for-profit or other sectors, all need to communicate with their customers. **Communications through promotional activities is an integral and essential part of the marketing mix**, part of an organisation's planned drive to satisfy its customers' needs.

Key concept

Marketing communications might therefore be understood as all forms of communication between an organisation and its customers and potential customers.

Action Programme 1

Make a list of the range of audiences that all organisations, large and small, need to communicate with in order to survive, grow and meet their various goals.

Marketing communications will involve **all communications** by an organisation with its **environment** and the various **stakeholders** who might influence it, **not just its customers**.

Marketing communications is one of the elements of the marketing mix, and is responsible for the communication of the marketing offer to the target market. It is the task of a **planned** and **co-ordinated** set of communication activities to communicate effectively with each of the target customer groups, wherever in the world they may be.

We must continually remind ourselves that we are not studying marketing communications strategies in isolation from the rest of the business or organisation. If they are to be successful, **marketing communications strategies must be co-ordinated with the overall planning process**. This is a very broad perspective and before we go any further we need to briefly consider the tools and methods of marketing communications.

The following diagram sets out the variety of promotional methods available to communicate with customers. These methods can be considered as a set of five, the **Marketing Communications Mix**.

These tools represent the deployment of **deliberate and intentional methods** calculated to bring about a favourable response in the customer's behaviour. The diagram represents the most obvious communication methods, though other parts of the marketing mix, including the product itself, pricing, policy and distribution channels, will also have decisive effects.

Choosing the correct tools for a particular promotions task is not an easy one. The process is becoming **more scientific** because of access to consumer and media databases. Matching consumer characteristics with media characteristics can be rapidly carried out and promotional budgets evaluated for different mixes. In the final analysis, however, the expertise of the marketing manager is vital.

Marketing communications can be considered in the context of the **exchange process**. Exchanges, or transactions, are central to much modern thinking in economics: all activity undertaken by individuals or organisations can be seen as a series of exchanges.

Key concept

> An **exchange** requires the participation of two or more parties, each offering something of value to the other. They enter freely into the exchange process. The relevance to marketing is obvious: buy something and you will have experienced an exchange.

Communication is central to the exchange process. The DRIP model is often used to explain this point.

(a) **Differentiates** between competing offerings, helping consumers to decide which exchanges to make, helping to prevent monopolies from developing and encouraging lower prices.

(b) **Reminds** customers of the benefits of past transactions and so convinces them that they should enter into a similar exchange.

(c) **Informs** and makes potential customers aware of an organisation's offering.

(d) **Persuades** current and potential customers of the desirability of entering into an exchange relationship.

Action Programme 2

Think of a product/service or brand and consider how the DRIP factors can be applied.

Communication can itself be the object of an exchange. In return for the consumer's interest and loyalty, communication is provided:

- As **entertainment**
- As **information**
- As a **vehicle** for transferring values and culture to different groups

Marketing at Work

'Ethical advertising' by, say, the Government's anti drink/drive campaigns over the Christmas period, can help to raise awareness of important social, political and environmental issues.

Cadbury's Roses' 'Thank you very much' campaign instilled values as well as selling the product.

An exam question asked under a previous syllabus asked for a discussion of the comment 'Young people are threatened by the evil use of advertising techniques that stimulate the natural inclination to avoid hard work by promising the immediate satisfaction of every desire' (Pope John Paul II). Arguments can be put forward that advertising is manipulative, that it encourages consumerism and wastes resources, that it creates an unfair barrier to entry and so hinders competition. Some people find it irritating and intrusive: they would say it spoils other forms of entertainment or that it trivialises serious issues.

The main aim of this chapter is to develop an understanding of the **various elements that influence the way individuals use information and make purchase decisions**. From this understanding it is possible to see how marketing communications can impact on customers and help them in the various decisions they need to make. We consider **organisational markets** in the following chapter.

1 Understanding how communication works

Marketing communications are used to **inform**, **remind**, **persuade** and **differentiate** an organisation and its products/services from those of its competitors.

An **understanding** of the way communication works is an important part of building skills and knowledge about marketing communications.

1.1 The communication process

P Kotler (1991) has put forward a simple 'radio signal' **model of the communication process** to provide a framework: Figure 1.1.

Figure 1.1: The radio signal or communication cycle model

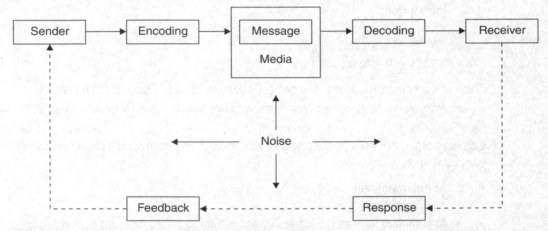

The elements of the model can be classified in the following way.

Element	Comment
Parties	
• Sender	Sends the message to the other party
• Receiver	Receives message
Communication tools	
• Message	Content of communication
• Media	Communication channels

Element	Comment
Communication functions	
• Encoding	Meaning is given in symbolic form (words etc) by sender
• Decoding	Receiver translates and interprets message
• Response	Receiver reacts to message
• Feedback	Part of receiver's response is communicated back to sender

FAST FORWARD

The **one-step** model of communication depicts communication as a linear process – but feedback and interaction are important parts of practical communications.

This model underscores many of the factors in effective communication. Senders need to understand the **motivation of their audiences** in order to structure messages that the audience will interpret correctly through the decoding process. The sender also has to ascertain the most **effective communication media** through which to reach the audience and must also establish effective **feedback channels** in order to find out the receiver's response to the message.

Action Programme 3

(a) Find some advertisements – watch TV for half an hour or flick through a newspaper or a magazine.

(b) Analyse each advertisement in the above terms. Consider who are the parties involved (*you* may not be the intended receiver), what communication tools are used, what sort of codes are used and how they will be decoded (for example by people in different income brackets or with different tastes) and what form feedback will take.

This communication process is **not carried out in isolation**. There are many senders competing for the attention of the receiver. As a result there is considerable noise in the environment and an individual may be bombarded by several hundred commercial messages each day.

Key concept

Noise is those factors that prevent the decoding of a message by the receiver in the way intended by the sender.

1.2 Opinion leaders and followers

FAST FORWARD

The **two-step** and **multi-step** models reflect the influence of other people on the communication process. Opinion leaders play important roles in bringing credibility, conviction and belief to the way people perceive and understand communications.

There is not just one receiver, **but many**, and the receivers may communicate with each other regarding the sender's message. By virtue of experience or social standing one particular receiver may influence the opinions of others regarding the product that is the subject of the message. This is known as **opinion leadership** and may lead to a **two-step flow of communication**, whereby mass messages are filtered through opinion leaders to a mass audience: Figure 1.2.

Opinion leaders are 'people within a reference group who, because of special skills, knowledge, personality traits or other characteristics, exert influence on others' in regard to a particular product or decision area (*Kotler et al, 1999*, p98).

Figure 1.2: Two-step flow of communication

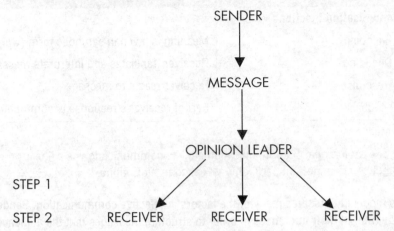

One of the marketer's tasks is to identify the relevant opinion leaders.

Opinion leaders are those who reinforce the marketing messages sent, and to whom other receivers look for information and advice.

Opinion formers are people who are designated as knowledgeable about a subject: their advice is credible (eg pharmacists provide advice about medicines).

In addition, **opinion leaders** may communicate a marketing message to those members of the group who may have missed the **original message**. The marketer's task in identifying opinion leaders is made more difficult by the fact that **opinion leadership is dynamic**. At one time it was believed that opinion leadership was confined to a few prominent members of society, but increased understanding of the concept has shown that a person may be an opinion leader in certain circumstances but an **opinion follower** in others.

Opinion leader (eg hifi enthusiast)	Opinion former (eg pharmacists)
Interested in a topic as a hobby	Part of job
Enthusiastic (eg likes gadgets)	Objective
Hard to target	Easy to target, as often known (eg all pharmacists are registered)

Note the two issues likely to be covered by exam questions:

- Characteristics of opinion leaders/formers
- Different approaches to communicating with them

This '**two-step**' approach contrasts to **Kotler's** simple model of communication identified earlier, which is a '**one-step**' model.

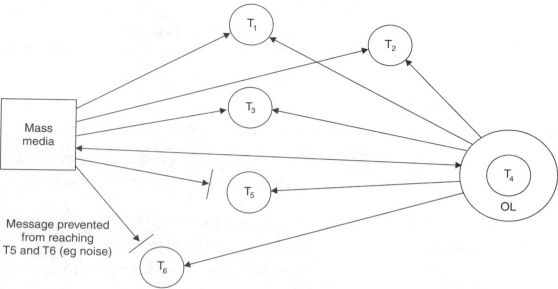

Figure 1.3: Two-step flow of communications (OL is an opinion leader)

It is possible to conceive communications flowing in a multitude of directions, from a variety of people within communication networks. This is referred to as a '**multi-step**' approach.

1.3 Word of mouth

It is easy to see from these models that opinion leaders/formers and the target audience must all influence each other. Where the message is delivered by someone of **credibility**, then **word-of-mouth communication** becomes extremely effective. To quote *Fill* (2002): 'Customers use word-of-mouth recommendations to provide information and to support and reinforce their purchasing decisions'.

Organisations therefore need to **target messages** at those individuals who are **most likely to volunteer positive opinions**, as this is likely to **encourage word-of-mouth recommendations.**

Exam tip

> Word-of-mouth communications featured on the December 2003 paper in the context of the fragrances and cosmetics sector.

1.4 The process of diffusion and adoption

An important contextual condition that affects marketing communication activity is the launch of new products and the propensity of consumers to respond to communication about new products.

Key concept

> An **innovation** refers to any good, service or idea that is perceived by someone to be new.

This is a subjective view, as a new product idea may have a long history but be an innovation to the person concerned. Innovations can be classified into three main groups.

Innovation	
Continuous innovation	The modification of an existing product rather than the invention of a completely new one. This causes the least disruption to established patterns of consumer behaviour.
Dynamically continuous innovation	Either the creation of a new product or the alteration of an existing product, but not significantly altering existing patterns of consumer buying or product use.
Discontinuous innovation	The introduction of a completely new product that alters existing consumer buying patterns in a radical way.

Action Programme 4

Can you think of products that fit into each of these three categories?

1.5 Adoption

Adopters of new products have been observed to move through the following five stages.

Stage of adoption	Comment
Stage 1: **Awareness**	The consumer becomes aware of the innovation but lacks information about it.
Stage 2: **Interest**	The consumer is stimulated to seek information about the innovation.
Stage 3: **Evaluation**	The consumer considers whether to try the innovation.
Stage 4: **Trial**	The consumer tries the innovation to improve his or her estimate of its value.
Stage 5: **Adoption**	The consumer decides to make full and regular use of the innovation.

The progression suggests that the **marketer of the innovative product should aim to facilitate consumer movement through these stages**. The process of adoption of innovation described here bears a remarkable similarity to the 'core' process of consumer buying behaviour. Indeed, when considering the adoption process, all we are considering is the consumer buying behaviour process for a new rather than an existing product.

1.5.1 Diffusion

Key concept

> **Diffusion** can be defined as the process by which an innovation is communicated over time among the individuals within society who comprise the target market.

Four key elements significant to the process of diffusion

- The innovation itself
- The communication processes and channels used
- The time at which individuals decide to adopt the product
- The social systems involved

At the heart of the diffusion process is the decision by an individual to adopt the innovative product or service. This process of adoption focuses on **the mental processes through which** an individual passes from first hearing about the innovation to final adoption.

Key concept

> **Adoption** is the decision of an individual to become a regular user of a product.

1.5.2 Categories of adopters

People differ markedly in their readiness to try new products. There are five identified categories of adopters, which are often described diagrammatically in terms of a normal distribution curve (showing their relative numerical importance), as follows: Figure 1.4.

BPP LEARNING MEDIA

Figure 1.4: The adoption curve

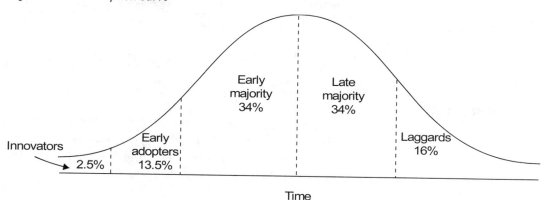

Characteristics of the various adopter groups

Measure	Comment
Innovators	• Eager to try new ideas and products • Higher incomes • Self confident
Early adopters	• Reliant on group norms • Oriented to the local community • Opinion leaders
Early majority	• Deliberate more carefully • Process of adoption takes longer • Positioned between the earlier and later adopters
Late majority	• Pressure to conform • Sceptical • Below average income and education
Laggards	• Independent • Tradition-bound • Lowest socio-economic status

The **time dimension** to the process of diffusion and adoption is important. The diagram suggests that each group learns by observing the previous group's behaviours and then adopts the behaviour itself. The marketer should therefore have a clear understanding of the dynamics of this process for his own industry.

1.6 Encouraging adoption

It is a common assertion that **90% of new products fail**. How, therefore, can a marketer ensure that his new product stands the best chance of success in the market? There are five **characteristics associated with the success of new products**.

Characteristics	Comment
Relative advantage	The extent to which the consumer perceives the product to have an advantage over the product it supersedes
Compatibility	The degree to which the product is consistent with existing values and past experiences of the potential customer

Characteristics	Comment
Complexity	The degree to which a new product is perceived to be complex and difficult to use
Trialability	New products are more likely to be adopted when customers can try them out on an experimental basis
Observability	A measure of the degree to which adoption of the product, or the results of using the product, is visible to friends, neighbours and colleagues. This process can be given added impetus if the product is seen to be used by celebrities or other role models. This factor obviously lends itself more to some products than others.

Action Programme 5

Apply this list of characteristics to the following innovations.

(a)   Mobile telephones
(b)   Banking by telephone or the Internet
(c)   Multimedia home entertainment
(d)   Quorn (fungus based food products)

1.7 Communications and the product life cycle

The consumer adoption process describes the way in which new products and services become accepted by different types of consumer over time. The **product life cycle** concept describes the rate at which this process takes place for different types of product.

Figure 1.5: A standard product life cycle

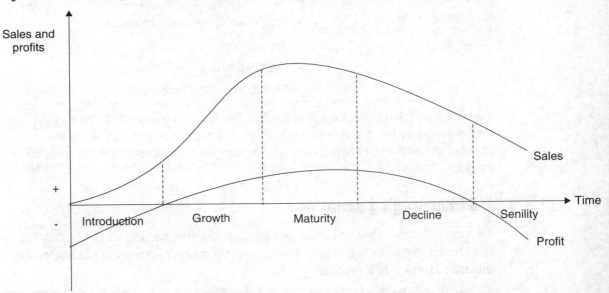

Figure 1.5 illustrates the different phases that products and services pass through over time. The length of time products take to move through the stages will be dependent upon the type of product, and a range of other marketing factors that determine how successful the product actually becomes.

Different kinds of communication will be appropriate at different stages

(a) Initially the objective will be to **create awareness** and will involve advertising, particularly for FMCG products. Sales promotion may also feature to gain acceptance and encourage repeat purchase.

(b) In **growth phases**, advertising will still be important but at a reducing percentage of sales.

(c) At maturity, more active **segmentation and targeting** becomes significant as competition intensifies and positioning and repositioning come to the fore.

(d) Although in many cases products do not decline, **sales may reduce** significantly, and promotional activity will probably reduce.

(e) For products where sales continue to be healthy, promotion will still be a major element of the marketing mix as brands seek to maintain or improve their positions by encouraging **brand switching**.

Organisations have a number of strategies at their disposal to influence customers to adopt innovations and, among these, marketing communication is obviously very important. For example, in markets where **continuous innovation** is the norm, organisations can encourage trial through **free samples** and **price promotions**.

Encouraging adoption for a discontinuous innovation is more problematic because the product cannot be purchased on a trial basis. Advertising may have to be used to promote awareness and communicate product features.

2 Consumer buying behaviour

Key concept

Consumer buying behaviour can be defined as, 'the decision processes and acts of individuals involved in buying and using products or services.' (*Dibb et al, 2001*).

The study of consumer buying behaviour by an organisation is important (*Dibb et al, op cit*) for a number of reasons.

(a) The **buyer's reaction** to the organisation's marketing strategy has a major impact on the success of the organisation.

(b) If organisations are truly to implement the marketing concept, they must examine the main influences on **what, where, when and how customers buy**. Only in this way will they be able to devise a marketing mix that satisfies the needs of the customers.

(c) By gaining a better understanding of the factors influencing their customers and how their customers will respond, organisations will be better able to predict the **effectiveness of their marketing activities**.

However, not all consumers behave in the same way. Decision making and purchase patterns of behaviour vary considerably within individuals and across product categories. This **complexity must be recognised** and **marketing communications adapted** to meet the needs of different customers.

3 Factors influencing consumer buying behaviour

In order to reach and influence members of the target audience it is crucial to understand the **context** within which customers receive and understand marketing messages.

The 'core' process of consumer buying behaviour described above will be influenced by a number of outside variables. These variables have been classified by *Wilson and Gilligan* (1997), as follows, with the focus progressively narrowing.

- Cultural
- Social
- Personal
- Psychological

Each factor will be considered in more detail separately, but it is essential to remember that they are not **mutually exclusive**. Marketers must have a clear understanding of how the various factors interact and how they influence buyer behaviour, both separately and in their totality.

Exam tip

> A question in the December 2007 exam asked you to explain how an understanding of buyer behaviour (in this case, consumer purchase of premium ice creams) would influence marketing communications. As you read on, think of the implications of different factors for communication decisions. What media? What messages?

3.1 Cultural factors

These are the most fundamental of the influencing factors, and include culture, subculture and social class.

Key concept

> **Culture** comprises the values and attitudes in the life adopted by people that help them to interpret and communicate with others, as members of a society.

Culture is largely the result of a learning process. As we grow up we learn a set of values, perceptions, preferences and behaviour patterns through socialisation in the family and other institutions such as school and work.

This broad set of values is then influenced by the **subcultures** in which we develop. Subcultural groups can be defined in terms of religion, ethnic characteristics, racial characteristics and geographical areas, all of which further influence attitudes, tastes, taboos and lifestyle.

A third cultural influence is that of **social stratification**, or **class**. The key characteristics of social class have been highlighted as follows.

(a)   People within a particular social class resemble each other more than they resemble those from other social classes.

(b)   Social class is determined by a series of variables such as occupation, income, education and values, rather than by a single variable.

(c)   Individuals can move from one social class to another.

3.2 Social factors

Within the context of culture, an individual is also influenced by a series of social factors, such as **reference groups**, family, social roles and status, all of which can have a direct effect on buying behaviour.

Reference groups are groups 'with which an individual identifies so much that he or she takes on many of the values, attitudes or behaviours of group members' (*Dibb et al, op cit*). Four types have been identified.

(a)   **Primary membership groups**, which are generally informal and within which individuals interact frequently(family, friends, neighbours, work colleagues).

(b)   **Secondary membership groups**, which tend to be more formal than primary groups and within which less interaction takes place (trade unions, religious groups and professional societies are examples).

(c)   **Aspirational groups**, to which an individual would like to belong.

(d)   **Dissociative groups**, whose values and behaviour the individual rejects.

Action Programme 6

The CIM is, presumably, one of your own aspirational groups. What other reference groups do you have? Divide them according to the above classifications.

3.2.1 The family

A major social influence is the family, particularly with regard to the roles and relative influence exerted by different family members. Research has indicated three patterns of decision making within the family.

- **Husband dominated**: life insurance, cars and television
- **Wife dominated**: washing machines, carpets, kitchenware and furniture
- **Equal**: holidays, housing and entertainment

Note that families now have many different forms and roles: unmarried partners, single-parent families, blended families and so on.

3.3 Personal factors

Influencing factors that can be classified as personal include such things as age and life cycle, occupation, economic circumstances and lifestyle.

Individuals will buy different types of product depending on their age. This is particularly relevant to such products as clothes, furniture and recreation. However, consumption may also be shaped by the stage of the **family life cycle** within which an individual falls.

A person's occupation will influence consumption and the task for marketers is to identify the occupational groups that have an above average interest in their products and services.

Buying patterns are also heavily influenced by an individual's economic circumstances. Kotler states that an individual's economic circumstances consist of:

- Spendable income: its level, stability and time pattern
- Savings and assets, including the percentage that is liquid
- Borrowing power
- Attitude toward spending versus saving

However, people coming from the same subculture, social class and occupation may lead completely different lifestyles.

Key concept

> A **lifestyle** is an individual's mode of living, expressed by, amongst other things, his or her attitudes and activities.

Marketers will search for relationships between their products and lifestyle groups. There are many different lifestyle classifications; two examples, from McCann-Erikson and Taylor Nelson, are given in the table in Action Programme 7 later in this chapter.

 Marketing at Work

Advertisers are failing to notice the growing population of over 50 year olds, according to research by Datamonitor. By 2025 there are expected to be 177 million in this age group in Western Europe.

Three groups of over 50 year old consumers have emerged:

'Woofs': well off older folk
'Youthfully spirited': less financially secure then 'woofs', but willing to experiment
'Self preservationists': older, more conservative than the other groups.

Companies are obsessed with youth, and the staff in advertising agencies are predominantly under 30.

FAST FORWARD

Analysis of this contextual element revolves around the way in which information (marketing communication messages) is **processed**, **interpreted** and **acted upon**. Therefore, **perception**, **motivation**, **learning** and **attitudes** are key psychological factors that need to be appreciated, as they apply to each target audience.

3.4 Psychological factors

The process of buyer behaviour is also influenced by four major psychological factors:

- Motivation
- Perception
- Learning
- Beliefs and attitudes

3.4.1 Motivation

Key concept

Motivation has been defined as a psychological force that energises, activates and directs behaviour towards goals.

Motivation arises from perceived needs. These needs can be of two main types – **biogenic** and **psychogenic**.

(a) Biogenic needs arise from physiological states of tension such as hunger, thirst and discomfort

(b) Psychogenic needs arise from psychological states of tension such as the need for recognition, esteem or belonging.

Most needs are not intense enough to motivate an individual to act immediately, but when aroused to a sufficient level of intensity the individual will be motivated to act in order to reduce the perceived tension. 'We prioritise the effort we make towards satisfying our needs, generally giving more time and effort to those, needs that have **higher costs and benefits**, and that are more **important, interesting and relevant** to us. (*Varey*, 2002, p50).

3.4.2 Theories of human motivation

Maslow's theory of motivation seeks to explain why people are driven by particular needs at particular times. Maslow (1954) argues that human needs are arranged in **a hierarchy** comprising, in their order of importance: physiological needs, safety needs, social needs, esteem needs and self-actualisation needs.

Maslow states that a person will attempt to **satisfy the most important need first**. When that need is satisfied it ceases to be a motivator and the person will attempt to satisfy the next most important need. For example, if you are hungry (a physiological need) you will venture out from your desk to get a sandwich.

Herzberg (1966) developed a 'two factor theory' of motivation that distinguishes between **factors that cause dissatisfaction and factors that cause satisfaction**. The task for the marketer is, therefore, to avoid 'dissatisfiers' such as, for example, poor after-sales service, as these things will not sell the product but may well unsell it. In addition the marketer should identify the major satisfiers or motivators of purchase and make sure that they are supplied to the customer.

Action Programme 7

(a) Look at the two tables below. Have you moved, or are you about to move, from one category to another? What about the members of your family and your friends and colleagues at work?

(b) See if you can think of five products or services that it would be easy to sell to a person in each of the lifestyle categories described.

(c) For each product or service identified in (b), devise a communications strategy that would encourage the person in question to try your company's brand.

Life-style categories

McCann-Erikson Men	McCann-Erikson Women	Taylor Nelson
Avant Guardians. *Concerned with change and well-being of others, rather than possessions. Well educated, prone to self righteousness.*	Avant Guardians. *'Liberal left' opinions, trendy attitudes. But out-going, active, sociable.*	Self-explorers. *Motivated by self-expression and self-realisation. Less materialistic than other groups, and showing high tolerance levels.*
Pontificators. *Strongly held, traditional opinions. Very British, and concerned about keeping others on the right path.*	Lady Righteous. *Traditional, 'right-minded' opinions. Happy, complacent, with strong family orientation.*	Social resisters. *The caring group, concerned with fairness and social values, but often appearing intolerant and moralistic.*
Chameleons. *Want to be contemporary to win approval. Act like barometers of social change, but copiers not leaders.*	Hopeful seekers. *Need to be liked, want to do 'right'. Like new things, want to be trendy.*	Experimentalists. *Highly individualistic, motivated by fast-moving enjoyment. They are materialistic, pro-technology but anti traditional.*
Self-admirers. *At the young end of the spectrum. Intolerant of others and strongly motivated by success. Concerned about self-image.*	Lively ladies. *Younger than above, sensual, materialistic, ambitious and competitive.*	Conspicuous consumers. *They are materialistic and pushy, motivated by acquisition, competition, and getting ahead. Pro-authority, law and order.*
Self-exploiters. *The 'doers' and 'self-starters', competitive but always under pressure and often pessimistic. Possessions are important.*	New unromantics. *Generally young and single, adopting a hard-headed and unsentimental approach to life. Independent, self-centred.*	Belongers. *What they seek is a quiet, undisturbed family life. They are conservative, conventional rule-followers.*
Token triers. *Always willing to try new things to 'improve their luck', but apparently on a permanent try-and-fail cycle. Includes an above average proportion of unemployed.*	Lack-a-daisy. *Unassertive and easy-going. Try to cope but often fail. Not very interested in the new.*	Survivors. *Strongly class-conscious, and community spirited, their motivation is to 'get by'.*

McCann-Erikson Men	McCann-Erikson Women	Taylor Nelson
Sleepwalkers. *Contented under-achievers. Do not care about most things, and actively opt out. Traditional macho views.*	Blinkered. *Negative, do not want to be disturbed. Uninterested in conventional success – in fact, few interests except TV and radio.*	Aimless. *Comprises two groups, (a) the young unemployed, who are often anti-authority, and (b) the old, whose motivation is day-to-day existence.*
Passive endurers. *Biased towards the elderly, they are often economically and socially disfranchised. Expect little of life, and give little.*	Down-trodden. *This group is shy, introverted, but put upon. Would like to do better. Often unhappy and pressurised in personal relationships.*	

3.5 Perception

Key concept

> **Perception** can be defined as a process by which people select and interpret stimuli into a meaningful picture.

The way consumers view an object could include their mental picture of a brand, or the traits they attribute to a brand. The way that a person perceives a situation will affect how they act. Possible differences in perception can be explained by three perceptual processes.

- Selective attention
- Selective distortion
- Selection retention

3.5.1 Selective attention

A receiver will not notice all the commercial messages that he comes into contact with, so the sender must design the message so as to **win attention** in spite of the surrounding noise. Repetition, size, contour, music and sexual attraction are features used to attract attention.

3.5.2 Selective distortion

In many cases receivers distort or change the information they receive if that information does not fit in with their existing beliefs. In other words, people hear what they want to hear. Selective distortion may take a variety of forms.

- Amplification (where receivers may add things to the message that are not there)
- Levelling (where receivers do not notice other things that are there).

The task of the sender is to produce a message that is clear, simple and interesting, what many refer to as **likeable**.

3.5.3 Selective recall and message rehearsal

A receiver will retain in memory **a small fraction of the messages** that are perceived and processed. The sender's aim, therefore, is to get the message into the receiver's **long-term memory**, because once in the long-term memory the message can modify the receiver's beliefs and attitudes. However, to reach the long-term memory the message has to enter the short-term memory, which has only a limited capacity to process information. The factor influencing the passage of the message from the short-term to the long-term memory is the amount and type of **message rehearsal** given by the receiver.

In message rehearsal the receiver elaborates on the meaning of the message in a way that brings related thoughts from the long-term memory into his short-term memory.

(a)   If the receiver's initial attitude to the object of the message is positive and he rehearses support arguments then the message is likely to be accepted and have high recall.

(b)   If the receiver's initial attitude is negative and the person rehearses counter arguments against the object of the message then the message is likely to be rejected, but it will remain in the long-term memory.

3.6 Learning

Learning concerns the process whereby an individual's behaviour changes as a result of their experience. Theories about learning state that learning is the result of the interplay of five factors.

- Drives
- Stimuli
- Cues
- Responses
- Reinforcement

(a)   A **drive is a strong internal force impelling action**, which will become a motive when it is directed to a particular drive-reducing **stimulus** object (the product).

(b)   **Cues are minor stimuli** (such as seeing the product in action, favourable reactions to the product by family and friends) that determine when, where and how the person responds.

(c)   If the purchase experience is rewarding, then the **response** to the product will be **reinforced**, making a repeat purchase the next time the situation arises more likely.

3.7 Beliefs and attitudes

Key concept

> A **belief** is a thought that a person holds to be true about something.

Beliefs are important to marketers as the beliefs that people have about products make up the brand images of those products.

Key concept

> An **attitude** describes a person's 'enduring favourable or unfavourable cognitive evaluations, emotional feelings, and action tendencies toward some object or idea' (*Kotler*, 1991).

Attitudes lead people to behave in a fairly consistent way towards similar objects. Attitudes can be regarded as a short-cut in the thought process by ensuring that people do not have to interpret and react to every object in a fresh way. Attitudes settle into a consistent pattern, and to change one attitude may entail major changes to other attitudes. *Varey* (*op cit*, p54) defines attitude as 'a learned tendency to respond to something in a consistently positive or negative manner .... Attitude is an evaluation: what we feel about a concept (brand, category, person, ideology and so on)'.

3.8 How to change attitudes

In changing attitudes, we can change:

- **Cognition**
- **Affectivity**
- **Conation**

Key concepts

> **Cognition**: what people think about a product
> **Affectivity**: what people feel about a product
> **Conation**: what people actually do; their behaviour

3.8.1 Changing the way people think

With regard to cognition, the aims of the marketing communicator would be:

- To **change beliefs** entirely
- To change the **relative importance** of existing beliefs
- To develop **new beliefs**

Messages that change cognition should then have a 'knock on' effect on the other two components, leading to an overall change in attitude: Figure 1.6.

Figure 1.6: Attitude change through cognition

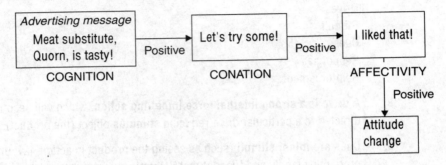

3.8.2 Changing the way people feel

Marketers can attempt to influence customers' feelings (**affectivity**) directly, before touching either beliefs or behaviour: Figure 1.7. The idea is to make the experience of using the product seem an enjoyable one (or a worthy, or exciting one).

Figure 1.7: Attitude change through affectivity

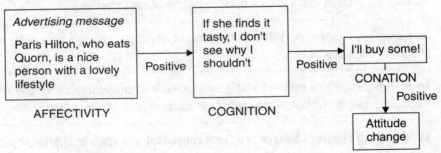

There are three main ways in which a message can change affectivity.

(a) **Repetition** of positive messages when the product is one in which the consumer is not much involved (eg washing up liquid).

(b) **Likeable advertising** means that the consumer is more inclined to like the product.

(c) **Classical conditioning** works by linking the product name with a stimulus that is liked by the consumer, such as music.

3.8.3 Changing the way people behave

Often a consumer will try or **experiment** with a product before either his beliefs or his feelings are changed, most usually because a product with fairly **low involvement** is **reduced in price**: Figure 1.8.

Figure 1.8: Attitude change through conation

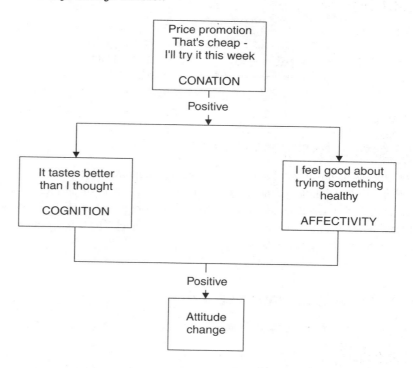

A question in the June 2007 exam asked you to explain how marketing communications could be used by a local council to change the attitudes of disadvantaged citizens (the 'customers' of the council) towards claiming benefits.

In your answer, you might have introduced the components of attitude, and their relevance to citizens' behaviour. You might then have explored practical ways of changing beliefs, affects and behaviours, in order to change the attitudes.

The examiner's reported noted that most candidates seemed to understand the attitude construct – but were unable to put it into practice to suggest ways of bringing about attitude change.

4 The consumer decision-making process

As the main aim of marketing communications is to influence consumers with regard to a specific product or service offered, it is essential that the marketing communications practitioner has some understanding of the process by which consumers reach decisions to buy or not buy.

Steps in **the buying process**:

Step 1 Need recognition

Step 2 Information search

Step 3 Evaluation of alternatives

Step 4 Purchase decision

Step 5 Post purchase evaluation

Action Programme 8

Before reading on, think about a recent purchase of a fairly major item that you have made. Did you go through the stages listed above? Explain what the need was and how you searched for information. How did you decide upon the eventual purchase, and has it been a success?

4.1 Step 1: Need recognition

The process begins when the buyer recognises a **need or problem**. This can be triggered by internal **stimuli**, such as hunger or thirst, or external stimuli, such as social esteem. If the need rises to a threshold level it will become a **drive**, and from previous experience the buyer will know how to satisfy this drive through the purchase of a particular type of product. The task for the marketer is to identify the stimuli that trigger a particular need, and use this knowledge to develop marketing strategies that trigger consumer interest.

4.2 Step 2: Information search

Once aroused, the customer will search for more information. The information search stage can be divided into two levels.

(a) '**Heightened attention**', where the customer simply becomes more receptive to information about the particular product category.

(b) '**Active information search**'. The extent of the search will depend on the strength of the drive, the amount of information available, the ease of obtaining additional information and the satisfaction obtained from the search.

The task for the marketer is to decide which are the major information sources that the customer will use and to analyse their relative importance. Kotler *et al* (*op cit*) suggests that **consumer information sources fall into four groups**:

- **Personal sources**: family, friends, neighbours, work colleagues
- **Commercial sources**: advertising, salespeople, packaging, displays
- **Public sources**: mass media, consumer rating organisations
- **Experiential sources**: handling, examining, using the product

A consumer will generally receive the most information exposure from commercial sources, but **the most effective information exposure comes from personal sources**. Each information source performs a somewhat different function, with consumers being informed by commercial sources and this information being legitimised (or not) by personal sources.

Through this information-gathering process the consumer will learn about competing brands and their relative pros and cons. This will enable the consumer to narrow down the range of alternatives to those brands that will best meet his or her particular needs: what has been called the **choice** or **evoked set**.

4.3 Step 3: Evaluation of alternatives prior to purchase

Trying to describe the process of evaluation of alternatives is not easy as there is no generally accepted single evaluation process. Most current models of evaluation are **cognitively** oriented: in other words they take the view that **the customer forms judgements largely on a conscious and rational basis**.

Kotler states that, as the consumer is trying to satisfy some need with the buying process, he will be looking for certain benefits from the product chosen and each product will be seen as a '**bundle of attributes**' with varying capabilities of delivering the benefits sought.

The consumer is likely to build up a set of **brand beliefs** about the position of each brand with regard to each attribute. The sum of these brand beliefs will make up the **brand image**. The consumer will most likely choose the brand that achieves the optimum balance between those attributes that are perceived to be the most important.

4.4 Step 4: Purchase decision

Having evaluated the range of brand choices the consumer may have formed a purchase intention to buy the most preferred brand. However, some factors could intervene between the purchase intention and the purchase decision. The first factor is the **attitude of others**. If, for example, a friend or relative of the consumer expresses a strong negative opinion regarding the brand choice, this may influence the consumer to change his or her mind. Purchase intention is also influenced by **unanticipated situational factors** that may intervene between purchase intention and decision. Such factors could include a change in financial circumstances such as redundancy, or circumstances in which some other purchase becomes more urgent.

4.5 Step 5: Post purchase evaluation

Having purchased the brand the consumer will experience some level of **satisfaction or dissatisfaction**, depending on the closeness between the consumer's product expectations and the product's **perceived performance**. These feelings will influence whether the consumer buys the brand again and also whether the consumer talks favourably or unfavourably about the brand to others.

5 Source effects influencing consumer behaviour

FAST FORWARD

The message to be delivered to target audiences must be perceived as **credible** if it is to be effective. The use of rational and/or image based appeals can assist the communication process.

5.1 Source effects influencing consumer behaviour

The source of the communication directly influences the consumer's acceptance and interpretation of a message. **Credibility** and **attractiveness** have been identified as the two major source factors influencing customers.

Key concepts

Source credibility is the level of expertise/trustworthiness that customers attribute to the source of the message, where expertise/trustworthiness is the ability to make valid statements about the characteristics and performance of a product. This **word of mouth** recommendation is a very significant form of communication.

The two elements are interlinked. For example, some spokespersons may be regarded as having high credibility in a particular field, but the trustworthiness of their product endorsements may be questioned because they are being paid by the advertiser.

Source attractiveness is determined by its likeability and its similarity to the consumer. Research has shown that when consumers perceive salespeople to be similar to themselves, they are more likely to accept and be influenced by the sales messages.

A five-mark question part in the December 2007 exam asked about the importance of source credibility for a large public service organisation trying to counter negative publicity about alleged mismanagement of a project. Which 'side' will the general public be more inclined to believe: the apparently objective news media – or the apparently self-interested organisation? Credibility can be enhanced by, for example, showing balance and objectivity on the issue, sharing transparency in giving information, gaining the endorsement of a trusted third party, and so on.

5.2 Balance of the message

Our understanding of the level of **involvement** that may exist in the target audience can be used to determine the overall balance of the message. Involvement may be defined as the degree of perceived relevance and importance of a brand choice or other decision. *Egan* (2004, p98) uses the alternative term **'salience'** to describe this level of importance or prominence. If there is **high involvement** then interested members of the target audience will **actively seek information**. Messages therefore tend to be **rational**, proclaiming product benefits and the key attributes.

Where there is **low involvement** the audience is not really interested and **needs to be drawn to the communication message**. In these cases, image-based appeals tend to be more successful and the use of **emotion** rather than logic predominates.

The strategic implication is that if **coordination** and **consistency** is to be achieved, then adherence to an emotional or rational approach has to be maintained throughout all the promotional tools.

There are a number of ways in which the informational and emotional based messages can be presented to audiences. These are referred to as **message appeals**. We look at this in more detail in Chapter 6.

6 Perceived risk

Allied to the concept of involvement is **perceived risk**.

Key concept

Risk is hard to define as it has precise meanings in different contexts. In marketing, risk relates to the possibility that the outcome of a decision will not have the desired affect or may make the situation worse. The amount of risk perceived in purchases varies from individual to individual and across product categories. By identifying the dominant forms of risk present at any one time it is possible to design messages that can help to reduce levels of perceived risk.

Risk	Comment	Dealing with it
Performance risk	Will the product function properly?	Guarantees money back
Financial risk	Can I afford it, is it good value?	Emphasise value for money, quality
Physical risk	Will the product harm me or other people?	Emphasise safety
Ego risk	Will the product satisfy my needs for self esteem and self image?	Aspiration groups
Social risk	Will significant others disapprove?	Suggest psychological rewards
Time risk	Have I the time to go shopping to buy this product?	Importance or convenience of product

Most individuals will experience a number of these risks when making purchase decisions. It is unlikely that all these risks will present at any one time. Once the dominant risks are identified marketing communications can be used to transmit messages that seek to reduce these risks.

(a) Should finance be an important factor, then interest free credit may help reduce this risk.

(b) If social risk is high then pictures of people smiling and giving approval to the person using the product will be effective.

Celebrity **endorsement**, the **approval** of opinion formers and **visual demonstrations** of the product/service in action are all important communication methods. Of course, one of the main methods is **branding**. Branding is a particularly powerful form of marketing communication as it allows individuals to assimilate product information quickly, identify levels of product quality and thereby reduce their levels of felt risk.

Relationship marketing (discussed in Chapter 11) is another way of reducing the perceived risk of a purchase. 'One reason why so-called high-risk purchases may benefit from relationship marketing strategies is that a relationship, over time, is likely to lower the perceived risk, as the consumer learns more about the terms and security of the arrangements, and, more generally, gets to know the supplier' (*Egan, op cit,* p99).

Exam tip

> We have begun this text with a consideration of buyer behaviour, since the syllabus indicates the importance for marketing communicators of developing a customer focus if they are to be successful. The theories need to be applied, rather than merely learned in isolation.

Chapter Roundup

- Marketing communications are used to **inform**, **remind**, **persuade** and **differentiate** an organisation and its products/services from those of its competitors.

- An **understanding** of the way communication works is an important part of building skills and knowledge about marketing communications.

- The **one-step** model of communication depicts communication as a linear process – but feedback and interaction are important parts of practical communications.

- The **two-step** and **multi-step** models reflect the influence of other people on the communication process. Opinion leaders play important roles in bringing credibility, conviction and belief to the way people perceive and understand communications.

- In order to reach and influence members of the target audience it is crucial to understand the **context** within which customers receive and understand marketing messages.

- Analysis of this contextual element revolves around the way in which information (marketing communication messages) is **processed**, **interpreted** and **acted upon**. Therefore, **perception**, **motivation**, **learning** and **attitudes** are key psychological factors that need to be appreciated, as they apply to each target audience.

- The message to be delivered to target audiences must be perceived as **credible** if it is to be effective. The use of rational and/or image based appeals can assist the communication process.

Quick Quiz

1   What does the acronym DRIP refer to?

D.........
R.........
I..........
P.........

2   What does 'encoding' mean when referring to the communications process?

A   Receiver translates and interprets message
B   Part of receiver's response is communicated back to the sender
C   Meaning is given in symbolic form by the sender
D   Receiver reacts to message

3   Opinion leaders are often part of a two-step flow of communication

True   ☐

False   ☐

4   Diffusion can be defined as the process by which an .... is communicated over .... among those within society who comprise the ....

5   Fill in the blanks in the statements below, using the words in the box.

When examining the various (1)........., we can identify five types. The first, (2)......., demonstrate an eagerness to try new ideas and products, and they are followed by the early adopters and early majority. The (3)........feel more pressure to conform, and so are a little more sceptical. Those who adopt the latest tend to have the lowest socio-economic status and are known as (4).......... Each group learns by observing the previous group's (5).......... and then (6)......... the behaviour itself.

Adopts	Late majority	Behaviour
Laggards	Adopter groups	Innovators

6   Name the four core variables influencing consumer buying behaviour.

7   When thinking about changing attitudes, the marketer may seek to change:

- *Cognition*: what people .... about a product
- *Affectivity*: what people .... about a product
- *Conation*: what people ....

8   There are six different types of perceived risk. What are they?

Answers to Quick Quiz

1   **D**ifferentiates

           Reminds

           Informs

           Persuades

2   C

3   True

4   Diffusion can be defined as the process by which an innovation is communicated over time among those within society who comprise the target market.

5   (1) Adopter groups (2) Innovators (3) Late majority (4) Laggards (5) Behaviour (6) Adopts

6
- Cultural
- Social
- Personal
- Psychological

7
- Cognition: what people know or believe about a product
- Affectivity: what people feel about a product
- Conation: what people do

8   Performance; Financial; Physical; Ego; Social; Time

Action Programme Review

1   Your list may include any number of the following.

    (a)   **Customers**, users (of competitor products/services).

    (b)   **Non users**, suppliers, distributors (such as wholesalers, dealers and retailers).

    (c)   **Employees**, head office staff.

    Financial service organisations, trade unions, the local community, the wider national or international community, trade and professional associations, local or national government bodies, the media .... to name a few.

2   You could try applying this to your own organisation or look to apply to a specific market sector and compare the way in which different competitors approach each aspect.

3   As you develop your studies and examine more closely the use of different promotional tools, come back to this exercise and see how it applies to them eg direct mail or PR.

4   Three suggestions:

    (a)   *Continuous innovation*: software packages such as Windows XP; these have to be similar enough to previous versions not to require extensive retraining by the user

    (b)   *Dynamically continuous innovation*: cheap electronic typewriters and PCs

    (c)   *Discontinuous innovation*: strictly speaking, this is more rare; the photocopier, or the fax machine or the video recorder are good examples

5   You might want to consider the role marketing communications could play in overcoming any perceived problem areas.

6   This list is likely to include groups which might be classified into business and personal categories. Can you identify any situations where these groups may have influenced your purchasing behaviour in either a business or personal context?

7   This exercise normally provides for an interesting discussion within a group situation. Try this with other members of your study group or some work colleagues.

8   When you have completed this, consider what were the major influencing factors on the purchase decision. Did reference group membership play a part?

Now try Question 1 at the end of the Study Text

Organisational markets, ethics and social responsibility

2

Syllabus content – knowledge and skill requirements

- Principal differences between consumer and organisational markets and how they impact on marketing communications (1.4)
- The importance for organisations of ethics and corporate responsibility, and their impact on brand reputation (1.5)

Introduction

This chapter continues the theme of understanding buying behaviour by describing the various elements that influence the way **organisations** use information to make their purchase decisions.

In this chapter we also focus on an area which is of increasing significance to marketers: the importance of **marketing ethics** and **social responsibility**. A lack of ethics can affect the purchasing decision process, and ultimately customer loyalty, both of which are central to successful marketing. In sections 8 and 9, we will develop the themes of social responsibility and 'green' issues.

1 Organisational buying behaviour

FAST FORWARD

It is vital for marketers to have an understanding of the **processes that customers go through when buying a product**. This applies equally when that customer is an organisation that is buying the product for use, further processing or resale.

Key concept

Organisational (or industrial) buying has been defined as 'the decision-making process by which formal organisations establish the need for purchased products and services and identify, evaluate and choose among alternative brands and suppliers' (*Webster & Wind*, 1972)

Kotler identifies a number of **differences between organisational and consumer markets** that mean that a modified approach needs to be taken when considering the process of buying behaviour.

(a) Organisational markets normally comprise **fewer buyers**, with those buyers often being very **concentrated** (a few buyers are responsible for the majority of sales).

(b) Because of this smaller customer base and the importance and power of larger customers there is generally a **close relationship between buyer and seller** in organisational markets, with a great degree of customisation and co-operation on product specification and other requirements.

A number of **demand factors** also influence the nature of organisational markets.

(a) Demand for industrial goods is ultimately **derived from the demand for consumer goods**. If the demand for these consumer goods slackens, then the demand for the industrial products that contribute to their production will also fall.

(b) The total demand for many industrial products is **inelastic**. In other words, it is not much affected by price changes.

(c) Demand for industrial products may also be quite **seasonal** and more **volatile** than that for consumer products.

The specific characteristics of organisational markets will vary according to the **types of organisation** that comprise the market. *Dibb et al* (2001) identify four types of organisational market.

Market	Comment
Producer markets	Organisations that purchase products for the purpose of making a profit, by using them to produce other products or by using them in their own operations. This may include buyers of raw materials and of semi-finished and finished items used to produce other products.

BPP
LEARNING MEDIA

Market	Comment
Reseller markets	Intermediaries such as retailers and wholesalers who buy the finished goods in order to resell them to make a profit. Other than minor alterations, resellers do not change the physical characteristics of the products they handle.
Government markets	National and local governments that buy a variety of goods and services to support their internal operations and to provide the public services that are within their remit, normally making their purchases through bids or negotiated contracts.
Institutional markets	Organisations that seek to achieve charitable, educational, community or other non-business goals.

2 The process of organisational buying behaviour

FAST FORWARD

The **organisational buying process** can be simply summarised as follows:

- Recognition of problem/need
- Information search
- Evaluation of alternatives
- Purchase decision
- Post purchase evaluation

This process follows the stages outlined below.

Stage 1   **Recognise the problem**: the stimulus may come from within or outside the firm.

Stage 2   **Develop product specifications** to solve the problem. People participating in the buying decision assess the problem, and determine what will be required to resolve or satisfy it.

Stage 3   **Search** for products and suppliers. The third stage of the process is similar to that of **information search**, utilising trade shows, trade publications, supplier catalogues, and soliciting proposals from known suppliers. This should result in a list of several alternative products.

Stage 4   **Evaluate products** in order to ascertain whether they meet the product specifications developed in the second stage.

Stage 5   **Select and order** the most appropriate product. In some cases an organisational buyer may select a number of suppliers in order to reduce the possibility of disruption. The order will then be made, often with specific details regarding terms, credit arrangements, delivery dates and technical assistance or after-sales service.

Stage 6   **Evaluate** the product and supplier performance against specifications regarding product quality and the performance of the supplier.

FAST FORWARD

The **extent to which an organisation engages in all these stages** will depend on the size, complexity and specific circumstances of the buying situation, and a range of influencing factors can be identified that could possibly affect the process. Such factors need to be recognised by marketers so that they are taken into account in marketing and promotional activity.

Again, as with consumer buying behaviour, the full buying process may not be applicable in all cases. **Three main types of organisational purchase can be identified**.

(a) **New task purchase**

The organisation is facing a need or a problem for the first time and the full organisational buying process will probably occur. As the problem has not been encountered before, the organisation will have to produce detailed specifications of both product and ordering routines. Given the fact that in many organisational markets there is a close and ongoing relationship between buyer and seller, these new task purchases can be important to sellers as they might be the start of a long relationship.

(b) **Modified re-buy**

Something about the buying situation has changed, but a lot still remains the same. Such situations may include circumstances where a buyer requires faster delivery, different prices or a slightly different product specification.

(c) **Straight re-buy**

The buyer routinely purchases the same products under the same terms of sale. In such situations the buying process will be truncated.

The implications of the types of buying situation for the stages of the organisational buying process have been summarised as follows.

	New task	Modified re-buy	Straight re-buy
Recognise problem	Yes	Yes	Yes
Develop specification	Yes	Possibly	No
Product/supplier search	Yes	Yes	Yes
Evaluate product	Yes	Possibly	No
Select product	Yes	Possibly	No
Evaluate performance	Yes	Possibly	No

2.1 The decision-making unit (DMU)

One of the major differences between consumer and organisational buying behaviour is the fact that **organisational purchase decisions are rarely made by a single individual**. This obviously has a significant influence on the buying process in the organisational context. Normally, purchasing decisions are made by a number of people from different functional areas, possibly with different statuses within the organisation.

Exam tip

This obviously complicates the process of marketing and selling the product and it is important that the marketer is fully aware of the composition of the buying group and the relative importance to the purchase decision of the individuals within it. This reflects the syllabus focus on a proper understanding of the customer (whether it be a consumer or an organisation). The Senior Examiner has emphasised that B2B contexts are – and will continue to be – emphasised in this exam: *always* check whether the customer in an exam question is an industrial or commercial buyer and focus clearly on B2B themes. Two questions in June 2006 directly concerned 'the B2B marketing communications mix', for example, and both the June and December 2007 exams had questions set in the context of B2B financial services marketing.

A framework for considering these issues was provided by *Webster and Wind*, (*op cit*), with the concept of the **decision making unit (DMU)**.

Key concept

The **decision making unit** is defined as 'all those individuals and groups who participate in the purchasing decision process, who share some common goals and the risks arising from the decisions.'

Webster and Wind suggested **six groups within the DMU**.

(a)   **Users**, who may initiate the buying process and help define purchase specifications.

(b)   **Influencers**, who help define the specification and also provide an input into the process of evaluating the available alternatives.

(c)   **Deciders**, who have the responsibility for deciding on product requirements and suppliers.

(d)   **Approvers**, who authorise the proposals of deciders and buyers.

(e)   **Buyers**, who have the formal authority for the selection of suppliers and negotiation of purchase terms.

(f)   **Gatekeepers** who, by controlling the flow of information, may be able to stop sellers from reaching individuals within the buying centre.

Action Programme 1

Whenever you have the chance – when visiting clients, when browsing in the newsagent, or at the dentist's or hairdresser's – browse through the trade magazines that you find (*Campaign, Farmer's Weekly, Banking World, Grocers' Weekly* or whatever).

What do you notice about the way products and services are marketed in such publications? Is more technical language used? Are the ads less 'glossy'? What do you learn about price and place?

The size, structure and formality of the DMU will vary depending on the specific situation. As *Wilson and Gilligan* (1997) state, however, the marketer has to consider five questions.

(a)   **Who** are the principal participants in the buying process?

(b)   In what areas do they exert the **greatest influence**?

(c)   What is their **level of influence**?

(d)   What **evaluative criteria** do each of the participants make use of and how professional is the buying process?

(e)   To what extent is **buying centralised** in large organisations?

Marketing at Work

Post-It-Notes

'Surprisingly, Post-It-Notes failed in concept, prototype and launch testing. In a last ditch effort, 3M sent the product to the secretaries/PAs of CEOs in large companies. They were asked to use the product and give feedback. In this case, the connectors were the secretaries/PAs .... Now just count the number of Post-It-Notes on your desk today!'

(*Smithson*, 2005)

3 Influences on organisational buying behaviour

Kotler (1991) identifies four main forces influencing the organisational buyer, shown below in order of progressively narrowing focus.

- Environmental
- Organisational
- Interpersonal
- Individual

Environmental forces include such factors as the level of primary demand, economic outlook, the cost of money, the rate of technological change, political and regulatory developments and competitive developments. All these environmental forces must be monitored so as to determine how they will affect buyers.

Each organisation has its own **objectives**, policies, procedures, organisational structures and systems, which may constrain the freedom of action of organisational buyers. This may in turn affect the decision-making process. For example, an organisation may insist on long-term contracts or may require special credit arrangements.

Interpersonal factors are important where the buying decision may involve a number of people. Within the buying group, the use of power and the level of conflict could significantly influence organisational buying decisions.

Individual factors are the personal characteristics of the individuals in the buying group such as age, education, personality and position in the organisation. These will affect the decision-making process, and the seller must be aware of their potential influence.

3.1 Organisational buyer behaviour matrix

An alternative framework for explaining the main influences and participants in the process of organisational buying behaviour has been put forward by the American Marketing Association: Figure 2.1.

Figure 2.1: The AMA model

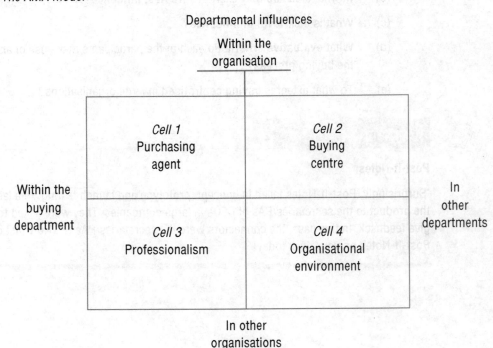

Cell 1: the purchasing agent. This represents the buyer, within the organisation and within the purchasing department. Various factors will influence the buyer, including social factors, price and cost factors, supply continuity and risk avoidance.

(a) **Social factors** include the relationships, friendships and antipathies that exist between buyer and suppliers and the extent to which these impinge on purchasing decisions. While in an ideal world such social factors should not influence decision making, they are, in reality, an important factor in the equation.

(b) **Price and cost factors** are obviously important and can include such things as the economic state of the buying organisation, the level of competition among suppliers, any cost/benefit analyses that might have been conducted, the purchasing budget and the personality and background of the purchasing agent (for example, an agent with an accountancy background may be more cost conscious).

(c) **Supply continuity** is a function of the number of suppliers that are available and the importance of the purchased item to the organisation.

(d) **Risk** avoidance is a common motivation for organisational buyers. The element of risk in the organisational buying decision can be considered along a continuum, ranging from the low risk of routine purchases to the high risk of new purchases involving high absolute or opportunity costs. Somewhere in the middle are reasonable risk situations, where the hazard involved with occasional purchases can be calculated to allow for reasonable risk minimisation or avoidance. **Buyers can typically cope with risk in a number of ways**:

  (i) Exchanging technical and other information with their customers and prospects

  (ii) Dealing only with those suppliers with which the company has previously had favourable experiences

  (iii) Applying strict (risk reducing) rules

  (iv) Dealing only with suppliers who have long established and favourable reputations

  (v) Introducing penalty clauses, for example for late delivery

  (vi) Multiple sourcing to reduce the degree of dependence on a single supplier

Cell 2: the buying centre. This cell equates to the decision making unit, where the focus is within the firm but between departments. Some of the influencing factors in this cell include organisation structure and policy, power, status and conflict procedures, and gatekeeping.

(a) With regard to **organisational structure and policy**, the place of the purchasing department within the organisation is very important as it will determine such matters as the level of influence and the reporting relationships.

(b) **Power, status and conflict procedures** relate to the degree to which the buyer or purchasing department wishes to change or maintain the status quo. For example, decentralisation and divisionalisation of the organisation may motivate outside departments to initiate their own buying decisions.

(c) Gatekeeping controls the **flow of information** in the organisation.

Cell 3: professionalism. This cell examines the influence of professional standards and practice in other organisations.

(a) **Specialist journals**, **conferences** and **trade shows** are likely to be the source of much professional knowledge. In addition, professional organisations usually attempt to set standards for professional conduct.

(b) **Word of mouth** communication can act as a potent force within the profession.

(c) **Supply-purchase reciprocity** refers to arrangements whereby two organisations reach an agreement to supply each other.

Cell 4: the organisational environment. This cell is concerned with factors outside the organisation, including economic, commercial and competitive forces, the political, social and legal environment, technological change, co-operative buying (through, for example, the formation of consortia), and the nature of the supplier.

3.2 Selection criteria

The issue of precisely **how** organisational buyers make the purchase decision, in terms of the selection criteria determining the choice of supplier, has been the subject of various pieces of research. Here are some important selection criteria.

- Delivery capability
- Quality
- Price
- Repair and after-sales service
- Technical capability
- Performance history
- Production facilities
- Help and advice
- Control systems
- Reputation

- Financial position
- Attitude toward the buyer
- Compliance with bidding procedures
- Training support
- Communications on the progress of the order
- Management and organisation
- Packaging
- Moral/legal issues
- Location
- Labour relations

4 Ethics and social responsibility

FAST FORWARD

Ethics are the moral principles and values that guide the thinking, decision making and actions of individuals and groups. Many ethical values form the basis for legislation that governs business activity. While ethics deals with personal moral principles and values, laws express the standards of a society that can actually be enforced in court. Ethics and legality are not necessarily congruent.

Social responsibility requires that organisations will not act in a way that harms the general public or that is thought to be socially irresponsible. It is because corporate decisions subsume marketing decisions that the **terms marketing ethics and social responsibility are often used interchangeably**.

Exam tip

The examiner noted in his comments on the December 2005 sitting that answers referring to questions about corporate social responsibility (CSR) need to be improved. There seems to be a lack of structural knowledge on CSR – the examiner said, "... I will certainly test this topic again and hope for more informed answers." CSR duly came up again in June 2006, asking *why* a company should seek to adopt CSR principles, and in June 2007, asking how CSR issues (for a financial services company) influence its marketing communications. Note that CSR is increasingly seen as a marketing issue – not just because marketing itself must be responsible, but because: marketing communications are used to promote responsible values within the organisation and to its stakeholders; and CSR credentials are an increasingly important brand attribute, which needs to be promoted to consumers.

4.1 The well-being of individuals and society

Critics of marketing argue that it is dedicated to selling products that are potentially damaging to the health and well-being of the **individual** or **society**. Examples include tobacco, alcohol, automobiles, detergents and even electronic goods such as computers and video recorders. It has been argued that even seemingly beneficial, or at least harmless, products, such as soft drinks, sunglasses or agricultural fertiliser, can damage individuals and societies. In traditional societies, new products can disrupt social order by introducing new aspirations, or changing a long established way of life.

How should the marketer react to these problems? There appears to be a clear conflict; what is profitable for a business organisation may not be in the interest of the customer, or the society within which the transaction is taking place. 'In general, businesses have become increasingly aware of the need to manage organisational **reputation** and many business leaders take the view that reputation is best achieved via a more inclusive approach which pays due recognition to the needs and rights of all **stakeholders**.' (*Worthington & Britton*, 2006, p450)

Key concept

> **Marketing ethics** are 'the moral principles and values that guide behaviour within the field of marketing, and cover issues such as product safety, truthfulness in marketing communications, honesty in relationships with customers and distributors, pricing issues and the impact of marketing decisions on the environment and society' (*Jobber*, 2007, p191).

4.2 Ethics and the law

Ethics deal with personal moral principles and values, but laws are the rules that can actually be enforced in court. Behaviour that is not subject to legal penalties may still be unethical.

Marketing at Work

For example, is it acceptable for the *RJ Reynolds Tobacco Company* in the USA to target Afro-Americans for a new brand of cigarette, when public health statistics show that this group has a high incidence of lung cancer and smoking related illnesses? The company maintains that it is operating within the law, but is it ethical?

We can classify marketing decisions according to ethics and legality in four different ways.

- **Ethical and legal** (eg the Body Shop and the concept of 'fair trade')
- **Unethical and legal** (eg 'gazumping')
- **Ethical but illegal** (eg publishing stolen but revealing documents about government activities)
- **Unethical and illegal** (eg employing child labour)

Marketing at Work

In June 2007, **Nike** unveiled an updated range of CSR goals.

'The firm, once famously criticised for poor conditions at supplier factories, says it wants to improve working conditions for the 800,000 people who manufacture its branded products. It hopes to eliminate the problem of excessive overtime by 2011.

'The company is also keen to increase the transparency of its supply chain operations by posting a list of the 700 factories it uses on the internet. The site will also explain the auditing tools it uses to examine its suppliers.

'It also intended to make its factories, shops and business travel climate neutral by 2011.

'[In May 2007], Nike signed a deal with a new supplier in Pakistan to make Nike footballs after problems with a different supplier last year. The contract has imposed strict guarantees on [the supplier] which is expected to meet nine workplace conditions, including making sure that employees are registered, paid hourly rates and eligible for social benefits, such as healthcare.'

Supply Management, 7 June 2007

Key concept

> An **ethical issue** can be defined as an identifiable problem, situation or opportunity requiring an individual or organisation to choose from among several actions that must be evaluated in terms of right and wrong.

4.3 Ethics in marketing

FAST FORWARD   Ethical issues can arise in relation to any of the elements of the marketing mix.

4.3.1 Product issues

Ethical issues relating to products usually revolve around **safety**, **quality**, and **value** and frequently arise from failure to provide adequate **information** in marketing communications to the customer. This may range from omission of uncomfortable facts in product literature to deliberate deception. A typical problem arises when a product specification is changed to reduce cost. Clearly, it is essential to ensure that product function is not compromised in any important way, but a decision must be taken as to just what emphasis, if any, it is necessary to place on the changes in product literature. Another, more serious, problem occurs when product safety is compromised. The potential for **product recall** becomes the issue here.

 Marketing at Work

When the French company **Perrier** discovered that its mineral water was in danger of contamination, it immediately withdrew all supplies, suffering huge losses. By acting ethically, the company's reputation was enhanced. **Coca Cola**, when faced with the same problem in Belgium, dithered, played down the issue, denied liability and suffered a huge blow to its image.

4.3.2 Promotion issues

Ethical considerations are particularly relevant to **promotional practices**. Advertising and personal selling are areas in which the temptation to select, exaggerate, slant, conceal, distort and falsify information is potentially very great indeed. Questionable practices here are likely to create **cynicism in the customer** and ultimately to preclude any degree of trust or respect for the supplier. It was because so many companies were acting unethically with regard to marketing communications that the Trade Descriptions Act 1968 came into being. Even taking into account the protection afforded to the consumer by such legislation, many think that persuading people to buy something they do not need is intrinsically unethical, especially if hard sell tactics are used.

Also relevant to this area is the problem of **corrupt selling practices**. It is widely accepted that a small gift such as a mouse mat or a diary is a useful way of keeping a supplier's name in front of an industrial purchaser. Most business people would however condemn the payment of substantial bribes to purchasing officers to induce them to favour a particular supplier. Where is the dividing line between these two extremes?

5 Ethical codes

FAST FORWARD

Some businesses have **published ethical codes**, specifying the ethical standards to which they adhere and setting out the standards that they expect all their staff to meet. The AMA has also published a *Code of Ethics.*

It is now common for businesses to specify their ethical standards. Some have even published a formal declaration of their principles and rules of conduct. This would typically cover payments to government officials or political parties, relations with customers or suppliers, conflicts of interest, and accuracy of records.

Ethical standards may cause individuals to act against the organisation of which they are a part. More often, business people are likely to adhere to moral principles that are 'utilitarian', weighing the costs and benefits of the consequences of behaviour. When benefits exceed costs, the behaviour can be said to be ethical. This is the philosophical position upon which capitalism rests, and is often cited to justify behaviour that appears to have socially unpleasant consequences. For example, food production regimes that appear inhumane are often justified by the claim that they produce cheaper food for the majority of the population.

The American Marketing Association has produced a **statement of the code of ethics** to which it expects members to adhere.

Code of Ethics

Members of the American Marketing Association (AMA) are committed to ethical professional conduct. They have joined together in subscribing to this Code of Ethics embracing the following topics.

Responsibilities of the Marketer

Marketers must accept responsibility for the consequence of their activities and make every effort to ensure that their decisions, recommendations, and actions function to identify, serve, and satisfy all relevant publics: customers, organisations and society.

Marketers' professional conduct must be guided by

1   The basic rule of professional ethics: not knowingly to do harm.
2   The adherence to all applicable laws and regulations.
3   The accurate representation of their education, training and experience.
4   The active support, practice and promotion of this Code of Ethics.

Honesty and Fairness

Marketers shall uphold and advance the integrity, honor and dignity of the marketing profession

1   Being honest in serving consumers, clients, employees, suppliers, distributors and the public.
2   Not knowingly participating in conflict of interest without prior notice to all parties involved.
3   Establishing equitable fee schedules including the payment or receipt of usual, customary and/or legal compensation or marketing exchanges.

Rights and Duties of Parties in the Marketing Exchange Process

Participants in the marketing exchange process should be able to expect

1   Products and services offered are safe and fit for their intended uses.
2   Communications about offered products and services are not deceptive.
3   All parties intend to discharge their obligations, financial and otherwise, in good faith.
4   Appropriate internal methods exist for equitable adjustment and/or redress of grievances concerning purchases.

It is understood that the above would include, *but is not limited to*, the following responsibilities of the marketer.

In the area of product development and management

- Disclosure of all substantial risks associated with product or service usage.
- Identification of any product component substitution that might materially change the product or impact on the buyer's purchase decision.
- Identification of extra-cost added features.

In the area of promotions

- Avoidance of false and misleading advertising.
- Rejection of high pressure manipulation, or misleading sales tactics.
- Avoidance of sales promotions that use deception or manipulation.

In the area of distribution

- Not manipulating the availability of a product for purpose of exploitation.
- Not using coercion in the marketing channel.
- Not exerting undue influence over the reseller's choice to handle the product.

In the area of pricing

- Not engaging in price fixing.
- Not practising predatory pricing.
- Disclosing the full price associated with any purchase.

In the area of marketing research

- Prohibiting selling or fund raising under the guise of conducting research.
- Maintaining research integrity by avoiding misrepresentation and omission of pertinent research data.
- Treating outside clients and suppliers fairly.

Organisational relationships

Marketers should be aware of how their behaviour may influence or impact on the behaviour of others in organisational relationships. They should not demand, encourage or apply coercion to obtain unethical behaviour in their relationships with others, such as employees, suppliers or customers.

1   Apply confidentiality and anonymity in professional relationships with regard to privileged information.
2   Meet their obligations and responsibilities in contracts and mutual agreements in a timely manner.
3   Avoid taking the work of others, in whole, or in part, and represent this work as their own or directly benefit from it without compensation or consent of the originator or owner.
4   Avoid manipulation to take advantage of situations to maximise personal welfare in a way that unfairly deprives or damages the organisation or others.

Any AMA members found to be in violation of any provision of this Code of Ethics may have his or her Association membership suspended or revoked.

(Reprinted by permission of *The American Marketing Association*)

The CIM's code is as follows. How do you think it compares to the AMA's?

(a)   A member shall at all times conduct himself with integrity in such a way as to bring credit to the profession of marketing and The Chartered Institute of Marketing.

(b)   A member shall not by unfair or unprofessional practice injure the business, reputation or interest of any other member of the Institute.

(c)   Members shall, at all times, act honestly in their professional dealings with customers and clients (actual and potential), employers and employees.

(d)   A member shall not, knowingly or recklessly, disseminate any false or misleading information, either on his own behalf or on behalf of anyone else.

(e)   A member shall keep abreast of current marketing practice and act competently and diligently and be encouraged to register for the Institute's scheme of Continuing Professional Development.

(f)   A member shall, at all times, seek to avoid conflicts of interest and shall make prior voluntary and full disclosure to all parties concerned of all matters that may arise during any such conflict. Where a conflict arises a member must withdraw prior to the work commencing.

(g)   A member shall keep business information confidential except from those persons entitled to receive it, where it breaches this code and where it is illegal to do so.

(h)   A member shall promote and seek business in a professional and ethical manner.

(i)   A member shall observe the requirements of all other codes of practice which may from time to time have any relevance to the practice of marketing insofar as such requirements do not conflict with any provisions of this code, or the Institute's Royal Charter and Bye-laws; a list of such codes being obtainable from the Institute's head office.

(j)   Members shall not hold themselves out as having the Institute's endorsement in connection with an activity unless the Institute's prior written approval has been obtained first.

(k)   A member shall not use any funds derived from the Institute for any purpose which does not fall within the powers and obligations contained in the Branch or Group handbook, and which does not fully comply with this code.

6 Corporate Social Responsibility (CSR)

FAST FORWARD

In the UK, there is a growing feeling that the concerns of the community ought to be the concerns of business. **Corporate Social Responsibility** (CSR) involves accepting that the organisation is part of society and, as such, will be accountable to that society for the consequences of its actions.

Key concept

The term **Corporate Social Responsibility** (CSR) is used to describe a wide range of obligations that an organisation may feel it has towards its secondary or external stakeholders, including the society in which it operates.

FAST FORWARD

Three key areas of social responsibility which have implications for marketers are **consumer issues**, **community issues** and 'green' issues.

Businesses and businessmen are also socially prominent, and must be seen to be taking a lead in addressing the problems of society. In the short term, responsibility is a very valuable addition to the **public relations** activities within a company. As pressure for legislation grows, **self-regulation** can take the heat out of potentially disadvantageous campaigns.

Recent studies in the US have shown that between 25% and 40% of the financial community take a company's record on social responsibility into account when making investment decisions. More and more, it is being realised that it is necessary for organisations to develop a sense of responsibility for the consequences of their actions within society at large, rather than simply setting out to provide consumer satisfaction. **Social responsibility involves accepting that the organisation is part of society and, as such, will be accountable to that society for the consequences of the actions which it takes**.

Three concepts of social responsibility are **profit responsibility**, **stakeholder responsibility** and **societal responsibility**.

6.1 Profit responsibility

Profit responsibility argues that companies exist to maximise profits for their proprietors. Milton Friedman asserts:

> 'There is one and only one social responsibility of business: to use its resources and engage in activities designed to increase its profits so long as it stays within the rules of the game – which is to say, engages in open and free competition without deception or fraud'.

Thus, drug companies that retain sole rights to the manufacture of treatments for dangerous diseases are obeying this principle. The argument is that intervention, to provide products at affordable prices, will undermine the motivation of poorer groups to be self-sufficient, or to improve their lot. Proponents of this view argue that unless the market is allowed to exercise its disciplines, groups who are artificially cushioned will become victims of 'dependency culture', with far worse consequences for society at large.

6.2 Stakeholder responsibility

Stakeholder responsibility arises from criticisms of profit responsibility, concentrating on the **obligations of the organisation to those who can affect achievement of its objectives**, for example, customers, employees, suppliers and distributors.

 Marketing at Work

Li & Fung Ltd, the Hong-Kong based global supply chain management group, addresses the issue of social responsibility:

'We understand that our customers today face an increasingly discerning group of consumers who are not only looking for quality and value, but are also concerned about how the goods are made. Compliance is a key element along all the steps of our supply chain. Through systematic inspection, audit and vendor education we help customers enforce their high standards throughout the factory base. We are a member of Business for Social Responsibility (www.bsr.org) and we also support the principles of the Global Compact (www.unglobalcompact.com).'

6.3 Societal responsibility

Societal responsibility focuses on the responsibilities of the organisation **towards the general public**. In particular, this includes a responsible approach to environmental issues and concerns about employment. A socially responsible posture can be promoted by:

- **Cause-related marketing**, when charitable contributions are tied directly to the revenues from one of its products

- Cause-related marketing as a branch of **affinity marketing**, by which a marketing organisation attempts to 'leverage the felt affinity, goodwill or brand name strength of a partner' (in this case, a charity or cause) to transfer loyalty to its own brand (*Suraminath and Reddy*, 2000, p382)

- **Fair trade marketing**. 'the developments, promotion and selling of fair trade brands and the positioning of organisations on the basis of fair trade ethos' (*Jobber*, 2007, p208)

The Body Shop, for example ensures that it offers fair prices to indigenous suppliers (Trade Not Aid) and other organisations have launched Fair Trade brands (eg Nestlé's Partners Blend Coffee and M&S's fair trade clothing).

 Marketing at Work

The charity **Barnardo's** ("Giving children back their future") enlists corporate support on its website (www.barnardos.org.uk).

'Barnardo's Corporate Relations Team has a proven track record in developing powerful, mutually beneficial partnerships with businesses.

'We bring to any partnership a charitable cause that is universally recognised and very well supported across all age ranges and social groupings.

'We can work with your company in a number of ways.

- Company partnerships
- Cause-related marketing
- Sponsorship
- Employee involvement
- Corporate donations
- Training challenges'

6.4 The social audit

Socially responsible ideas may be converted into actions through plans developed in the course of a **social audit**. Companies develop, implement and evaluate their social responsibility through a social audit, which assesses their objectives, strategies and performance in terms of this dimension. Marketing and social responsibility programmes may be co-ordinated.

 Action Programme 2

What do you think a social audit might involve?

In the USA, social audits on environmental issues have increased since the Exxon Valdez catastrophe in which millions of gallons of crude oil were released into Alaskan waters. The **Valdez principles** were drafted by the Coalition for Environmentally Responsible Economics to focus attention on environmental concerns and corporate responsibility. They encourage companies to behave responsibly towards the environment.

(a) Eliminate pollutants, minimise hazardous wastes and conserve non-renewable resources

(b) Market environmentally safe products and services

(c) Prepare for accidents and restore damaged environments

(d) Provide protection for employees who report environmental hazards

(e) Appoint an environmentalist to their board of directors, name an executive for environmental affairs, and develop an environmental audit of their global operations, which is to be made publicly available

6.5 *Why* be socially responsible?

Managers need to take into account the effect of organisational outputs into the market and the wide **social community**, for several reasons.

(a) The modern **marketing concept** says that in order to survive and succeed, organisations must satisfy the needs, wants and values of customers and potential customers. Communication and education have made people much more aware of issues such as the environment, the exploitation of workers, product safety and consumer rights. Therefore an organisation may have to be seen to be responsible in these areas in order to retain public support for its products.

(b) There are skill shortages in the labour pool and employers must compete to attract and retain high quality employees. If the organisation holds a reputation as a socially responsible employer it will find it easier to do this than if it has a poor '**employer brand**'.

(c) Organisations rely on the society and local community of which they are a part for access to facilities, business relationships, media coverage, labour, supplies, customers and so on. Organisations which acknowledge their responsibilities as part of the community may find that many areas of their operation are facilitated.

(d) Law, regulation and Codes of Practice **impose** certain social responsibilities on organisations, in areas such as employment protection, equal opportunities, environmental care, health and safety, product labelling and consumer rights. There are financial operational **penalties** for organisations which fail to comply.

Economist *Milton Friedman,* however, argued that the social responsibility of business is **profit maximisation**. The responsibility of a business organisation – as opposed to a public sector one – is to maximise wealth for its owners and investors. This does not mean that the business will not be socially responsible, but it will be so out of 'enlightened self interest', protecting its corporate image, ability to retain staff and so on.

Mintzberg (1983) argues that:

- A business's relationship with society is not only economic, because a business is an open system with many other non-economic impacts: employees, image, information, environmental effects

- Social responsibility helps to create a social climate in which the business can prosper in the long term

7 Consumer and community issues

FAST FORWARD

Green marketing is founded on responsibility for the community and **sustainability** – the idea that society must be aware of the consumption of resources, so that the environment can continue to provide a supply of inputs and absorb the products of consumption.

The consumer movement can be defined as a collection of organisations, pressure groups and individuals who **seek to protect and extend the rights of consumers**. The movement originated in a realisation that the increasing sophistication of products meant that the individual's own judgement was no longer adequate to defend against inappropriate marketing.

Marketing at Work

Four basic consumer rights were identified by US President John Kennedy.

(a)   **The right to safety**. Consumers expect that the products they purchase will be inherently safe to use. This right is bolstered in many countries by extensive product liability legislation.

(b)   **The right to be informed**. It is not acceptable for marketing communications to suppress important information or make false claims.

(c)   **The right to choose**. Companies should not attempt to stifle competition or make comparisons difficult by, for instance, restricting the information they make available.

(d)   **The right to be heard**. Complaints should be dealt with fairly, effectively and speedily.

The main consumer protection body in the UK is the **Office of Fair Trading**. The Director of Fair Trading has a number of roles.

- To promote competition
- To encourage the adoption of codes of practice
- To curb anti-competitive practices
- To issue licences under the Consumer Credit Act
- To administer the Estate Agents Act

As well as government bodies, there are voluntary associations. Chief of these in the UK is the **Consumers' Association** (CA).

(a)   *Which?* magazine is published by the CA every month. It contains detailed reviews of products and services. Each product review features detailed breakdowns of the performance of competing products in a number of tests. Whilst readership of *Which?* magazine is limited, its findings are widely reported in the media.

(b)   The CA provides its members with **legal advice**, even acting for members in some cases, regarding malpractice or poor service.

(c)   The CA also **lobbies Parliament and ministers** on matters such as product safety, labelling and advertising honesty.

There are a number of other organisations and groups representing consumer interests.

- National Consumer Council (a government sponsored body)
- National Federation of Consumer Groups
- National Association of Citizen's Advice Bureaux

Some industries have panels of individuals appointed to represent the consumer interest. This is particularly true of utilities.

7.1 Consumer protection legislation

- Trade Descriptions Act 1968
- Fair Trading Act 1973
- Unfair Contract Terms Act 1977
- Food Act 1984
- Weights and Measures Act 1985
- Consumer Protection Act 1987

BPP
LEARNING MEDIA

7.2 Community issues

Marketers and organisations are members of a community which expects them to contribute to its well-being. Areas which the marketer might consider as suitable for supporting community growth, and increasing community satisfaction, include education, the arts and disadvantaged groups. The organisation also has a responsibility towards its own employees, which is recognised by modern employment protection legislation and health and safety regulations.

Recognition of community issues can also have a long-term benefit for the organisation. It can generate **goodwill and publicity** and perhaps affect the attitudes of potential customers.

 Marketing at Work

The Metropolitan Police in London selected interactive mobile services firm Buongiorno to handle an email marketing campaign aimed at cutting time wasting calls. Two million non-urgent calls are received each year, diverting resources from real emergencies.

The first stage encouraged 250,000 Londoners to consider several situations, and reinforced the idea that none were worthy of a 999 call.

Londoners who provided their mobile phone number were sent the number of their local police station via SMS, for storing on their phone until needed. They could opt in to receive further information.

Jonathyn Smith of Buongiorno said, 'It is fulfilling to use our marketing and technical capabilities and experience on a project that has the ultimate objective of improving community life. The recognition of the power of new media is also very positive....delivering a fully integrated marketing campaign is an ideal way of reaching the target audience.'

Brand Republic, Revolution UK online, March 25 2003

Exam tip

When thinking about ethics in the context of a *Marketing Communications* exam question, think about how you, as a marketing communicator, can enhance your appeal to the ethical consumer. Here are some ideas.

- Identify and position your product to a specific target audience

- Formulate and publish your policy for the benefit of both customers and staff. This announces to the world that "We are prepared to be judged against what we say we will do"

- Use third party endorsement, such as the Fairtrade Mark, supported by advertising and promotion

- Use public relations to reinforce the market position

There are risks associated with an avowedly ethical stance. Your company could make itself a target for allegations of hypocrisy. Perhaps more significantly, ethical judgements may not be shared by the different cultures that international companies market to. Attitudes to animal welfare, for example, are not universal.

8 Green issues

Public awareness of the connections between industrial production, mass consumption and environmental damage is higher than it has ever been, with information flooding out through the mass media and sometimes generating profound public reaction. Modern marketing practice, then, needs to reflect awareness of these concerns, and is being changed by the issues that they raise. In particular, food scares, when badly handled (as in the case of BSE in the UK), have caused great damage to primary producers and retailers. When handled well (as, for instance, in the scare over the mineral water Perrier – see above), little damage to sales is caused, and the company or industry may even emerge with an enhanced reputation.

8.1 Green concerns

The modern 'green' movement is animated by concerns over pollution, overpopulation and the effects of massive growth on the finite resources of the earth. A series of ecological disasters in the past twenty-five years highlighted links between big business and environmental damage, including:

- the Union Carbide plant at Bhopal, India
- the Chernobyl nuclear reactor in Ukraine
- the Exxon Valdez oil spill in Alaska
- the torching of the Kuwaiti oilfields at the end of the Gulf War

According to green thinkers, conventional economics has failed to deal with the problems of overproduction. Green economists have tried to put together an economics based on alternative ideas.

- Monetary valuation of economic resources
- Promoting the quality of life
- Self reliance
- Mutual aid
- Personal growth
- Human rights

8.2 The impact of green issues on marketing practices

8.2.1 Environmental impacts on business

(a)   **Direct**

   (i)   Changes affecting costs or resource availability
   (ii) Impact on demand
   (iii) Effect on power balances between competitors in a market

(b)   **Indirect**. Examples are pressure from concerned customers or staff and legislation affecting the business environment.

8.2.2 Green pressures on business

Consumers are demanding a better environmental performance from companies. In recent surveys, it has been demonstrated that around three-quarters of the population are applying environmental criteria in many purchase decisions.

(a)   **Green pressure groups** have increased their influence dramatically.

(b)   **Employees** are increasing pressure on the businesses in which they work, partly for ethical reasons.

(c)   **Legislation** is increasing almost by the day. Growing pressure from the green or green-influenced vote has led to mainstream political parties taking these issues into their programmes.

(d)   **Environmental risk screening** has become increasingly important. Companies in the future will become responsible for the environmental impact of their activities.

 Marketing at Work

Coca-Cola and Pepsi were fined $4,000 each by India's Supreme Court after painting advertisements on 'ecologically sensitive' rock faces along a highway through the Himalayas. Although such a site may have seemed an attractive idea in terms of generating awareness, the choice of medium backfired for the companies' reputations (even if the fines were tiny).

Head office of both companies claimed not to be aware of what their local franchisees were doing, but this lack of control did not constitute an acceptable excuse.

8.3 Sustainability

Key concept

Sustainability requires that a company only uses resources at a rate that allows them to be replenished, and confines emissions of waste to levels that do not exceed the capacity of the environment to absorb them.

Policies based on sustainability have three aims:

- To pursue equity in the distribution of resources
- To maintain the integrity of the world's ecosystems
- To increase the capacity of human populations for self-reliance

 Marketing at Work

The news and marketing press is full of examples of 'green' branding and industry response to green pressures. Keep an eye out yourself: here's just a small sample:

- Leading detergent manufacturers (such as Procter & Gamble and Unilever) are attempting to raise their green credentials – and profits – by developing environmentally friendly laundry products. (*Euromonitor*, 8 March 2007)

- The Virgin Group announced in 2006 that it would apportion 100% of all its transport related profits over three years into an enterprise called Virgin Fuels, to research renewable energy sources and bio-fuels. This is partly in response to pressures on the airline industry to reduce carbon dioxide emissions – but it also earned Virgin 'Top ethical brand' status.

- Organic food and drink sales have been steadily increasing in the light of public concern over genetically modified foods, toxicity in foods, mad cow disease and so on. Mintel predicts 72% growth by 2010. (*What's New in Marketing, May 2007*)

- The Toyota Prius, the first gas-electric hybrid vehicle gained initial recognition through celebrity endorsement, but is also on the 'Top Ten Ethical Brands' list for 2006. (www.medinge.com)

- General Electric, America's biggest corporation, has set a mission of 'defining the cutting edge in cleaner power and environmental technology'. It has promised by 2010 to double its research spending on cleaner technologies; to double its sales of environment-friendly products; and to reduce its emission of greenhouse gases by one per cent.

8.4 Green marketing

There are strong reasons for bringing the environment into the business equation. The green consumer is a driving force behind changes in marketing and business practices. Green consumption can be defined as **the decisions related to consumer choice that involve environmentally-related beliefs, values and behaviour**. There is extensive evidence that this is of growing importance to business:

- Surveys that indicate increased levels of environmental awareness and concern
- Increasing demand for, and availability of, information on environmental issues
- Value shifts from consumption to conservation
- Effective PR and marketing campaigns by environmental charities and causes

8.4.1 Segmenting the green market

Profiles of green consumers show that the force of green concern varies. Many consumers have not resolved the complex, confusing and often contradictory messages which are being sent out by various interest groups in this area. Broadly, females are more environmentally-aware than males, and families with children are more likely to be concerned about making green consumption choices. The evidence also shows that consumers are becoming both more aware and more sophisticated in their approach.

Marketing diagnostics has developed a **typology of green consumers** that identifies four main groups.

(a) **Green activists** (5 – 15% of the population) are members or supporters of environmental organisations.

(b) **Green thinkers** (30%, including the activists) seek out green products and services, and look for new ways to care for the environment.

(c) **Green consumer base** (45 – 60%) includes anyone who has changed behaviour in response to green concerns.

(d) **Generally concerned** (90%) claim to be concerned about green issues.

Studies show that consumer behaviour varies in greenness according to the information that is available about the product, the regularity of purchase, the price-sensitivity of the purchase involved, the degree of brand loyalty to existing brands, the availability of substitutes and the credibility of green products.

Exam tip

Successful green marketing for the marketing communicator
(a) Understand the environmental issues which are relevant to the company, customer, products and market environment.
(b) Evaluate the degree to which green product attributes fit consumer needs.
(c) Develop strategies that identify and effectively meet consumer needs and competitor challenges in relation to green issues.

8.4.2 Marketing planning

Marketing plans need to be reconsidered in the light of **new environmental priorities**. Certain areas will require redefinition.

- Strategic product/market objectives
- Markets
- Market share, customer satisfaction and competitor comparisons
- Performance and technical aspects of product performance and quality

All of these aspects will have to be fitted within **a view of the company's performance that takes account of environmental responsibilities**. In addition, the traditional criteria for evaluating success or failure, and the parameters within which they operate, may well have to be redrawn.

Timescales also have to be lengthened considerably, since products are now evaluated in terms of their long-term effects, as well as the impact of production processes. Programmes designed to clean up environmental impacts often take a long time to become fully operational.

Getting marketing's 4Ps right leads to profit, according to orthodox ideas. Green marketing insists that the mix must be evaluated in the terms of four Ss: Figure 2.2.

- **Satisfaction** of customer needs
- **Safety** of products and production for consumers, workers, society and the environment
- **Social** acceptability of the products, their production and other activities of the company
- **Sustainability** of the products, their production and other activities of the company

Figure 2.2: The Green Marketing Process (from Peattie, (1992))

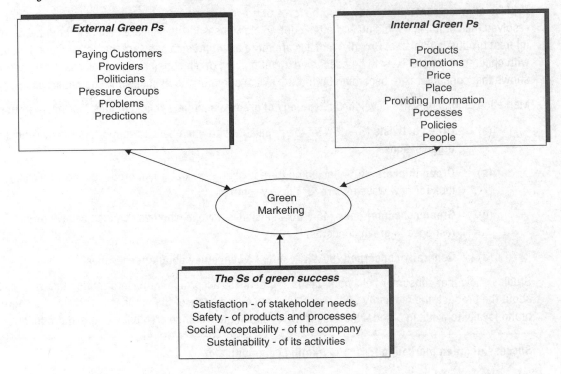

 Marketing at Work

Co-op asks members for sustainability ideas

'The Co-op is to ask its four million members in the UK what it should do about sustainability.

The supermarket collective is consulting its members to develop an ethical food policy that will underpin the business's strategy on issues such as sustainable sourcing, food labelling and community support. Members are being asked to consider the impact of their proposals, because if supply chains become localised in a desire to reduce "food miles" and carbon footprint, it will affect the group's suppliers in the developing world.

Peter Marks, chief executive of the Co-op, was critical of other retailers' attempts at sustainable policies. 'We are determined not to pursue lazy thinking, such as airplane logos on air-freighted produce," he said "Our members will help establish our ethical priorities for the next three to five years.'

Barry Clavin, the Co-op's ethical policies manager, told SM it was too early to judge what responses would concentrate on, but they would affect suppliers. He added that the important thing was to follow through on commitments once they had been made.

The Co-op has carried out surveys on similar issues before, but never on this scale. It was the first UK supermarket to stock Fair trade bananas in 2000, and all its stores are powered by green electricity.'

Supply Management, 20 September 2007

Action Programme 3

What are the implications of green issues for services marketing?

Since the profit motive has been blamed for generating wasteful and environmentally damaging over-consumption, the **not-for-profit (NFP) sector** would seem to be intrinsically greener. On the other hand, free market enthusiasts argue that not having to make a profit is more likely to promote waste and inefficiency, since the discipline of competition is absent.

Even within the NFP sector, there are likely to be varying factors at work. For instance, government departments are more likely to feel a responsibility for the environment than smaller NFP organisations.

9 Strategies for social responsibility

An organisation can adopt one of **four types of strategy** for dealing with social responsibility issues.

9.1 Proactive strategy

A **proactive strategy** involves taking action before there is any outside pressure to do so, and without the need for government or other regulatory intervention. A company that discovers a fault in a product and recalls the product without being forced to do so acts in a proactive way. 'Building coalitions with all stakeholders keeps the company abreast of ..... regulations, issues , debates, technology and attitudes.' (*Gummesson*, 2002, p123).

9.2 Reactive strategy

A **reactive strategy** involves allowing a situation to continue unresolved until the public, government or consumer groups find out about it. The company might already know about the problem. When challenged, it might deny responsibility, while at the same time attempting to resolve the problem. In this way, it seeks to minimise any detrimental impact.

9.3 Defence strategy

A **defence strategy** involves minimising or attempting to avoid additional obligations arising from a particular problem. There are several defence tactics.

- Legal manoeuvring
- Obtaining support from trade unions
- Lobbying government

9.4 Accommodation strategy

An **accommodation strategy** involves taking responsibility for actions, probably as a result of either encouragement from special interest groups or a perception that a failure to act will result in government intervention. The essence of the strategy is action to forestall more harmful pressure.

This strategy falls somewhere between a proactive and a reactive strategy. McDonalds has developed a nutrition-centred advertising campaign in an attempt to appease nutritionists and dieticians who were pressing for detailed nutritional information to be provided on fast food packaging. Action before the pressure arose would have been proactive; action after government intervention in response to the pressure would have been reactive.

 Marketing at Work

In 2007, **Marks & Spencers** launched a new CSR programme called **'Plan A'** (so called because 'There is no Plan B'), built on five CSR 'pillars':

- *Climate change:* eg reducing energy-related CO2 emissions from stores and offices; supporting farmers who are investing in small-scale renewable energy production; piloting 'eco-stores'; monitoring the carbon footprint of the food business; and encouraging consumers in more eco-friendly washing of clothing products.

- *Waste:* eg engaging customers in reducing carrier bag usage and recycling clothing; reducing use of packaging, increasing use of recycled materials; improving recycling rates for construction waste and coat hangers. (The target is to send zero waste to landfill from M & S operations.)

- *Sustainable raw materials:* eg promoting animal welfare in fashion and food production (eg implementing lower stocking densities for chicken); increasing use of Fairtrade and organic cotton and recycled polyester; and increasing sales of organic foods.

- *Fair partner.* eg extended use of Fairtrade certified products; supporting local farmers; creating a Supplier Exchange to involve suppliers in Plan A; raising money in the community (for Breakthrough Breast Cancer and Save the Children); updating commitments on labour standards; and working with overseas suppliers to help them develop 'ethical model factories' to identify and share best practice.

- *Health:* eg removing artificial colourings and flavourings from 99% of food products; reducing salt levels; introducing front-of-pack FSA 'traffic lights'; and training shop floor staff as 'healthy eating assistants'.

M&S is involving stakeholders, including employees, suppliers and customers (asking them to sign 'pledges' of commitment to each of the five pillars). Its website gives case studies for the various pillars, and updates on progress.

Marks & Spencer.com

Chapter Roundup

- It is vital for marketers to have an understanding of the **processes that customers go through when buying a product**. This applies equally when the customer is an organisation buying the product for use, further processing or resale.

- The **organisational buying process** can be simply summarised as follows:
  - Recognition of problem/need
  - Information search
  - Evaluation of alternatives
  - Purchase decision
  - Post purchase evaluation

- The **extent to which a consumer engages in all these stages** will depend on the size, complexity and specific circumstances of the buying situation and a range of influencing factors can be identified that could possibly affect the process. Such factors need to be recognised by marketers so that they are taken into account in marketing and promotional activity.

- **Ethics** are the moral principles and values that guide the thinking, decision making and actions of individuals and groups. Many ethical values form the basis for legislation that governs business activity. However, while ethics deals with personal moral principles and values, laws express the standards of a society that can actually be enforced in court. Ethics and legality are not necessarily congruent.

- Ethical issues can arise in relation to any of the elements of the marketing mix.

- Some businesses have **published ethical codes**, specifying the ethical standards to which they adhere and setting out the standards that they expect all their staff to meet. The AMA has also published a *Code of Ethics*.

- In the UK, there is a growing feeling that the concerns of the community ought to be the concerns of business. **Corporate social responsibility** (CSR) involves accepting that the organisation is part of society and, as such, will be accountable to that society for the consequences of its actions.

- Three key areas of social responsibility that have implications for marketers are **consumer issues**, **community issues** and **'green' issues**.

- **Green marketing** is founded on responsibility for the community and sustainability – the idea that we must be aware of the need for resources to be marshalled and monitored so that the environment can continue to provide inputs and absorb the products of consumption.

Quick Quiz

1   Define organisational buying.

2   Fill in this grid:

Type of organisational market	Characteristic
P......................	Organisations that purchase products for the purpose of making a ....
R......................	.... such as retailers and wholesalers who .... the finished goods in order to .... them
G......................	Buy goods and services to support their internal operations and to provide ....
I......................	Seek to achieve charitable, educational, community or other .... goals.

3   What are the six stages of the organisational buying process?

4   Match the six actors within the DMU (user, influencer, decider, approver, buyer, gatekeeper) to their respective roles:

   (a)   Help define the specification and evaluate the available alternatives: ....
   (b)   Control the flow of information to the buying centre: ....
   (c)   Initiate the buying process and help define purchase specifications: ....
   (d)   Authorise the proposals of deciders and buyers: ....
   (e)   Responsibility for deciding on product requirements and suppliers: ....
   (f)   Authority for the selection of suppliers and negotiating purchase terms: ....

5   When discussing ethics and marketing, there appears to be a .... : what is profitable for a .... may not be in the interest of the ....

6   Give an example of a business practice which is both unethical and illegal.

7   How does stakeholder responsibility differ from profit responsibility?

8   What are the four S's of the green marketing mix?

S...............................	S.....................................
S..............................	S.....................................

BPP LEARNING MEDIA

Answers to Quick Quiz

1   The decision-making process by which formal organisations establish the need for purchased products and services and identify, evaluate and choose among alternative brands and suppliers.

2

Type of organisational market	Characteristic
Producer	Organisations that purchase products for the purpose of making a profit.
Reseller	Intermediaries such as retailers and wholesalers who buy the finished goods in order to resell them.
Government	Buy goods and services to support their internal operations and to provide public services.
Institutional	Seek to achieve charitable, educational, community or other non-business goals.

3   *Stage 1.*   Recognise the problem
    Stage 2.   Develop product specifications to solve the problem
    Stage 3.   Search for products and suppliers
    Stage 4.   Evaluate products relative to specifications
    Stage 5.   Select and order the most appropriate product
    Stage 6.   Evaluate the product and supplier performance

4   (a)   Influencer
    (b)   Gatekeeper
    (c)   User
    (d)   Approver
    (e)   Decider
    (f)   Buyer

5   Conflict; business organisation/company; customer

6   Employing child labour

7   Stakeholder responsibility arises from criticisms of profit responsibility, concentrating on the obligations of the organisation towards all of those who can affect achievement of its objectives (for example, customers, employees, suppliers and distributors).

8

Satisfaction of customer needs	Safety of the products
Social acceptability of the products	Sustainability of the products

Action Programme Review

1   The result or answer to this activity will depend on items that you have chosen. You are likely to have concluded that while the advertisements will often continue to be 'glossy', they tend to be based upon satisfying needs for information about product functionality, price and distribution rather than more emotional, image-based appeals.

2   • Recognising society's expectations and the rationale for engaging in socially responsible activity
     • Identification of causes or programmes that are congruent with the mission of the company
     • Determination of objectives and priorities related to this programme
     • Specification of the nature and range of resources required
     • Evaluation of company involvement in such programmes, past, present and future

3   Service providers have traditionally thought that green issues are less relevant to them than to other types of business enterprise. Although service enterprises typically do have less environmental impact than other types of business, they still consume resources and generate waste. They still face the same choices in their selection of suppliers, their investments and their contribution to the welfare of staff and customers. In fact, the very proliferation of green marketing practices is creating a growing demand for business services such as environmental auditing, green training, waste management and pollution control specialists.

Now try Question 2 at the end of the Study Text

Part B
Co-ordinated marketing communications

3

The planning framework and budget

Syllabus content – knowledge and skill requirements

- The main parts of a marketing communications planning framework and the principal linkages between the various elements (2.13)
- The main methods used to determine a marketing communications budget (2.14)

Introduction

As we have seen in previous chapters, some basic principles apply to all types of co-ordinated marketing communications. Marketers must be aware of how these can be expected to work in the marketplace. They cannot control all the information that customers gather and process about products, but nevertheless marketing organisations must use these principles of communication in order to develop an effective **co-ordinated marketing communications plan**, and thereby exert some form of control.

Such plans are vitally important in the modern market, because the marketing mix variables on which marketers have traditionally relied to distinguish themselves from their rivals (product design, lower prices, distribution channels etc) have been changed by the march of technology (see Chapter 10 for more on this). Competitors can copy what is done quicker than ever before.

It could be that **marketing communications** is one area where it is still possible to differentiate your product or service – making the customer believe what you want him to believe about your company, product, brand or service. As a result, those responsible for marketing communications face some major tasks:

- Who should receive messages
- What the messages should say
- What image of the organisation/brand the receivers should retain
- How much is to be invested in the process
- How the messages are to be delivered
- What actions receivers should take
- How the whole process should be controlled
- To determine what was achieved

The nature of the **prevailing market conditions** is an important **context** that needs to be considered when planning and developing marketing communications activities.

Like all other areas of business activity, marketing communications needs careful housekeeping. The **amount of money available** is the key constraint on marketing communications, and there is growing pressure on total communications expenditure. This is because of fluctuating world economies and increasing media costs, but also because methods of measuring the effectiveness of spending have been improved, and wastefulness is more transparent.

So in the final part of this chapter we consider **who sets the budget and how**, and what can be done to control expenditure and get the best value for money.

1 The business context

FAST FORWARD

In order to be effective, the development of marketing communications must take place within the context of the prevailing **corporate**, **business and marketing strategies**.

An organisation's interaction with the various markets in which it operates is, of course, crucial. In order that its marketing communications be effective it is necessary to understand the conditions and elements that prevail in specific markets.

(a)   Is the market **expanding or contracting**?

(b)   What are the **values and beliefs** held by the target audience towards your products and those of your competitors?

(c)   What are the attitudes of **intermediaries**?

(d)   What is the nature of **competitive communications**?

These elements (and others) constitute the business context.

2 Corporate strategy and business strategy

> **Corporate strategy** is concerned with identifying the scope of activities and markets with which the company wishes to be associated.

The direction in which a company will move forward will be dependent upon a number of factors.

- The nature of the changing environment
- The existing and future resource capabilities of the organisation
- The strategies adopted by competitors
- The expectations and values of the management and workforce
- The maintenance of a competitive position within the market

2.1 The strategic triangle

One way of looking at this is from the perspective of the three main players, as in the 'strategic triangle', so called by Japanese management consultant *Kenichi Ohmae* (1983): Figure 3.1.

Figure 3.1: The strategic triangle

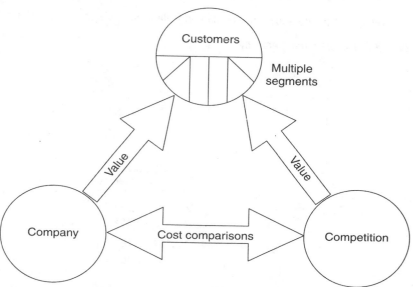

Once the corporate strategy has been decided, this may then be translated into a **business unit strategy**. Business unit strategy is concerned with how individual strategic business units will compete within their chosen market.

Functional strategies (or operational strategies) encompassing marketing, finance, production and personnel will then be created to support the corporate or individual business unit strategy. As part of the marketing mix, a promotional strategy will be devised that will integrate into the strategic marketing plan and contribute to the fulfilment of business unit objectives.

The framework within which the promotional strategy operates is built upon prior decisions regarding product policy, segmentation and targeting (see Sections 5 and 6). As a consequence, should any of these decisions be fundamentally flawed, the promotional strategy will be somewhat restricted. Creative advertising may sell a product once, but should the product not meet customer expectations, it may not sell it again.

This example highlights the contribution that a promotional strategy makes **within the overall corporate strategy**. It also shows how corporate level or business level decisions provide the framework within which the promotional plan can function.

3 Marketing communication objectives

As we have already emphasised, the nature of marketing communications strategy has to be viewed within the context of an **overall marketing strategy**, since a promotional strategy cannot exist in isolation. Prior to the promotional strategy being decided, the company will make a series of **corporate** and/or **business unit** decisions that will determine the nature of the overall marketing strategy. It is this which will then lay down the parameters within which a promotional strategy will be developed.

Each level of the organisation has a **hierarchy** of:

- Objectives
- Strategy
- Tactics

The tactics of the upper level then become the objectives of the next level down in the organisation. The levels we can usually consider are:

- Corporate (and then business unit, if separately managed)
- Functional (including marketing)
- Activity (including marketing communications)

These relationships are shown in the Planning Hierarchy (*Majaro*, 1993): Figure 3.2.

Figure 3.2: The planning hierarchy

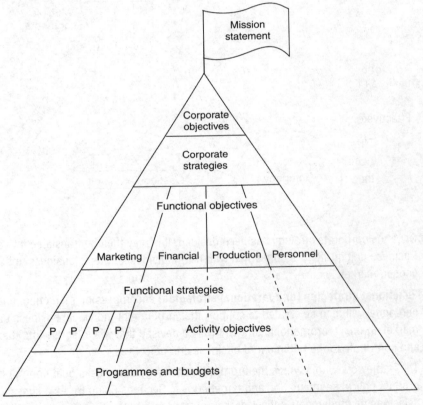

An organisation's mission statement is a description of its long-term vision and values. Mission statements have become increasingly common because they can provide clear guidance to managers and employees on the future direction of the organisation. In particular the mission statement can be used to develop the hierarchy of objectives that link long-term vision and values with specific objectives at each level of the organisation.

In order to deliver an effective plan, it is important to **establish marketing communications objectives**. These will involve variables such as perception, attitudes, developing knowledge and interest or creating new levels of prompted and spontaneous awareness.

It should be clear that for our purposes there are three different forms of objectives: corporate, marketing and marketing communications objectives. Collectively these are referred to as **promotional goals** or **objectives**: Figure 3.3.

Figure 3.3: Promotional objectives

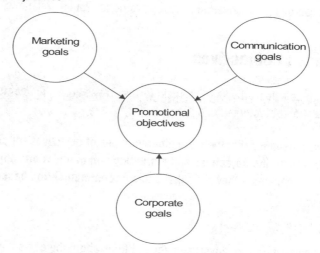

3.1 Promotional objectives

Promotional objectives need to be stated in such a way that it is easy to understand what is to be achieved and what was achieved.

Effective objectives have a number of key attributes.

- They need to be **specific** in that they must be capable of communicating to a target audience (**who**), a distinct message (**what**), over a specified time frame (**when**). Promotional objectives must therefore include:

    - Identification of the **target audience**
    - A **clear message**
    - **Expected outcomes** in terms of trial purchase or awareness
    - A measurement of **results**
    - Mechanisms for **monitoring and control**

- They need to be **measurable and therefore quantifiable**. Statements such as 'increase consumer awareness' are vague, whereas 'increase awareness of the 55 – 65 year age group from 40% to 80%' is more precise and capable of measurement.

- They need to be **achievable** or realistic given the time and resources available. Purely from an internal company perspective, if sales are targeted to increase by 25% over a designated time period then manufacturing capacity will have to be secured to meet this target. Likewise, attempting to gain additional shelf space within a retail outlet will require that additional resources are devoted to the sales force, to sales promotions and to advertising.

- They need to be **relevant**, or aligned with corporate strategic direction and objectives. An unaligned target would tend to ignore the competitive and environmental forces affecting the company, the available resources at the company's disposal, the time frame in which the objectives have to be achieved and the need to present a coherent, consistent image to the outside world. Relevance is a cornerstone of **integrated** marketing communications

- Finally, they need to be set with a defined **time period**. Although a plan of action may be drawn up for a year, it will be the case that the plan will be reviewed against target, for example monthly or quarterly, so as to enable corrective action to be taken.

These principles of **SMART** (**s**pecific, **m**easurable, **a**chievable, **r**elevant and **t**imed) objectives apply not only to the overall communication strategy but also to the setting of objectives for each tool within the **promotional mix**. Once the overall communication strategy has been set then individual (yet co-ordinated) plans need to be devised for each of the five main promotional tools. Using the SMART principle, objectives can be set for advertising, sales promotion, public relations, direct marketing and personal selling.

3.2 Types of objectives

FAST FORWARD ▶▶

The goals to be achieved take three main forms. These are **sales**, **communication** and **corporate communication objectives**.

Earlier it was identified that there are different types of objectives (or goals). These are **corporate objectives**, **marketing objectives** and **marketing communications objectives**. Each consists of one of two main components – they are either **sales** or **communication based**.

Action Programme 1

Select a television or print advertisement and think about the goals it attempted to achieve.

One of the first things that you might have thought was that to increase sales was the main goal. What other elements might the advertisers be seeking to achieve?

Is it fair to expect marketing communications to achieve all the marketing plan's objectives?

3.2.1 Sales goals

If you ask most people what the goal of marketing communications is, then most will respond 'to increase sales'. Ultimately this (and profit) is an important outcome, but ask yourself this: are sales generated by marketing communications alone? What role does each of the other elements of the marketing mix play? How will sales vary if a competitor reduces its prices or you increase yours? What impact do marketing channel and product availability play in sales performance? **Marketing communications is important but it is not the sole contributor to marketing success or failure**.

One further difficulty associated with sales goals concerns the **impact of past promotional activities**.

Key concept

> This is referred to as the **adstock effect**. Sales today might be the result of last year's (month's, week's) communications. The customers were not ready to buy then, but the significance of the communication enabled them to store salient messages and use them when they were ready. Setting sales-based goals fails to account for this important point.

Sales goals are important and performance can be determined in terms of sales volumes, sales value or revenue, market share, or profitability measures such as return on investment (ROI). They are a useful management aid as they are easy to comprehend and measurement is straightforward.

3.2.2 Communication goals

In earlier chapters we explored ideas about how marketing communications might work. The essence of **sequential models** such as the AIDA is that in order to achieve a sale, each buyer must move, or be moved, through a series of steps. These steps are **essentially communication-based stages** whereby individuals learn more about a product and mentally become more disposed towards adjusting their behaviour in favour (or not) of purchasing the item.

Awareness is an important state to be achieved as without awareness of a product's existence it is unlikely that a sale is going to be achieved. To achieve **awareness** people need to see or **perceive** the product, they need to **understand** or **comprehend** what it might do for them (benefits) and they need to be **convinced** that such a purchase would be in their best interest. To do this, there is a need to develop suitable **attitudes** and **intentions**.

3.2.3 Corporate communication goals

Analysis of the organisational context will have determined the extent to which action is required to communicate with members and non-members. Corporate communications, particularly with employees, and corporate branding to develop the image held by key stakeholders, should be integral to such co-ordinated marketing communication campaigns. These tasks form a discrete part of the communication programme. In addition to this, it is the responsibility of the communication programme to **communicate the mission and purpose of the organisation in a consistent** and understandable form. In addition, the organisation needs to be able to listen and respond to communications from its stakeholders in order that it are able to adjust its position in the environment and continue to pursue their corporate goals.

4 Marketing planning

Marketing communication strategies are intended to support and deliver the marketing objectives. **Marketing objectives are prepared and articulated through a marketing plan**. This document acts as a cornerstone for the development of effective marketing communications: Figure 3.4.

Figure 3.4: Marketing communications planning framework

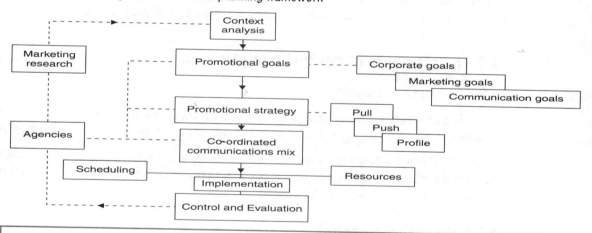

Exam tip

This framework should ideally be learnt, as it can be applied to most questions about marketing planning. Mere recitation of the framework is not enough – you need to be able to extract the communication issues associated with it and discuss them in the context of the question.

More generally, it represents a structure whereby marketing communications plans can be developed for use in your other studies, and in the workplace. Whether you work for a large multinational, a not-for-profit organisation, a medium sized service sector organisation or a small independent trading company, the structure is equally applicable.

4.1 Context analysis

There are **five** main contextual areas that need to be considered when developing marketing communication campaigns. These are the **business**, **customer**, **stakeholder**, **organisational** and **external contexts**.

It should be clearer now that **each marketing communications programme is developed in unique circumstances**. It is vitally important that the contextual conditions are analysed in order that any factor that may influence the content, timing or the way the audience receives and interprets information may be identified and incorporated within the overall plan.

In order to help provide for a systematic appraisal of the prevailing and future conditions, a context analysis is recommended when formulating a marketing communications programme. This consists of a review of the various sub-contexts.

Main sub-contexts:

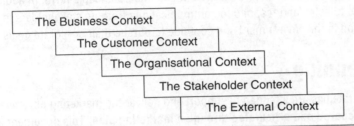

Exam tip

This framework is not prescriptive, and other frameworks and factors can be introduced, reflecting the organisation or brand and its particular conditions at any one moment. You may wish to utilise this framework to help develop your understanding and familiarity with this concept.

4.2 The elements of context analysis

4.2.1 The business context

This part of the analysis involves a consideration of the markets and conditions in which the organisation is operating, which are of prime concern for the co-ordinated marketing communication programme.

Competitors' communications, general **trading conditions** and trends, the organisation's **corporate and marketing strategies**, a detailed analysis of the **target segment's** characteristics and a **brand audit** are the primary activities associated with this context.

4.2.2 The customer context

Here the emphasis is upon understanding **buyer behaviour** and the decision-making processes that buyers in the market exhibit. The objective is to isolate any key factor in the process or any bond that customers might have with the product/brand. This can then be reflected in any communication.

4.2.3 The stakeholder context

Co-ordinated marketing communications recognises that there are **audiences other than customers** with whom organisations need to communicate. For example, members of the marketing channel, the media, the financial community, local communities and shareholders all seek a dialogue with the focus organisation. The strength and duration of the dialogue may vary but messages need to be developed and communicated and the responses need to be understood and acted upon wherever necessary.

4.2.4 The organisational context

The characteristics of the organisation can impact heavily on the nature and form of the communications they enter into. It is important, therefore, to consider the **culture and the strength of identity the workforce has with the organisation**. This is of absolute importance if truly co-ordinated communications are to be forged. In order to appreciate the strength of this sub-context think about the way the staff of different companies communicate with you as a customer. Internal and external audiences communicate with each other and this is a significant part of co-ordinated marketing communications.

4.2.5 The external context

Co-ordinated marketing communications is influenced by a number of factors in the wider environment. These political, economic, social and technological elements are largely uncontrollable by organisations, for example economic conditions or the laws and regulations. Nevertheless, they can shape and determine what, when and how messages are communicated to audiences.

Exam tip

Marketing communications occur in particular contexts. It is vital when developing strategy and writing communication plans to understand the prevailing contextual conditions. It is also good exam practice to imagine the different forces and restraints operating on marketers. Consider for example the following circumstances.

- Launching new products
- Reviving a flagging brand
- Price competition
- Introducing a new variant
- A new competitor enters the market
- Regulations change
- Promotional budget is slashed

Linkages within the marketing communications planning framework (*Fill*, 2002)

Element:	Derived from:
Objectives	The marketing plan (including the competitor analysis) in context • Business • Customer • Stakeholder • Internal
Strategic balance (3Ps)	An understanding of the brand, the needs of the target audiences (including employees and other stakeholders) and the marketing goals.
Brand/product positioning	The perception, attitudes and motivations of users and non-users.
Message content and style	An understanding of the level of involvement, perceived risk, DMU analysis, information processing styles and positioning intentions.
Promotional tools and media	An analysis of the target audience and their media habits, involvement and preferences, media compatibility, competitor analysis and resource review.

Exam tip

> The examiner may well test understanding of the planning process. This might be through the preparation of a marketing communication plan. However, you might be asked to explain the linkages between the various parts of the plan or asked to focus on the key strategic elements. Whatever the tasks required, students are advised strongly to develop their understanding of this framework and to practise its application to mini-case questions.

4.2.6 Summary

(a) The essence of the **marketing communications planning framework** (MCPF) is that the process begins with an attempt to understand the **context** within which the communications are expected to work. This is referred to as **context analysis**. This leads to the determination of objectives for the marketing communications activities: for example, an increase in the number of people who are aware of a new product offering.

(b) From this point, a focused communication strategy is developed. This is then supported by the development of suitable **messages** and the formulation of suitable **promotional mixes**.

(c) **Human and financial resources** need to be assessed before a schedule is determined and the plan implemented.

(d) The final part of the process is to **investigate what has been achieved** in the campaign, and to use that knowledge as an input into the context analysis as the cycle is repeated for the next promotional exercise.

5 Segmenting the market

Within this framework, an understanding of the **target audience** is fundamental to marketing communications.

Key concept

> The **target marketing process** (TMP) consists of segmenting the market, targeting particular segments and then positioning the offer in the selected segment in order to achieve the marketing goals.

We have included information about segmentation here as it is an important part of the promotional plan, although you will be familiar with much of this material.

5.1 Market segmentation

FAST FORWARD

> The overriding requirement for modern marketing is better **targeting**. This means aiming at the proper segment of the market. Common criteria for market **segmentation** are geography, demographics, geodemographics, behaviour and psychographics.

Key concept

> **Market segmentation** is the process of breaking down the total market into segments that share common properties, that is, customers who behave in a similar way and who can be reached by similar strategies.

The overriding requirement for modern marketing is **better targeting at specific segments**. This applies to a range of activities including the location of a new retail superstore, the stocking of a range of products, the placement of an advertisement in a newspaper and the launching of a new product into the market. The key aim is to communicate effectively with as many people as possible within a given market, while minimising the waste in communicating with those people in whom the organisation is not interested.

5.2 Bases for segmentation

The major issue surrounding the debate on market segmentation is the criteria upon which markets are segmented. There are five main **bases upon which markets can be segmented**:

- Geographics
- Demographics (including socio-economics, age, race, religion)
- Geodemographics
- Psychographics (including attitudes, interests, opinions and lifestyle)
- Behaviour (including benefits sought, brand loyalty/usage rates, situation specifics)

5.2.1 Geographic segmentation

Geographic segmentation is possibly one of the easiest forms of dividing markets into individual segments. This form of segmentation depends upon there being discernible disparities in consumer buying behaviour between one region and the next.

5.2.2 Demographic segmentation

Demographics encompass age, sex, education, income, occupation and family composition. Consumption of holidays and of clothing provide good examples of segmentation based upon age. An important element within this form of segmentation is the **family life cycle**. *Wells and Gubar* (1966) established the nine-stage family life cycle outlined below.

Stage of life cycle	Characteristics
1 Bachelor stage: young single people living at home	Have limited or no financial commitments. Buy stereos, cars and fashion conscious.
2 Newly married couples. Dual incomes, no children	Financially well off, tend to buy consumer durables.
3 Full nest 1: youngest child under six	Cash position is low, savings are minimal. Purchase toys, clothes, baby foods and some white goods.
4 Full nest 2: oldest child over six	Returning to dual incomes, savings improving; purchasing bicycles, computers, holidays.
5 Full nest 3: older married couples with dependent children	Financially more secure, some children working, increased ability to purchase desirables and luxury goods.
6 Empty nest 1: children left home and head of household still in work	House ownership at a peak, savings at a maximum; purchase holidays and spend more on recreation and home improvements.
7 Empty nest 2: older married, no children at home, husband and wife retired	Reduction in income, dependent upon pension, savings and investments. Health conscious and buy medical products.
8 Solitary survivor in the workforce	Income high.
9 Solitary survivor, retired, dependent	Income at its lowest, may sell home, may require attention.

The **changing political and social environment** and altering attitudes and expectations are impinging upon this analysis. The traditional associations between age and lifestyles are changing, requiring a new marketing focus.

Some examples include:

(a)   More women are having children later in life

(b)   Older people are now more likely to engage in leisure and sports pursuits later in their lives, as well as embarking upon new challenges, such as education

(c)   There is a rising incidence of divorce, and so there are more single parent families

(d)   Many young couples are leaving it later and later to get married

(e)   The need for increased financial awareness and planning at a younger age will affect disposable income in earlier years (ie stages 2 and 3), while improving financial spending power in later years (stages 6 and 7). This has been brought about by the prospect of cutbacks in state pensions. Many more people have taken out their own pensions policies. This has provided the opportunity for financial institutions to promote a wide range of products to younger age groups.

One of the more common means of demographic segmentation is by **socio-economic grading**. This involves characterising a market by occupational status, related specifically to the head of the household. Commonly referred to as the AB/C1/C2/DE classification, it is based on the National Readership Survey and assumes that buying behaviour is related to occupational types.

A:	Upper middle class	C2	Skilled working class
B:	Middle class	D:	Manual workers
C1:	Lower middle class	E:	Those at the lowest level of subsistence

This approach has some major weaknesses.

(a)   It tends to ignore income, especially dual incomes where both the husband and wife are in employment.

(b)   Concentration on the 'head of household' occupation wrongly assumes that buying behaviour by other family members will be related to this.

(c)   While comparisons between the highest and lowest categories may afford some benefits, comparisons between the middle groups are somewhat less useful.

Nonetheless, this basis is still widely used because the main newspapers present their readership profiles in this manner and because the information that supports this system is relatively easily obtained.

5.2.3 Geodemographics

Geodemographics (locality marketing) can be defined as the analysis of people according to where they live. It relies on the concept that people live in relatively homogenous neighbourhoods, and that these neighbourhoods are capable of classification.

5.2.4 Widely-used geodemographic systems

(a)   **ACORN** (A Classification Of Residential Neighbourhoods) divides up the entire UK population in terms of the **type of housing** in which they live. For each of these areas, a wide range of demographic information is generated and the system affords the opportunity to assess product usage patterns, dependent upon the research conducted within national surveys. There are 54 separate groupings, including the following examples.

(i)   Wealthy suburbs, large detached houses
(ii)   Private flats, elderly people
(iii)   Gentrified multi-ethnic areas
(iv)   Rural areas, mixed occupations
(v)   Council areas, residents with health problems

(b)   **MOSAIC**. This system also analyses information from various sources including the **census**, which is used to give housing, socio-economic, household and age data; the **electoral roll**, to give household composition and population movement data; **postcode address files** to give information on housing and special address types such as farms and flats; and the CCN files/Lord Chancellor's office to give **credit search information** and bad debt risk respectively (formally known as JICNARS).

 Marketing at Work

Circular Distributors ("Number one at getting your message home") claims to be the leader in Britain in delivering advertising leaflets and free samples door to door: it claims to deliver over one and a half billion items a year to households all over the country. Their web address is www.cdltd.co.uk.

The company uses Mosaic, a geodemographic system that splits UK residents into a number of consumer types, categorised by income levels, addresses (grouped into postcode areas) and tastes as indicated by certain products and services.

As a general rule, for instance, people in Merseyside spend 20 per cent more per head on toys and other products for children (such as prams) than people elsewhere in the UK. In Surrey, people are 20 per cent less likely to visit pubs regularly and only half as likely to go to wine bars as the average British citizen.

Using this type of data, split up into much smaller areas comprising around 700 or so households, Circular Distributors can decide which areas of Britain are most likely to be receptive to the specific promotional offers that clients want dropped through people's letterboxes on a targeted basis.

In this way, for example, literature related to special deals in a cut-price supermarket would find its way to poorer households in a run-down inner city area, while wealthier families in the suburbs might receive leaflets asking them to take expensive holidays.

Source: *Financial Times*

5.2.5 Behavioural segmentation: benefits sought

Benefit segmentation relates to the different benefits being sought from a product or service by customer groups. Individuals are segmented directly according to their needs. This form of segmentation assists the marketer in developing distinct and personalised strategies aimed at specific users, based upon their existing consumption of a product or service.

Individuals can be categorised by usage patterns (whether they are light, medium or heavy users of a product or service). The TGI (Target Group Index) helps to identify these groups for a wide range of products and services. For example, banks and other financial institutions are introducing incentive schemes for customers when using their credit cards. This potentially allows heavy users of the service to amass points and convert them into gifts.

5.2.6 Behavioural segmentation: situation specific

Situation specific segmentation refers to the actual situation in which consumption of the product takes place. Dependent upon the situation, it would appear that a different form of the product may be appropriate, or even an alternative brand. For example, the purchase of ice cream may vary in relation to the following situations:

- A special occasion
- Everyday consumption by the family
- An outdoor picnic
- In a restaurant
- In groups or alone

In each of these situations the consumer will evaluate alternative product types and brand offerings. Where the evaluation of brands takes place, the attributes of each brand will also vary in importance depending upon the situation in which consumption takes place. Part of the communication process is to keep the brand at the forefront of the consumer's evoked set, and to emphasise the situation specific benefits of the product.

Action Programme 2

Nestlé manufactures a range of confectionery products that fit with this situation specific typology. These include Quality Street, After Eights and Kit Kat. For each of these products:

- Identify the situation for which they are purchased
- Identify the target groups
- Evaluate the communication techniques used for each product

5.2.7 Psychographics

An individual's activities, interests, opinions and values represent that person's lifestyle. Quantitative measures of lifestyle are known as psychographics.

Psychographic segmentation provides a richer analysis of the consumer than is provided by simple demographic segmentation. It does not replace demographic segmentation but enhances it, and in so doing provides the opportunity to target individual consumers more precisely within a specific geographic area.

Marketing at Work

A major tour operator in the UK recognised the difference between demographics and psychographics and the implications for developing a promotional strategy. Two families living next door to one another, with similar family life cycles and income profiles, might demonstrate different attitudes to holidays. One family might be keen on package holidays abroad, while the other family prefers camping and walking holidays. **The two families have similar demographic profiles but contrasting psychographic lifestyles**. The consequence is a need for alternative communication strategies.

Lifestyle segmentation groups people in relation to how they spend their time and money. Traditional socio-economic groupings aggregate individuals in terms of their occupation. Recent lifestyle analysis deals with how people spend their money rather than how much they earn. *Young and Rubicam*, the international advertising agency, developed an alternative segmentation system, the Four Cs (Cross-Cultural Consumer Classification), which identified the following groups.

Group	Characteristics
Mainstreamers	• Brand conscious • Seek security/reliability • Risk averse • Buy British
Aspirers	• Image conscious • Seek individual recognition • Conspicuous consumption • Fashion oriented
Achievers	• Career oriented • Achieved personal success • Like to be in control • Personal wealth
Reformers	• Value of life • Highly educated • Independent • Family oriented

The major problem with psychographics is that, unlike other segmentation approaches, it is difficult to assign any form of specific measures. Although it is possible to identify the number of males aged 24-35 in a given area earning £25,000 per annum, it is almost impossible to estimate how many are fun-loving, carefree and fashion-oriented. Nonetheless, this does not prevent advertising agencies portraying these and other characters as part of the communications message. Psychographics today within the advertising industry is inextricably tied in with other demographic and economic descriptions.

Action Programme 3

With reference to Young and Rubicam's Four Cs, identify recent advertisements on television that refer to each of the groups specified. For each one, evaluate to what extent the characteristics portrayed are similar and identify other factors that are indicated.

5.3 Criteria for effective segmentation

FAST FORWARD

To determine whether a segment is worth pursuing, the market needs to consider the **size, measurability, access, uniqueness of response, stability and actionability** of the segment.

One of the **problems** of market segmentation is determining **to what extent definable market segments are worth pursuing**, especially when considering the development of an individual promotional campaign. There are a number of criteria that need to be satisfied in order for a market segment to be deemed commercially viable.

One of the first questions to be asked concerns **size** or **substantiality**: whether the market is of sufficient size to justify attention. Will the segment generate sufficient demand and hence sales to help create the required return from the sector? This will depend to some extent on the resources at the disposal of the company.

Morgan, the family run car manufacturer, which produces fewer than 10 cars a year, finds the segment in which it competes lucrative, while Ford and GM would undoubtedly find this market unprofitable.

Measurability. The market segment needs to have characteristics that will assist in measuring the market potential. It is necessary to establish whether there are discrete groups of people with relatively homogeneous buying habits.

Access. A necessary prerequisite is that the market is capable of being accessed both for distribution and promotion. A fairly scattered market segment in terms of geographic penetration would lead to wasted promotional expenditure if it appealed to only 10% of the market. Modern direct marketing techniques, however, reduce the potential waste, especially if the market segment can be easily identified.

Uniqueness in response. The market segment identified must exhibit similar behavioural characteristics. The individuals making up the segment should all respond in a similar way to a targeted marketing strategy.

Stability. For any company to divert resources to a particular market segment that has been identified, it must reassure itself that the segment will remain fairly stable over a long enough time period to warrant specific marketing attention.

Actionability. This is the degree to which marketing programmes can be formulated for attracting and servicing segments.

A marketing programme to expand the volume of sales for existing Rolls Royce models by attracting people on average incomes is obviously *not* actionable. If Rolls Royce chose to expand its targets, a new product would need to be developed.

6 Market targeting

FAST FORWARD

The basic options in targeting are **undifferentiated** or **mass** marketing, **differentiated** marketing, **concentrated** marketing and **customised** marketing. The approach is selected on the basis of **cost/benefit** analysis.

Once the market has been segmented along the relevant bases, the marketing manager must decide which market to target. The target market decision relates to the selection of the specific segment or segments towards which the promotional effort will be focused. The firm has four options (Figure 3.5):

- **Undifferentiated** marketing
- **Differentiated** marketing
- **Concentrated** marketing
- **Customised** marketing

Figure 3.5: Targeting options

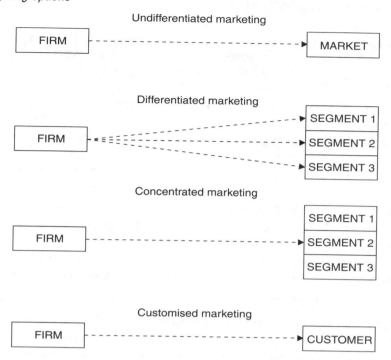

(a) **Undifferentiated or mass marketing** occurs where an organisation tends **to ignore the differences that exist within a market, and aims to provide a standard product or service to a wide variety of customers**. It is more appropriate for some product forms (for example, Intel computer chips) than others.

(b) **Differentiated marketing** acknowledges the differences that exist in customer tastes. **A separate marketing mix is developed for each identifiable market segment**. This strategy is quite **common in large companies**, and is reflected in a trend towards multiple product offerings. **Kellogg's**, the breakfast cereal manufacturer, adopts multiple marketing strategies to accommodate the requirements of a diverse market, including children, adults, families, the health conscious, and weight watchers.

(c) **Concentrated marketing focuses attention solely upon a distinct customer group** to the exclusion of all others. The aim is to concentrate on one segment and focus resources on excellence. Examples include Ferrari (car manufacturer) and Steinway (piano manufacturer), where the company targets individuals and/or groups on one or a combination of characteristics, such as income or age. The danger of concentration is that a market can dry up with amazing rapidity.

(d) **Customised marketing** refers to the extent to which organisations will move towards individually-tailored products to meet individual customer needs. Some car manufacturers are working towards computer-generated cars that will reflect the personal whims and desires of the customer. Financial products offered by the banking and financial sector are increasingly reflecting the need for tailoring to individual financial circumstances.

The marketer usually selects one of these approaches via a **cost/benefit analysis**. The marketer expects to generate additional revenue from a segment by satisfying the needs of that group, and by developing effective promotional activities that better match that segment. In doing so, the marketer incurs additional costs for new advertisements, promotions, sales force activities and public relations campaigns. The marketer will only choose to develop a new segment if the **incremental revenues generated exceed the incremental costs of serving that segment**.

6.1 Effective positioning

Positioning of a product is concerned with how it creates and establishes an image in the minds of consumers and how it is evaluated against competing products. Positioning may be according to attribute, price and quality, use or application, product user, product class or competition.

According to the basic principles of marketing, products and services are created to solve customer 'problems' (that is, to satisfy needs and wants) and provide benefits. Thus, to be effective, **positioning must promise the benefit the customer will receive**, create the expectation, and offer a solution to the customer's problem. If at all possible, the solution should be different from and better than the competition's solution.

Key concept

> **Positioning** is about how the target market perceives the presentation of the product/service relative to competing products. It is what is in the minds of the target audience.

Positioning should be a single-minded concept, an umbrella from which everything else in the organisation flows. Perhaps the most important aspect of positioning is that **a company should not try to be all things to all people**.

Properly targeted, single-minded positioning affects everything a product does or stands for. Positioning affects policies and procedures, employee attitudes, customer relations, complaint handling, and the myriad of other details that combine to make up the customer's experience.

There must be a consistency among a company's various offerings and it is the positioning statement that guides this consistency.

6.1.1 Tests of effective positioning

- The position must be **believable** in the customer's mind.
- The **product must deliver that promise** on a consistent basis.

There is no point in implementing a particular positioning strategy just because a market analysis reveals that an **opportunity exists**. For instance, if an analysis reveals a potential opportunity for a high-quality premium-priced positioning strategy, the first thing to ask is **whether your company** is suited for such an approach.

It is imperative that everyone in the company 'buys into' the strategy. In other words, the positioning strategy should permeate the entire organisation, from the CEO to the sales force to the delivery driver.

6.2 Developing a successful positioning strategy

This process must be continuous to keep up with changes in the environment, including the changing needs of the customer and the competitors' tactics.

6.2.1 Market positioning

Market positioning is the first step.

Key concept

> **Marketing positioning** is defined as the process of identifying and selecting markets or segments that represent business potential, to determine the criteria for competitive success.

This must be based on a thorough knowledge of the needs, wants, and perceptions of the target market, along with the benefits offered by the company's products or services.

- What is **important** to the target market?
- How does the target market **perceive the product**?

- How does the target market **perceive the competition**?
- What **attributes** should a product use to **differentiate** itself?

The reality is that if the target market does not perceive the image, the image does not exist. If the target market does not believe that what the product has to offer is a benefit, it is not a benefit. If the target market doesn't believe that the benefit can be delivered, promises are meaningless. If the benefit isn't important to the target market, it isn't important. If the benefit is not perceived as being different from that of the competition, then differentiation has not succeeded. **In short, images, benefits, and differentiation are solely the perception of the customer, not the perceptions of production managers or marketers**.

6.2.2 Psychological positioning

This step utilises communications to convey a product's identity and image to the target market. It converts customer needs into images and positions a product in the customers' minds.

Key concept

> **Psychological positioning** is a strategy employed to create a unique product image with the objective of creating interest and attracting customers.

There are two kinds of psychological positioning: **objective positioning** and **subjective positioning**.

(a) **Objective positioning**

   (i)   **What is it?** Objective positioning is concerned, almost entirely, with the objective attributes of the physical product. It means creating an image about the product that reflects its physical characteristics and functional features.

   (ii) **How is it used?** If a product has some unique feature, that feature may be used to position the product objectively, to create an image, and to differentiate it from the competition.

   (iii) **Drawbacks**. Less successful objective positioning occurs when the feature is not unique. This is why many product promotions fail to create a distinct image or successfully differentiate the product. One of the first rules of effective positioning is uniqueness.

(b) **Subjective positioning**

   What is it? Subjective positioning is concerned with subjective attributes of the product. Subjective positioning is the **image, not of the physical aspects of the product, but of other attributes perceived by the customer** (that is, attributes that do not necessarily belong to the product but to the customer's mental perception). These perceptions and the resulting images may not necessarily reflect the true state of the product's physical characteristics. They may simply exist in the customer's mind and not all customers' imaginings will agree with a particular perception or image. What the marketer hopes is that the people in the **target market will agree on a favourable image,** whether or not the image is true.

6.3 Positioning strategies

Marketers may decide to select the most appropriate of the following strategies, depending on the information gathered during market and psychological positioning. (There is some overlap between the strategies: for instance superb after-sales service could be offered simply as a customer benefit or as something that a competitor does *not* offer).

- Attribute, feature or customer benefit
- Price and quality
- Use or application

- Product user
- Product class dissociation
- Competitor

Action Programme 4

For each of these positioning strategies, identify a product and/or a service that fits into the category.

Positioning by **attribute or feature** involves positioning the product by clearly identifying it **with a distinct set of attributes that distinguish the product within the market**. BMW, the German car manufacturer, while positioned within the luxury end of the car market, makes constant reference to the engine performance and design as part of their positioning statement. Likewise, Volvo the Swedish car manufacturer has for many years positioned itself on safety features incorporated into the design of the car.

Another way to differentiate yourself from the competition is by providing **a unique range of services**. Depending on the characteristics of your local market, unique capabilities could include 24-hour operations, free pickup and delivery, or electronic commerce (online file transfer and on-demand output).

Exceptional customer service can be another differentiator. For obvious reasons, customers prefer vendors who follow their instructions and offer a simple ordering system, on-time delivery, easy problem-resolution, timely and accurate invoicing, and personalised service.

Marketing at Work

Positioning and differentiation strategies online

It has been suggested that, in an online context, retailers can position their products relative to competitor offerings according to four main variables: product quality, service quality, price and fulfilment time.

(These positioning options have much in common with *Porter's* competitive strategies of cost leadership, product differentiation and innovation.)

The aim of positioning is to develop a perceived advantage over rivals' products. In an e-marketing context the advantage and positioning can be communicated by developing an **online value proposition (OVP)**. For maximum effectiveness the OVP should clarify:

- A clear differentiation of the online proposition compared to the conventional offline proposition.

- A clear differentiation of the online proposition from competitors based on cost, product innovation or service quality.

- Target market segment(s) that the proposition will appeal to.

- How the proposition will be communicated to website visitors, and in all marketing communications.

- How the proposition is delivered across different parts of the buying process

- How the proposition will be delivered and supported by resources.

6.3.1 Price and quality

Price and quality are becoming increasingly important as companies attempt to offer more features, better value and improved quality at competitive prices.

Price. Some companies go for the bottom line: they attract customers by being the lowest cost service providers in the market. They do this by having highly efficient operations, so their cost-per-unit (eg per square foot, per page, etc) of output is the lowest. This does not necessarily mean those businesses spend less money than their competitors. For example, the price leader in a given market will probably do the most advertising, but because of the high volume of work the advertising helps bring in, the business will achieve the lowest cost per unit. However, a low-price positioning strategy always requires a high volume of business.

Quality. A company that provides exceptional quality to its customers can command a higher price for its services than its less quality-conscious competitors. However, quality is a variable that customers may take for granted after a while. When a competitor offers those customers a lower price, some of them might give the competitor a try, and may find out they 'get what they pay for'.

If a company intends to sell its quality programme in order to charge higher prices for its services, then it must be willing to invest the time and money required to live up to the higher expectations of its customers. If it creates expectations of superior quality but fails to deliver, few customers will give the company a second chance.

6.3.2 Use or application

In the third case, the company attempts to position its product or service by deliberately associating it with a specific **use or application**. Kellogg's, the cereal manufacturer, in striving to defend its market position and increase sales, has positioned its main product Corn Flakes as an 'any time of day food', and not just to be eaten at breakfast.

6.3.3 Product user

Positioning by virtue of product user associates the product with a particular class of user.

It is possible to position a company brand against a product class or an associated product class, claiming that yours is different from the rest. Heinz, which produces a range of 'Weight Watcher' foods, is positioning these against normal but more calorific foods.

6.3.4 Competitors

A **competitor's position** within a market may be used as a frame of reference in order to create a distinct positioning statement. Avis car rental used the slogan 'We're number 2, so we try harder'. Here the market leader is being used as a reference point to create a competitive statement. The key determinant for the marketer is whether claims made within a promotional campaign which use blatant comparisons can be substantiated through better quality, service, value and cost.

This approach is used when it is necessary to meet the competition head-on; to bring out differences between products. For example, Visa credit cards competed with American Express by showing examples of places from around the world that do not accept American Express but do accept Visa.

 Marketing at Work

Ice cream success is in the difference

The premium ice cream sector had been dominated by the sophistication of the **Haagen-Dazs** brand, and previous challenges had come to ground after challenging head on with similar approaches to branding and communications. Having established brand presence via limiting distribution and selective use of PR, **Ben and Jerry's** finally took on Haagen-Dazs but chose a very different approach. Rather than promote luxuriousness via sexual connotations which had been the Haagen-Dazs theme, B&J's built a position based on humour.

The communications aim to remain true to the original brand positioning of the niche, loveable underdog. The success of the brand led to its acquisition by the giant food group Unilever.

6.4 Perceptual product mapping

The use of **perceptual maps** can assist the positioning decision.

Part of the positioning strategy involves **mapping the competing products** within a defined product class so that specific gaps may be identified into which the company may place a new product offering. These perceptual product maps identify the attributes that are strongly associated within a given product class. For example, Figure 3.6 is a hypothetical product map that may be appropriate for the shampoo market.

Figure 3.6: Hypothetical product positioning map 'Hair shampoo'

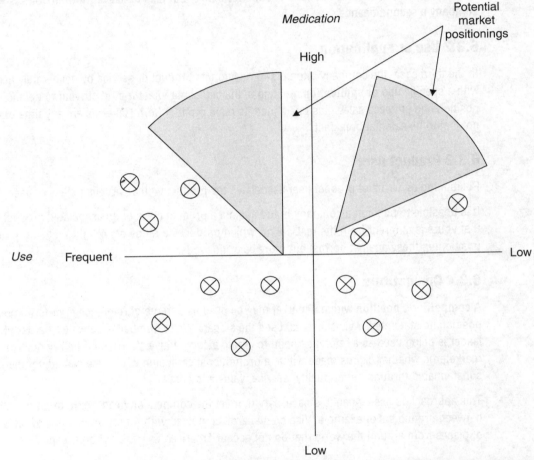

By plotting the competing products on this map, it would be possible to identify the gaps that exist within the market, and enable new products to be positioned accordingly in the mind of the consumer. Since the map illustrated is only two dimensional, it must be remembered that other factors will need to be taken into consideration, such as price, which will undoubtedly affect the optimal marketing mix employed for the new product.

Exam tip

When considering the importance of marketing planning for the exam, remember that the ultimate success of any promotional strategy will be dependent upon a **number of inter-related factors**, such as the creative stance adopted, choice of media, sales training and so on.

However, these issues are dependent upon two main strategic choices, made **at the planning stage**:

- The **chosen segment** in which the company will compete
- The **nature of the positioning statement**, which will influence consumer choice.

These two issues will determine to what extent the company is able to create for itself a definite competitive edge within its chosen market.

7 How to decide budgets

FAST FORWARD

Methods of budgeting:

- Spending an arbitrary amount
- Spending all you can afford
- Determining the spend on a historical basis
- Matching competitors' expenditure
- The percentage of sales method
- By experiment and testing
- By modelling and simulation
- The objective and task method

Action Programme 5

For several organisations with which you are in contact, carry out a review of how they decide their marketing communications budgets. Determine if there are any similarities and decide what the reasons are for any variety in methods. Comparing data with friends and colleagues at college will be valuable, but don't give out confidential information.

There is no one uniform method of deciding what to spend on marketing communications. This is not so surprising. The following are some of the considerations that can affect the amount of expenditure.

- What variety of marketing communications is to be used?
- What tasks are to be undertaken?
- How competitive is the marketplace?
- How well known is the organisation?
- Are there any special requirements?

7.1 Costs to be budgeted

- Air time and broadcast media
- Space and printed media
- Production costs
- Staff salaries
- Overheads and expenses

7.2 Theoretical approaches to budgeting

Theoretical approaches to setting budgets, for example by marginal costing approaches, have not found favour in industry because the effects of **any marginal increase on expenditure are likely to be swamped**, or at least hidden, by many other marketing variables. The effects of any expenditure will have both long-term and short-term effects. It is worthwhile emphasising the view here that **marketing communications should be treated as an essential long-term investment**.

Methods of deciding budgets have been developed over a period of time and, in the absence of clearer guidance, are useful in approaching a budget decision for the first time. After several years' operations it is possible to use experience to make decisions. One, or a combination of the following methods can be used to approach the problem.

- Completely arbitrarily
- All you can afford
- Historical basis
- Matching the competition
- Percentage of sales
- Experiment and testing
- Modelling and simulation
- Objective and task method

7.2.1 Completely arbitrarily

There are many examples of budgets being set in an apparently **arbitrary way by senior management**. There may be a link between the personality of the decision maker and the level of expenditure. This link may not be obvious to people elsewhere in the organisation.

7.2.2 All you can afford (usually a minimum)

This often applies to a new company starting up or to an existing company advertising for the first time. The conscious decision has to be taken to forgo immediate profits or to forgo an investment in another area in favour of an investment in marketing communications. This often means investing at a minimum level. This will necessarily limit the scope of the work, however, and limit the results to be achieved.

7.2.3 Historical basis

We have already indicated that with experience managers are able to form their own judgement of the effectiveness or otherwise of particular expenditure levels and different promotional methods. Year-on-year figures provide the basis for following trends and making decisions accordingly.

(a) The **danger of inertia**: a temptation just to keep it the same, in which case all the elements of the environment and the costs associated with the task facing the organisation are ignored.

(b) A slight improvement is to use a **media multiplier**, which at least recognises that **media rate card costs** may have increased.

7.2.4 Matching the competition

In many cases an organisation is trying to reach exactly the same customers through exactly the same channels. In order to obtain a certain market share it is then necessary to match the competition and particularly the market leader.

7.2.5 Percentage of sales method

The percentage of sales is a commonly used method of determining a marketing communications budget because:

- It is easy to calculate
- It is precise

- It can be quickly monitored
- It can be varied in progressive steps
- It appears logical
- It is financially safe

However, the percentage chosen should be conditioned by other variables (not least by whether the market is a consumer or industrial one) and it should be dependent upon how competitive the market is. The following figures are based on experience of different accounts.

Percentage of sales on total communications budget

State of competition	Consumer markets	Industrial markets
No competition	1%	0.5%
Little competition	2%	1%
Average competition	5%	2%
Heavy competition	10%	3%

Action Programme 6

Use the above table to determine the approximate marketing communications budget for a number of market situations with which you are familiar. Include consumer and industrial markets.

[Key skills for marketers: Using financial information]

Action Programme 7

What do you think is the logical flaw associated with the percentage of sales method as an effective technique for budget allocation?

If all companies in an industry use a similar calculation then expenditure will approximate to market share positions. However, it must be clear that the real position is very complex and sales are the result of marketing communications and not the other way round. The method is in reality over-simplistic but does form a good basis of calculation.

Once a sales forecast has been made, the approximate budget level can be obtained. It can then be moderated for special circumstances such as the degree of competition experienced in the previous year or expected in the next year.

7.2.6 Experiment and testing method

This method involves selecting a set of matched markets. Different final promotional budgets can be set for each of these markets and the results carefully monitored. The resulting levels of awareness and sales delivered can be compared. For example, this method can be used to evaluate alternative media schedules. Problems associated with this method include:

- The cost of conducting the experiment
- The time it takes to get results
- The premature informing of competitors
- The fact that markets can never be completely matched

7.2.7 Modelling and simulation method

With advancing use of computer databases and more precise promotional media it is possible to build models to forecast the likely performance of different media schedules. There are likely to be an increasing number of PC-based modelling programs available which will allow a number of business variables to be examined including:

- Sales levels
- Purchase frequency
- Awareness levels
- Profits achievable

Problems associated with modelling include time and cost and the validity of the chosen model.

7.2.8 The objective and task method

FAST FORWARD

The **objective and task method** is the most rigorous. As its name suggests, this entails determining the marketing communications objectives, determining the tasks necessary to achieve those objectives and determining the cost of each element.

The objective and task method is probably the one which is most **logical and appropriate** to the complex situation found in planning marketing communications programmes. Basically the logic of the method is as follows.

```
┌─────────────────────────────┐
│   Determine the marketing   │
│  communications objectives  │
└─────────────────────────────┘
              ↓
┌─────────────────────────────┐
│  Determine tasks necessary to│
│   achieve these objectives  │
└─────────────────────────────┘
              ↓
┌─────────────────────────────┐
│   Determine the cost of cash │
│            element          │
└─────────────────────────────┘
```

This approach is simple to understand and it embodies some elements of the marginal cost approach, but this time in conjunction with carefully considered and linked objectives and tasks. It is necessary to be realistic about the objectives and accurate in the costing of the tasks.

Action Programme 8

To demonstrate the logic and difficulty of this method, choose a marketing communications problem with which you are familiar:

- Define the precise marketing communication objectives
- Determine the tasks necessary to achieve these objectives
- Cost out the problem both in terms of the individual tasks and in total

7.2.9 Ten steps in applying the objective and task method

Step 1   Define marketing and promotion objectives

Step 2   Determine the tasks to be undertaken

Step 3   Build up expenditure by costing the tasks

Step 4   Compare the results against industry averages

Step 5   Compare the results as a percentage of sales

Step 6   Reconcile differences between steps 3, 4 and 5

Step 7   Modify estimates to meet company policies

Step 8   Specify when expenditures are to be made

Step 9   Maintain an element of flexibility

Step 10   Monitor actual results against these forecasts

Action Programme 9

Compare the advantages and disadvantages of the various methods that can be used to determine the appropriate levels of marketing communication budgets.

8 Strategic considerations

You may notice, say, that you see British Telecom ads far more frequently than ads for most of its competitors such as the cable companies' telephone services. BT is, of course, the largest player in the market. But then, French car ads are more often to be seen than ads for Japanese cars, yet the Japanese have a larger share of the market. How can we analyse these strategies?

8.1 Advertising to sales ratios (A/S ratios)

One of the important factors that always needs to be considered is the amount spent on communications by competitors. It can be difficult determining the amount spent by competitors on **below-the-line** activities, although accurate guesstimates can often be made by those actively involved in the market.

Above-the-line activities can be measured (data bought from various marketing research agencies) and can be used to gain an insight into possible strategies.

The A/S ratio for an industry provides a benchmark against which it is possible to determine how much should be spent or stimulate consideration of why certain amounts have been spent.

Key concept

> The **A/S ratio** is different for each market sector. It is calculated by working out the total amount spent on advertising (usually at rate card cost) as a proportion of the sales in the market. Therefore, if sales in a market are valued at £150 million per year and the amount spent on advertising is £14 million then the A/S ratio is said to be 9.33%.

Part of the strategic decision is to decide whether an individual company's A/S ratio should be higher or lower than, or the same as (at equilibrium with) the industry average.

(a)   **Reasons to spend more** might be that a **new product or variant** is being introduced to the market so greater effort is require to **develop awareness** (reach).

(b)   **Reasons to underspend** the industry average might include trying to maintain an established market position or **directing spend to other products** in the portfolio or deciding to **put more work below-the-line**.

8.2 Share of voice

Key concept

> Within any market the total of all advertising expenditure (adspend), that is, all the advertising by all the players, can be analysed in the context of the proportions each player has made to the total. This is **Share of voice**.

If one advertiser spends more than any other then more of their messages will be received and therefore stand a better chance of being heard and acted upon. If a brand's **share of market (SOM)** is equal to its **share of voice (SOV)** an equilibrium can be said to have been reached.

It is possible that organisations can use their advertising spending either to maintain equilibrium (SOV = SOM) or to create disequilibrium.

The following matrix (Figure 3.7) shows how different spending strategies are appropriate depending on your competitors' share of voice and your own share of market.

Figure 3.7: SOV/SOM matrix

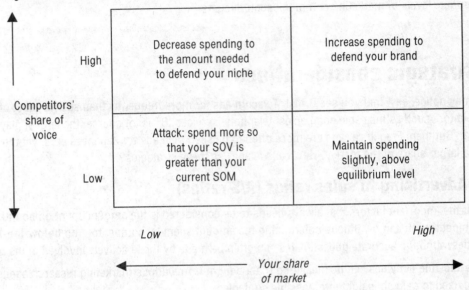

Note that careful monitoring of the fortunes of competitors is needed: if you know that a competitor is spending large sums on restructuring, then they may not be in a position to retaliate to a sudden advertising burst by your company.

9 Controlling the budget

Budgetary control is essential because of the large sums involved. In essence this involves establishing satisfactory measures of the effectiveness of the marketing communications process.

Marketing communication budgets may be very substantial and have a major effect on profitability. Controlling the effectiveness of the budget may be difficult if not impossible. What is possible is to use normal budgetary control techniques in marketing expenditure, and to review its effectiveness regularly, even if this is only by means of informed judgement: Figure 3.8.

Figure 3.8: Controlling the budgets and effectiveness

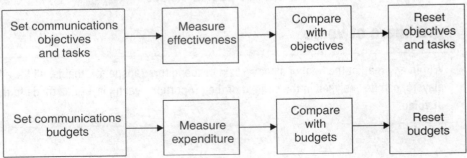

Chapter Roundup

- In order to be effective, the development of marketing communications must take place within the context of the prevailing **corporate**, **business and marketing strategies**.

- **Promotional objectives** need to be stated in such a way that it is easy to understand what is to be achieved and what was achieved.

- The goals to be achieved take three main forms. These are **sales**, **communication** and **corporate communication objectives**.

- There are **five** main contextual areas that need to be considered when developing marketing communication campaigns. These are the **business**, **customer**, **stakeholder**, **organisational** and **external contexts**.

- The overriding requirement for marketing in today's modern markets is better **targeting**. This means aiming at the proper segment of the market. Common criteria for market **segmentation** are geography, demographics, geodemographics, behaviour and psychographics.

- To determine whether a segment is worth pursuing, the market needs to consider the **size**, **measurability**, **access**, **uniqueness of response**, **stability and actionability** of the segment.

- The basic options in targeting are **undifferentiated** or **mass** marketing, **differentiated** marketing, **concentrated** marketing and **customised** marketing. The approach is selected on the basis of **cost/benefit** analysis.

- **Positioning** of a product is concerned with how it creates and establishes an image in the minds of consumers and how it is evaluated against competing products. Positioning may be according to attribute, price and quality, use or application, product user, product class or competition.

- The use of **perceptual maps** can assist the positioning decision.

- **Methods of budgeting**:

    - Spending an arbitrary amount
    - Spending all you can afford
    - Determining the spend on a historical basis
    - Matching competitors' expenditure
    - The percentage of sales method
    - By experiment and testing
    - By modelling and simulation
    - The objective and task method

- The **objective and task method** is the most rigorous. As its name suggests, this entails determining the marketing communications objectives, determining the tasks necessary to achieve those objectives and determining the cost of each element.

- **Budgetary control** is essential because of the large sums involved. In essence this involves establishing satisfactory measures of the effectiveness of the marketing communications process.

Quick Quiz

1   'In order that its marketing communications be effective it is necessary to understand the conditions and elements that prevail in specific markets' – this statement refers to an organisation's customer context.

   True   ☐

   False ☐

2   Which three C's make up the 'strategic triangle'?

   C..........

   C..........

   C..........

3   Which one of the following statements is correct?

   A   Marketing communications are a type of 'noise'
   B   Marketing communications should never be directed against competitors
   C   The promotional plan is totally independent of the overall corporate strategy
   D   Creative advertising will always be able to sell a product

4   Pick the correct four words from the six options given.

   Prior to the promotional (1) .... being decided, the company will make a series of (2) .... decisions that will determine the nature of the overall (3)........... It is this which will then lay down the parameters within which a (4) .... strategy will be developed.

Promotional	Marketing strategy	Customers
Strategy	Noise	Corporate

5   Promotional objectives need to be specific. What 'W' word can be used to summarise each of these?

   • Capable of communicating to a target audience: **W**.....
   • A distinct message: **W**.....
   • Over a specified time frame: **W**.....

6   What are the five elements of context analysis?

7   What does 'MCPF' stand for?

8   Match these definitions to the processes they describe – positioning, target marketing process or segmentation?

   (a)   Breaking down the total market into segments that share common properties

   (b)   How the target market perceives the presentation of the product/service relative to competing products.

   (c)   Segmenting the market, targeting particular segments and then positioning the offer in the selected segment in order to achieve the marketing goals.

9   List three ways of setting a marketing budget.

10 If total sales in a market are valued at £300 million and the amount spent on advertising is £25 million, what is the A/S ratio?

Answers to Quick Quiz

1   False. This statement describes the business context.

2   Company, customers, competition

3   A

4   (1) Strategy; (2) Corporate; (3) Marketing strategy; (4) Promotional

5   • Capable of communicating to a target audience: Who
    • A distinct message: What
    • Over a specified time frame: When

6   Business, customer, organisational, stakeholder, external

7   Marketing Communications Planning Framework

8   (a)   Segmentation
    (b)   Positioning
    (c)   Target marketing process

9   Check your answer against Section 7

10 8.33%

Action Programme Review

1   Marketing communications can most effectively be expected to achieve objectives related to increasing awareness levels and changing attitudes and behaviour patterns. Increasing sales or market share is dependent on other marketing factors such as product acceptability, price and distribution.

2   Another example you could have considered is Cadbury's Roses, where the buying situation in advertisements has involved a sense of guilt or obligation on the part of the giver. Many products in this category are purchased as gifts for differing reasons rather than for personal consumption. You may also consider here the role of point of sale displays as an influencing factor in the purchase decision process.

3   Try undertaking this task by examining advertisements for products in the same category eg alcoholic drinks or cars. You can identify which brands are being promoted to the different classifications.

4   Try to identify similar kinds of products or services from competing companies. How does their approach to positioning vary? A skim through one of the Sunday newspaper supplements will show a range of different advertisements for motor cars that are all aimed at the same target audience but from a variety of positioning platforms.

5   Having identified the different approaches to budgeting, what are the significant differences in the way in which the budget is spent? It will be interesting to compare the different kinds of businesses and the way in which different kinds of communication tools are used.

6   You will be able to identify sales turnover figures from company Annual Reports. Also look at market sector reports from Mintel or Keynote.

7   The main deficiency of the percentage of sales method is that it turns the traditional cause and effect relationship on its head.

Promotion causes sales. Hence, the amount of sales is a function of the amount spent on promotion. The strict implementation of the percentage of sales method means that the promotional spend becomes a function of the level of sales. Therefore, if sales decrease, then the amount spent on promotion is also decreased, whereas it might be wiser to keep the promotional spend constant in the face of declining sales.

The problem in forecasting future sales is the uncertainty of knowing what resources will be available to achieve the sales targets. Hence, this method should only be used to determine how much needs to be spent if conditions remain static. Beyond that, the budget needs adjusting in view of the new objectives.

8   This could involve looking at your own organisation or use a past examination paper mini case study.

9   This can be achieved by checking back to the points made in this chapter.

Now try Question 3 at the end of the Study Text

Promotional tools

4

Syllabus content – knowledge and skill requirements

- The effectiveness of each of the promotional tools using appropriate criteria such as cost, communication effectiveness, credibility and control (2.2)
- The meaning of the terms above-, through- and below-the-line (2.3)
- The role of each of the promotional tools within a co-ordinated marketing communications mix (2.4)

Introduction

Exam tip

There are a variety of tools that can be used to communicate with audiences. This chapter will remind you of the salient points about each tool.

An understanding of the promotional tools and the ways in which they work is essential. What is most important is an appreciation of the way in which the tools can be co-ordinated in order that consistent and meaningful messages may be presented to target audiences.

This knowledge can be examined in a number of ways. One of the more obvious approaches is through the preparation of a marketing communications plan. Other ways include direct questions on co-ordination or the effectiveness of promotional tools.

Read *Campaign*, *Marketing Week*, *Marketing* and other trade journals on a regular basis and look out for case histories that track the use of a selection of promotional tools.

1 An overview of the promotional tools

FAST FORWARD

There is a substantial **range of promotional tools** from which the marketer can choose. The skill involves not only choosing the appropriate tools, but choosing the appropriate **combination** of tools.

In this part of the Study Text the aim is to make you more familiar with the very broad range of promotional tools and to provide some guidelines for **choosing the most appropriate promotional mix**. With promotional tools this is not an easy job, because usually it is not just one tool that is required but a combination.

Having chosen a suite of promotional tools, and allocated them as either **primary** or **secondary**, it is important to be able to **co-ordinate** them in a comprehensive and **cost effective** whole.

1.1 The range of promotional tools

The range of promotional tools continues to grow. The variety of media that can be used for **above-the-line** campaigns has expanded, both in the printed advertising field and in the broadcast field. There are literally thousands of publications aimed at different target groups. In the broadcast field the number of television stations steadily increases through satellite, cable and digital television and the number of commercial radio stations has also grown considerably.

Key concepts

Above-the-line campaigning is advertising placed in paid for media, such as the press, radio, TV, cinema and outdoor sites. The 'line' is one in an advertising agency's accounts, above which are shown its earnings on a commission basis, from the buying of media space for clients.

Below-the-line promotion involves product-integral and negotiated sales incentives, such as packaging, merchandising, on-pack discounts and competitions and so on. (Agency earnings on a fee basis are shown below the 'line' in their accounts.)

The diagram on the next page shows the range of tools that can be used to influence a customer or potential customer. These tools represent the use of **intentional methods calculated to bring about a favourable response in the customer's behaviour**. The diagram represents the most obvious promotion methods, though other parts of the marketing mix, including the product itself, pricing, policy and distribution channels, will also have decisive effects.

Action Programme 1

(a) Actually read your junk mail, wander around the supermarket, read the paper, watch TV, and start collecting those leaflets that are constantly posted through your letterbox. How many examples of the tools shown below can you find? Be on the alert constantly for real-life examples and illustrations that you could use in your examination answers.

(b) Were you influenced by any of the examples that you found? Did you respond? You should be able to analyse your reasons.

(c) Can you think of (or better, find examples of) any other promotional tools, not shown in the diagram below?

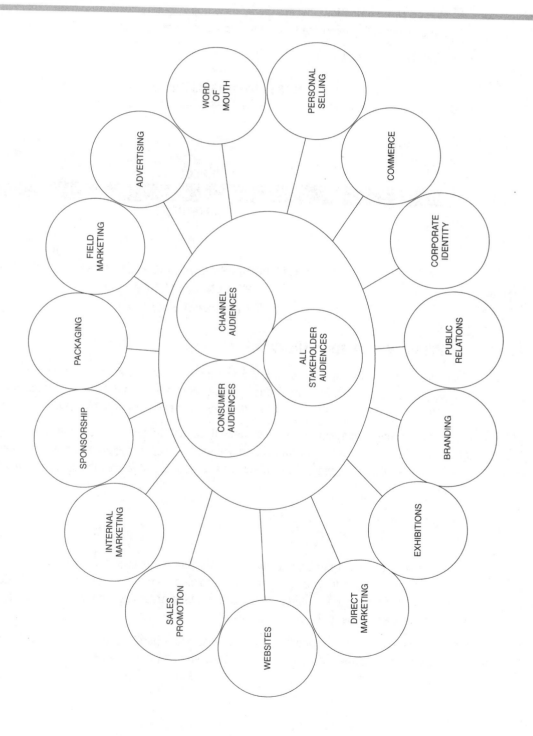

Figure 4.1: Promotional tools

There have been **major changes** in the way organisations communicate with their audiences. New technology, new media and changes in the way that people spend their time (working from home, shopping habits and leisure patterns etc) have meant that companies have to find new ways to reach people. **Direct marketing** (see Section 9) is now a more significant part of the marketing plan for many products, along with interactive forms such as the Internet (see Section 10).

The traditional emphasis on heavy mass above-the-line advertising has given way to more highly targeted campaigns. Below-the-line, and even what *Fill* (2002) terms '**through-the-line**' promotion (Figure 4.2) is now far more common. To quote Fill:

"The shift is from an **intervention-based approach** to marketing communications (one based on seeking the attention of a customer who might not necessarily be interested), towards **permission-based communications** (where the focus is upon communications with members of an audience who have already expressed an interest in a particular offering)."

Figure 4.2: 'Through the line' promotion

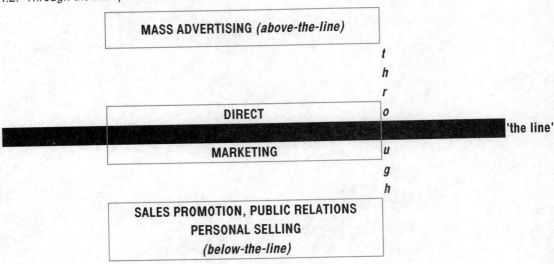

1.2 Primary and secondary roles

What should already be clear is that influencing customers and potential customers is a complex business. Discussions of buyer behaviour have shown that there is not just one process that influences the customer but a whole series. It follows therefore that each promotional tool will have a variety of roles.

In terms of making management decisions and allocating budgets it is possible to consider promotional tools in two broad categories of **primary** and **secondary** roles. For example, in a consumer campaign it may be that television is used as the main vehicle for launch, which is then sustained by a longer-lasting poster campaign.

 Action Programme 2

A mobile phone company ran a campaign of TV ads featuring a romance along the lines of the Nescafé Gold Blend couple. Then they ran a competition showing viewers extracts from the first series of ads and offering a prize to those who could put the extracts in the order in which they originally appeared. This (we were told) was a prelude to the second series of ads.

What are the primary and secondary promotional activities here? What do you think the prize was? Can you classify other campaigns that you have witnessed in a similar way?

The choice of primary promotion tool can also be influenced by the stage of the **product life cycle (PLC)**.

1.2.1 The PLC and developing promotional strategy

According to the PLC model, each of the stages from introduction to decline have different strategic requirements from their promotional activities.

Promotional Activities	Introduction	Growth	Maturity	Decline
Strategic focus	Strong push then pull for awareness	Pull to differentiate	Pull and push to sustain loyalty and exposure through reassurance	Some pull to remind core users
Public relations	X		X	
Advertising	X	X	X	
Direct marketing		X	X	X
Personal selling	X	X	X	X
Sales promotion	X		X	

The table above sets out the **strategic focus for each phase,** and the main promotional activities to be considered. What the table does not show is the way the promotional tools are used to support a push as opposed to pull approach. One particular benefit of the PLC is that it is possible to overlay the various stages of the process of **diffusion**. Through this it is possible to identify the **different types of buyer** involved with the product at each stage and through this fine tune the appropriate message and media.

1.2.2 Introduction

For consumer brands this phase is critical as the primary need is to **secure trade acceptance** (and hence shelf space) and then build **public (target audience) awareness**. Sunny Delight was developed by Procter & Gamble in consultation with major multiple grocers. When the product was launched the multiples accepted the brand as it had been developed partly to their specification on price, ingredient and packaging/size.

1.2.3 Growth

During growth, promotional activity is used competitively to **build market share**. Customers are normally willing to buy, having been made aware, but their problem becomes one of **brand choice**. Marketing communications should therefore be used to **differentiate and clearly position** the product such that it represents significant value for the customer.

1.2.4 Maturity

Once the rapid growth in a market starts to ease, the period of maturity commences. The primary characteristic of this stage is that there is little or no growth. The battle therefore is to **retain customer loyalty**. To do this, sales promotions are often used, to encourage trial by non-users and to reward current users.

Marketing at Work

Hoover has to reposition itself due to the market entry by Dyson with a technically superior product. Sales promotions alone therefore may not be sufficient, and a whole repositioning programme may be necessary to sustain a brand in competitive conditions.

1.2.5 Decline

As sales start to decline it is normal practice to withdraw a great deal of promotion support. **Direct marketing** and a little well targeted advertising to **remind** and **reassure** brand loyalists is the most commonly used.

Exam tip

Use of the tools of the promotional (or communications) mix over the life of a product featured on the Pilot Paper and again in the December 2006 exam (in the specific context of a automotive accessories retailer), so it is worth thinking about which tools may be appropriate at which stage of the life cycle.

2 How to co-ordinate the tools

FAST FORWARD

The choice should be made within the overall context of the **promotional objectives** and the strategies that have been determined.

All the promotional elements must be **co-ordinated** if the maximum effect is to be achieved.

Promotion work aims to influence customers favourably towards your organisation's products or services. It is necessary to co-ordinate all the promotional elements to achieve the maximum influence on the customer.

Having recognised the need for co-ordination, it is necessary to consider some more **practical steps to ensure that co-ordination** occurs. Figure 4.3 shows that co-ordination can be a conscious choice **during the planning process**, and it can also be a necessary part of the review and revision process.

Figure 4.3: Integration of promotional tools into planning

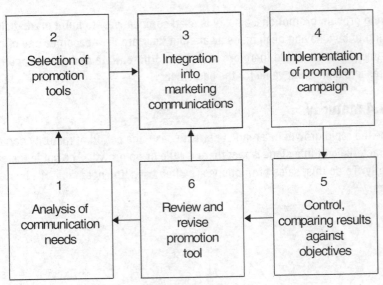

Figure 4.4 below demonstrates the use of measures that can be taken to ensure co-ordination. The first three involve asking questions about the **effectiveness**, **economy** and **efficiency** of the promotion tools. The efficiency can be forecast in the pre-campaign phase and then measured by means of tracking studies during the campaign. This will lead to a review, revision and further co-ordination of the promotion tools.

Figure 4.4: Criteria for integrating promotion tools

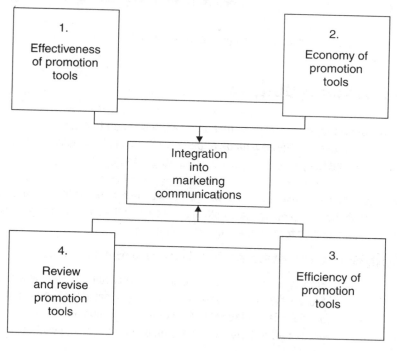

It is worth keeping the whole promotional mix in mind, because questions may ask you to select a mix for a given task or organisational context. The case study question in June 2007, for example set the task of a local council's getting disadvantaged citizens to apply for benefits: separate question parts addressed (a) the media and tools that can be used for the campaign and (b) the key messages that would need to be given.

3 Advertising

Advertising may be defined as non-personal paid-for communications targeted through mass media with the purpose of achieving set objectives. Advertising is a means of reaching large audiences in a cost-effective manner. Personalised feedback from an advertising message is not usually obtained.

The purpose of advertising is to achieve set objectives. These objectives will vary depending on the following factors.

- The result of the context analysis
- The nature of the product or service to be advertised
- The stage it has reached in its life cycle
- The marketplace in which it operates
- The role advertising is to play

Action Programme 3

Choose some television or print advertisements and try to work out what each one might be trying the achieve. What type of goals might there be?

Advertising is discussed in detail in Chapters 6 and 7.

4 Personal selling

Key concept

> **Personal selling** is an oral presentation by a salesperson to a customer with the aim of gaining a sale through persuasion. The advantage of personal selling is that technical detail can be given to the customer, and the product can be demonstrated if necessary.
>
> (www.learn.co.uk)

All organisations have employees with responsibility for contacting and dealing directly with customers and potential customers. These employees, known as the **sales force**, provide a vital function to the organisation as they form a direct link to the buyers.

An organisation has a choice as to how it **organises itself for selling**.

(a) Employ a direct sales force, consisting of full - or part-time paid employees who work exclusively for the company. This type of sales force may, in turn, consist of two groups: **inside sales personnel** who conduct their business from the company premises via the telephone, or **field sales personnel** who travel and visit customers.

(b) An organisation could employ a **contractual sales force**, which could comprise sales agents, dealers or brokers who are paid a commission on the sales they generate.

Irrespective of the type of sales force a company may use, the sales force needs the support of other groups within the organisation if it is to operate efficiently and effectively. The activities of the following groups impact upon the effectiveness of the sales force.

(a) **Top management** who can be increasingly involved in the selling process, particularly with big orders or key accounts.

(b) **Technical sales personnel** who supply technical information and service to the customer before, during or after the sale of the product.

(c) **Customer service representatives** who provide installation, maintenance and other services to the customer.

(d) **Office staff** including sales analysts, administrators and secretarial staff.

Selling increasingly regarded as a **team effort** involving all these groups.

4.1 The tasks in the selling process

Personal selling is probably the area of the promotional mix that has the most stereotypes attached to it. The image of the 'travelling salesman' is an enduring one. However, the term sales representative covers a broad range of positions, which vary tremendously in terms of tasks and responsibilities.

Role	Comment
Order collector	The salesperson's job is predominantly to deal with routine orders, normally through telemarketing.
Order taker	The salesperson passively takes orders from the customer. This can be further divided into *inside* order takers, such as shop assistants, or *outside* order takers, such as those salespeople who call on regular customers to take an order periodically. The customer has already been persuaded to use the product, or has been using the product in the past.
Pre-order caller	The salesperson is not expected or permitted to take an order but is expected to build goodwill or educate the customer in the use of the product. Medical representatives from pharmaceutical companies may fall into this category.
Order supporter	The salesperson's main skill is the application of his technical knowledge relating to the product.
Order getter	The salesperson has to stimulate demand and creatively sell tangible or intangible products.

The 'degree of difficulty' of the salesperson's tasks increases the nearer the person gets to being an order getter. However, the art of 'selling' in its narrowest sense is only one of a number of tasks that the salesperson could perform. A salesperson could perform as many as seven different activities (*Kotler et al*, 1999).

Activity	Comment
Prospecting	The salesperson may gather additional prospective customers in addition to sales leads generated by the company on his behalf.
Communicating	Communicating information to existing and potential customers about the company's products and services can take up a major proportion of the salesperson's time.
Selling	'The art of salesmanship', encompasses approaching the customer, presenting, answering objections and closing the sale.
Servicing	A salesperson may provide various services to the customer, such as consulting about their problems, rendering technical assistance, arranging finance and expediting delivery.
Information gathering	The salesperson can be a very useful source of marketing intelligence because of his or her links with the end customer. Many salespeople are responsible for supplying regular reports on competitive activity within their particular sales area.
Allocating	The salesperson may assist in evaluating customer profitability and creditworthiness, and may also have to control the allocation of products to customers in times of product shortages.
Shaping	An increasingly important role is to help build and sustain relationships with major customers.

While a salesperson may engage in all these tasks from time to time, **the mix of tasks will vary according to the purchase decision process, company marketing strategy and the overall economic conditions of the time**. For example, the skills needed for a straight rebuy situation (where the customer has bought the same product in the same way in the past) will be totally different from those required to develop a new account.

Exam tip

> A question in the June 2007 paper asked you: (a) to evaluate the effectiveness of personal selling as compared with advertising, in a B2B setting (electronics manufacture) and (b) to suggest how personal selling messages could support stages of the organisational purchase decision process (see Chapter 2).

Sales force activity must also be undertaken within the context of the organisation's overall marketing strategy.

(a)   For example, if the organisation pursues a '**pull**' strategy, relying on massive consumer advertising to draw customers in to ask for the brand, then the role of the sales force may primarily be a servicing one, ensuring that retailers carry sufficient stock, allocate adequate shelf space for display and co-operate in sales promotion programmes.

(b)   Conversely, with a '**push**' strategy, the organisation will rely primarily on the sales force to sell the brands to intermediaries, who will then assume the main responsibility for selling on the brands to the end customer.

The mix of a salesperson's tasks may vary with the prevailing economic conditions. For example, in times of product shortage the art of selling may not be as important. However, such a view neglects the other roles of the salesperson that will be of greater importance in such circumstances, such as allocating, counselling customers, communicating company policy to customers and perhaps selling other products that are not in short supply.

 ## Marketing at Work

One of the key advantages of personal selling, is the ability to allow customers to try or sample a product before they buy, reducing the perceived risk of the purchase decision. An emerging concept is '**tryvertising**', advertising in ways that allow and encourage product trial.

Three ways to 'tryvertise' in 2008 and beyond.

- Opened in July 2007, *Tokyo's Sample Lab* (www.samplelab.jp) is a members-only space that invites consumers to sample and test new products. More than 100 people lined up for the opening, paying a modest ¥300 registration fee and a ¥1000 annual membership fee. In addition to retail shelves stocked with merchandise, the space features a powder room where women can sit down to try beauty products. Besides trying everything out in the shop, members can take home up to five items per visit. To harvest their precious feedback, Sample Lab asks visitors to fill out surveys about the products they've tested.

- While promoting goods and services through friendly get-togethers is nothing new, *House Party* (www.houseparty.com) has given the concept a radical makeover. Unlike traditional sales parties, hosts don't sponsor events to earn a cut of the profit, nor are company representatives or consultants present to pitch their wares. Instead, anyone can apply to hose a party through the House Party website. Hosts get freebies, samples and special offers, plus access to party planning tools. For each campaign, House Party aims to book at least a thousand parties across the US to take place on the same day. This bundles the buzz and exponentially increases the effect of word of mouth advertising following an event.

- Food and beverage marketers have long known that there's nothing quite like sampling to convince a consumer to try something new, but the high cost and limited reach of traditional sampling campaigns are often prohibitive. Enter *First Flavor* (www.firstflavor.com), which converts flavours into 'Peel 'n' Taste' strips that can be mass-distributed in broad-scale campaigns in stores or magazines. Packaged in thin, tamper-evident pouches, the dissolving taste strips enable shoppers and readers to taste a new product or flavour. First Flavor's strips are produced in bulk quantities of 100,000 to 10 million or more, and quantity-based pricing ranges from seven to 40 US cents per

BPP LEARNING MEDIA

strip. Other possible uses for the strips include direct mail, product-on-product and in-store coupon dispensing applications.

Marketing, March 2008, p46

5 Sales promotion

Key concept

> The Institute of Sales Promotion (ISP) defines **sales promotion** as 'a range of tactical marketing techniques, designed within a strategic marketing framework, to add value to a product or service, in order to achieve a specific sales and marketing objective.'

(a) Sales promotion encompasses a range of techniques appropriate for targeting **consumers**, for instance via price reductions, competitions or gifts with purchases. However, **trade and sales force incentives** are also implied under the general heading of sales promotion.

(b) Sales promotion is viewed by the ISP as a tactical promotional tool. The majority of companies will use sales promotion as a means of achieving a **short-term objective**, for instance to gain short-term sales volume or to encourage trial and brand switching by a rival manufacturer's consumers.

(c) Although it is used as a tactical tool, sales promotion works within a **strategic marketing framework**. Sales promotion should start with due regard to the strategic objectives for the brand.

(d) Sales promotion always seeks to **add value** to a product or service. Thus consumers are offered something extra for their purchase, or the chance to obtain something extra.

Sales promotion includes the notion of both **sales pull** and **sales push** techniques. As we have seen, sales pull techniques incentivise the consumer to buy. Sales push techniques ensure that the distribution pipeline is well loaded, and sales are pushed along the distribution chain.

Exam tip

> Be aware of the potential for confusion between the terms *promotion* (used as a synonym for communication techniques in general) and *sales promotion* (which is a specialist term reserved for the specific techniques described here). In examinations some candidates read the question paper very quickly and mistake a question on sales promotion for one on promotional techniques in general. This unfortunate slip can result in a candidate scoring virtually no marks.

5.1 Sales promotion objectives

Examples of consumer sales promotion objectives.

- **Increase awareness** and interest amongst target audiences
- Achieve a **switch in buying behaviour** from competitor brands
- **Incentivise consumers** to make a forward purchase of your brand
- **Increase display space** allocated to your brand in store
- **Smooth seasonal dips** in demand for your product
- Generate a **consumer database** from mail-in applications

Exam tip

> Objectives of promotional activity were a feature of the December 2003 paper: in particular, brand development and encouraging purchase. A December 2006 Section A question asked, more generally, how a communications campaign could make the shift from conveying brand values and identity to a more definite 'call to action' – encouraging customer *experience* of the brand. You might identify sales promotion techniques as one option for achieving this.

Sales promotion objectives will link into overarching marketing and marketing communications objectives.

Marketing objective	To increase brand X market share by 2 percentage points in the period January to December 2006.
Marketing communications objective	To contribute to brand share gain of 2% in 2006 by increasing awareness of X from 50% to 70% among target consumers.
Sales promotion objective	To encourage trial of brand X among target consumers by offering a guaranteed incentive to purchase.

Action Programme 4

Tesco and Sainsbury issue a type of loyalty card that shoppers present when they reach the check-out. Points are awarded for sums spent over a minimum amount and these are added up each quarter. Money-off vouchers to be used against future grocery bills are sent to the shopper's home. What do you think is the value of this?

6 Public relations

6.1 Definitions

Key concept

The Institute of Public Relations has defined **public relations (PR)** as 'the planned and sustained effort to establish and maintain goodwill and mutual understanding between an organisation and its publics'.

The Public Relations Consultants Association (PRCA) says that:

'Public relations is the name given to the managed process of communication between one group and another. In its purest form it has nothing to do with marketing, advertising or "commercialism". It will, however, often promote one group's endeavours to persuade another group to its point of view and it will use a number of different methods, other than (although often alongside) advertising to achieve this aim'.

6.2 The scope of PR

The scope of public relations activity is very broad.

- Government – national, local, international
- Business and industry – small, medium, large
- Community and social affairs
- Educational institutions, universities, colleges
- Hospitals and health care
- Charities and good causes
- International affairs

Whilst the specific practice of the discipline of public relations will vary from sphere to sphere (and indeed, from organisation to organisation), there are numerous separate types of activities that the PR practitioner may carry out at some time.

- Counselling based on an understanding of human behaviour
- Analysing future trends and predicting their consequences
- Research into public opinion, attitudes and expectations and advising on action
- Establishing and maintaining two-way communication
- Preventing conflict and misunderstandings

- Promoting mutual respect and social responsibility
- Harmonising the private and public interest
- Promoting goodwill with staff, suppliers and customers
- Improving industrial relations
- Attracting good personnel and reducing labour turnover
- Promoting products and services
- Projecting a corporate identity

From this list of activities it can be seen that the scope of **public relations activity**, if implemented effectively, should **embrace the whole organisation**. A number of criteria have been put forward in an attempt to define what constitutes 'excellent' public relations within an organisation.

- Programmes should be managed strategically
- There should be a single integrated public relations department
- Public relations managers should report directly to senior management
- Public relations should be a separate function from marketing
- The senior public relations person should be at board level
- Communication should adhere to the 'two-way symmetrical model' (see below)

6.3 Four models of PR

This last factor relates to the way in which public relations is practised. Given the diversity of the role of PR as emphasised above, it is logical to consider different ways in which PR could be practised. A framework for considering this has been propounded by *Grunig and Hunt* (1983), who suggest that there are four models of public relations practice. Each model will be considered in turn.

6.3.1 Press agency/publicity

The role of PR is primarily one of **propaganda**, spreading the faith of the organisation, often through incomplete, half-true or distorted information. Communication is one-way, from the organisation to its publics: essentially telling the publics the information the organisation wants them to hear.

6.3.2 Public information

In this model the role of PR is the dissemination of **information**, not necessarily with a persuasive intent. As Grunig and Hunt state, 'the public relations person functions essentially as a journalist in residence, whose job it is to report objectively information about his organisation to the public'.

6.3.3 Two-way asymmetric

Grunig and Hunt describe the main function of the two-way asymmetric model as scientific persuasion, using social science theory and research about attitudes and behaviour to persuade publics to accept the organisation's point of view and to behave in a way that supports the organisation. The aim is to achieve the maximum change in attitudes and behaviour.

6.3.4 Two-way symmetric

In the two-way symmetric model the **PR practitioner serves as a mediator between the organisation and its publics** with the aim of facilitating mutual understanding between the two. If persuasion occurs it is as likely to persuade the organisation's management to change its attitude as it is to persuade the publics to change theirs.

Public relations is, therefore, the **management of an organisation's reputation with its publics**, and this management involves a close consideration of the relationships involved. The organisation can be either reactive or proactive in its management of these relationships.

(a)   **Reactive PR** is primarily concerned with the communication of what has happened and responding to factors affecting the organisation. It is primarily defensive, with little or no responsibility for influencing policies.

(b)   In contrast, **proactive public relations practitioners** have a much wider role and thus have a far greater influence on overall organisational strategy.

Inevitably some techniques will be more appropriate in certain circumstances with certain types of publics than others. It is possible, therefore, to classify the different types of techniques or media according to the type of project areas in which they appear to be most effective. The most frequently used techniques are as follows.

(a)   **Consumer marketing support techniques**

    (i)   Consumer and trade press releases
    (ii)   Product/service literature
    (iii)   Promotional videos
    (iv)   Special events (in-store competitions, celebrity store openings)
    (v)   Consumer exhibitions
    (vi)   In-house magazines for sales staff, customers and/or trade
    (vii)   Salesforce/distributor incentive schemes
    (viii)   Sport and, to a lesser extent, arts sponsorships

 ### Marketing at Work

Sports sponsorship was worth £460 million in the UK at the end of 2002. This figure is still a long way from that spent on conventional advertising, but it is a sign of a resilient sector. It is no longer the 'poor relation' of other marketing initiatives, nor is it necessarily the first activity to be axed in an economic downturn.

The public has a high level of acceptance of sponsorship, with many recognising that if there is no sponsorship, there will be no event at all. Spiralling costs have meant that sponsors are increasingly prepared to consider involvement at the grass roots level rather than the higher cost, 'glamour' events. This in turn encourages the development of sport over the long term, and appeals to today's socially responsible consumer who is looking for genuine involvement to overcome his cynicism about corporate motives. The Football Association in the UK, for instance, now has a limited number of sponsorship partners, who are expected to get involved at all levels of the game. To quote Martin Cannon of the Institute of Sports Sponsorship:

'Perhaps the one certainty of the coming year is that the growth of auditing and evaluation services that have been developed in the recent past will continue apace. To survive, sponsorships will not just have to be seen to be successful, they will have to be clearly and unequivocally proven successes with a measurable impact on the achievement of sponsors' objectives.'

Adapted from *What's New in Marketing*, online, 2003

(b)   **Business-to-business communication techniques**

    (i)   Corporate identity design
    (ii)   Corporate literature
    (iii)   Corporate advertising
    (iv)   Trade and general press relations, possibly on a national or international basis
    (v)   Corporate and product videos
    (vi)   Direct mailings
    (vii)   Sports and arts sponsorships
    (viii)   Trade exhibitions

(c) **Internal/employee communications techniques**

    (i)   In-house magazines and employee newsletters
    (ii)   Employee relations videos
    (iii)   Formal employee communications networks and channels for feedback
    (iv)   Recruitment exhibitions/conferences
    (v)   Speech writing for executives
    (vi)   Company notice boards
    (vii)   Briefing meetings

(d) **Corporate, external and public affairs techniques**

    (i)   Corporate literature
    (ii)   Corporate social responsibility programmes, community involvement
    (iii)   Trade, local, national and possibly international media relations
    (iv)   Issues tracking
    (v)   Management counselling
    (vi)   Local or central government lobbying
    (vii)   Industrial lobbying
    (viii) Facility visits
    (ix)   Local/national sponsorships

(e) **Financial public relations techniques**

    (i)   Financial media relations on both a national and international basis
    (ii)   Design of annual and interim reports
    (iii)   Facility visits for analysts, brokers, fund managers, etc
    (iv)   Organising shareholder meetings
    (v)   Shareholder tracking research

While this is not a comprehensive list, it does give an indication of the many types of PR techniques that can be used in various circumstances and how certain techniques will re-occur in various settings. Media relations, for example, is used in virtually all areas of activity.

Exam tip

> A December 2007 question asked you to suggest how Public Relations activity could be used specifically to counter negative media coverage. Think what could be done *reactively* in such a situation (to get more positive messages out there) and what could be done *proactively* (to ensure that media are 'on your side' or consult you before breaking negative stories).

7 Direct marketing

The aims of direct marketing are to **acquire and retain customers**. Here are two further definitions.

Key concept

> The Institute of Direct Marketing in the UK defines **direct marketing** as 'The planned recording, analysis and tracking of customer behaviour to develop relational marketing strategies'.
>
> The Direct Marketing Association in the US defines direct marketing as 'An interactive system of marketing which uses one or more advertising media to effect a measurable response and/or transaction at any location'.

It is worth studying these definitions and noting some key words and phrases.

	Comment
Response	Direct marketing is about getting people to send in coupons, or make telephone calls in response to invitations and offers.
Interactive	It is a two-way process, involving the supplier and the customer.
Relationship	It is in many instances an on-going process of selling again and again to the same customer.
Recording and analysis	Response data are collected and analysed so that the most cost-effective procedures may be arrived at. Direct marketing has been called 'marketing with numbers'. It aims to take the waste out of marketing.
Strategy	Direct marketing should not be seen merely as a 'quick fix', a 'one-off mailing', a promotional device. It should be seen as a part of a comprehensive plan stemming from clearly formulated objectives.

Direct marketing helps create and develop direct relationships between you and each of your prospects, between the consumer and the company on an individual basis. It is a form of direct supply, embracing both a variety of alternative **media channels** (like direct mail), and a choice of **distribution channels** (like mail order). Because direct marketing removes all channel intermediaries apart from the advertising medium and the delivery medium, there are no resellers, therefore avoiding loss of control and loss of revenue.

7.1 Components of direct marketing

Direct marketing encompasses a wide range of media and distribution opportunities.

- Television
- Radio
- Direct mail
- Direct response advertising
- Telemarketing
- Statement stuffers
- Inserts
- Take-ones
- Electronic media
- Door to door
- Mail order
- Computerised home shopping
- Home shopping networks

In developing a comprehensive direct marketing strategy, organisations will often utilise a range of different yet complementary techniques.

Direct mail tends to be the main medium of direct response advertising. It has become the synonym for it. The reasons for this is that other major media, newspapers and magazines, are familiar to people in advertising in other contexts. Newspaper ads can include coupons to fill out and return, and radio and TV can give a phone number to ring (DRTV is now very common). However, direct mail has a number of strengths as a direct response medium.

(a) The advertiser can target down to **individual level**.

(b) The communication can **be personalised**. Known data about the individual can be used, while modern printing techniques mean that parts of a letter can be altered to accommodate this.

(c) The medium is good **for reinforcing interest stimulated by other media** such as TV. It can supply the response mechanism (a coupon) that is not yet available in that medium.

(d) The opportunity to use **different creative formats** is almost unlimited.

(e)   **Testing potential is sophisticated**: a limited number of items can be sent out to a 'test' cell and the results can be evaluated. As success is achieved, so the mailing campaign can be rolled out.

The cornerstone upon which the direct mailing is based, however, is **the mailing list**. It is far and away the most important element in the list of variables, which also include the offer, timing and creative content.

A **database** is a collection of available information on past and current customers together with future prospects, structured to allow for the implementation of effective marketing strategies. Database marketing is a customer-oriented approach to marketing, and its special power lies in the techniques it uses to harness the capabilities of computer and telecommunications technology. Building accurate and up-to-date profiles of existing customers enables the company to:

(a)   Extend help to a company's target audience

(b)   Stimulate further demand

(c)   Stay close to them: recording and keeping an electronic database memory of customers and prospects and of all communications and commercial contacts helps to improve all future contacts

 Marketing at Work

Database applications

Computers now have the capacity to operate in three new ways that will enable businesses to operate in a totally different dimension.

'Customers can be tracked individually. Thousands of pieces of information about each of millions of customers can be stored and accessed economically.

Companies and customers can interact through, for example, phones, mail, e-mail and interactive kiosks. ... for the first time since the invention of mass marketing, 'companies will be hearing from individual customers in a cost-efficient manner'.

Computers allow companies to match their production processes to what they learn from their individual customers – a process known as 'mass customisation' which can be seen as 'the cost-efficient mass production of products and services in lot sizes of one'.

There are many examples of companies which are already employing or experimenting with these ideas. In the US Levi Strauss, the jeans company, is taking measurements and preferences from female customers to produce exact-fitting garments. The approach 'offers the company tremendous opportunities for building learning relationships'.

The Ritz-Carlton hotel chain has trained staff throughout the organisation to jot down customer details at every opportunity on a 'guest preference pad'.

The result could be the following: 'You stay at the Ritz-Carlton in Cancun, Mexico, call room service for dinner, and request an ice cube in your glass of white wine. Months later, when you stay at the Ritz-Carlton in Naples, Florida, and order a glass of white wine from room service, you will almost certainly be asked if you would like an ice cube in it.'

Source: *Financial Times*

7.2 Telemarketing as a co-ordinated marketing activity

Telemarketing is the planned and controlled use of the telephone for sales and marketing opportunities. Unlike all other forms of direct marketing it allows for immediate two-way communication.

7.2.1 Role of telemarketing

(a) **Building, maintaining, cleaning and updating databases.** The telephone allows for accurate data-gathering by compiling relevant information on customers and prospects, and selecting appropriate target groups for specific product offerings.

(b) **Market evaluation and test marketing**. Almost any feature of a market can be measured and tested by telephone. Feedback is immediate so response can be targeted quickly to exploit market knowledge.

(c) **Dealer support**. Leads can be passed on to the nearest dealer, who is provided with full details.

(d) **Traffic generation**. The telephone, combined with postal invitations, is the most cost effective way of screening leads and encouraging attendance at promotional events.

(e) **Direct sales and account servicing**. The telephone can be used at all stages of the relationship with the prospects and customers. This includes lead generation, establishing buying potential for appropriate follow-up and defining the decision-making process.

(f) **Customer care and loyalty building**. Every telephone contact opportunity can demonstrate to customers that they are valued.

(g) **Crisis management**. If, for example, there is a consumer scare, immediate action is essential to minimise commercial damage. A dedicated hotline number can be advertised to provide information and advice.

8 The Internet and e-commerce

FAST FORWARD

The **Internet** is the name given to the technology that allows any computer with a telecommunications link to send and receive information from any other suitably equipped computer.

Most Internet activity in the UK is **business-to-business** related.

Exam tip

You can count on exam questions coming up that cover the case for Internet-based marketing and the use of digital technology. The December 2007 exam, for example asked how on-line/digital communications could be used by a medium-sized organisation (low budgets), specialist brand (premium ice creams) sold through an expanding franchise with a network (need to build connections).

The Internet is the name given to the technology that allows any computer with a telecommunications link to send and receive information from any other suitably equipped computer. Terms such as 'the net', 'the information superhighway', 'cyberspace', and the 'World Wide Web (www)' are used fairly interchangeably.

Access to the Internet is becoming easier and easier: most new PCs now come pre-loaded with the necessary software and developments in telecommunications networks will eventually render modems unnecessary. The decision to use the **Internet and related digital technologies** for either the whole or as a part of the business operations is a **strategically significant decision**.

The Internet can be used by organisations for business-to-consumer and/or business-to-business purposes. In the UK some 80% of Internet activity is **business-to-business related**, although as more members of the public get online and telephone and access costs reduce, this divide should narrow.

8.1 Websites

Most companies of any size now have a 'site' on the Net. A site is a collection of screens providing information in text and graphic form, any of which can be viewed simply by clicking the appropriate button, word or image on the screen. The user generally starts at the site's 'home page', which sets out the contents of the site. For instance, Penguin UK has a home page that includes the following options.

 Marketing at Work

The Penguin Home Page (www.penguin.co.uk)

- New releases
- Today @ Penguin
- Book of the Day
- Author of the Day
- Penguin Prize Winners

- Book of the day
- Bestsellers
- What We're Reading
- Affiliates

By clicking on 'Bestsellers' you can browse and order top selling books from the Penguin catalogue.

(Website accessed 29 June 2006)

8.1.1 Audience profile

The Internet is reckoned to be currently the fastest growing communications medium in Britain. It is thought that use is growing at between 10% and 15% per month. Estimates of the number of Internet users vary widely: one survey found that 63% adults in Britain had Internet access, or 37 million users. Many net users use it both at work and at home.

8.1.2 Internet Service Providers (ISPs)

Connection (if not available through a user's organisation) is made via an Internet Service Provider (ISP). The user is registered as an Internet subscriber and pays a monthly fee. If access is via telephone line, telephone charges may also be payable.

ISPs such as America Online (AOL) and Tiscali provide their own services, in addition to Internet access and email capability. For instance, AOL also offers a main menu with options such as Life, Travel, Entertainment, Sport, Kids.

There are many ISPs offering a combination of cost and performance. Many now also offer 'broadband' (very quick) access via cable or ADSL modem.

8.1.3 Browsers and search engines

Most people use the net through interface programs called **browsers**. Internet Explorer and Mozilla Firefox are two examples. Surfing the net is done using a **search engine** such as Yahoo! or Google. These guide users to destinations throughout the world: the user simply types in a word or phrase such as 'beer' to find a list of thousands of websites that contain something connected with beer.

8.2 Promotion: banner advertising

FAST FORWARD

A lot of the advertising on the Internet takes the form of **banner ads**.

Companies such as Yahoo! make money by selling advertising space. For instance, if you type in 'beer' an advertisement for Miller Genuine Draft will appear, as well as your list of beer-related sites. If you click on the advertisement you are taken to the advertiser's website, perhaps just to be told more about the product, perhaps to be favourably influenced by the entertainment provided by the site, or perhaps even to buy some of the product. The advertiser may get you to register your interest in the product so that you can be directly targeted in future. At the very least advertisers know exactly how many people have viewed their message and how many were interested enough in it to click on it to find out more.

8.3 Email as a promotional tool

FAST FORWARD

Email is cheap, targeted and can be sent to millions of people at relatively little cost. It is therefore of great interest to marketers, but there is increasing concern at the prevalence of 'junk' e-mail.

There are various uses of email.

- To advertise a product/service, usually with a link to a website.
- To update a subscriber to a product/service with useful information
- To confirm an order
- To invite users to write in or to respond to a helpline

Unsolicited email is probably more intrusive than traditional 'junk mail', though less so than the telephone. However, bad use of email can have the habit of upsetting large numbers of people, to the extent that in Europe regulation is felt to be needed.

8.3.1 Curbing the cost of junk email

The European Commission have published a report entitled 'Unsolicited Commercial Communications and Data Protection', which highlights the significant issues of concern surrounding the use of email for consumer targeting. The report estimates that in future the cost of downloading unsolicited emails could reach £6.4 billion a year. Regulations covering the use of direct mail are relatively clear in most countries with opt in/out clauses and mail preference services. The situation online is far from clear. Issues surrounding costs to recipients present a different aspect to this form of communication. Unwanted direct mail can be thrown away whereas email incurs costs in viewing and downloading from the Internet.

'Spamming' – the process of sending millions of unsolicited messages at one go – creates major problems for recipients imposing high costs. Emailing is an attractive form of communication for marketers, being both cheap, fast and effective.

In Europe, four separate directives cover unsolicited email but are considered to be unclear and inconsistent. To date five countries (Austria, Denmark, Finland, Germany and Italy) have legislated for opt-in systems which allow for email to be sent to consumers who have indicated they want to receive them. However, the 'policing' of this issue is complex and it will take some time to arrive at any kind of international agreements.

8.3.2 Internal communication: intranets

The idea behind an 'intranet' is that companies set up their own mini version of the Internet, using a combination of the company's own networked computers and Internet technology. Each employee has a browser, and a server computer distributes corporate information on a wide variety of topics and also offers access to the global net.

Potential applications include daily company newspapers, induction material, online procedure and policy manuals, employee web pages where individuals post up details of their activities and progress, and internal databases of the corporate information store.

8.4 Marketing and e-commerce

E-commerce is about transactions involving the exchange of goods and services, for payment, using the Internet and related digital facilities.

Internet marketing is about the application of the Internet and related digital facilities to help determine and satisfy marketing objectives.

Before we look at some of the strategic issues associated with marketing communications and the Internet, it is important to establish what is meant by some key terms, namely, **e-commerce** and **Internet marketing**.

E-commerce is about transactions involving the exchange of goods and services, for payment, using the Internet and related digital facilities.

Internet marketing is about the application of the Internet and related digital facilities to help determine and satisfy marketing objectives.

Although Internet marketing is not concerned with the mechanics associated with payments and security, the boundaries between e-commerce and Internet marketing are becoming blurred. As a result of this these phrases will be used interchangeably.

8.5 Strategic issues

The Internet **facilitates interactivity and a two-way dialogue** that no other method of communication can support.

The development of an interactive facility requires a major shift away from conventional commercial activities. This is often achieved in three phases.

	Comment
Presentation	The use of a website to enable visitors/customers to **access information**, provides an opportunity to stand out from competitors and **enhance corporate image**. It is an opportunity to illustrate the organisation's products and services. This facility is often referred to as brochureware.
Interaction	This phase is characterised by **two-way communication**. Questions and answers flow between the system and the user. Visitors to the site are able to enquire more deeply than at the presentation stage and **information about the visitor** is logged and stored on a **database** for future reference and for both on and offline communications.
Representation	When this phase is reached the organisation will have replaced parts of its commercial activities with **full online transactions**. The organisation's traditional commercial trading methods and channels may still be in place and the new interactive facility provides a complementary and/or alternative method for particular market segments.

It should not be assumed that all organisations move through each of these phases and if they do, it is at different speeds. Those that do migrate do so according to a number of variables, including the **nature of the markets in which they operate**, their strategy, technical resources, their attitude to risk and competitive pressures.

Internet technology can also be used strategically to enable communication with particular audiences.

(a)   The **Internet** itself enables public access to an organisation's website.

(b)   An **intranet** refers to a private internal network which is normally used to enable communication with employees.

(c)   **Extranets** allow particular external audiences such as distributors, suppliers and certain customers access to an organisation's facilities.

The Internet offers two main marketing opportunities, namely **distribution and communication**. The ability to reach customers directly and so avoid many channel intermediaries reduces transaction costs and is a prime goal for most organisations.

The use of the Internet as a communications medium is equally attractive. It is more than a medium as it **facilitates interactivity and a two-way dialogue** that no other method of communication can support. Unlike other forms of communication, dialogue is induced by the customer, the speed and duration of the communication is **customer controlled** and the intensity of the relationship (with the online brand), is again customer managed. All the traditional tools of the promotional mix can be deployed over the Internet, with varying degrees of success, but it appears that **offline marketing communications are required to support** the online communications and facilities. A combination of off and online communications need to be determined if the overall communications are to fulfil the **DRIP** roles that we discussed earlier in this Study Text.

Exam tip

> Examiner's Reports for this paper consistently urge students to think about the integration of any communications or media mix they propose: on-line and off-line media are both required to reach target audiences, and should be used in ways that support each other.

8.5.1 The Internet and the buying process

FAST FORWARD

> The Internet can be used to support stages in the **buying process**.

The use of the Internet can perhaps be best observed when set alongside the purchase decision process. See the table below.

Use of the Internet to support stages in the Buying Process

Awareness

Not very effective at generating awareness and needs the support of offline communications to drive visitors to the site.

Positioning

As a means of presenting features and benefits the web is very good once a prospective customer has determined a need for a supplier search and is looking to compare offerings.

Lead generation

Once an active search commences leads can be obtained and used to reach prospects in the future.

Purchase decision support

By carrying vast amounts of information at low cost, websites provide good opportunities to impress visitors and build credibility.

Facilitate purchase

Through the provision of basic transaction facilities (credit card payment) sales should not be lost once a decision to buy has been made.

Post purchase support and retention

Through the provision of free customer support and advice, levels of cognitive dissonance in customers can be reduced. Feedback from customers, email updates about product developments and the use of sales promotions to stimulate repeat site visits can improve reputation, enable cross selling and promote favourable word of mouth recommendations.

8.6 E-commerce and website management

To be successful a **website** should do the following.

- **Attract visitors**
- **Enable participation**
- **Encourage return visits**
- **Allow for two-way information sharing**

Management need to attend to three main decisions concerning their Internet and digital related facilities. These are their **development, maintenance and promotion**. All of these use resources and management need to be clear about the level of support that is appropriate. One of the key concerns is the website itself. To be successful the website should do the following.

(a)   **Attract visitors** – with online and offline methods

(b)   **Enable participation** – interactive content, and suitable facilities to allow for transactions

(c)   **Encourage return visits** – design targeted at needs of particular segments, free services and added value facilities

(d)   **Allow for two-way information sharing** – personalisation reflecting visitor preferences, direct marketing and information retrieval provide visitors with the information they are seeking

Exam tip

The December 2007 exam included a question on how the design and use of a website could assist (ie support or enhance) the marketing communication of a B2B financial services provider. Such a question includes issues of enhanced communication and relationship through direct electronic channels; e-commerce and e-supply potential; and design issues (ie how can the website be made most effective and attractive to B2B customers?).

A similar question was set in June 2007, but with the 'twist' that a company's direct web marketing competed with its channel intermediaries, causing relationship problems: worth bearing in mind as a potential downside!

8.7 Business-to-business e-commerce

Many observers are taking the view that the future of Internet marketing lies in the **business-to-business** (B2B) sector. The belief is based on the premises that:

(a)   Selling low value items to consumers requires significant spending on advertising and promotion and costly back up systems.

(b)   Consumers expect free content

(c)   Businesses that look for quotes can massively increase their source of suppliers, nationally and globally

(d)   Suppliers have a wider market to appeal to

B2B is therefore expected to break down barriers and enhance supply chain management.

Marketing at Work

Traditional manufacturing companies around the world have moved into e-commerce. Many have formed alliances to create their own online marketplace, especially in the automobile, aerospace and chemicals industries.

One example is the Australian Automotive Network Exchange (AANX).

The automotive industry relies on Just In Time (JIT) manufacturing in which the production of goods occurs with the minimum amount of waste in both time and resources. JIT puts pressure on all points of the supply chain to reduce inefficiencies in transportation, processing inventory and other business processes.

To facilitate JIT, the automotive industry is developing a fast and reliable communications network so that the shareholders – manufactures, suppliers, importers, dealers – can share information. This is called the Australian Automotive Network Exchange (AANX). It is am industry-driven initiative supported by the Federal Chamber of Automotive Industries, the Federation of Automotive Products Manufactures and the Motor Trades Associates of Australia. The four major car manufactures – Ford, Holden, Mitsubishi and Toyota – are also engaged.

AANX operates as an Internet-based infrastructure that allows users to send data to each in a reliable and confidential manner. It requires collaboration across company boundaries on the standards and protocols, in particular those concerning security, as the network will be used to transmit business – critical and competitive information. AANX is designed to send computer-aided design files and a range of media such as product management systems, electronic data interchanges and file sharing.

Combining resources to create a single automotive industry network for Australia will reduce effort and complexity. It also delivers shared benefits such as lower costs, consolidated network links, reduced operating costs, lower acquisition/maintenance costs, faster business cycles deployment, simpler roll-out of future technologies and increased service quality levels.

AANX enables Australian companies to tap into the global automotive networks and thus boost export opportunities and import efficiencies. These networks include North America, Europe, Japan and Korea. AANX is also working to achieve critical mass within its domestic market and to position the Australian automotive industry to take advantage of the potential offered by e-commerce.

From the website of the Australian Government Department of Communications, Information Technology and the Arts, accessed 3 July 2006

8.7.1 Benefits of using the Internet in e-commerce

Benefit	How generated
Loyalty	Faster response
Productivity	Better management of the supply chain
Reputation	Depends on competition, and ability of web-based strategies to offer real customer benefit
Costs	Generally lower; easier for customers to obtain information

Exam tip

Students are required to understand how Internet marketing can (and should) impact on marketing communications. Ideas about the Internet, intranets and extranets will be tested, normally through the mini-case questions. Individual specific knowledge about banner advertisements or the role of portals for example is not required. It is necessary to understand the strategic significance of Internet technologies, the impact they may have on current commercial systems and marketing activities and the role traditional marketing communications will continue to have in the strategic promotional activities of organisations.

There are two sides to this topic. A question in December 2002 under the old syllabus turned the issue on its head by asking students why luxury goods markets tend *not* to rely on online sales activity.

Chapter Roundup

- There is a substantial **range of promotional tools** from which the marketer can choose. The skill involves not only choosing the appropriate tools, but choosing the appropriate **combination** of tools.

- The choice should be made within the overall context of the **promotional objectives** and the strategies that have been determined.

- All the promotional elements must be **co-ordinated** if the maximum effect is to be achieved.

- The **Internet** is the name given to the technology that allows any computer with a telecommunications link to send and receive information from any other suitably equipped computer.

- Most Internet activity in the UK is **business-to-business** related.

- A lot of the advertising on the Internet takes the form of **banner ads**.

- **Email** is cheap, targeted and can be sent to millions of people at relatively little cost. It is therefore of great interest to marketers, but there is increasing concern at the prevalence of 'junk' e-mail.

- **E-commerce** is about transactions involving the exchange of goods and services, for payment, using the Internet and related digital facilities.

- **Internet marketing** is about the application of the Internet and related digital facilities to help determine and satisfy marketing objectives

- The Internet **facilitates interactivity and a two-way dialogue** that no other method of communication can support.

- The Internet can be used to support stages in the **buying process**.

- To be successful a **website** should do the following.

    - **Attract visitors**
    - **Enable participation**
    - **Encourage return visits**
    - **Allow for two-way information sharing**

Quick Quiz

1   What range of promotional tools is available?

2   What is through-the-line promotion?

   A   Advertising placed in paid-for media
   B   Communication with an audience that has already expressed an interest
   C   Any form of advertising which reduces profits
   D   Sales incentives such as packaging and merchandising

3   Suggest promotional strategies (pull and/or push) for the different phases of the product life cycle:

Phase	Strategy
Introduction	
Growth	
Maturity	
Decline	

4   Choose the most appropriate words from the grid to fill in the gaps:

Sales promotion includes the use of both pull and push techniques. Sales pull techniques (1) .... the (2).......... to buy. Sales push techniques ensure that sales are pushed along the (3) ....

Direct selling	Incentivise	Advertising
Distribution chain	Consumer	DMU

5   Direct marketing encompasses a wide range of opportunities. How many can you recall from the list in Paragraph 7.1?

6   What are three advantages of email as a promotional tool?

7   What are we talking about here?

   (a)   .... is about transactions involving the exchange of goods and services, for payment, using the Internet and related digital facilities.

   (b)   .... is about the application of the Internet and related digital facilities to help determine and satisfy marketing objectives.

8   How might Internet marketing generate increased customer loyalty?

Answers to Quick Quiz

1   Check your answer against the diagram following Paragraph 1.1

2   B

3

Phase	Strategy
Introduction	Strong push, then pull for awareness
Introduction	Pull to differentiate
Maturity	Pull and push to sustain loyalty
Decline	Some pull, to remind core users

4   (1) Incentivise (2) Consumer (3) Distribution chain

5   Check your answer against Paragraph 7.1

6   • Cheap
    • Targeted
    • Can be sent to millions of people quickly

7   (a)   E-commerce
    (b)   Internet marketing

8   It may lead to faster response times, that encourage customers to visit your website again and again in the expectation of superior service.

Action Programme Review

1   You will find it useful to maintain files of these examples. Try and find examples relating to differing market sectors including consumer products, services, public sector and not for profit. At your place of work collect examples based on business-to-business marketing communications. Collect examples for the same companies over a period of time. This will illustrate different use of communication tools and identify changes in strategy and tactics over time.

2   How does this approach differ from other companies in this sector? How was this co-ordinated with other communications activities by One-to-One?

3   Consider the goals in relation to business, marketing and communications strategies.

4   On the launch of its 'Clubcard' Tesco said that it was a way of saying thank you to customers and that it wanted to 'recreate the kind of relationship that existed between consumers and local shops half a century ago'.

    In practice, however, the schemes give supermarkets the chance to build up a massive database containing customers' names, addresses and detailed information on individual shopping habits. But did they really encourage loyalty? No. Safeway decided that the considerable expenditure in the loyalty card scheme could be better spent on sales promotions targeted at local level (eg leafleting of local households). Safeway reported substantial increases in sales – but this has to be set against the fact that Tesco, still using the Clubcard, is the UK's most successful retailer.

Now try Question 4 at the end of the Study Text

5

Pull, push and profile

Syllabus content – knowledge and skill requirements

- The key characteristics associated with push, pull and profile strategies (2.9)
- The main characteristics of key accounts and the stages and issues associated with key account management (2.10)
- How co-ordinated marketing communications can be used to develop key account relationships (2.11)
- How marketing communications can be used to launch new products, support brands, maintain market share, develop retention levels, encourage customer loyalty and support internal marketing within the organisation (2.12)

Introduction

The focus of this part of the marketing communication process is to consider the emphasis of the marketing strategy – the balance between the need to communicate with consumers, with distributors and with all other stakeholders.

Type of Audience		Message Focus
1.	Consumers and business-to-business customers	Products and services
2.	Members of the marketing channel, such as dealers	Products and services
3.	All stakeholders, in order to raise the visibility of the organisation	The organisation

These approaches are referred to as the **3Ps of marketing communication**:

1.   **Pull** communication strategies
2.   **Push** communication strategies
3.   **Profile** communication strategies

FAST FORWARD

> **Pull**, **push** and **profile strategies** are not mutually exclusive. In practice, all three strategies are used, but the balance between the three strategies will vary, according to the needs of each programme.

Exam tip

> Communication strategy is a reflection of the objectives and positioning requirements set earlier in the marketing plan. 'Push', 'pull' and 'profile' strategies are not exclusive to each other and it is perfectly acceptable to choose an element of all three approaches, depending upon what needs to be achieved. Do not forget that they can all be used in the international context.

 Marketing at Work

Continental, the German tyre group, uses a combination of 'push' and 'pull'.

*   **Push to**: the OE (original equipment) market, by supplying tyres to the big car manufacturers
*   **Pull via**: replacement tyres, with consumers tending to opt for the same brand

The tyre-fitting trade plays a large role in the route to the customer. Continental carries out a lot of 'push' activity here, with incentive programmes, training and education to make sure that the fitters understand the brand segments (premium, quality, economy, budget, own-label). A greater challenge was to get consumers to think about tyres as more than those black things attached to their cars. TV and press advertising in Europe sought to change this perception.

Adapted from Marketing Business, January 2002

1 Pull based communication strategies

FAST FORWARD

> **Pull based programmes** are targeted at **end user consumers** and **business-to-business customers**. **Branding** is often used as pull strategy as it is possible to convey a great deal of information in a concise way.

Key concept

> A **pull strategy** is used to generate and sustain a dialogue with end user customers.

These might be consumers or they might be business-to-business customers, where the customer is the end user and does not move the product on through the marketing channel. **Pull strategies encourage end-users to demand the product from the distributors**, pulling the product through the distribution network.

Where a pull strategy is specified, then the promotional mix and the message and media combination will need to be co-ordinated. This will be explored later.

Typical strategies are to create higher levels of **product awareness** (spontaneous or prompted).

Action Programme 1

In order to ensure that the target market develops appropriate **attitudes** towards the brand, so that it has the best chance of being selected, the marketer has a range of options. Fill in the table below with your ideas as to what these options could entail.

Option	What does this mean?
Modifying the brand	
Altering beliefs about the brand	
Altering beliefs about competitors' brands	
Altering the importance of attributes	
Calling attention to neglected attributes	
Shifting the buyer's ideals	

A particular pull strategy that has been developed and refined over many years is **branding**.

2 Branding and customer retention

Branding originated as a means of differentiating products from commodities but it has come to be of major importance for reasons far wider in power and implication, especially since the introduction of mass media. In many markets it has taken over the role previously held by the direct selling operation.

2.1 What is a brand?

The following is a useful definition of a successful brand.

Key concept

A **brand**:

- is an identifiable product, service, person or place
- augmented so that the buyer or user perceives
- relevant, unique, added values, which
- match the buyer's/user's needs closely

The brand contributes the added value and can be seen as adding 'clothes' to a naked product.

Lancaster & Withey (2005) suggest that a product, and its attributes, can be seen at different levels: Figure 5.1

Figure 5.1: Augmented product concept

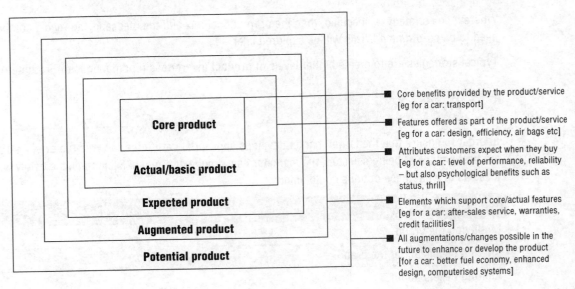

The **core product** satisfies the **basic need** of the customer, which is then built upon with **actual product** features and the **augmented product** 'embellishments'.

Action Programme 2

Apply this model to a Jaguar car. What are the core, actual and augmented elements of this particular product?

Another simple way of describing the difference between **commodities** and **brands** is shown in Figure 5.2.

Figure 5.2: Commodity or brand?

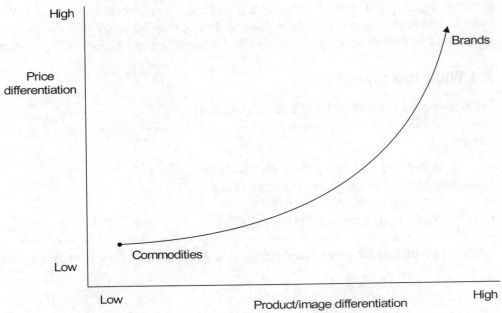

Branding encourages the consumer to associate certain attributes with a product. It differentiates very similar products into distinct segments of the market.

The process of differentiation through branding allows the marketer to establish a unique position for a package. Thus goods that in fact have very close substitutes, as in fmcg markets, can be positioned as though there was very limited competition.

Brands are no longer simply a convenient device to differentiate, they are of importance in their own right. It is often the brand that is bought, not the product.

The underlying justification for a brand is that it **builds profits**.

BASIC PRODUCT

↓

INVESTMENT IN BRANDING

↓

SUSTAINABLE ADVANTAGE

↓

MARKET SHARE INCREASE

↓

ECONOMIES OF SCALE

↓

INCREASED PROFITABILITY

↓

LONG TERM BRAND VALUE

2.1.1 Types of brand

Type of brand	Comment
Individual brand name	This is the option chosen by Procter & Gamble, for example, who even have different brand names within the same product line, eg Bold, Tide.
Blanket family brand name for all products, eg Hoover, Heinz	This has the advantage of enabling the global organisation to introduce new products quickly and successfully. The cost of introducing the new product in terms of name research and awareness advertising will be reduced.
Separate family names for different product divisions	This is the option for the global organisation with 'inconsistent' product lines where a single brand name is not appropriate.
The company trade name	(For example, Kellogg's Corn Flakes, Rice Krispies). This option both legitimises (because of the company name) and individualises (the individual product name). It allows new 'names' to be introduced quickly and relatively cheaply.

2.2 Branding strategies

There are three main elements associated with successful branding: **differentiation, added value** and **integration**.

2.2.1 Differentiation

Through branding it is possible to differentiate a product from its competitors, make it distinguishable and **readily identifiable**. It has been suggested that differentiation is a four part process as shown below.

Product	Comment
Generic product	Core product, nothing added (functional aspects only)
Expected product	Minimal value expected by buyer (features, design, packaging and price)
Augmented product	Value that surpasses a buyer's basic expectations (service, guarantees, add-ons, delivery and availability)
Potential product	Binding buyers to the branded item (brand name, quality and value perceptions, reputation)

 Marketing at Work

'A brand that illustrates *personality* perfectly is Paul Newman's Own, a well-defined brand that is reflective of the great man himself. There is a unique equity in his tongue-in-cheek humour that can resonate across various categories. His quirkiness creates a strong connection *on pack* and allows for visually compelling facings on shelf. Do people even interact with buying home brand? Do they even look at the pack other than to make sure it's peas not beans (sometimes you have to look hard to tell)? A bit harsh, perhaps, but it is a minimal involvement sort of gig. Modern-day branders aim for maximum *involvement*, always.

Brands can also bring activities outside their product and packaging to the party. Paul Newman's Own has *positive brand reinforcement* associated through making donations to charities for over 14 years. Nothing to do with the quality of produce, the taste or the colour of the label but rather a confirmation of generosity of spirit embodied in the brand itself. The feeling is further enhanced through the use of a Paul Newman's Own notebook-styled *interactive website* full of news, charity updated and recipes. The consumer now has a reason to keep connected that it also puts them in an ideal place to hear about what's new.'

Ad News + Packaging News, Pack Design Special, March 2008 p8

2.3 Added value

Branding needs to add value so that the consumers perceive a **meaning** in a brand that is **relevant** to them. This can be achieved through the way buyers perceive the performance of the brand, the psychosocial meanings attached to a brand and the level of **brand name awareness**.

	Comment
Perceived Performance	A function of the overall perceived quality and presence of important or significant attributes (eg Dyson).
Psychosocial meanings	A deduction of the social implications of brand ownership (eg Marlboro cigarettes and the differences between German/French cars).
Level of brand awareness	This can range from a state of unawareness through passive, active and top-of-mind awareness levels. This last stage is reached when the brand name becomes **synonymous** with the product category as with Walkman and Hoover.

2.3.1 Integration

For a brand to survive, the communications underpinning it must be consistent, uniform and reinforcing, so that it is very clear what it stands for.

2.4 Branding and marketing communications

Exam tip

Section A of the December 2003 paper contained a question on *brand support* for a leading cosmetic and fragrance company. The June 2006 exam also set a compulsory question on the selection of a communications mix for a *brand launch* (this time, shampoo). In December 2007, it was how marketing communications could be used differently to support national brands and local brands (in this case, ice creams sold through local ice cream parlours – as opposed to national brands such as Streets or Haagen-Dazs). Bear in mind that, even if the question isn't explicitly about brand strategy, a brand (or brand family) might be involved – or opportunities to *create* a brand might exist. Add branding issues to your list of things to bear in mind when reading an exam scenario.

The main idea behind branding is that **a basic product can be converted with marketing communications into a brand**. These communications can take one of two main approaches.

Approach	Comment
Functional	The aim is to provide information about the attributes and benefits associated with brand ownership. This is common where persuasion is important and where involvement and levels of perceived risk are also high.
Expressive	Emotions and feelings are central to the message and the prime goal is to develop audience likeability for the communication. Where involvement is low and perceived risk is minimal, it is common practise to try to engage the audience on an emotional level.

2.5 Brand strategies

Brand strategies may be summarised as follows.

Branding strategy	Description
Line extensions	Use of the same brand name to introduce new flavours, forms, colours and package sizes.
Brand extensions	Use of an existing brand name to launch new products in other categories (eg Mars into Mars Ice Cream, Honda into lawn mowers).
Multibrands	The introduction of additional brands into a particular market (eg Electrolux owns Frigidaire, Kelvinator, Westinghouse, Zanussi, White and Gibson).
New brands	The development of a new product into a market where none of the company's current brands would be applicable (eg Kellogg's entry into sportswear).

Branding strategy	Description	
Co-brands	Occurs where two (or more) established brands combine together to generate increased impact. There are a number of variants:	
	Ingredient co-branding	Volvo advertises that it uses Michelin tyres, Intel and Nutrasweet are other brands which are promoted within a brand.
	Same-company co-branding	When a company promotes two or more of its own brands in the same sector.
	Joint Venture co-branding	Microsoft sponsorship of the NSPCC charity.

The relevance of branding does not apply equally to all products.

(a) The cost of intensive brand communications, principally advertising to project a brand image nationally, may be prohibitively high.

(b) Goods or services that are sold in large numbers, on the other hand, promote a brand name by their existence and circulation.

Where a brand image promotes an idea of quality, a customer will be disappointed if his or her experience of a product fails to live up to expectations. **Quality control** is therefore an important element in branding policy. It is especially **a problem for service industries** (eg hotels, airlines, retail stores) where there is less possibility than in a manufacturing industry of detecting and rejecting the work of an operator before it reaches the customer.

 Marketing at Work

An article on *brand strategy* in *B and T* magazine (June 2007) compared brand management to parenting.

'I know a fair few of our clients who believe that brand management is a command and control activity. You define the target audience, craft your brand's proposition to appeal, and place your communication with military precision to win them over …

[But] any notion you can 'manage' a brand in this fluid, consumer-empowered and media-diffracted age is ridiculous. Today, powerful brands are made and consumed by the same people – their customers…

New channels, brand experiences, personalisation and modes of consumption mean that today's consumers can engage and shape their preferred brands in ways that were unthought of five years ago. Think Apple stores, viral marketing, online customisation of everything from jeans, to mobile phones, cars, holidays and home furnishings. Blog sites from dissatisfied customers and YouTube uploads of brand experiences from delighted Emirates first class passengers achieve more than the last well-planned and executed campaign.

This is a new world and your brand is engaged in a *constant, uncontrollable dialogue* with consumers in a thousand contexts at once.

So what are the lessons for modern branding?

• Set values and be consistent, but don't try and micro-manage your brands.

• Understand the context they are consumed in and inform their behaviour to be appropriate in each setting.

- Listen, as much as you dispense wisdom and opinion. Invite dialogue and co-creation.

- Forget brand tracking – there are much better measures of salience/relevance.

2.6 Customer retention

Arguably, this is another 'pull-based strategy', predicated on the notion that 20% of customers provide 80% of profits. Research by Frederick Reichheld, a management consultant at Bain & Co, found a high correlation between customer retention and company profitability. Retained customers are more profitable than new customers because: they cost less to obtain; they are amenable to cross-selling and up-selling (adding revenue); they cost less to serve; and they are a cost-effective source of word-of-mouth publicity, recommendations and referrals (*Reichheld*, 1996).

We discuss customer retention in more detail in Chapter 11.

2.6.1 Impact on marketing communications

(a) Customer retention requires internal (employees) as well as external marketing, in order to create a culture of excellent customer service

(b) Development of loyalty programmes (eg Air Miles) and communication of these to consumers

(c) More use of direct marketing (perhaps the Internet) to known customers to leverage the potential of trust and contact

(d) The main communications burden may be carried out by service staff

(e) Use of messages to reinforce 'barriers to exit' (*Egan*, 2004): emphasising familiarity, costs of finding alternatives, loss of loyalty rewards, legal barriers (eg minimum contract periods), emotional attachment to the brand 'community' and so on.

Exam tip

Exam questions will require you to use examples. We could cite Tesco as one where, in the long run, customer retention is a virtuous circle; if less money need be spent attracting new customers this represents a significant advantage over competitors and frees financial resources for other marketing activity (such as price cuts).

3 Push based communication strategies

Push based programmes are directed at **members of the marketing channel** where trust and commitment are essential ingredients for effective communications. **Key account management** techniques serve to help communications with strategically important accounts.

Communication with members of the marketing channel, such as **dealers and retailers**, is absolutely vital if sufficient **exposure and visibility** are to be obtained for the product. Without suitable distribution it is unlikely that the marketing objectives will be met.

It is therefore important to determine a promotional strategy to reach channel members in order to maximise the impact of a co-ordinated marketing communications approach. This strategy is referred to as a **Push Communications Strategy**: Figure 5.4.

Figure 5.4: Push based communication strategies

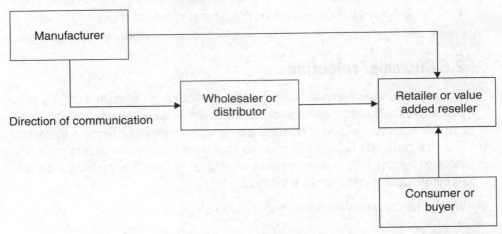

> A **push strategy** requires the identification of distributor needs and, through a combination of elements, an attempt to meet and satisfy these needs in order that both the supplier and the distributor are able to achieve their respective goals. The focus is on the intermediary.

Members of a marketing channel might be **independent** organisations and have their particular goals, but they choose to work together and are therefore **interdependent** and share a common goal: consumer/customer satisfaction.

Understanding the needs of the people who make up the decision making unit and then communicating effectively is an essential aspect of the push approach. Partnership success is achieved through co-ordination, trust, participation and the quality of information shared.

3.1 Key account management (KAM)

Key account management is an approach to determining which customer accounts are strategically important. These may be large revenue-driven accounts or they might be accounts that offer access to new markets or new technology, be competitively significant or represent a geographic advantage.

> **Key accounts** are perceived to be strategically meaningful and the communications (primarily personal selling) are geared to sustaining and developing the relationship between the two parties.

Relationships with key accounts unfold and develop through a series of phases.

Stage	Activity
Pre KAM	Identification of potential key accounts
Early KAM	Tentative agreements and probing
Mid KAM	Account review and senior management involvement
Partnership KAM	Joint problem solving and sharing of sensitive information
Synergistic KAM	Synergy of shared values and a one entity perspective
Uncoupling KAM	A positive move recognising that there is no further value in the relationship

There is more on key account management in Chapter 11 in the context of **relationship marketing**.

4 Profile based communication strategies

Profile strategies aim to influence the **way the organisation, as a whole, is perceived** by either a small or large range of stakeholders. These strategies serve to develop the visibility and credibility of an organisation. **Crisis management techniques** are an aspect of this, as are corporate branding and associated image activities.

The context analysis may have uncovered issues concerning the way the organisation is perceived by a range of stakeholders, perhaps as a result of an **ethical issue or crisis that has struck the company** and the associated **media comment**. In these circumstances, one of the objectives of the marketing communications strategy will be to correct or adjust the perception held by influential stakeholder audiences.

The extent of the perception gap will have been uncovered during the analysis of the organisation context. This in turn should have been articulated as a corporate communication objective.

Key concept

> A **profile strategy** addresses how the corporate entity is perceived by a range of stakeholder audiences. For example, it is quite common for an organisation to develop a communications campaign that is targeted at the financial markets and the stock market in particular. This is referred to as investor communications.

4.1 Corporate identity

Corporate identity and corporate image are two different facets of the profile development strategy. Increasingly organisations are adopting the phrase **corporate branding** as a substitute for corporate identity.

Corporate identity is about the way an organisation communicates with its audiences. There are two main forms of communication: those that are planned and pre-determined by the organisation, and those that are unplanned and unexpected.

The individual communication methods that make up these planned and unplanned communications are referred to as cues.

(a)   Examples of **planned cues** are letterheads, logos, signage, product quality and the behaviour and level of knowledge of employees.

(b)   Examples of **unplanned cues** are media comment, the cleanliness of the company's vehicles and any actions taken by competitors and consumer groups that may reflect or directly relate to the organisation.

Action Programme 3

Identify three corporate communication campaigns and the cues used by each to communicate with the different audiences.

The way in which these cues are perceived frames the way an individual sees and understands an organisation and helps form the image they have of an organisation.

Corporate identity therefore is about how an organisation presents itself. Corporate image is what an audience believes an organisation to be as a result of their understanding of the cues. Sometimes the perception of these cues is correct and sometimes it is not correct. This may be because of the quality of either corporate communications or corporate performance. **Corporate reputation** is an extension of corporate image.

'No Logo' by Naomi Klein is anti-branding and 'anti-multinational'. She considers that by their very nature multinationals aim to destroy difference and impose a homogeneous culture on the world. Corporate ethics is therefore seen as a cynical, halfhearted exercise. For example, oil companies trading on their green and ethical intentions have been undermined by allegations of human rights abuses.

4.2 Corporate communication strategy

As well as communicating about its individual products and services, the company may wish to pursue a corporate communication strategy. This can take either of two forms.

(a)   First, it can be a simple corporate communication campaign aimed at improving the company's identity and subsequently its image.

(b)   Secondly, it may be a campaign whereby the company associates itself with a current and topical social issue.

Action Programme 4

Identify two major companies which have developed corporate campaigns related to social issues. What do you consider to be the benefits and potential problems associated with such a strategy?

4.3 Crisis communications

Closely allied to corporate identity is the field of **crisis management** (communications). Company image and reputation can be severely tarnished or even ruined if a response to a crisis is deemed inappropriate.

Marketing at Work

The initial response by Mercedes when its then prototype vehicle the A-Class turned over when driven by journalists was to deny that there was a problem. That denial, which lasted eight days, turned into a crisis as 3,000 orders were lost and the media refused to let go of the problem. The reputation of Mercedes was dented for the first time in a long time and only the acceptance of the problem, and a public statement about the actions the company was to take with regard to production and design, alleviated the pressure on the company.

Some crises can be anticipated, perhaps because of the nature of the business environment in which an organisation operates. For example, hospitals can plan for bed shortages caused by epidemics or local accidents. Airlines plan meticulously to cope with air accidents although their incidence is relatively rare. However, the kidnapping of a senior executive cannot be anticipated with such clarity and neither can product sabotage and other seemingly unprovoked attacks on an organisation.

The following table sets out the phases through which most crises pass (*Hainsworth & Meng*, 1988). The duration of each phase will vary, depending upon the nature of the disaster and the quality of the

Disaster phase	Actions
Scanning	Scanning of the environment to pick up signals that might herald a disaster. Identify the nature of different crises that might hit the organisation. Where and when will it affect the organisation? Devise alternative crisis programmes for differing disasters. Establish appropriate communication channels, internally and externally. Chief Executive to formalise the programme and establish its significance throughout the organisation.
Pre-impact	Preparation of a specific crisis plan accompanied by the deployment of crisis teams in order to minimise the effects, and to inform stakeholders of the proximity of the crisis. Select key senior personnel and delegate responsibility. Instigate training programmes as necessary.
Impact	Implementation of the plan and continued communication with key stakeholder groups. The aim is to neutralise and localise the effect of the crisis but not to hide or diminish its significance. Maintain close contact with the media and provide stakeholders with access to specific personnel. Anticipate questions, do not speculate, use facts when answering questions and track media comment.
Readjustment	The speed of recovery is partly dependent upon the strength of the company's image/reputation before the crisis struck. However, internal and external (media, police) investigations characterise this phase. The organisation's attitude must remain consistent, positive and concerned.

 Marketing at Work

On Friday 19 February 2005, the Food Safety Agency (FSA) ordered the recall of more than 350 brands containing chilli powder coloured with Sudan 1, a red synthetic dye commonly used to colour shoe polishes and petrol.

Sudan 1 has been shown to cause cancer in mice and in tests on human liver cells. The substance has been banned from food use in the USA since 1918 and was banned as a food dye in 1995 by the European Union.

The dye was contained in a chilli powder used by Premier Foods to produce a Worcester Sauce. The sauce was in turn included in a variety of food products such as ready meals, soups and sauces.

The red chilli is reported to have come from India in 2002 as part of a 5 ton assignment.

Premier Foods started to use the chilli powder in September 2004 to make to make its Crosse and Blackwell Worcester sauce.

UK tests failed to uncover the presence of the potentially hazardous substance in the food chain. However, product tests in Italy did detect the presence of Sudan 1 in Worcester sauce.

The sequence of events, as drawn from a variety of publications, seems to be as follows:

28 January 2005   Italian company informs Premier Foods about Sudan 1 in its Worcester sauce.

2 February 2005   Premier Foods reports situation to local environmental health authorities.

7 February 2005	Environmental Health officers confirm findings.
10 February 2005	FSA demands a list of companies supplied with the Worcester sauce for use in other products.
14 February 2005	FSA receives list from Premier Foods of 200 companies whose products included Sudan 1.
18 February 2005	FSA announces recall of 359 brands affected by Sudan 1

Premier Foods did not carry out tests on the chilli powder but obtained written assurance from its supplier that the consignment was free of Sudan 1.

From a marketing perspective, consideration might be given to whether Premier Foods has a process entailing the above mentioned four phases.

Chapter Roundup

- **Pull**, **push** and **profile strategies** are not mutually exclusive. In practice, all three strategies are used, but the balance between the three strategies will vary, according to the needs of each programme.

- **Pull based programmes** are targeted at **end user consumers** and **business-to-business customers**. **Branding** is often used as pull strategy as it is possible to convey a great deal of information in a concise way.

- **Push based programmes** are directed at **members of the marketing channel** where trust and commitment are essential ingredients for effective communications. **Key account management** techniques serve to help communications with strategically important accounts.

- **Profile strategies** aim to influence the **way the organisation, as a whole, is perceived** by either a small or large range of stakeholders. These strategies serve to develop the visibility and credibility of an organisation. **Crisis management techniques** are an aspect of this, as are corporate branding and associated image activities.

Quick Quiz

1   What are the 3Ps of marketing communications?

2   Pull strategies encourage end-users to demand the product from the distributors.

   True   ☐

   False ☐

3   Fill in the gaps in this definition, using the words from the grid below.

   A successful brand:

   - is an (1) ………. product, service, person or place
   - (2)………. so that the buyer or user (3)……….
   - relevant, unique, (4) ………., which
   - (5)………. the buyer's/user's (6) ………. closely

Needs	Perceives	Added value
Identifiable	Matches	Augmented

4   What are the three main elements associated with successful branding?

5   Branding is appropriate for all products in all circumstances.

   True   ☐

   False ☐

6   It is important to determine a promotional strategy to reach channel members in order to maximise the impact of a co-ordinated marketing communications approach. This strategy is referred to as a .... communications strategy.

7   Which statement is correct? Key account management:

   A   Justifies managers in ignoring those customers who only order small amounts
   B   Is an approach to determining which customer accounts are strategically important
   C   Is not important in industrial markets
   D   Only really happens in advertising agencies

8   A profile communication strategy addresses how the corporate entity is perceived by a range of stakeholder audiences.

   True   ☐

   False ☐

Answers to Quick Quiz

1   Pull communication strategies
   Push communication strategies
   Profile communication strategies

2   True

3   (1)   Identifiable
   (2)   Augmented
   (3)   Perceives
   (4)   Added value
   (5)   Matches
   (6)   Needs

4   Differentiation, added value and integration

5   False. For example, the cost of intensive brand communications, such as advertising to project a brand image nationally, may be prohibitively high.

6   Push

7   B

8   True

Action Programme Review

1

Option	Comment
Modifying the brand	Redesigning the product so that it offers more of the attributes that the buyer desires.
Altering beliefs about the brand	Pursued if the consumer underestimates the qualities of the brand.
Altering beliefs about competitors' brands	Would be appropriate if the consumer mistakenly believes that a competitor's brand has more quality than it actually has.
Altering the importance of attributes	Persuade consumers to attach more importance to the attribute in which the brand excels.
Calling attention to neglected attributes	Where the brand excels in these attributes. ('Have you forgotten how good they taste?').
Shifting the buyer's ideals	The marketer would try to persuade consumers to change their ideal levels for one or more attributes.

2   For a Jaguar car, the 'core' is transport from A to B. The 'actual' product is a mechanical/electrical/electronic machine in certain colours built with certain features such as leather seats. The 'augmented' component adds the history and tradition of the Jaguar name and heritage.

3   Look for campaigns from companies involved in similar fields and examine how they differ. Give some consideration to the possible differences in the objectives set.

4   Financial services companies such as the Cooperative Bank have developed campaigns based on their ethical investment strategy. Tesco, the food retailer, has been involved in promotional activity aimed at raising funds to provide computers in schools. Such strategies may find favour with different stakeholder groups and enhance corporate image. Drawbacks may include criticism if, for example, the Cooperative Bank is seen to be investing in an area or in a company where negative issues have been raised by pressure groups.

Now try Question 5 at the end of the Study Text

Key media – concepts and effectiveness

6

Syllabus content – knowledge and skill requirements

- Primary and secondary media (online and offline) and their main characteristics (2.6)
- Key media concepts (reach, frequency, duplication, GRPs, flighting) and the principal approaches used to measure media effectiveness (2.7)
- Information and emotional based advertising messages and the concept of likeability (2.8)

Introduction

In this chapter, we look at primary and secondary advertising media.

(a) We will start by outlining the general criteria involved in **media selection**

    (i) **Criteria** by which the effectiveness and efficiency of media can be evaluated

    (ii) How the major media can be **compared** with each other

(b) We will then look at the characteristics of each of the **major media** (online and offline) in turn, and at how opportunities to advertise in each can be evaluated.

With this chapter we are still concerned with the most heavily weighted (50%) area of the syllabus, covering *Co-ordinated Marketing Communications*. There is a concentration on 'the tools and media used to communicate co-ordinated messages to target audiences'. This is a development of your knowledge of the marketing planning framework from Chapter 3.

1 Media selection

FAST FORWARD

Media selection should be made in accordance with the organisation's **advertising objectives** on the following criteria:

- The size of the audience/circulation
- The type of audience (in relation to the target audience)
- The opportunity of the audience to use the medium
- The effort required to use the media
- The audience's familiarity with the medium
- The selectivity/segmentation allotted by the medium
- The suitability of the medium's technical characteristics for the message
- The suitability of the medium's perceived function for the message
- The cost-effectiveness of the medium
- The medium's susceptibility to testing and measurement

The general criteria for selecting a medium to convey the promotional message to the appropriate audience are as follows.

- The advertiser's specific **objectives** and plans
- The **size of the audience** that regularly uses the medium
- The **type of people** who form the audience of the medium
- The **suitability** of the medium for the message
- The **cost** of the medium in relation to its ability to fulfil the advertiser's objectives
- The susceptibility of the medium to **testing** and **measurement**

1.1 The planning of an advertising campaign

(a) The identification of the **target audience**: Who are they? Where are they? Which demographic group do they fall in? What are their interests, media consumption habits, buying patterns, attitudes and values?

(b) The specification of the **communication** or promotional message. What do you need to say, and in what way, in order to impact on the audience in such a way as to achieve your marketing goals?

(c) The setting of **targets**: What is the marketing goal to which the advertising can contribute? What do you expect the ad to achieve and at what cost? What aspects of the audience's thinking or behaviour do you wish to change, and how will you recognise and measure that change if and when it occurs?

1.2 Balance of the message

As we first saw in Chapter 1, our understanding of the level of involvement that may exist in the target audience can be used to determine the **overall balance of the message**. If there is **high involvement**, messages tend to be **rational** (or **information based**), proclaiming product benefits and the key attributes. Where there is **low involvement** the audience are not really interested and the use of **emotion** (or **image**) predominates.

There are a number of ways in which these **information** and **emotional based messages** can be presented to audiences. These are referred to as **message appeals** and some of the more common approaches are outlined below.

1.2.1 Information based (rational) appeals

Issue	Comment
Factual	The benefits are presented using reasoned, factual arguments (eg nicotine patches).
Slice of life	Allow the target customer to identify with the characters and a common problem. Brand X is then perceived as a suitable solution (eg washing powders).
Demonstration	Show the audience how the product solves a problem (eg floor cleaners, before and after use).
Comparative	Through comparison it is possible to achieved enhanced status and superiority (eg credit and charge cards).

When a rational approach to advertising is used, the aim is to inform, persuade and arouse interest and preference. Some of the key factors in information-based appeals are:

(a) **Factual content** with perceived balance, objectivity, reasoned argument or 'proof' (eg through demonstration or expert endorsement).

(b) **Targeting** the perceived needs and interests of the target audience.

(c) **Source credibility** (as discussed in Chapter 1), so that customers believe in the trustworthiness and/or expertise of the people identified with the message to make valid statements about the product/service. This involves a number of source effects.

    (i) Spokespersons may be selected for high credibility in the relevent field (ie not just 'celebrity')

    (ii) Credibility may be lessened by the awareness that spokespersons are paid by the advertiser.

    (iii) Perceivable objective endorsements (eg by third parties or consumer organisations) are highly valued.

    (iv) Interpersonal influence, using consumers' own networks and reference groups, is highly effective. *'Word of mouth'* endorsement can be stimulated (eg by product trial and 'tell a friend' incentives for off-line messages, and/or viral marketing tools for on-line messages, such as 'send to a friend', recommendation lists, 'blogs' or product journals, on-line reviews and so on.)

The rewards of being a trusted and recommended brand

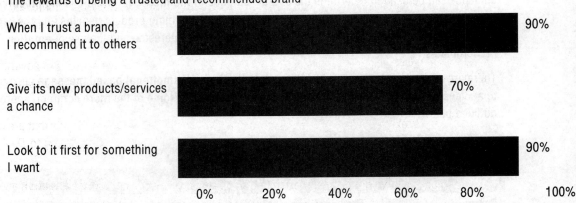

When I trust a brand, I recommend it to others	90%
Give its new products/services a chance	70%
Look to it first for something I want	90%

0%   20%   40%   60%   80%   100%

1.2.2 Emotional based appeals

Issue	Comment
Fear	The suggestion of physical danger or social rejection might be alleviated through use of the brand (eg life assurance, drink driving, anti-dandruff shampoo).
Humour	Attention and mood can be maintained by relaxing the target audience (eg Batchelors Super Noodles).
Animation	For low interest products/services animation can attract attention and convey complex products/issues in a novel manner (eg Revenue & Customs Self Assessment, Tetley Tea Bags).
Sex	Used primarily to attract attention and to be salient (eg Diet Coke, Wonderbra, Citroen Xsara).
Music	Provides campaign continuity and a degree of differentiation through recognition (eg Ford Cougar, Peugeot 406).
Fantasy	Used to engage an audience and to encourage the question 'what is going on here?' (eg Bristol & West Building Society, Silk Cut, Ericsson).

Action Programme 1

Using a variety of media, identify two examples of all the message appeals listed above. Can you identify anything that is common to your selections?

When an **emotional approach** to advertising is used, the aim is that the consumer will develop positive feelings about the product being advertised. The role of what is termed **likeability** becomes paramount. People need to enjoy the advertisement at the same time as finding it credible. According to *Fill* (2002) those advertisements that are remembered have certain characteristics. These characteristics add up to making an advertisement 'likeable'.

(a)   The **product is different** or new

(b)   The **advertisement itself is 'different'** or interesting

(c)   The message proclaims something that is **personally significant and relevant** to the consumer (Fill gives the example of a car advertisement seen by someone who is already planning to go out and buy a car the next day)

Researchers have isolated likeability as the only meaningful indicator of the success of advertising. Likeable messages are more likely to be **stored in the long term memory**, and retrieved when the customer is ready to make a purchase.

In an online context, the concept of likeability can also be applied to **websites**. Those that are enjoyable to visit and use are more likely to be remembered and revisited. In conclusion, according to *De Pelsmacker et al* (2000):

'Ad likeability might be an important factor because of its ability to **attract attention** and **facilitate information processing**. Peripheral cues such as humour, music, animals and children may attract attention, **induce curiosity,** which leads consumers to watch the whole ad, and induce a favourable attitude towards the ad, which can lead to a **favourable brand attitude**.'

Exam tip

The Section A question in December 2006 asked you to explain the terms 'source credibility' and 'likeability' and how they could be developed in advertising messages by a bakery. (You may be aware of recent campaigns by real-life bakery chain "Bakers Delight" using their own staff in 'home-made', up-beat TV and press ads, for example.) This followed a June 2006 question on the characteristics of rational and emotional based messages (using examples from the grocery market) and the use of word of mouth. Similarly, the December 2007 exam included a question on the importance of source credibility (in correcting negative media publicity) *and* on the charged issues of rational and emotional messages and how they could be used (to promote a sports centre). Don't neglect these aspects of marketing communications – because the examiner is obviously serious about testing them!

1.3 The size and type of the audience

FAST FORWARD

Media research is designed to provide data on circulated audience reach and media habits.

Each medium reaches a certain number and 'type' (demographic group, market segment, interest group) of people. There is a trade-off between the size and relevance of the available audience.

(a)   General-interest, national mass-market medium (such as a national newspaper or television) will have the largest **circulation figures**, but may not reach the highest percentage of a particular market segment.

(b)   **Segmentation** may be possible through the scheduling and placing of ads in large-scale media (for example, in special-interest sections or supplements in the press, or by programme preference in TV).

(c)   **Targeted media** may reach a smaller population, but a higher percentage of the target audience.

(i)   **Local or regional media** (in the catchment area)

(ii)   **Specialist magazines** and journals related to the target audience

(iii)   Media that fit the **'media habits'** of the target audience

Action Programme 2

Brainstorm a list of media that might be suitably targeted (by factors in the media themselves, or in the media habits of the target audiences) for advertising the following products/services.

(a)   A local garage offering car service, maintenance and parts

(b)   An up-market restaurant

(c)   A software package for use by accountants (based on UK law and regulation)

(d)   A new brand of washing powder

(e)   A microchip for use in engineering applications

The effective audience of a medium and therefore the competitiveness of different media is influenced by the following factors.

(a)   **Opportunity to use the medium**. The potential audience will not be able to use TV during working hours, or magazines while driving, or cinema over breakfast. Radio in the morning and TV in the evening have bigger effective audiences.

(b)   **Effort required to use the medium**. People usually use the medium that will cost them least effort. Print media require the ability to read and concentrate: television is comparatively effortless.

(c)   **Familiarity with the medium**. People consume media with which they are familiar: hence the survival of print media, since the education system is still predominantly print-orientated. Electronic media are, however, gaining ground.

(d)   **Segmentation by the medium**. The print media currently has the greatest capacity for segmentation into special-interest audiences. Commercial television segments the audience to a limited extent through programming, and cable/satellite television to a greater extent, through the proliferation of channels. Some media only charge in proportion to the segment that is targeted, which is more cost effective than paying for the full circulation.

Action Programme 3

What opportunity, effort and familiarity issues might you consider when appraising the following media?

(a)   A newly launched radio station

(b)   Daytime television

(c)   Posters on buses

(d)   Web pages

Media research is designed to provide advertisers with detailed information on the size and composition of the audience for relevant media, and the reading and viewing habits of the different types of people. Media planners (the people in advertising agencies who plan how to deploy the main-media advertising budget) use as much reliable research data as they can obtain. Here are some examples.

(a)   The National Readership Survey (formerly JICNARS) for major newspapers and magazines

(b)   BARB (the British Audience Research Bureau) for television

(c)   RAJAR (Radio Joint Audience Research) for radio

(d)   JICPAS for posters

(e)   The Screen Advertisers' Association for cinema

A marketing organisation may wish to commission or carry out its own research into the media habits of its customers and potential customers.

1.4 The suitability of the medium for the message

Certain media 'do' certain things better than others. You might bear this in mind.

(a) **The technical characteristics of the medium**. The success of a medium depends on its ability to identify and offer the benefits that its technical characteristics are best suited to provide: television for images and demonstrations, cinema for fantasy and visual impact, radio for music and participation, print for detailed information.

(b) **The perceived function of the medium**. Media users look to different media to perform different functions in their lives: information/education (world news, local events, specialist instruction) or entertainment (music, sport, escapism, community contact). These perceptions of a medium's functions and strengths will influence the orientation of its audience towards advertising messages.

(c) **The impact/realism of the medium**. One of the strengths of television is the impact to be derived from its realistic merging of sight and sound.

1.5 Cost and value for money

FAST FORWARD

Cost comparisons are usually made on the basis of 'cost per thousand' (people reached, or impacts).

Cost in itself is not a helpful criterion (unless it rules out a medium by virtue of its exceeding the spending budget). What advertisers need to know, in order to compare and evaluate media meaningfully, is the following.

- How many relevant people are reached?
- How many times and how effectively?
- For how much?

The conventional criteria of value for money measurement is **cost per thousand people reached** by a medium. If an advertisement in a newspaper with a circulation of 2 million readers costs £7,000, the cost per thousand is £3.50.

'Cost per thousand' is a common **inter-media comparison**-measuring device. However, it is only a crude measure, which does not take everything into account.

(a) The **targeting or relevance** of the audience reached by different media (or in different issues or time slots)

(b) The **potential impact** of an advertisement in different media (its size or length, colour or black and white, positioning in the publication or programme schedule, proximity to competing ads)

(c) **Extended or repeated exposure** to the ad (if people use the medium frequently, or pass it on to friends)

(d) **Selective exposure** to the ad (for example, people may not read the whole paper or magazine, or may leave the room during TV commercials)

The different media have their own methods of allowing for these factors when promoting their effectiveness to advertisers, and we will look at some of them – such as television ratings – later in this chapter.

1.6 Susceptibility to testing and measurement

FAST FORWARD Possible scheduling options include **continuity**, **flighting** and **pulsing**.

Testing, or measuring the effectiveness of advertisements is the only sure way to know what 'works' in terms of gaining a response. The same ad run in different media can demonstrate the comparative effectiveness of the media, while different ads (size, position, timing, layout, response methods, headlines) in the same media can indicate the most effective form of the promotional message.

Some media are better for testing ads than others and if this is important to you, you will need to ask yourself the following questions.

(a)   How **quickly** do I want our tests to yield results? (A daily publication produces response more quickly than a weekly.)

(b)   How **effectively** does the medium allow me to elicit direct responses? (Will it carry a direct-response coupon, or memorable telephone number?)

(c)   Will I be able to **attribute** increased enquiries/sales to their source in a particular ad? (Coded coupons, tracking, for example).

1.7 A general comparison of major media

The next three pages show some of the ways in which you might usefully evaluate advertising media.

Medium	Advantages	Disadvantages
Newspapers (daily metropolitan/ national)	• 'Mass' medium: large audience in single exposure • Targeted sections (auto, home, computers etc) • Reader navigation: seeking news, information • Short lead time for production: accept ads 24-48 hours before publication • Flexibility of ad size • Tangibility of ad (can be torn out and kept) • Multiple readers/users • Allows detailed information (prices, phone numbers etc) • Allows (still) images • Allows response mechanisms (eg captions)	• Circulation does not mean readership: wasted circulation paid for • Print/image reproduction of variable quality • No exclusivity: ad may be next to competitor's • Costs loaded for preferred positions • Short life-span of news
Newspapers (local/free)	• Low cost • Geographical targeting • High local readership • Special sections (especially local real estate, entertainment etc)	• Circulation of free papers/weeklies not always monitored/audited • Variable editorial content • Subject to weather and junk mail rejection if letterbox dropped

Medium	Advantages	Disadvantages
Magazines	• High circulation (major titles) • Targeted audiences (specialist) • High quality reproduction (colour photography etc) • Potential high prestige • Reader motivation (selection, subscription) • Long shelf life and multiple use/readership • Tangibility, detail, images, response mechanisms (see newspapers)	• High costs of production • Hyper-segmentation (by interest and geography, may be insufficient circulation to support local outlets) • Long lead times: copy/artwork required 1 – 3 months before publication, can be inflexible
Television	• 'Mass' medium: large audience at single exposure, almost universal ownership/access • Detailed monitoring of exposure, reach, viewer habits • Allows for high degree of creativity • Realism: impact of sound + sight + movement • High-impact visual images reinforce retention • Allows demonstration • Flexibility as to scheduling • Allows association with desirable products	• Most expensive of all media costs • High production costs • Lack of selectivity (except via programming) of audience • Lack of opportunity: does not reach commuters/workers • Long lead times for booking and production: penalties for withdrawal: inflexibility • Passive, unmotivated audience: 'zapping' by video fast-forward and remote controls erodes reach
Radio	• 'Mass' medium: wide coverage/access • Audience selectivity (local/regional) programme style/variety/content) • Opportunity: radio is portable – in-home, in-car, on public transport, shops, offices – even jogging • Function: high usage for morning news, home 'companionship', background • Personal (and potential for participation) • Highly competitive costs of air time and production • Can be backed by personal DJ promos	• May be passive 'background' noise: low attention, retention • May be 'cluttered' by announcers/DJ promotions • Sound only: no tangibility (pressure on retention of message), no shelf-life or 'pass on' circulation, no demonstration, no coupons, limited details

Medium	Advantages	Disadvantages
Outdoor media (poster sites, bus stops, buildings etc)	• Flexible: sites, duration of lease • Comparatively low cost • Opportunity: exposure to commuters, shoppers	• Difficulty of verification of exposure/response • Subject to weather • Opportunity: site specific • No audience selectivity (except by site)
Cinema	• Glamorous • High impact (large size, highly visual, loud sound, high quality) • Captive audience (no TV 'zap' factor) • Can segment by local area	• High cost • Opportunity: site/time specific • Poor verification of response • Limited number of people reached per exposure
Internet	• Principally sight, but with sound and colour further possibilities are developing • Interactive, permitting direct response • Able to track audience movements • Message permanent, and can be downloaded	• Generally poor viewership • Consumer confidence in security low (but improving) • Possible to direct audience to information, but can be difficult to gain large audience without support from other media • Not yet a mainstream media with broad customer appeal • Speed of access depends on sophistication of technological link • No universal computing language yet agreed

The following is a broad SWOT analysis comparing some of the major media.

Medium	Applications	Targeting	Testing	Cost per contact	Response speed	Response %	Response volume
Press	– Lead generation – Direct sales – General awareness – Support for other activities – Boost store traffic	Medium	Medium	V low	Fast	Low	High
Radio	– Awareness – store and event traffic boost – lead generation (high ticket business-to-business)	Medium to poor	Poor	High	Medium	V Low	Low
TV – general	– Awareness – Store traffic boost	Medium to poor	Poor	High	Fast	Low	Low

Medium	Applications	Targeting	Testing	Cost per contact	Response speed	Response %	Response volume
TV – direct response	– Lead generation (high ticket items) – Direct sales (low ticket items) – Support for other activities	Medium	Poor	Low	Fast	Low	Medium
Posters	– Awareness – Store traffic boost	Poor	Nil	V low	Slow	Nil	Nil
Inserts	– Lead generation – Direct sales (especially non cash-with-order sales	Good	V Good	Low to medium	Fast	Medium to low	High
Direct Mail	– All (weakest where prospects 'cold', no suitable list available)	V Good	V Good	V High	Medium	High	Medium

Exam tip

There will almost certainly be a question in the exam asking you to recommend a media mix (as in June 2006 June 2007 and December 2007) and/or to discuss the advantages and disadvantages of one or more media, and/or to compare and contrast two or more media. In December 2006, for example, you were asked to compare/contrast the effectiveness of sales promotion and advertising (note that you need to distinguish and define your terms clearly!), and to discuss the advantages and disadvantages of outdoor and print media (for a ferry operator). In June 2006, you had to compare/contrast the effectiveness of advertising versus direct marketing and personal selling, and discuss the advantages/disadvantages of cinema and print media (for a city council awareness campaign). In December 2007, it was comparing and evaluating broadcast and outdoor media (for a railway operator targeting car drivers). In June 2007 it was evaluating radio and consumer magazines (for an animal protection charity). Get to grips with this material now!

1.8 Media scheduling

When are the messages to be communicated to the target audience? This depends on a number of factors.

(a) **Objectives** of the campaign. If these are short term, then a concentrated burst will be best. Longer-term objectives can probably be satisfied by a less intense campaign.

(b) It is important to reach the consumer at or very near the **point of purchase**.

(c) The **level of involvement** is important. For high involvement purchases, less repetition is needed than for low involvement, where the message needs to be more frequent.

(d) The **characteristics of the target audience** will also dictate scheduling times – when their favourite programmes are on television, for instance.

(e) The size of the promotional **budget** is also a key factor.

The following **scheduling options** have been identified.

1.8.1 Continuity patterns

These represent **regular and uniform** presentation of advertisements for **reminder** purposes, generally on mature products and fmcgs, where no additional information is needed by the customer prior to purchase. The danger with this type of scheduling is that where the budget is limited, resources may be spread too thinly over the period during which the advertisement is running.

1.8.2 Flighting patterns

Flighting means **concentrating advertising in only a few periods**, allowing advertisers to spread resources over a longer period of time. No campaign is run at all in some months, in order to be able to spend more during times of peak demand. For that reason it is appropriate in situations where there is a **varying demand** for the product, or there is likely to be a sudden requirement for some kind of competitive response. Other situations where flighting may be appropriate include:

- Major sales promotions
- A response to adverse publicity
- One-off market opportunities
- Seasonality (such as tour operators advertising summer holidays in the depths of winter)
- Launch of new products
- Promotion of a particular event

1.8.3 Pulsing

The disadvantage of a flighting pattern is that the target customers can easily forget messages during times of no advertising. A **pulsing** pattern represents a combination of both flighting and continuous presentation. A certain level of advertising takes place during the whole period, with levels increased at certain times of the year. This is a 'safe' pattern, but is also likely to be comparatively **expensive**. The key advantage of pulsing stops target customers from forgetting, building awareness and providing a barrier in the customer's memory against competitor advertising.

2 Press or print media

Press or print media includes:

- **Newspapers**: daily and weekly, morning and evening, national and regional
- **Magazines**, periodicals and journals: general appeal, special interest and trade

2.1 Circulation and readership figures

The **Audit Bureau of Circulation (ABC)** provides audited figures of the actual circulation of major newspapers and magazines. This figure is often the basis of advertising rates. It offers only partial information.

(a)   There may be many **more readers than purchasers**. People may pass a publication on to others to read, or it may be perused by many people in dentists' waiting rooms or hairdressers. It is the estimated **readership** that interests the advertiser. The **Readership Survey** publishes the average readership per issue.

(b)   Readership data is also available on what **types of reader** consume various publications, with what frequency and in what manner (all the way through or some sections only).

2.2 Types of press ads

Print media offer different types of advertising.

(a) **Classified advertising**. The classified sections of publications offer small spaces for text-only ads. The advantage is that classified space is very cheap, and the publication usually typesets the ad for you. The disadvantage is the difficulty of attracting attention with so much competition and so little space: icons, headline, styles and impactful/incentive copy are required to make an ad stand out.

(b) **Semi-display advertising** allows you to use borders, typographic features and illustrations to attract attention (although on a crowded page, white space and simplicity may be more effective). Small ads in the Yellow Pages are a good example.

(c) **Display advertising** offers further opportunity for creativity: the advertisers design and provide their own artwork or film, constrained only by the technical specifications (size, colour) of the publication. Full-colour magazine ads are a good example. 'Long copy' advertisements break the usual simple visual style of display advertising by including lots of detailed information.

(d) **Advertorials** are advertisements presented as edited copy, in order to take advantage of the perceivably objective authority of editorial matter. Features on health and beauty, advice, house and garden are often advertisements for the products and services 'reviewed' or 'recommended'.

(e) **Loose inserts or 'drop outs'** are printed leaflets (produced by the advertiser) inserted into magazines and newspapers. They usually work out 4 or 5 times more expensive than advertising space – but draw up to 5 or 6 times as many responses as a full-page advertisement.

Marketing at Work

Car manufacturers often use long copy display ads for their cars. Full-page advertisements include detailed technical specifications and engineering drawings of the cars' driving and safety features. Such extensive copy is often effective for very expensive products, because it provides sufficient information to support an expensive purchase decision – and to justify or rationalise the purchase as a 'good' decision, not merely based on desire or snobbery.

Contrast this with purely visual display ads – often with no copy at all.

2.3 Press ad rates

Print media is bought in **column inches** (or centimetres) or standard **page divisions** (quarter, half or full page, or 'junior' page). The cost/rate differs.

- The **size** of the ad
- The number of **colours** in the ad and the production quality of the publication
- **Position** of the ad for which a premium may be charged
- The **readership** number of the publication
- The **potential for readership** targeting or niche marketing
- The **prestige** of the publication and the spending power of its readership.

2.4 Positioning press ads

Media research into **'traffic per page'** (the reading and noting of different pages in a print publication) suggests the following.

- **Early pages** are read more than late pages (depending on editorial content)
- **Right-hand pages** have higher noting scores than left-hand pages
- **Pages opposite relevant or popular editorial content** do better than pages opposite other advertising and less read editorial content.

Cover space is particularly sought after because of its high visibility, and usually also because the covers are printed on better quality paper for colour production. The outside front cover is likely to be most expensive, followed by outside back, inside front (especially if opposite the contents page) and inside back.

2.5 Scheduling of press ads

FAST FORWARD

Reach refers to the size of the audience which is exposed to an ad, both net (number of people reached) and gross (including cumulative multiple exposures).

Frequency refers to the number of times an ad is run; opportunities to see (OTS) the ad.

The approach to **scheduling** requires a combination of the following concepts.

(a) **Reach or exposure** – how many of the right type of people see the ad

(b) **Frequency** – how many times people see the ad. It does not cover the quality of the exposure or whether any impact was made on the audience.

With press advertising, in some circumstances it is generally advisable to repeat an ad more often.

- if the ad is **small** (and may not be noticed by all readers at one exposure)
- if the publication is **high circulation** (so the ad may not be noticed by all readers)
- if the product or ad is **interesting** (and will therefore continue to attract attention)

Even so, the **law of diminishing returns** operates with repeated exposure. As the ad reaches a higher proportion of the relevant audience, more often, the rate of response levels off. Awareness of the company or offer increases with repetition, but the rate of direct response to individual ads (via coupon or response line) falls: the 'easiest' prospects have already been reached.

Exam tip

> The examiner, in his comments on the December 2005 sitting, noted that "candidates sitting this paper must understand the different qualities of each of the classes of mainstream media and be able to show how the media decision is affected by the campaign objectives and the message to be conveyed". Media selections or recommendations always need to be related to the context of the question. You may also be asked to discuss contextual issues: in June 2006, for example, two questions asked you to identify distinctive aspects of a B2B marketing communications mix – and media selection would be a key part of this discussion.

3 Broadcast media

Traditional broadcast media include:

- Radio
- Television

3.1 Radio

The perceived function and image of **radio** is an important factor in the response to radio advertising. Radio is a personal and 'intimate' medium which encourages relationship and trust: according to the Radio Advertising Bureau (www.rab.co.uk), people are more likely to believe what they hear on radio than what they see on television. **Local radio** has a particularly close 'community' image. National radio stations are aimed more at a particular type of listener.

Radio tends to form the **background** to other activities. This enables it to have a wide reach (since it can be listened to while driving, working, jogging), but also lessens listeners' attention to and retention of advertising messages. The lack of visual images is also a disadvantage, but can be overcome by different techniques: the use of dialogue, mood, drama, humour and curiosity.

Radio ads are usually bought in series of 15 second or 30 second '**slots**'. Because of the high 'portability' of radio, there may be a wider range of off-peak scheduling opportunities.

 Marketing at Work

The **Radio Advertising** Bureau highlights these terms on its website (www.rab.co.uk).

Term	Explanation
TSA	Total Survey Area: the area covered by a station's signal.
Campaign reach	The number of listeners who hear at least one ad in a particular campaign – either expressed in thousands, or as a percentage of the population.
Frequency (Opportunities to Hear or OTH)	The average number of times a listener will hear a campaign ad, usually during a week.
RAJAR	Radio Joint Audience Research. The official measurement system for both BBC and commercial radio audiences.
Listening	Listening to a station may be measured either in terms of how many listeners tune in each week (reach), or in terms of how much listening there is in each week (hours).
Weekly reach	The number of listeners who tune in to a station at some point during a week, expressed as a percentage of the TSA.
Weekly hours	The total amount of listening (measured in hours) that a station accounts for. So, if commercial radio has a 51% share, 51% of *all* radio listening is to a commercial station.

3.1.1 Listenership figures

RAJAR (Radio Joint Audience Research Ltd) release quarterly reports showing what percentage/volume of the population listens to commercial radio, at what times and for how long, with breakdowns for each radio station. Around 25% of the UK population listens to national commercial radio, and 50% to local commercial radio, in the course of a week, for an average 15 hours per week. Over 70% of 15 – 34 year olds listen to commercial radio and almost the same proportion of business people and housewives with children.

Although such figures do not indicate whether people hear or take in any ads that may air during their listening hours, there are several positive indicators that radio can perform well in this respect.

- **Prompted recall of radio ads** is 80% of that of TV ads
- Radio listeners report that they **do not generally switch stations** when ads come on
- An average weight campaign on radio will reach each consumer **four times a week**
- **Talk-back radio** has a high response rate, even late at night

3.2 Television

The **Independent Broadcasting Authority (IBA)** controls commercial TV (and radio) in the UK, and licenses a number of regional companies.

Because of the **high exposure**, **glamour** and **audio-visual impact** of television, it has become the favoured medium for launching new products, raising brand awareness and building brand loyalty, re-positioning brands and also motivating the employees and supply chain partners of the advertising organisation. (This perception is encouraged by advertising agencies, whose **commission** on TV airtime is many times higher than on print space and other media.)

A major recent trend is in the development of **direct response TV advertising**, in which the viewer is given a telephone number and invited to call for more information or to place an order. This used to be perceived as down-market and American, but research now shows that it promotes an image of the organisation as organised, financially sound and willing to be readily accessible to customers. Direct response advertising has also enabled detailed measurement of the effectiveness of ads on different stations, at different times, in different formats.

3.2.1 Viewership figures

FAST FORWARD

Ratings are measurements of television audiences, which multiply reach by frequency (or OTS) to give the probable coverage and repetition of an ad, with (TARPs) or without (GRPs) breakdown by demographic criteria.

As with radio, it is a complex matter to access not just how many sets are owned and switched on at particular times, but how many people are actually watching – let alone consciously taking in what is being transmitted.

The size of the television audience for a given programme (and advertising) is measured in **ratings**: rating points, or **TVRs**. One TVR point represents 1% of all homes that have a TV set in the region to which the programme is broadcast. Ratings are used by TV stations to monitor the popularity of their programmes, and to set advertising rates. The advertiser pays for the number of TVRs allocated to given advertising spots.

(a) A programme with 20 TVRs is seen by 20% of homes with a TV. This is the number of people who will (in theory) see an ad once.

(b) If you placed an ad in four programmes, each with a rating of 20 TVRs, you would achieve 80 TVRs. However, some homes might have seen the ad all four times, while others may have missed it altogether. You need to distinguish between **reach** and **frequency** (the number of times the ad is run, and therefore the number of **opportunities to see it, or OTS**).

(c) **Gross Rating Points (GRPs)** are a measure of probable reach multiplied by probable frequency. If you buy 280 GRPs, about 70% of households should have 4 opportunities to see your ad.

(d)   **Target Audience Rating Points (TARPs)** measure reach and frequency against specific demographic audiences, across a wide range of criteria (geographic, gender, age, socio-economic bracket).

These are the most effective guide for advertisers, since they allow the media planner to devise a schedule which will deliver the largest relevant audience for the available budget: the gross cumulative exposure of the campaign to the target audience can be assessed on the standard cost-per-thousand basis.

Key concepts

> **Reach** refers to the size of the audience which is exposed to an ad, both net (number of people reached) and gross (including cumulative multiple exposures)
>
> **Frequency** refers to the number of times an ad is run, opportunities to see (OTS) the ad; or 'impacts'
>
> **Ratings** are measurements of television audiences, which multiply reach by frequency (or OTS) to give the probable coverage and repetition of an ad, with (TARPs) or without (GRPs) breakdown by demographic criteria.

Exam tip

> These key concepts (reach, frequency and opportunities to see) were featured in a question on the Pilot Paper, and again in June 2006.

The lowest cost per thousand is not necessarily the best schedule: one recommendation is the purchase of at least 250 – 300 TVRs, giving 70% coverage and a minimum of three OTS, in order to make a TV campaign worthwhile.

Statistically valid and helpful for comparison as ratings are, they still give only limited information: they count 'pairs of eyes' not responsiveness to ads. Detailed **qualitative media research** is required to indicate people's media habits.

- **Leaving the room** during commercial breaks
- Using the **remote control** to change channel to avoid ads
- **Videoing** TV programmes and fast-forwarding through commercial breaks

Further testing will be required to gauge **awareness and recall** of specific ads.

3.2.2 Scheduling TV ads

In addition to TARPs, which suggest where and when to schedule ads in order to reach an optimum number of target viewers an optimum number of times, the advertiser should consider the following.

(a)   **Daytime audiences** are more responsive. Direct responses to TV ads are greatest between 12 noon – 2pm and 2pm – 4pm on weekdays.

(b)   Audiences show greater recall of ads at the **beginning** of a long commercial break. The more ads they see, the lower the recall of each.

(c)   Audiences tend to watch through commercial breaks in the **middle of TV programmes**, because they do not want to miss any of the programme. However, viewers are reluctant to take action in response to ads during the programme, so direct-response ads are more successful during **end breaks.** (Most people respond within 15 minutes of the ad spot.)

(d)   Advertising guru David Ogilvy suggests that while most advertisers use 30-second ads, 90-second or even two minute ads can be more effective (as with long-copy press ads) especially for complex or expensive products.

(e)   Very short (10-second) ads can also be effective, and offer much higher TARPs for the available budget, since you can get more exposures. However, the greater impact of longer commercials usually offsets the reduced TARPs which longer ads deliver.

(f)   Repetition of ads increases TARPs, but is subject to the law of **diminishing returns**. It is essential for the message to sink in, but people easily become habitual and cease to notice or be motivated by the ad.

(g)   One strategy is to have a **set of related ads** that can be rotated, reinforcing but varying the message.

3.3 Duplication of broadcast advertisements

Those who are exposed to an advertisement only once are said to provide **unduplicated reach**. When a target is exposed to two or more overlapping advertisements, this is referred to as **duplicated reach**.

As part of the consideration of the **effectiveness of a media plan**, and related to the concept of frequency, it is important to think about **how many times a message should be repeated**. This goes back to points (f) and (g) above.

There is general agreement that there should be at least three OTS (opportunities to see) or opportunities to hear.

- First exposure: "What is this?" (seeking **understanding**)
- Second exposure: "What does this mean to me?" (**recognition**)
- Third exposure: "Oh, I remember" (**prompting action**)

Members of a target audience buy several magazines, and watch more than one television programme. They are exposed to many media vehicles. Those who are exposed to an advertisement only once are said to provide **unduplicated reach**.

When a target is exposed to two or more overlapping advertisements, this is referred to as **duplicated reach**.

Duplicated reach is obviously more expensive than unduplicated reach, and so any media plan needs to specify how much of each type of reach is required.

3.4 Digital television

Digital TV allows viewers to obtain in-depth information about products and services, via their remote control.

Digital television also offers opportunities for better targeting and segmentation. In theory, TV companies will be able to target particular advertisements to particular areas. However, this type of interactivity is still in its early stages. There is wariness by some marketers about becoming too intrusive.

Exam tip

The impact of digital based technologies on marketing communications is a specific syllabus topic. As an indication of how it may be examined, a question set in June 2002 under the old *Integrated Marketing Communications* syllabus asked candidates about the use of interactive TV, and how customers might be encouraged to use it again and again. New media and digital technologies were also examined in June 2005, June 2006 (in the context of supporting personal selling in a B2B market) and December 2006 as a tool for enhancing channel relationships. The December 2006 exam also contained a compulsory question asking for recommendations for the scenario organisation (a bakery) to develop its on-line marketing communications. The examiner has stated that although traditional media remain 'critical' and will continue to be tested, digital and new media will be of increasing interest.

Marketing at Work

The advent of digital television, where the viewer is in control, not only of the programmes he or she watches, but also their level of involvement with the content, may offer vast opportunities for marketers.

Broadcasters need material to fill their programmes, and specialist PR agencies are starting to emerge, dedicated to producing TV coverage which promotes brands via tailored footage of, for example, motor shows and fashion shows.

Action Programme 4

All other things being equal, and subject to detailed research, at what time of day, or in what kind of programme, might you advertise the following products on TV?

- Shoe polish
- Home disinfectant
- Car repairs
- Chat/introduction lines

4 Other media

4.1 Outdoor media

Poster advertising is one of the oldest media for consumer goods advertising. Sites on walls, hoardings and bus shelters can be leased for a fee per calendar month. In addition, many vehicles (buses, trucks and taxis) now carry external advertising, and some are tailor-made to do so (advertising 'floats'). Trains and buses also offer internal advertising positions. Size and visibility of the sites are the main consideration.

Action Programme 5

The posters medium is sometimes given the more general name of 'outdoor'. See if you can think of examples other than large poster sites. It may help if you go for a walk round your town and take a notepad.

Marketing at Work

" **Live demos in Singapore taxis**

'Sony Ericsson has installed live demo units in taxis around Singapore, allowing users to test the sights and sounds of its new W810i Walkman Phone. In the installation, the W810i is mounted on the back of the passenger seat with a set of headphones for passengers to listen to the phone's sound quality. The campaign is supported by print and cinema campaigns.'

B&T, 19 May 2006

4.2 Cinema

Cinema advertising takes advantage of high audio-visual impact and a captive audience but still requires a high quality and entertainment value.

Cinema advertising best suits 'lifestyle' products.

- **Branded consumer goods** with high style and profile, aimed mainly at young adults (such as jeans and alcohol)
- **Local services** in the area of the cinema (particularly restaurants)

4.3 New media

Technology has widened the range of advertising media to include the following.

(a) **Videos** including informational instructional videos and advertising accompanying entertainment videos

(b) **Teletext** (usually via sponsoring of relevant types of information that the target audience might access)

(c) **Enhanced CD and CD-ROM** (especially for selling merchandise related to the information or entertainment contained on the CD)

(d) **Websites**. Internet shopping and other transactions are on the increase, as issues of payment security are sorted out. Websites with product/service information and related links vary in sophistication, but can provide an attractive **audio-visual and interactive** experience of promotional messages. In addition, they offer an opportunity for customers to access basic information that they might be reluctant to ask about over the phone.

(e) **SMS** (mobile phone) text messaging, ring tones and screen savers. This is a huge advertising growth area, especially now that mobile telecommunications has been integrated with the Internet – SMS marketing is low-cost, easy to use, highly personal and compelling (especially in youth markets) – but it does have to be done on a 'permission' basis.

(f) **Merchandise media** (eg printed mouse mats, T-shirts)

(g) **Interactive kiosks and displays**, eg for catalogues, store searches, 'virtual' fashion fitting rooms and so on.

 Marketing at Work

Stay awake to 'new media' – both hi-tech/digital and low-tech but inventive. Advertisers are buying space on everything from retail food-court table tops, to sky (using sky-uniting) – and even people (eg marketing tattoos!).

One major trend is on-line media featuring user-generated content, as a grass roots or viral marketing tool. Examples include websites such as YouTube, auction sites such as e-Bay, and the user features (favourites lists, reviews, weblogs) on sites such as Amazon.com.

Go on-line regularly to see what your favourite – or the 'hottest' – brands are doing. Check out a variety of sites, from Virgin to Kelloggs, Apple, Dyson, FedEx and so on.

[Key skill for marketers: Using ICT and the Internet]

5 Advertising on the Internet

FAST FORWARD

Online promotion uses communication via the Internet itself to raise awareness. This may take the form of links from other sites, targeted email messages or banner advertisements.

The opportunities to reach target audiences are now many and varied, but **just because they exist, that does not mean that they have to be used**. The purpose of advertising is to 'inform, influence or persuade' (CIM), regardless of the media used. To quote from the CIM again:

> 'Matching medium to audience demands that the marketer consider a number of criteria, some of which will be more important than others depending on the campaign aims and objectives. These include cost, ability to reach the audience and creative ability of the medium.'

Marketing at Work

Online advertisements are becoming ever more attention seeking. Animation, video and audio are moving the field beyond the normal banner advert. A company called *Eyeblaster.com* has facilitated the development of brash and noisy online advertising. The new formats are giving scope for greater creativity.

Newspapers, which invested heavily in putting their content online, are at the forefront of experimenting with the new formats to attract advertising revenue to their sites.

The use of interactive banner adverts is also increasing, adding value to the advertisement by providing services such as:

* Entering a destination to show the cheapest fare
* Filling in an e-mail address to receive further information

So the Internet has become a medium for carrying advertising in its own right. The same principles that we have already discussed in this chapter, centred around **matching medium to audience**, still apply. Companies need to be sure that the web provides the right environment and audience profile to meet marketing objectives.

The most common form of web advertising occurs when the advertiser uses a range of sites to drive visitors to a corporate site: Figure 6.1.

Figure 6.1: Driving web visits (Source: www.marketing-online.co.uk)

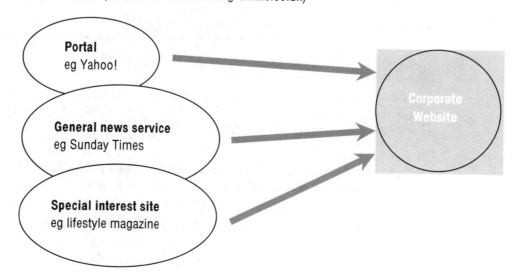

Companies are still learning what works with web advertising, and what does not. There are two basic types of promotion associated with the Internet, **online** and **offline**.

Key concepts

> **Online promotion** uses communication via the Internet itself to raise awareness. This may take the form of links from other sites, targeted email messages or banner advertisements.
>
> **Offline promotion** uses traditional media such as TV or newspaper advertising to promote a website address (URL).
>
> A **banner advertisement** is "a typically rectangular graphic displayed on a web page for purposes of brand-building or driving traffic to a site. It is normally possible to perform a click through to access further information from another website. Banners may be static or animated". Banner adverts can be targeted at a particular audience.
>
> *Source:* www.marketing-online.co.uk

Here are some examples of banner advertisements.

 ## Marketing at Work

'A new study claims a quarter of young broadband users have creatively participated with brands online and a further 56% would be likely to, challenging the 1-9-90 theory that 1% of users create, 9% comment on, and 90% view creative consumer content.

The survey, carried out by MediaLab, targeted around 11,000 16 to 35-year-olds in 22 markets around the world, including Australia, the US, UK, Russia, Mexico, India, China and Singapore. The study aimed to address the question of how marketers can adapt their brand communications in the digital world to remain relevant and have a positive effect on their brand.

MediaLab found that the chief motivator for *creative consumer participation* (CCP) is the expectation of involvement in product trials and receiving free samples from the brand, while the main barriers to participation were having to make a purchase and time constraints.

"Time, energy and money are commonly known to be the most desired resources of people today", read the report. "It is important to avoid costing too much of any of these to ensure quality consumer participation."

While half of all respondents said they would fee more positive about a brand that invited them to participate online, only 5% said they would fee less positive.

As Unilever has learned, the democratic nature of the internet means the power to invigorate or damage a brand is increasingly finding its way into the hands of consumers. Its Dove skincare and Axe deodorant brands have come under fire in online forums and channels such as YouTube, for charges ranging from sexism (Axe) to hypocrisy (Dove's Campaign for Real Beauty, which was accursed of using retouching).

Conversely, Nike ("Join the Chain" campaign) and Mentos and Diet Coke (via various YouTube "experiment" videos) have enjoyed huge "word-of-mouth success as a result of either insightful strategy or pure good fortune.

Nikki MacLennan, 'Brands enjoy more on-line involvement' *Ad News* (Australia), 16 May 2008, p26

5.1 Placing and paying for banner advertising

Banner advertising can generally be placed through a traditional agency. It is typically paid for according to the number of users who view the web page. Cost is calculated as **cost per thousand ad impressions**.

5.2 Measuring the effectiveness of Internet advertising

This is based upon the behaviour of web users. When using the Internet, users will go through several stages:

- **Be exposed** to a message (for example, through a banner advertisement)
- Look for **more information** by clicking on the banner
- **Go to the web page** of the advertiser

Based on this sequence, different types of ad effectiveness have been identified (listed by *De Pelsmacker* (2000)). These can be measured for different online advertisements of the same advertiser, on a daily basis if required, to monitor web ad effectiveness.

- Total **ad impressions** (number of contacts made by the ad)
- '**Click throughs**' (contact by a user with advertisement)
- **Ad transfer** (successful arrival of a user at the advertiser's website)

5.3 Other online advertising methods

These include:

(a) **Promotion in search engines and directories** (such as Yahoo!). Your company may want to have its company website listed when a user types in a specific keyword, such as 'office equipment'. To achieve this, your website should be registered with each of the main search engines (Yahoo!, MSN, Infoseek, Netscape, Google, for example).

(b) **Links from other sites**. This involves making sure that your site is linked to as many related sites as possible.

(c) **Using email** for advertising new products directly to customers.

(d) **User-generated content and communities**: discussion groups, user reviews, web logs (blogs), user-uploaded content (eg YouTube), user groups and so on.

6 Measuring media effectiveness

There are number of different approaches and tools for measuring the effectiveness of **marketing communications** or a particular **campaign** or **media plan**.

6.1 Media exposure

Media exposure refers to the amount, duration and frequency with which the organisation, brand or marketing message is featured across all communications media (or particular media segments): in other words, how much 'air time' the message or brand is getting. This may be measured by:

- The **media schedule**: that is, the amount of TV, cinema and radio advertising 'spots', pages of print advertising and poster sites the organisation has purchased over a period (or for a particular campaign). The advertising agency should provide this information, together with published **reach data**: viewer figures or ratings (for TV), listener figures (for radio), audited circulation and estimated number of readers per publication (for print media). This may be supplemented by *actual* measured exposure: for example, number of hits on the website, or number of viewers of a TV programme.

- Number of **mentions** in the news and information media, online discussion boards, blogs, promotion of sponsored events, and other essentially uncontrolled communications. This is usually monitored by specialist media monitoring or 'Share of Voice' agencies.

- **Cost per reach**: eg cost per thousand listeners/readers/viewers.

6.2 Campaign measurement

The success of a particular marketing communications campaign can be fairly scientifically measured by pre-campaign and post-campaign testing: the differences in the two sets of results should (theoretically) be attributable to the campaign.

Pre-and post-testing may use a variety of quantitative and qualitative techniques, including:

- **Results**: increases in sales (or donations, say); increases in enquiries, responses or website visits; increase in repeat orders or order value; and so on. (We discuss these measures below.)

- **Survey questionnaires or depth (one-to-one) or focus group interviews.** These methods can direct questions to more complex information about the impact of the campaign on the target audience: awareness of the campaign/brand; recall and recognition of the campaign/brand; what messages were understood from the campaign; the congeniality (likeableness) of the campaign/brand; perceptions and attitudes to the campaign/brand and so on.

Recall tests are designed to measure how much of the content of marketing messages members of the target audience remember. They can be used to measure the 'memorability' of advertising, press/publicity, sponsorships and branding campaigns – both before the campaigns run (pre-testing, using mock-ups) and afterwards (post-testing).

Survey or panel interviewees may be asked what advertisements and other communications they remember or have noticed. (This is called unprompted or unaided recall.) They may then be reminded of some details of the campaign, such as the theme of a series of advertisements or press articles, and asked what else they remember, or which ads/articles in the series they remember (prompted recall).

Recognition tests are similarly used to test the *penetration* of advertising and other marketing messages: how much of the target audience have they reached? Survey or panel interviewees are asked to look through newspapers, magazines or journals they have already read, and to identify which marketing messages they remember.

Marketing at Work

Jobber (*op cit*, p539) offers the case study of charity **Christian Aid**, and its national 'Christian Aid Week' fundraising campaign in 2005. This shows the depth of information that can be gathered on the success of a particular campaign.

'Every year NOP carries out before (pre-) and after (post-) research on the effectiveness of Christian Aid Week using a UK representative sample and a street-based questionnaire...

'Detailed results included:

- Significant shift in awareness of Christian Aid achieved by the 2005 campaign (pre-campaign compared to post-campaign): 8% increase in spontaneous awareness, 13% increase in total awareness.

- Awareness of Christian Aid advertising in 2005 higher than in 2004: 13% increase in spontaneous awareness; 6% increase in total awareness.

- The advertising in 2005 was seen as interesting and increased positive perceptions of Christian Aid: it made 4 out of 10 respondents laugh; it wasn't the sort of advertising expected from Christian Aid; it was seen as different from other charity advertising.

- Recall of advertising content was very encouraging.

- 70% of those who responded directly to Christian Aid Week advertising were new contacts.

- The main messages were communicated well. Respondents understood the message as: giving a poor family a chicken is better than giving them an omelette (30%); Christian Aid invests in things that multiply (19%); Christian Aid helps people to help themselves (18%); Christian Aid helps people in the third world stand on their own two feet (14%).

- Overall, Christian Aid Week donations were higher in 2005: the house-to-house envelope collection broke the £15 million (€21 million) for the first time and £100,000 (€140,000) was raised online.'

6.3 Results-based measurement

Exposure, recall and recognition are all very well – but if the target audience doesn't *do* anything, or do anything *different*, as a result of marketing communications, you know that *something* about the communication mix or media plan isn't working...

The success of the marketing communications activity can be measured by its effects, in relation to specific results-focused objectives.

- **Increased sales.** You might, for example, set as your campaign objective 'To produce direct sales of £X,000': that is, orders are to be received from people replying directly to the advertisement totalling this amount or more. In order to attribute sales directly to marketing communications, you need to identify what prompted a person to make a purchase: this can be done with direct response order forms or coupons (identifying media, date, campaign and so on), or by sales staff asking 'Where did you hear about us?' type questions.

- **Response rates.** You might, for example, set as your campaign objective: 'To produce enquiries from genuinely interested potential customers at a cost of not more than £X per enquiry'. Response rates can be most easily measured by using direct response advertising: different identification codes, telephone numbers, email addresses or website entry points may be advertised in different media, say, so that responses can be directly attributed to them. In other cases, however, it may be difficult to gather data on exactly what people are responding to. (It may also be difficult to define what a 'genuinely interested potential customer' is: that is, whether the response constitutes an engaged, qualified prospect or 'lead' – or just a casual enquiry that will not result in a sale.)

- **Inquiry tests:** comparison of the number of inquiries generated by particular media, and 'cost per inquiry' ie cost of the media divided by the number of inquiries generated.

- **Conversion rates:** how many responders, enquirers, prospects or sales leads actually become customers by committing to a purchase. This measure usefully recognises the unprofitability of generating responses/enquiries which do not convert into sales.

- **Repeat orders.** Repeat purchase is a useful measure of the effectiveness of relationship marketing communications and loyalty programmes (discussed later in this Text), in creating loyal long-term customers.

- **Order value.** Another of the aspirations of relationship marketing is to improve the profitability of loyal customers, which comes not just from repeat orders but from orders of increasing size and value. Order value is a useful measure of the effectiveness of cross-selling and up-selling activity, and of relationship marketing communications in general: higher-value orders may reflect the development of trust in the relationship, in both consumer and B2B markets.

6.4 Evaluating different marketing communications tools

As a final round-up, here are some sample measures for evaluating the effectiveness of particular marketing communications tools and campaigns. (Not intended to be comprehensive: just some ideas…)

Advertising and direct mail	Awareness, recall and recognition testing Congeniality (likeability) to the target audience Attitude surveys Media exposure: viewer/listener/circulation figures Cost per 1,000 target audience reached Cost per direct sale, inquiry or response generated Pre- and post-measurement of sales, enquiries, order value etc Advertising industry/media awards User comment on or sharing of ad content (eg on YouTube) Monitoring hits on web advertising, banner ad clicks etc.
Sales promotion	Increased consumer sales during the promotion period Increased intermediary sales during trade promotion period First-time intermediary sales from the trade promotion Number of coupons, vouchers, competition entries received Quality customer data gathered and input to database Cost per sale or response generated
Public rations	Media exposure Research/testing of audience awareness of key messages Research/testing of audience attitudes and perceptions Sales recovery after crisis communication Specific audience measures eg: • Focus group awareness of a publicity campaign • Reduction in employee turnover • Positive coverage in financial and other media • Increased trade in shares • Endorsement (or less opposition) from pressure groups • Change in government policy in line with lobbying

Exhibitions	Awareness of brand in industry, trade press
	Media exposure at or related to the exhibition
	Number of visitors to the stand
	Number of new qualified leads generated
	Contacts later converted to sales, supply contracts or alliances
	(An Exhibition Industry Federation survey found that the average time to convert an exhibition lead to a sale was seven months, and in some cases, two years or more…)
	Cost per sales (or other value) generated
Sponsorship	Awareness of sponsorship and brand
	Direct sales and enquiries (if attributable to the sponsorship)
	Media exposure arising from the sponsorship
	Cost per sale or response generated

Chapter Roundup

- **Media selection** should be made in accordance with the organisation's **advertising objectives** on the following criteria:

  - The size of the audience/circulation
  - The type of audience (in relation to the target audience)
  - The opportunity of the audience to use the medium
  - The effort required to use the media
  - The audience's familiarity with the medium
  - The selectivity/segmentation allotted by the medium
  - The suitability of the medium's technical characteristics for the message
  - The suitability of the medium's perceived function for the message
  - The cost-effectiveness of the medium
  - The medium's susceptibility to testing and measurement

- **Media research** is designed to provide data on circulated audience reach and media habits.

- **Cost comparisons** are usually made on the basis of 'cost per thousand' (people reached, or impacts).

- Possible scheduling options include **continuity**, **flighting** and **pulsing**.

- **Reach** refers to the size of the audience which is exposed to an ad, both net (number of people reached) and gross (including cumulative multiple exposures).

- **Frequency** refers to the number of times an ad is run; opportunities to see (OTS) the ad.

- **Ratings** are measurements of television audiences, which multiply reach by frequency (or OTS) to give the probable coverage and repetition of an ad, with (TARPs) or without (GRPs) breakdown by demographic criteria.

- Those who are exposed to an advertisement only once are said to provide **unduplicated reach**. When a target is exposed to two or more overlapping advertisements, this is referred to as **duplicated reach**.

- **Online promotion** uses communication via the Internet itself to raise awareness. This may take the form of links from other sites, targeted email messages or banner advertisements.

Quick Quiz

1   Fill in the gaps using the words in the grid below:

The general criteria for selecting a medium to convey the promotional message to the appropriate audience are as follows.

- The advertiser's specific (1) ....
- The (2) .... of the audience which regularly uses the medium
- The (3) .... who form the audience of the medium
- The (4)........ of the medium for the message
- The (5).......... of the medium in relation to its ability to fulfil the advertiser's objectives
- The susceptibility of the medium to (6) ....

Testing & measurement	Type of people	Size
Cost	Objectives	Suitability

2   What are the two types of message appeal?

3   Researchers have isolated 'likeability' as one of the most meaningful indicators of advertising success.

True ☐

False ☐

4   The conventional criteria of value for money measurement is cost per thousand people reached. If an advertisement in a newspaper with a circulation of 3 million readers costs £21,000, the cost per thousand is:

A   £6.30
B   £3.50
C   £7
D   £21

5   Give one advantage and one disadvantage of the use of a national newspaper for advertising.

6   Fill in the gaps using the grid below:

(1)   .... refers to the size of the audience which is exposed to an ad

(2)   .... refers to the number of times an ad is run

(3)   .... are a measure of probable reach multiplied by probable frequency.

(4)   .... measure reach and frequency against specific demographic audiences, across a wide range of criteria (geographic, gender, age, socio-economic bracket).

Target audience rating points (TARPs)	Reach
Gross rating points (GRPs)	Frequency

7   What is duplicated reach, and why is it important to the process of media scheduling?

8   'Click throughs' are measures of:

A   The number of contacts made by an Internet advertisement
B   The direct contact by a user with an advertisement
C   Successful arrival of users at an advertiser's website
D   The number of banner advertisements seen by a use

Answers to Quick Quiz

1   (1) Objectives (2) Size (3) Type of people (4) Suitability (5) Cost (6) Testing & measurement

2   Information and emotion-based appeals

3   True. Likeability seems to lead directly to favourable brand attitudes.

4   C.   (£21,000 divided by 3,000)

5   *Advantage*:   mass medium to reach lots of people
     Disadvantage: short life span (generally only one day) so your ad may be missed

6   (1) Reach (2) Frequency (3) Gross rating points (4) Target audience rating points

7   When a target is exposed to two or more overlapping advertisements, this is referred to as duplicated reach. Duplicated reach is more expensive than unduplicated reach, and so any media plan needs to specify how much of each type of reach is required.

8   B.

Action Programme Review

1   Include these examples in the files you are keeping of differing communications activities.

2   (Suggestions only)

(a)   Local radio (in car), bus stop, poster sites (driver visibility), local paper 'Auto' section.

(b)   Local cinema (evening session, adult-appeal film), local paper 'Food' section, Good Food Guide (regional listing), local radio (classical music/news programmes?)

(c)   UK Accountancy journals (various), Underground Station posters in financial districts, direct mail.

(d)   Commercial TV (especially daytime for housewives, poster sites (shopper visibility), women's and household magazines. (Assuming mainly female buyer decision.)

(e)   Trade (engineering journals, Research/home Website of inventor

3   (a)   Opportunity and effort are good with radio: effortless background, portable etc. Familiarity may be a constraint where station newly launched: listeners may not want to switch from old favourites, may not be able to recall frequency.

(b)   Daytime TV: minimal effort and good familiarity with regular users, but limited opportunity if target audience includes workers/school-age commuters.

(c)   Bus posters: minimal effort (depending on size, length of copy, sight lines: can be a strain to read bus posters), good familiarity, good opportunity because moving around (outside posters) but limited by bus users only (inside).

(d)   Web pages: high effort (to search, wait, use hypertext queries etc, requires technological know-how) improving familiarity (biased towards young computer-literate), limited opportunity by virtue of technology, access and expertise required.

4   (a)   Assuming mainly professional male buyers, next to business news, news or evening/weekend sports.

(b)   Assuming mainly female buyers/decision makers, daytime (cost effective), home/lifestyle programmes, prime time soaps (eg for launch).

(c)   Assuming car-owner buyers, not during commuting hours: driving/car programmes, motor sports, home/lifestyle (women buyers).

(d)   Assuming single buyers, late-night television.

5   Here is a suggested approach to the activity:

- Categorise the types of sales promotion into groups. Are certain types of promotion a characteristic of certain product categories?

- Are all the promotions appropriate to the products? Why?

- Try to distinguish objectives of the different promotions. What are they and, in your opinion, are they being achieved?

Now try Question 6 at the end of the Study Text

7

The international context

Syllabus content – knowledge and skill requirements

- The main issues concerning the use of marketing communications in an international and global context, such as media availability, culture, religion, education and literacy (2.15)

Introduction

Different viewpoints exist concerning the **globalisation of markets**. On the one hand, there is the argument that consumers are converging in tastes (aided by global technological advances such as the Internet) and that companies have an opportunity to market standardised products worldwide. An alternative view is that consumer markets are fragmenting and that products and services need to be adapted to individual preferences.

Key concept

'**Globalisation** of markets' is an expression that relates to:

- *Demand*: tastes, preferences and price-mindedness are becoming increasingly universal.

- *Supply*: products and services tend to become more standardised and competition within industries reaches a worldwide scale.

- *Multinational corporations* (ie those with operations in more than one country): trying to design their marketing policies and control systems appropriately so as to provide global products for global consumers.

This chapter begins by addressing a key question: to globalise or not to globalise? Then we go on to discuss various aspects of national differences.

1 Cross border marketing communications

FAST FORWARD

The international marketing communicator needs to decide **whether or not it is appropriate to standardise** communications across markets.

1.1 A global village?

Factors contributing towards the globalisation of markets include the following.

- (a) More **sophisticated consumers** who holiday outside their home country and are willing to experiment with non domestic products and services.

- (b) The trend towards **elimination of political, trade and travel barriers** worldwide.

- (c) The **internationalisation of broadcast and print media** (for example, cross border satellite transmission means consumers receive common programming).

- (d) The **saturation of domestic markets**, leading companies to search for growth for their goods and services in new markets.

1.2 Vive la difference?

Standardisation may suit companies, but may not be what consumers are seeking. An alternative view is that consumer markets are fragmenting rather than converging. Consumers are seeking to express themselves as individuals and do not want to be treated as part of a homogeneous mass. Products and services should therefore be **adapted** to individual country markets.

These two conflicting opinions provide a starting point for any consideration of international marketing management.

- (a) It is unlikely that the majority of companies competing outside their own home market will be able to standardise their marketing mix completely.

(b)   Nor is it likely that they will choose to adapt their marketing mix totally for each country in which they operate.

(c)   The nature of the product or service, consumer buyer behaviour and competitive market environment will all dictate the appropriate strategy to adopt.

Marketing at Work

Consumers in India are acutely price sensitive. They will think nothing of spending an entire morning scouting around to save five rupees. As a result, India has the largest 'used goods' market in the world. Most washing machines in the Punjab are used to churn butter, and the average washing machine (conventionally deployed) is over 19 years old.

"What many foreign investors don't understand is that the Indian consumer is not choosing between one soft drink and another; he's choosing between one soft drink and a packet of biscuits, or a disposable razor", says Suhel Seth of Equus Red Cell, an advertising company.

What this means for foreign investors is that they must price cheaply, and therefore source almost everything locally, to keep costs down.

There are other problems. Standard refrigeration becomes pretty useless when acute power shortages occur. Most consumable goods perish pretty quickly in the climate. And the country's fragmented regional culture means advertisers have to focus on common ground (such as music, Bollywood and cricket).

Is it worth the effort? Investors say that overcoming such obstacles has equipped them for success in any market in the world.

Adapted from the *Financial Times*, April 2002

2 Cultural considerations

FAST FORWARD

Companies operating outside their home markets need to be aware of the implications of **cultural differences** for all aspects of the marketing mix. Verbal and non verbal communications, aesthetics, dress and appearance, family roles and relationships, beliefs, learning and work habits are dimensions of culture of particular relevance to communications.

Marketing communicators need to be particularly sensitive to culture if messages are to work in global markets.

We absorb the culture of our home society as we grow up. Our family, our religious institutions, and our education system all play a part in passing culture from one generation to the next. Some behaviours and customs learned early in life are likely to remain resistant to the best marketing or promotional efforts. For instance, attitudes and behaviour with respect to particular foodstuffs can be culturally ingrained.

Culture evolves. Although core cultural precepts are passed from one generation to the next, the values of society do change. Before the Second World War, a 'marriage bar' existed in white collar occupations such as clerical work and teaching. When a single working woman married, she was expected to give up her job to look after her husband. This social norm seems inconceivable to us today.

Various **dimensions of culture** are relevant to the international marketing communicator:

*   Verbal and non verbal communications
*   Aesthetics
*   Dress and appearance
*   Family roles and relationships

*   Beliefs and values
*   Learning
*   Work habits

These are now discussed in detail.

2.1 Verbal and non verbal communication

Common-sense dictates that care must be taken when translating copy from one language to another. A catchy phrase in the home market may not work so well elsewhere. A literal translation of an advertising slogan, 'as American as apple pie' would be meaningless in many countries.

Usually, agencies will aim to interpret and adapt in order to capture the spirit of a communication message, rather than relying on a mechanical word for word translation.

Most agencies will buy in the services of a translation house when required. This will usually ensure that translation is carried out by someone who speaks the vernacular language of the country in question, an important point given that languages are in constant evolution. If an agency subsidiary or local company office exists in the overseas market, it can also be helpful to incorporate their advice. Back translation, where the copy is translated back into English, can be a final precaution.

It may be difficult to decide exactly which language to choose for translation purposes. The official language of China is Mandarin, but a large proportion of Chinese living in the south of the country have Cantonese as their native tongue. In Canada, although the majority of the population speak English, packaging must include a French translation.

An additional consideration is that of the **space required for foreign language text**.

Brand and product names must be assessed for their suitability in international markets. Mars changed the name of their *Marathon* chocolate bar to *Snickers* in 1990 to facilitate their global communications strategy. A different approach is demonstrated by companies who choose to go with different names in different markets. For instance Ford's Mondeo name works well in European markets, where the 'world' association comes across powerfully. In the US market however, the car is called the Contour.

Sometimes the phonetic sound of names can cause a problem. The French soft drink Pschitt would have obvious disadvantages in the English-speaking world (*Jobber*, 2007).

People communicate both by using language and by their use of **non verbal signals**. A shake of the head to British people means 'no', and a nod yes. This convention is reversed in some cultures.

Spatial zones can communicate. In Western societies, we give work colleagues or acquaintances a large zone of personal space. Only family and close friends will enter an individual's near zone. If a colleague comes too close, our reaction is to back off, as our personal space is being invaded. This is not so in some Far Eastern countries, where space is at a premium and people have far less privacy. There, it is acceptable to stand far closer to others.

2.2 Aesthetics

Attitudes towards different design and colour aesthetics vary around the world. A fragrance or toiletries carton decorated with chrysanthemum flower graphics would not be a success in France, where the flowers are traditionally associated with funerals. Similarly, the colour white, which carries connotations of freshness, purity and fragility in the UK, is the colour of mourning in China.

Different cultures will have grown up with their own rules about visual representation. The idea of showing a figure partially out of frame is well known in Europe. In much of Africa by contrast, figures that go over the edge of their frame transgress the cultural rule about how pictures should look. Similarly, a bird's eye view of a sail boat in a Gilbey's Gin advert was not understood by any of the 600 consumers interviewed in a West African project exploring how advertising was decoded.

2.3 Dress and appearance

Dress, be it formal or social, is very much constrained by culture. Advertisers need to be aware of cultural dress codes when deciding if an execution prepared in one market will be acceptable in another. In Europe, for instance, adverts for shower and bath products will often depict a semi-nude model. Such executions would be out of the question in the Middle East, where women can only appear in advertisements if carefully attired.

2.4 Family roles and relationships

Family has always been the dominant agent for transmitting culture. However, it may be that family influences are on the decline, at least in Westernised societies. It is now the norm to talk about the nuclear family, geographically isolated from grandparents and other relatives. Single parent families are also on the increase. This contrasts with many third world countries, where the extended family lives in a tight knit community.

Family roles can differ greatly from country to country. Recent television adverts in the UK have shown fathers shopping in the supermarket with their children (Bisto); fathers washing children's clothes while their wives are out (washing powder commercial); and men cooking happily in the kitchen (Sainsbury's). In countries with more rigid gender codes, these executions might be either absurd or offensive.

2.5 Beliefs and values

Beliefs and values evolve from religious teachings, family structures and the pattern and nature of economic development in that society. In our culture, material well being is important, people tend to be defined (and define themselves) by their work roles, individualism and equal opportunities are held dear and time is a precious commodity. Different cultures may put a different emphasis on these values. Any communications imagery designed to be used internationally should therefore be scanned for underlying values or beliefs that are culture specific.

2.6 Learning

The level of education within a culture is an important factor for the international marketing communicator. Low literacy levels will mean that verbal methods of communication take precedence over visual ones. Press advertising and direct marketing may have to be ruled out. Packaging may need to be simplified, and point of sale and sales promotion techniques handled with care.

In some societies, education emphasises the value of rote learning. In others, critical thinking is encouraged. This may affect the way in which information is transmitted within a market.

2.7 Work habits

Not all societies conform to the Monday to Friday, 9.00am till 5.00pm work routine. In Hong Kong, the working week extends until Saturday lunchtime. In some parts of Southern Europe, it is usual to work from very early in the morning until early afternoon. Workers then go home for a siesta.

2.8 Advertising culture

In addition to being sensitive to a country's culture in general, marketers should be aware of the level of a country's advertising literacy. Advertising in any national culture develops over time, and so any country can be described as having either high or low advertising literacy. Thus, imported advertising can be inappropriate because the advertising of country A is at a different stage of development from that of country B.

2.8.1 Five levels of advertising development

Level	Comment
Least sophisticated	The emphasis is on the manufacturer's description of the product. Messages are factual and rational with much repetition. Product or pack shots take prominence.
Unsophisticated	Consumer choice is acknowledged so emphasis switches to the product's superiority over the competition (eg products that wash whiter, feel softer).
Mid point	Consumer benefits are emphasised, rather than product attributes. Executional devices may include the use of celebrity endorsements or role models may give demonstrations, for example a dentist endorsing toothpaste products.
More sophisticated	Brands and their attributes are well known, so need only passing references (perhaps by way of a brief pack shot or logo). The message is communicated by way of lifestyle narrative (eg Gold Blend couple; Bisto family).
Most sophisticated level	The focus is on the advertising itself. The brand is referred to only obliquely, perhaps at a symbolic level (eg Silk Cut; Benson & Hedges). Consumers are believed to have a mature understanding of advertising, and are able to think laterally in order to decode messages.

Action Programme 1

Choose a country that is quite dissimilar to your own. You could perhaps choose somewhere that you have visited on holiday, or that a friend, relative or colleague has visited and told you about. Using the headings listed at the beginning of Section 2, compile a list of similarities and differences between the culture of the foreign country and that of your own.

Ideally, this should be conducted as a class exercise, so that you can pool your experiences.

3 Media considerations

FAST FORWARD

Planning and buying media across borders can be a complex task. Media availability can vary greatly from country to country. Media conventions that apply in a home market may not apply elsewhere.

Exam tip

Media is a complex, highly specialised area within marketing communications. International media is even more of a minefield and therefore the CIM does not expect students to have expert knowledge within this field. **What can be expected, however, is a grasp of the factors influencing media choice in overseas markets** (this is the subject of a question on the Pilot Paper), and some understanding of the practical problems that may be experienced when planning the use of media. The December 2003 Section A case study question contained an element on the influence of an international marketing strategy on marketing communications.

The UK is a media rich country that offers a great variety of choice to the advertiser. Press is a well segmented sector with over 6,000 consumer and trade and technical magazines, as well as the national and regional newspaper titles. Commercial television now includes terrestrial and satellite channels. Radio as a sector is strengthening, with both local and national stations. Cinema and outdoor are mature mediums.

This diversity is not always mirrored in overseas markets. **Media availability can vary greatly from country to country**.

Trying to gain a perspective on the international media scene is a frustrating task. Different sources give conflicting information because of different definitions and different methods of data collection that have been used. Any facts that are collected tend to become dated very quickly because of the dynamic nature of the media sector. Whatever information is gained from secondary sources will always need to be double checked for accuracy in the home market itself.

3.1 Press

The first point to check when contemplating press as a media option, is the **literacy levels prevailing within the country**. The majority of European nations have literacy rates of 98% or 99%. By comparison, the literacy level quoted for Hong Kong is 77%, for Egypt 44% and for India 41%.

In the UK, there are a large number of national newspaper alternatives (24 at the last count). Although some countries are similarly well served with national papers from which to choose (eg Germany, Finland), others have more of a tradition of reading strong daily regional papers.

The UK has one of the world's largest **trade and technical press sectors**, with business-to-business advertisers being particularly fortunate in the choice available to them. A strong trade press sector, however, tends to go hand in hand with a strong economic industrial base. Less developed nations may have few, if any, trade media vehicles.

It is wise to preview any candidate title before going ahead with a decision to include it on the media schedule. This will help in gaining an understanding of the editorial stance of the publication and give an impression about the calibre of the competitive advertising. It also allows the intending advertiser a chance to gauge the quality of media reproduction.

There is some debate about whether truly international press options exist. Serious business journals such as *Time*, *Newsweek*, and the *Economist* are widely available, as are women's titles with different national editions (eg *Marie Claire*, *Cosmopolitan*, *Elle*). General interest magazines such as *Reader's Digest* and in-flight magazines reach many markets. However, such publications are likely to be read by only a niche business and professional or lifestyle group. To reach the less wealthy, less well travelled wider population, other local media will have to be accessed.

 Action Programme 2

In Germany, where more advertising money is spent in magazines than in any country other than in the USA, the main classifications are supplements, 'ad mags', consumer magazines, customer magazines, and trade and technical journals. Supplements are loose inserts in newspapers or periodicals with a magazine format and with many pages printed in four-colour. The principal types are programme, quality, special topic, and trade and technical. Programme supplements, the most widely read, are published once a week and carried in daily newspapers. Editorial content is largely concentrated on previews of radio and television programmes. Quality supplements are found in some of the major newspapers and are largely read by males in managerial and professional positions. Special topic supplements come out at irregular intervals with various carriers. Trade and technical supplements focus on topics of interest to readers of the specialised journals in which the supplements are placed.

Imagine you are a media buyer and have, say, six different products or services that you want to advertise in German magazines. What products/services would you place where?

3.2 Television

Before TV can be included on the media options list, two important questions need to be answered.

- How extensive is television ownership?
- Do commercial stations exist?

In the UK, 98% of households have a television. In India, by comparison, television ownership is low, as purchase of the cheapest set is beyond the means of the majority. However, television watching may be a group activity and so while ownership is low, reach might be higher.

The opportunities for television advertisers seem overwhelming in Italy, where there are several licensed national TV channels and several hundred local TV stations. Advertisers face a different sort of problem in Norway. The first terrestrial commercial channel started broadcasting in September 1992. Before that date, the only television advertising seen by Norwegians was on satellite stations.

Satellite television is perceived to offer good opportunities for reaching wide audiences across national boundaries. MTV, the pan-European music station, targets 16 – 34 year olds and is received in 27 different countries.

3.3 Outdoor

The UK lags behind many European countries in its use of posters as an advertising medium. Outdoor offers a good opportunity to communicate to international target groups, as copy tends to be minimal and visuals are key.

3.4 Cinema

Cinema may not always be experienced in the same way around the world. In some countries, cinema is viewed in outdoor theatres. There can also be dramatic variations in the quality of the films which are screened. Both these factors may affect how advertising is received by cinema goers.

3.5 Radio

While the cost of purchasing a television set is prohibitive in some nations, radio ownership seems to be ubiquitous around the world. In most countries, radio plays the role of support medium.

3.6 Media planning and buying

As well as the usual media planning considerations (campaign objectives, target markets, media availability, budgets), there may be specific factors which need to be taken into account when planning in international markets. For a food product, media scheduling will need to take account of climatic and seasonal characteristics of individual countries.

Some international print media may be purchased from the home country market via international media representatives. Other media may have to be bought by a local country agent, acting for the advertiser.

Media buying practices can vary from country to country. In the UK, published ratecard costs tend to be negotiable downwards. Other countries may be less flexible in negotiations.

4 Legal considerations

Laws and regulations governing marketing communications must obviously be observed. Each country will have its own set of restrictions that apply to advertising, packaging, sales promotion and direct marketing.

In the EU alone, there are a number of significant differences regarding the regulation of advertising between member states. A Gossard TV commercial came under scrutiny in the UK for its risqué execution. In France, the problem was not the generous display of cleavage, but the fact that the advert was set in a bar where alcohol was being consumed. There is a ban on TV alcohol adverts and the Gossard ad needed to be re-edited to fall in line with French restrictions.

In some countries, restrictions apply to the use of non native models and actors. This can mean that advertising has to be reshot for specific countries.

Packaging regulations can vary. In a number of European markets, the push towards environmentally-friendly packaging has resulted in far more stringent rules than those that apply in the UK. In Denmark, soft drinks may not be sold in cans, only in glass bottles with refundable deposits.

Direct marketing is an area under threat from EU legislation. In the UK, direct marketers must offer consumers the choice of **opting out** of receiving further mailings. Recent European legislation requires marketers to give consumers the choice of **opting into** direct mailings (permission marketing) for email, fax and other electronic mass messaging formats. Elsewhere in the world, opt-out regulations and 'Do not call' registers (for telemarketing) are also being tightened.

4.1 Cross border advertising

The **European Commission** maintains that there must be overriding reasons relating to the public interest for imposing additional national rules on communications, and these rules must be 'proportionate' to the public interest objectives. However, to test the validity of current national restrictions on commercial communications through the courts takes several years for each case. Many regard national advertising restrictions as thinly veiled protectionism.

Marketing at Work

National restrictions

'Sweden forbids all advertising aimed at children under 10; Greece bans TV toy advertising between 7am and 10pm; some countries require ads for sweets to carry a toothbrush symbol; others have rules intended to curb advertisers from encouraging children to exercise 'pester power'.

'The same maze of national rules exists when it comes to promoting alcohol, tobacco, pharmaceuticals and financial services.

'There are proposals to set up a new body to deal with these issues, which are felt to be significant barriers to cross border trade.

'Early meetings of the new body would examine national differences in sales promotions and sponsorship regulations ... On sponsorship, for example, the Netherlands was singled out as having particularly restrictive curbs on events sponsorship, while the UK and Denmark were seen to impose strict rules on broadcasting.

'Price advertising and discounting is another area likely to get early attention. Measures are so disparate that cross-border campaigns using discounts are all but impossible ... In Germany, cash discounts are limited to 3% and the advertising of special offers is also restricted. Austria, Belgium and Italy also have strict regimes. In contrast, in Scandinavia, where the advertising law is more closely linked to consumer protection rather than unfair competition considerations, price advertising is encouraged – Swedish law, for example, promotes comparative price advertising between traders '

Source: Financial Times

5 Standardisation vs adaptation

Strategies appropriate for companies operating in international markets (*Keegan*, 2002) include:

(a) **Standardise** product/standardise communication (for example, Coca-Cola).

(b) **Standardise product/adapt communication** (Horlicks is promoted as a relaxing bedtime drink in the UK and as a high protein energy booster in India).

(c) **Adapt product/standardise communication** (washing powder ingredients may vary from country to country depending on water conditions and washing machine technology. However, the communication message of clean clothes is the same).

(d) **Adapt product/adapt communication**.

(e) **Invent a new product** to meet the needs of the market.

Action Programme 3

Over the next few months as you work towards the exam, scan the marketing and advertising trade press alongside the quality papers for examples of products and services that adopt the different strategies listed above. You will be able to generate your own list of current examples to illustrate points you make in the examination. Examiners welcome up-to-date relevant examples that demonstrate that you keep abreast of current practice.

Advantages of standardising communications include the following.

(a) **Economies of scale** can be generated. A single worldwide advertising, packaging or direct mail execution will save time and money.

(b) A **consistent and strong brand image** will be presented to the consumer. Wherever users see the brand, they will be reassured because the messages received will be the same.

(c) A **standardised communications policy** allows for **easier implementation** and control by management.

(d) Good **communications ideas are rare** and should be exploited creatively across markets.

Arguments against standardising communications include the following.

(a) Any standardisation policy assumes consumer needs and wants are identical across markets.

(b) Centrally-generated communications concepts may prove to be inappropriate for the specific culture of the local market (or indeed any market that may see the advertisement and take offence, as the example overleaf illustrates.)

(c) Media channel availability and infrastructure varies widely from country to country.

(d)   A country's level of educational development may prevent a standardised approach. For instance, a press campaign featuring detailed copy would be a non starter if literacy levels were low.

(e)   Legal restrictions may prove to be a stumbling block. For example, France does not allow any advertising of alcohol on television; cashback sales promotion offers are not allowed in Italy or Luxembourg.

(f)   Standardisation may encourage the 'not invented here' syndrome, so that local management become lacklustre about creative ideas and communications policies imposed from above.

(g)   Different countries have economies which may be much more or much less developed than others. Factors that need to be considered are as follows.

    (i)   What is the level and trend in per capita income?
    (ii)   Is the balance of payments favourable or unfavourable?
    (iii)   Is inflation under control?
    (iv)   Are the exchange rates stable?
    (v)   Is the currency easily convertible?
    (vi)   Is the country politically stable?
    (vii)   How protectionist is the country?
    (viii) Who controls distribution channels?

 Marketing at Work

Diageo's blunder

An advertisement on the London Underground in December 2002 for Smirnoff offended the Taiwanese. It showed a picture of an item with the label "Made in Taiwan" and the caption "Warning – this gift will break down on Christmas morning". Taiwan, so long a byword for inferior manufacturing quality, is now one of the leading high-tech manufacturers in the world. The Taiwan government was considering an outright ban on Diageo products.

Diageo was trying to achieve distinctiveness in a 'noisy' market, but this must never come at the expense of social responsibility and international awareness. This is a difficult line to tread – to appeal to one segment, you might risk offending others. Joking is always risky!

So Diageo found itself plunged into crisis management, despite the fact that its marketing code includes the provision: 'Don't use anything likely to be considered gratuitously offensive or demeaning to either gender, or to any race, religion, culture or minority group.'

6 International communications alternatives

It is all too easy to focus on advertising and packaging as the prime communicators in international campaigns. However, sales promotion, public relations, sponsorship, exhibitions, direct marketing and personal selling can all play a part.

6.1 Sales promotion

Sales promotion encompasses a range of techniques appropriate for targeting consumers, for instance via price reductions, free gifts, or competitions. Trade and sales force promotions are also implied under the general heading of sales promotion.

Different countries have their own **local restrictions** concerning different sales promotional devices. For instance, collector devices are a familiar method of encouraging repeat purchase in the UK. However, they are not allowed in Germany, Luxembourg, Austria, Norway, Sweden and Switzerland. Petrol forecourt promotions are very familiar to drivers in the UK, but following a vicious sales promotions battle between petrol companies in 1989, the Malaysian Government banned sales promotion of petrol.

Sales promotions that are to run across a number of different countries must tap into common tastes, interests and activities. As has been seen from the section on culture, this may not be an easy task.

6.2 Public relations

The UK's Institute of Public Relations describe public relations as, 'the planned and sustained effort to establish and maintain goodwill and mutual understanding between an organisation and its publics'. Publics can include:

- Customers
- Shareholders
- Employees
- Suppliers
- Trade intermediaries
- The local community
- Media
- Government
- Pressure groups

The importance of any one group will vary from country to country, which will mean that **public relations campaigns are unlikely to be completely standardised** across markets.

There is some debate as to whether public relations can be standardised at all. There is wide disparity in the sophistication of PR from country to country, as well as the usual list of cultural, language, media and legal barriers. The **political context** of individual countries may also affect the extent to which different public relations techniques can be used.

6.3 Sponsorship

Sponsorship seems a particularly appropriate means of communicating internationally. Internationally televised sporting events have an appeal that crosses borders and cultures, as football, rugby and cricket matches often show.

6.4 Exhibitions

Trade fairs and exhibitions are an effective means of initial business-to-business contact, providing an opportunity for producers, distributors, customers and competitors to meet. Where specialist exhibitions take place, rival companies from across the globe are likely to gather under one roof, offering an excellent opportunity for international buyers to compare offerings and place orders.

Exhibitions allow companies to display goods and mount demonstrations and trials. They can be good as a mechanism for image building, especially in new markets. Exhibitions provide a means for supporting local distributors and agents and allow direct contact with customers. There is also the chance to conduct competitor and customer market research.

Detailed evaluation of exhibition results should be carried out in order to fine tune future plans.

6.5 Direct marketing

International direct marketing has been growing slowly over the last decade. Factors driving the move to international direct marketing include the following.

(a) The growth in sophistication of computer and **database technology**

(b) The increasing availability of suitable **consumer or business listings**

(c)   Growth of **international media**, which can be used for direct response advertising

(d)   The perceived **accountability** of direct marketing campaigns compared with other communications campaigns

(e)   The ease with which direct marketing campaigns can be **tested in advance** in order to maximise their effectiveness

(f)   Improving **skills** of direct marketing agencies

(g)   Increasing **willingness of the consumer** to purchase items directly

(h)   Increasing use of **internationally accepted credit cards**

On the other hand, there are a number of factors restraining the move to international direct marketing.

- Lack of telephone and postal **infrastructure**
- Lack of road and rail penetration to facilitate **distribution**
- Lack of **suitable media** to use to target consumers
- Lack of **consumer and business lists** in some countries
- The threat of increasingly strict **legislation** concerning the use of consumer information
- **Consumer backlash** against what is seen as junk mail

6.6 Personal selling

Many of the communications tools described above will rely on integration with the personal selling function. For instance, certain types of consumer sales promotion will require **sales force support** to gain trade acceptance. Likewise, direct marketing campaigns will create sales leads that require follow up. Personal selling is therefore a likely requirement of most markets.

Companies may use **agents or distributors** to act in a sales capacity. Alternatively, a company may establish its own branch offices abroad with a team of local salespeople.

Personal selling will be particularly important in industrial markets, where products are high value and complex, or in markets where purchasing is controlled by government agencies.

Exam tip

Students answering exam questions on international aspects of communications tend to focus on advertising and packaging as the prime promotional vehicles. Examiners welcome answers that demonstrate that other options such as sales promotion, public relations, sponsorship, exhibitions, direct marketing and personal selling have been considered. Meanwhile, don't panic: you are generally invited to discuss the context of a country of your choice!

7 Multinational communications agencies

When selecting an agency to handle communications on an international basis, any decision would take into account the differences in approaches to communications discussed in this chapter.

Often the decision making process will be influenced by the structure of the client company and how far they **devolve** marketing responsibility on a regional basis. Some elements of the communications strategy and branding may be handled centrally, whereas implementation is dealt with 'locally', where more detailed knowledge with regard to media and other context issues can be applied.

For many of the larger multinational and global companies such as Coca Cola, Heinz or Procter & Gamble there is a need to deal with agencies who have sufficient resources of their own to handle the size of budgets being allocated. As there has been consolidation taking place among multinational businesses through acquisition and merger, this has also been happening among communications businesses. Between them, companies such as WPP handle a significant share of the world's advertising billings.

These agencies have grown partly by success in winning new business but also through the acquisition of other agencies in different parts of the world.

Other agencies offer multinational services to clients by being part of networks. They maintain independence as individual companies but via informal and sometimes formal collaborations, they can provide client services in different geographic markets. Sometimes clients may appoint a 'lead' agency who will hold ultimate responsibility for planning and co-ordination of agencies in different markets.

Advances in new technologies make the process of handling the communications needs of sophisticated multinational clients more straightforward but may not always replace the need for 'local' knowledge.

Chapter Roundup

- The international marketing communicator needs to decide **whether or not it is appropriate to standardise** communications across markets.

- Companies operating outside their home markets need to be aware of the implications of **cultural differences** for all aspects of the marketing mix. Verbal and non verbal communications, aesthetics, dress and appearance, family roles and relationships, beliefs, learning and work habits are dimensions of culture of particular relevance to communications.

- **Planning and buying media across borders can be a complex task**. Media availability can vary greatly from country to country. Media conventions that apply in a home market may not apply elsewhere.

- **Laws and regulations** governing marketing communications must obviously be observed. Each country will have its own set of restrictions that apply to advertising, packaging, sales promotion and direct marketing.

Quick Quiz

1   One aspect of globalisation concerns the efforts by multinational corporations to design (1)...........
    which provide global (2)......... for global (3).......... . Fill in the gaps.

2   The internationalisation of broadcast and print media is one of the factors driving the internationalisation
    of markets. Is this true, and if so, why?

3   Various dimensions of culture are relevant to the international marketing communicator. See if you can
    recall them from Section 2.

    C..........
    A..........
    D..........
    F..........
    B..........
    L..........
    W..........

4   Which of the following statements is true? (There may be more than one)

    A   Literacy levels only vary to a small extent between countries, so using the press is always going to
         make sense

    B   Literacy levels are important when considering press as a media option

    C   Media availability varies greatly from country to country

    D   In flight magazines reach many people in many markets and so are an invaluable mass advertising
         media

5   List some advantages of standardising communications.

6   Why might sponsorship be a particularly effective form of international marketing communications?

7   Which one of the following statements is true?

    A   It is not necessary to research every international market, as some will be very similar to the
         domestic market

    B   Research can help with the evaluation of the success of a campaign

    C   Laws and regulations change so often that it is impossible, and unnecessary, for a marketer to
         keep up with them

    D   Standardised marketing communications will always be better than adapted ones, because they are
         cheaper

8   Fill in the gaps using the words from the grid below:

    Some advertising agencies offer (1).......... services to clients by being part of (2).......... They maintain
    (3).......... as individual companies, but via collaborations they can provide client services in different
    (4).......... markets.

Geographic	Contact	Account management
Multinational	Networks	Independence

Answers to Quick Quiz

1   (1) Marketing policies; (2) Products; (3) Consumers

2   True. For example, cross border satellite transmission means consumers in different countries receive common programming. Also, consumers are now more sophisticated and have increased exposure to other cultures via the broadcast and other media. This expands their tastes and preferences and makes 'international' products more attractive.

3   **C**ommunications (verbal and non-verbal)
        Aesthetics
        Dress (and appearance)
        Family roles and relationships
        Beliefs and values
        Learning
        Work habits

4   B and C

5   Check your answer against Section 5

6   International sporting events, such as the Football World Cup, attract audiences from many different cultures.

7   B

8   (1) Multinational; (2) Networks; (3) Independence; (4) Geographic

Action Programme Review

1   Once you have completed this, consider the implications for differences in approach to marketing communications.

2   What differences would there be if you were promoting these products or services in the UK or another market?

3   Your own research.

Now try Question 7 at the end of the Study Text

Evaluating marketing communication activities

Syllabus content – knowledge and skill requirements

- The effectiveness of co-ordinated campaigns (2.5)
- The effectiveness of marketing communications activities, tools, media and campaigns (2.16)

Introduction

In the exam, you will frequently be asked to provide examples of, and *evaluate*, campaigns of different kinds: we look at some different contexts and markets in this chapter. You may also be asked to discuss *how* you would go about evaluating the effectiveness of a particular campaign or mix of tools/media: this was a compulsory question in June 2006, for example. Determining methods of feedback/measurement for control are also part of marketing planning: remember to include them (briefly) in any marketing or MC plan you are asked to outline.

1 Understanding communications effectiveness

FAST FORWARD

Industrial marketing communications strategies can be very different from consumer campaigns. There are differences in such areas as purchase motivation, customer needs, product specifications, level of customer service needed and so on. This calls for different approaches in employing the various promotional tools.

1.1 A summary of marketing communication effectiveness

Communications are designed to meet three objectives.

Awareness	Increase brand **awareness** and establish brand **recognition**
Trial	Stimulate **trial purchase**
Reinforcement	Stimulate and **reinforce** brand **loyalty**

To succeed in achieving these goals, communications must:

- Gain attention
- Communicate a message
- Reinforce and improve attitudes to the brand
- Obtain the audience's liking for the message and its execution

There are two elements to the evaluation of the effectiveness of marketing communications campaigns (*Fill*, 2002).

(a) **Developing and testing** the messages themselves: **guidance** through **pre-testing**.

(b) Measuring the overall **impact and effect** of the message: **quantitative** evaluation after the campaign (**post testing**).

Key concepts

Pre-testing is aimed at ensuring that the final creation will meet advertising objectives. It involves the showing of unfinished commercials to help to refine them. Focus groups may be used.

Post testing measures recall and recognition of a completed campaign, perhaps by counting the number of promotional coupons returned.

The difficult part is measuring the effectiveness of the marketing communications process. The following are some possible techniques.

Marketing communications methods	Examples of measurements
Personal selling	Sales targets; productivity; costs
Public relations	Editorial coverage; awareness; opinions
Direct marketing	Enquiries generated
Advertising	Brand awareness
Sales promotion	Stock turnover
Exhibitions	Contacts made
Online communications	'Click-throughs'

The following table shows possible *advertising effectiveness measures*.

Type of measure	Advertising related	Product related
Laboratory measures (Respondent aware of testing)	*Pretesting panels* • Consumer panels • Portfolio tests • Readability tests • Physiological measure eg eye tracking	*Pretesting* • Theatre tests • Hall tests • Laboratory scores
Real world measures (Respondent unaware of testing)	*Pretesting* • Dummy advertising • Inquiry tests • On air tests *Post testing* • Recognition • Recall tests • Association measures	*Pre and post procedures* • Sales tests • Test markets

Exam tip

Candidates should be able to use suitable examples to demonstrate the points they are making. The age of an example is not important, nor is the culture or country from where the examples are drawn. What you must do is give more than a description. You should show your understanding through a structured interpretation and evaluation of a campaign. You are encouraged to keep up-to-date by reading the business press and, in particular, trade magazines such as *Marketing*, *Marketing Week* and *Campaign*. These contain regular reviews of marketing communications activities including varying campaigns from different types of organisations. You are also encouraged to obtain and study case histories in more detail than you would normally find in such sources.

Action Programme 1

For a campaign of your choice answer the following questions. (You might have to do this in an exam.)

(a) Describe the organisation concerned and its competitors.
(b) What factors and issues have shaped the campaign?
(c) What are the marketing communications objectives?
(d) What are the main elements of the communication strategy?
(e) How can you measure the effectiveness of the campaign?

2 Consumer communication case studies

The cases used here are presented in a format that would provide a framework for marketing communications planning:

- Situation analysis
- Communications objectives
- Marketing communications strategy
- Communications tactics – promotional mix
- Action – implementation
- Control – measurement and evaluation

 Marketing at Work

Walker's Crisps: Gary Lineker

Situation

In 1989 Walkers and Smiths Crisps moved under the umbrella of PepsiCo Foods International. In 1993, the two brands were merged. With a turnover in the region of £300 million, Walkers Crisps had become the biggest single food brand in the UK.

By August 1994, Walkers had experienced two years of double-digit growth, and the brand's share had reached 22%, over three times that of its nearest branded rival. However, there were several clouds looming on the horizon:

- Plateauing distribution
- Success of promotions
- Advertising uncertainties.

Marketing communications objectives

To maintain volume and share growth on a par with that achieved in the previous two years, primarily through ROS (rate of sales) growth. In particular it needed to do this in two ways:

(a) Theme advertising that would work harder than before and would generate ROS increases in its own right.

(b) Through promotional advertising that would be part of the same campaign and hence more strongly branded than before, and that would generate even more pronounced short-term ROS uplifts than the previous promotional advertising.

Marketing communications strategy

In March 1993 Walkers had embarked on a successful series of 'Instant Win' promotions, producing unprecedented uplifts in volume and ROS. 'Instant Win' promotions were seen as another engine for dynamic growth. But it was unclear how important the novelty factor was to their success, and whether repetition would see declining effectiveness over time, and it seemed inevitable that competition would try to copy them.

There was little doubt that the promotional advertising had been successful in boosting sales. However, to protect the salience of Walkers' own promotions in the face of copying by competitors, stronger branding of the 'Instant Win' promotions was felt to be desirable, best achieved by a single brand umbrella bringing promotional and theme advertising together.

When Walkers put the advertising account out to pitch in mid 1994, it was to develop an co-ordinated brand campaign incorporating new theme and promotional advertising.

It was decided to create advertising that would appeal to a mass audience of adults as well as children. From qualitative research conducted amongst crisp-lovers of all ages, 'irresistibility' was identified as the quality that embodied everything they most enjoyed about snacking. It was shorthand for the perfect crisp. A creative vehicle that would generate PR and media coverage was desired. Given the importance of fame and the need for a mass audience, TV was chosen as the main medium.

The idea for the campaign can be summarised as 'Walkers are so irresistible they make even nice guys turn nasty when it comes to crisps'.

What set the idea apart was the thought of casting ex-England and Leicester footballer Gary Lineker as the nice guy turned nasty.

As the ambassador and genuine 'nice guy' of the game, Gary was as attractive to mums as to kids. His well-publicised return from playing in Japan offered unique PR opportunities. Most important of all, his down-to-earth personality and roots in Walkers' Leicester heartland provided a seamless fit with the desired brand personality and the unpretentious values to be established.

Tactics

Prior to the 1996 IPA Awards five TV executions had been produced in the series including two for further 'Instant Win' promotions:

Execution	Airdate	TVRs	Objective
'Welcome home'	Jan 95	472	Launch improved cheese & onion
'Nun'	Mar 95	520	Support 'Instant cheque' promotion
'Garymania'	May 95	451	Launch Crinkles range
'Dial-a-Prize'	Sept 95	361	Support 'Dial-a-Prize' promotion
'Salt & Lineker'	Jan 96	553	Launch improved S&V flavour

Action

From the outset, the Lineker campaign generated an amount of TV and press coverage much in excess of anything previously seen in the market. TV coverage ranged from News at Ten to Fantasy Football League, The Big Breakfast and How Do They Do that? Press coverage appeared in all national press, from *The Times*, *The Independent* and *Daily Telegraph*, to the *Daily Mail*, *Daily Mirror* and the front page of *The Sun* ... twice.

Control

Analysis of growth in different advertised varieties of Walkers crisps, showed that the advertising clearly influenced consumer behaviour. Two econometric models showed directly that the advertising was responsible for a large proportion of the brand's growth. The part played by other variables showed no other activity could have been responsible for the effect claimed for advertising.

The marketing objectives of sustaining volume and increasing market share growth were successfully exceeded.

Volume grew by 22.5% in the year following Gary Lineker's appointment.

Walkers continue to use Gary Lineker in their ads. The equivalent campaign for the sister brand ('Lays') in Australia uses the tennis star Pat Rafter.

Action Programme 2

This is an co-ordinated campaign. Identify as many features of integration as you can, both from the above or from your own experience of the Walker's brand.

Marketing at Work

Dulux reveals true colours

Situation

Historically, Dulux the paint manufacturer had used advertising to associate the brand with white and 'Natural Hints' ranges. If they were to achieve ambitious targets for 1999, focus on the coloured paint sector was also required. Paint sales were expected to grow at the expense of wallpaper and the coloured sector was important as it was the most profitable sector and likely to see a significant proportion of the forecast growth. Brighter colours were more fashionable as a result of programmes such as Changing Rooms, which particularly appealed to a younger target audience. The image of Dulux was safe and respected but irrelevant to the younger market.

Target audience

Focus was placed on the under 35s for a number of reasons. Unless younger customers could be attracted this would lead to longer-term loss of share as these were the customers of the future. First-time house purchase was on the increase, fuelled by lower interest rates creating younger home owners. It was also the sector where Dulux had the lowest share and therefore most opportunity for growth. Further segmentation targeted females who were seen to be the decision makers and to seek consumers with a more adventurous mindset in order to move away from the 'safe' image.

Promotional mix

A TV campaign spearheaded the repositioning efforts, demonstrating the range of colours available and the consumer need this range met. The theme was bright, bold and controversial, very different to the gentle and romantic execution of earlier advertising.

A website allowed consumers to test different paint mixes and advise on suitability for different surfaces and calculate the quantity required. PR included a challenge to personalities to dye their hair for a day in aid of charity. Further media coverage arose from a body-painted naked lady visiting key media offices with the famous Dulux dog to deliver specially created paint mixes.

Measuring effectiveness

Tracking studies four months into the campaign showed a 12% increase in the numbers agreeing that Dulux 'had the widest range of colours' and a 15% rise in those agreeing that Dulux 'always has the right colour for you'. As a result of the campaign, over 80% of those recalling the ads remembered the key message that Dulux can 'match the colour you want'.

In February 2000, Dulux volume share topped own label (Homebase /B&Q)sales for the first time.

From an article in *Marketing Business,* February 2001

Marketing at Work

Last laugh for Skoda

Situation

For years the butt of jokes based on the car's unreliability, the success of the brand over the last two years provides a remarkable example of how to turn a brand around. Even after motoring journalists began praising the improvements made in product design and engineering, sales hardly moved. The advertising was doing little to overcome brand prejudice and although drivers might have recognised that the product had improved, they would still not want to be seen driving a Skoda. It was further recognised that the pan-European approach that had been taken did not reflect the fact that the brand meant something different in each market.

BPP
LEARNING MEDIA

Budget constraints

A reduced promotional budget compared to earlier launches made the task even more of a challenge when launching the new Fabia model. £4.5 million was half of the £9 million Toyota spent on launching the Yaris and little more than a third of the £17 million spent by Renault on relaunching the Clio.

A risky approach

There was little doubt that it would take something different to change consumer attitudes toward the brand not made easier by the low budget available. The Fallon advertising agency created a campaign with the strapline 'It's a Skoda. Honest'. This centred on reducing the gap between consumer expectations and reality using self-deprecating humour in seeking revaluation of the brand. Research of the concept proved positive.

Promotional mix

£2.85 million was spent on a TV campaign, supported by £600,000 spent on posters and £274,000 in colour press. PR was used to extend and amplify the message and further activity included retail staff training and high profile location product placement.

Measuring effectiveness

In addition to improving sales of most models and creating a waiting list for the new Fabia, significant changes in attitude toward the brand were achieved.

Before the campaign 54% of people agreed that Skodas were better than they were commonly perceived. This increased to 79% after the campaign. Only 20% said they could imagine themselves driving a Skoda before the campaign with this increasing to 33% after.

The success of the communications has prompted Skoda to seek further improvements by building their database and nurturing customers (who may currently be warming to the brand), closer to point of purchase.

From an article in *Marketing Business*

3 Business-to-business communications strategies

Although the principles of marketing communications are the same for both consumer and industrial markets, there are significant differences in the details of how promotion is carried out. We saw this in earlier chapters.

In particular, the targets in industrial markets are usually more specific and promotional budgets are usually more limited. In order to understand these differences it is valuable to look again at the major differences between industrial (or business) marketing and consumer marketing.

	Area	Industrial marketing	Consumer marketing
1	Purchase motivation	Multiple buying influences / Support company operations	Individual or family need
2	Nature of demand	Derived or joint demand	Primary demand
3	Emphasis of seller	Economic needs	Immediate satisfaction
4	Customer needs	Each customer has different needs	Groups with similar needs
5	Nature of buyer	Group decisions	Purchase by individual or family unit

	Area	Industrial marketing	Consumer marketing
6	Time effects	Long term relationships	Short term relationships
7	Product details	Technically sophisticated	Lower technical content
8	Promotion decisions	Emphasis on personal selling	Emphasis on mass media advertising
9	Price decisions	Price determined before Terms are important	Price substantially fixed Discounts are important
10	Place decisions	Limited number of large buyers, short channels	Large number of small buyers Complex channels
11	Customer service	Critical to success	Less important
12	Legal factors	Contractual arrangements	Contracts only on major purchases
13	Environmental factors	Affect sales both directly and indirectly	Affect demand directly

3.1 Business decision-making process

Perhaps the most significant differences are the nature of the **buying motivation** and the linked nature of the buying decision process. In industrial buying there are many motivations. These stem partly from the technical use of the product but also from financial, security of supply and, to a lesser degree, emotional reasons.

Decision makers		Buying motivation
1	Operations Manager	Uses the product in the organisation's processes – wants efficiency and effectiveness.
2	Technical Manager	Often has to test and approve the product – wants reliability.
3	The Managing Director	May approve major expenditure or change of supplier.
4	The Purchasing Manager	Approves conditions of purchase. Monitors supplier performance.
5	Legal Manager	Draws up or approves legal contracts with supplier.
6	Finance Manager	Approves expenditure and controls debt payment.
7	Health and Safety Manager	May have a role to play with hazardous supplies.

3.2 Implications for marketing communications strategy

It will be obvious that marketing communications strategy for industrial marketing must reflect this considerably more complex decision-making process.

3.2.1 Strategic importance

Business or industrial marketing can be regarded as involving more strategic decisions in its implementation. Consumer products, by definition, are mass market products often purchased in a routine and habitual manner. This is unlikely to be the case in industrial marketing. Business customers have differing needs and in some cases these needs may be conflicting within the organisation. Identifying business needs is complicated by having to deal with different decision makers within the company.

3.2.2 Impact of time

The length of time involved for the purchase evaluation and for the life of the product is much greater in industrial markets. Consumers often make buying decisions on the spur of the moment. Industrial buying decisions may take over one year. This then alters both the type of marketing communications and the relationships between the buying and selling organisations.

3.2.3 The buying organisation

Business buyers have several different methods of organising purchasing, and this can affect communication strategy. Some firms purchase on a highly centralised basis. This allows for maximum price advantage and negotiation strength because of economies of scale. Other organisations allow decentralised purchases, which leads to local needs being better met. In these cases, two different forms of selling organisation are needed and the communication strategy needed to reach the right person will be different in each case.

3.2.4 Variety of products and services

The variety of products in business markets is extremely large. Business products vary from product inputs to items for resale. They can be broken down into three main types.

- Capital equipment (major purchases of fixed assets)
- Production inputs (becoming part of the buyer's process)
- Business supplies/services (ongoing use by the buyer)

Again, each type of purchase will need a different communications strategy.

3.3 The business-to-business communications mix

Figure 8.1 shows the relative importance of differing elements of the promotional mix between consumer and industrial markets. These differences are reflected in developing marketing communication strategies for industrial markets.

Exam tip

> When exam questions ask about the 'B2B (marketing) communications mix', this is what they mean. You should be able to apply this (as relevant to specific contexts) to any B2B micro-scenario.

Figure 8.1: Relative importance of promotional elements

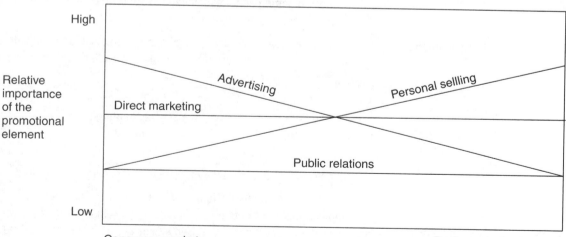

The clearest difference is the importance of personal selling in industrial markets because of the complex decision-making process, the differing industrial needs and the higher value of individual purchases. Advertising, though still important, is less so than for consumer marketing. The diagram also shows that both public relations and direct marketing have important continuing roles in both consumer and industrial marketing. It is clear from the above list that the methods to communicate with industrial markets will be of a much greater variety than for consumer markets. This in turn means that industrial marketing decisions can be really challenging and **the need for effective co-ordinated marketing communications is important**.

The range of promotional methods is described below.

Method	Comment
Personal selling	This is a major component of industrial marketing because of the need to deal with technical and other issues on a face-to-face basis.
Internal selling	Increasingly it is recognised that a salesperson has an internal role to play in representing his customers' needs to the company.
Internet	The use of the Internet for e-commerce is perhaps more highly developed in industrial marketing than in the consumer sector. Advertising and online catalogues are just two of the ways that it can be used. Many companies have also set up electronic links with suppliers and customers for such functions as automatic ordering.
Advertising	A wide variety of publications exist which can be used to target individual market sectors including: (i) trade journals (ii) business press (iii) directories Advertising is used to create awareness, provide information, generate leads, assist channel members and sometimes to sell off the page.
Telemarketing	Telemarketing has been proved to be a very cost effective method of order processing, customer service, sales support and account management.
Direct mailing	Direct mail, another form of direct marketing, has been used by industrial marketers for a long time but its use has substantially increased. It can be used to provide information and generate enquiries. It can be tailored to individual customer needs.
Public relations	Sometimes in industrial markets this is referred to as publicity. It often focuses on getting editorial coverage in appropriate magazines but it has a wider role of building customer relations.
Sales promotion	Sales promotion is an important area of communication in industrial markets. There are a wide range of methods that are of well established use in industrial campaigns. • Literature • Exhibitions • Videos • Discounting • Events • Business gifts • Trade shows Technical literature is clearly important in specifying the product. Complicated equipment can be captured on video and applications shown. Trade shows and exhibitions continue to grow in importance. Discounting and special price promotions are used extensively in industrial markets. Business gifts continue to have their value if not used excessively.

3.4 Evaluating the effectiveness of personal selling

This hinges around measuring the **inputs** made (the effort and costs by the sales force) against the **outputs** achieved (*Fill*, 2002). The key measure, **productivity**, is the ratio of inputs to outputs. Increasing emphasis is also being placed upon the **profitability** of each salesperson.

(a) **Activities**

    (i)   Sales calls
    (ii)   Presentations made
    (iii)   Expenses   } these can be measured against organisational standards
    (iv)   Cost of samples
    (v)   Time taken

(b) **Knowledge and skills inputs**

    (i)   Depth of product knowledge
    (ii)   Presentations skills   } less easily evaluated, but very important (and likely to become more so)
    (iii)   Customer relationships
    (iv)   Market knowledge

Ratios are often used to measure the performance and productivity of a salesperson or the sales force as a whole. They can also be used to **benchmark** against industry standards.

4 Marketing communications for service organisations

FAST FORWARD

The marketing of **services** is similar to the marketing of products in many ways, but there can be differences because of such factors as professional and legal constraints, the nature of capacity available, and the buying process itself. Personal selling is more important.

4.1 Similarities to product marketing

The promotion of goods and services have many similarities.

- The **role of promotion** in meeting marketing objectives
- The need to **design** effective promotions
- The **managerial challenge** of efficient implementation
- The broad **choice** of methods and media
- The **agencies** available to support promotion

Promotional objectives for services are related to those for products, as the following examples show.

- Build awareness and interest in the service and the service organisation.
- Communicate and portray the benefits of the services available.
- Build and maintain the overall image and reputation of the service organisation.
- Advise customers of new channels.
- Advise customers of special offers or modifications to the service.
- Persuade customers to use or buy the service.

4.2 Service communications

In spite of these similarities there are significant differences caused by the special nature of services. *Grönroos*, (2000), draws attention to some of the complexity in service communication: Figure 8.2.

In service markets there are four **elements of the service** that need to be taken into account in planning.

- The **core service concept** and any auxiliary service
- The **accessibility** of the service
- The **interactive communications** that take place in delivering the service
- The **influence of the consumer** and other consumers receiving the service

Four promotional methods are then used to influence the customer.

- Traditional selling
- Advertising and direct marketing
- Public relations and sales promotions
- The communication aspects of pricing policy

Figure 8.2: Model of service communications

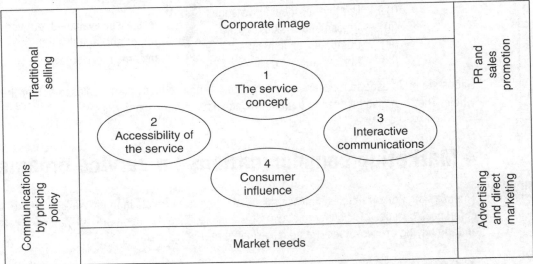

There are differences in promotion necessitated by the characteristics of service industries and services companies (*Cowell*, 1989).

Characteristics	Consequences
Lack of market orientation	Managers are untrained, unskilled and unaware of the role of promotion.
Professional and ethical constraints	Places limitations on certain promotion methods. Sometimes legal restrictions.
Small scale of many service organisations	Limits size of promotion budgets.
Nature of capacity available	Capacity for delivering the service may be limited. Promotion may produce too much demand.
Attitude to promotion methods	Limited knowledge of and attitude to wide range of promotion methods.
Nature of the service	Services may be very specific, which excludes mass advertising.
Consumer attitudes	Consumers may rely on subjective judgements made at the point of service delivery.
Buying process	The need to develop a professional relationship with the service provider makes customer care important.

4.3 Guidelines for service marketing

These differences lead to a number of guidelines that must be considered when designing communication campaigns for service markets.

(a)   Use **clear unambiguous messages** to communicate the range, depth, quality and level of services.

(b)   **Emphasise the benefits of the services** rather than their technical details.

(c)   **Only promise what can be delivered**, to avoid disappointment.

(d)   **Advertise to employees,** as they are particularly important in many people-intensive services.

(e)   Obtain **maximum customer co-operation** in the service production process, as the service is often an interactive system.

(f)   Build on **word of mouth communication** from one satisfied customer to another.

(g)   Provide **tangible evidence to strengthen promotional messages**. Use well known personalities to support the messages.

(h)   Develop **continuity in promotion** by the use of consistent and continuous symbols, themes, formats or images.

(i)   **Remove post purchase anxiety** by reassuring the buyer of the soundness of choice, especially where there is no tangible product.

(j)   **Personal selling** becomes more important in the promotion of services

4.4 Differences in selling goods and selling services

Issue	Comment
Customer's purchase perception of services	• Customers view service as having less consistent quality • Service purchasers have higher risks • Service purchasing is less pleasant • When services are bought greater consideration is given to the particular salesperson • Perception of the service company is an important factor when deciding to buy a service
Customer's purchase behaviour with services	• Customers may do fewer price comparisons with services • Customers give greater consideration to the particular seller of services • Customers are less likely to be influenced by advertising and more by personal recommendations
Personal selling of services	• Customer involvement is greater • Customer satisfaction is influenced by the salesperson's personality and attitude • Salespeople may have to spend more time reducing customer uncertainty

5 Marketing communications for non profit organisations

FAST FORWARD

In **non profit marketing communications** there is likely to be less money available, messages are likely to be subjected to greater scrutiny and the objectives of the communication will be quite different from those applying in consumer marketing. The major categories of non profit communicators are political parties, social causes, the government, religious bodies and professional bodies.

The major principles of marketing communications for non profit organisations are the same as for consumer and industrial marketing. There are, however, considerable differences of emphasis. The sum of money available for organised communication may be less. Public scrutiny of policies may be higher.

Marketing at Work

In the face of a severe shortfall in revenue (due to wildly optimistic forecast visitor numbers) the amount of grant funding to the New Millennium Experience Company rocketed to £628 million. Sir John Bourne of the National Audit Office said in a report:

> "Building and opening the Millennium Dome on the very short timescale required was a tremendous achievement. But the New Millennium Experience Company has experienced severe financial difficulties this year and has required considerable additional lottery funding.

> The main cause of these difficulties is the failure to achieve the visitor numbers and income required. The targets were highly ambitious and inherently risky leading to a significant degree of financial exposure on the project. In addition, the task of managing the project has been complicated by the complex organisational arrangements put in place from the outset, and by the failure to establish sufficiently robust financial management."

What went wrong? The whole issue illustrated the need for proper marketing communications planning. Strong negative word-of-mouth also had an impact. The following general points should have been considered.

- Promotional strategies to attract visitors (pull strategy), communicate with those issuing tickets (push strategy), and promote the image of the 'Dome' and that of the Millennium Experience Company (Profile Strategy), should have been fully co-ordinated.

- Messages should have been adapted to the various audiences.

- Promotional strategies should have taken into account financial constraints imposed by the fact that this was funded in the main through public money. Sales were likely to fall short of targets if insufficient money and time was invested in marketing.

Adapted from CIM material

Categories of non profit communications include the following.

- Political party communications
- Social cause communications
- Charitable communications
- Government communications
- Religious communications
- Professional body communications
- Other private non profit communications (hospitals, universities, museums and so on)

5.1 Communication objectives for NFP campaigns

Almost certainly there will be a different set of **communication objectives**.

- Making target customers **aware** of a product, service or social behaviour
- **Educating** consumers about the offer or changes in the offer
- **Changing beliefs** about negative and positive consequences of taking a particular action
- **Changing the relative importance** of particular consequences
- Enlisting the **support** of a variety of individuals
- Recruiting, motivating or rewarding **employees or volunteers**
- Changing **perceptions** about the sponsoring organisation
- Influencing **government bodies**
- Preventing the **discontinuity** of support
- **Proving benefits** over 'competitors'
- **Combating** injurious rumours
- **Influencing** funding agencies

5.2 Frameworks for NFP messages

Once the non profit marketer has developed the broad objectives for the communications plan the next step is to decide specific messages. These messages may be developed within one of the three frameworks.

(a) **Rational, emotional and moral framework**

(i) Rational messages pass on information and serve the audience's self interest. For example messages about value, economy or benefits.

(ii) Emotional messages are designed to develop emotion to shape the desired behaviour. For example with fear, guilt, shame appeals to stop doing things like smoking, drinking, taking drugs or overeating.

(iii) Moral messages directed at the audience's sense of right or wrong. For example, to support a cleaner environment or equal rights or help the under-privileged.

 Marketing at Work

EShopAfrica.com is a website dedicated to selling the wares of African craftsmen. As well as the products themselves, the site features information about tribal traditions and personal stories about the craftsmen themselves.

Difficulties with credit card payments to Africa (the financial infrastructure is relatively underdeveloped) and the fact that the products can be obtained far more cheaply from bulk import/export businesses has meant that the site has struggled to break even. According to the site's founder, this misses the point of the venture.

The site is aimed at improving the lot of the craftsmen, and its avowed primary goal is to create sustainable businesses for five artisans a year. It aims to tap the snobbery market, and specifically that customer segment that is social/ego oriented and which seeks out the original and unusual at a premium price. This premium price can be seen by the customer to directly benefit an African craftsman and so the customer can feel good about him or herself.

Action Programme 3

Can you foresee any problems with the eShopAfrica promotional strategy? Is it sustainable in the long term, even if it is effective now?

(b)   **Reward and situation framework**

(i)   There may be four types of reward: rational, sensory, social or ego satisfaction rewards.

(ii)   Rewards may result directly from use, or indirectly from the products in use, or be incidental to use. For example, think about the various rewards offered by cars with catalytic converters.

(c)   **Attitude change framework**

(i)   Changes in the importance of one or more outcomes

(ii)   Changes in the beliefs about one or more outcomes

(iii)   Adding new positive outcomes

Having decided what messages to transmit it is then necessary to decide the style of promotional execution. The following styles are appropriate for consumer goods advertising but can easily be adopted for non profit organisations.

5.2.1 Example: health education

Styles	Execution
Slice of life	Family doing healthy activities throughout the day
Life-style	Father and daughter off jogging early in morning
Fantasy	Dream of winning a marathon
Mood	Exercises in a field of wild flowers
Musical	Exercises to modern music
Personalities	Using a well known successful sports personality
Technical expertise	Quoting performance capability in exercises
Scientific evidence	Showing the benefits of less illness and greater longevity
Testimonial evidence	Members of the public give views on benefits

5.3 Media used by NFP organisations

Method	Comment
Paid advertising	Non profit organisations may have limited funds but this can still be an effective route even on low budgets, as the Save the Children Fund campaign showed. Alternatively the budget may be boosted by obtaining commercial sponsorship.
Unpaid (public service) advertising	Media owners may provide airtime or press space on a free of charge basis as a public service. However, there is little control over this and the times or spaces may occur at unpopular times or places.

Method	Comment
Sales promotions	Short term incentives to encourage purchases or donations. Market control is strong and promotions are often newsworthy (for example, Red Nose Day or Poppy Day promotions).
Public relations	Many of the stories of non profit organisations are of considerable interest. They may feature in the press or the broadcast media. Control over the message is good and feedback is possible.
Personal selling and communications	Staff at all levels of the non profit organisations should be trained in personal communications. They will often have the opportunity to 'sell' to their supporters and possible benefactors.

5.3.1 Direct marketing

This is a medium increasingly being used by non profit organisations, particularly arts foundations and charities. It has seven important **advantages for non profit marketers**.

(a)   It can be very focused for maximum effect on the target market.

(b)   It can be private and confidential. This is especially important when dealing with sensitive issues.

(c)   There is less direct regulation on direct mail promotions. In the past charitable advertising in the broadcast media has been limited.

(d)   Cost per contact and cost per response is low and controllable, which is important where funds have to be used wisely.

(e)   Results are clearly measurable and can make the programmers more accountable.

(f)   Small scale tests of proposed strategies are feasible.

(g)   The effectiveness of direct marketing can be assessed in terms of behaviour (ie orders, donations, requests for membership).

5.4 Behaviour channels

Non profit campaigns often call for **behavioural changes** on the part of the target audience. It is for this reason that it is valuable to monitor the effectiveness of such a campaign using a modification of the hierarchy of effects model. The model shown below (Figure 8.3) has been adapted for a campaign to encourage the use of contraceptives to aid family planning.

Figure 8.3: Contraceptive campaign – social behaviour change model

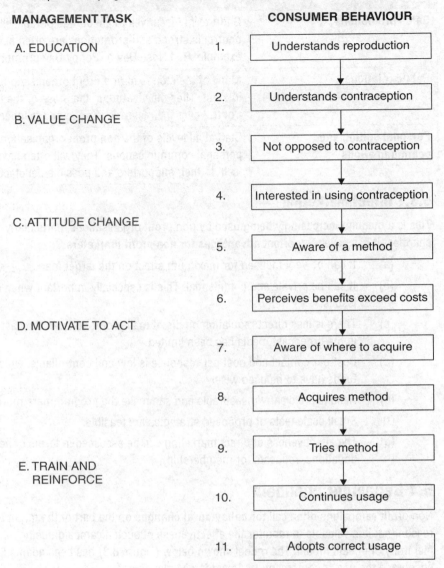

Marketing at Work

Campaign Title: NSPCC – Full Stop

Context

Business

The NSPCC set up a five vision programme to tackle the problem of child abuse, head on. This programme sought to:

- Set up an investigative service to run in parallel with the police
- Promote quality parenting
- Work with schools and teacher training colleges
- Develop children-friendly communities
- Work for cultural and legislative change

External

An independent national commission of enquiry had reported that 'child abuse and neglect can almost always be prevented, provided the will to do so is there'.

Organisational

- The financial resources necessary to implement the five visions were limited.
- There was a strong culture and drive to be successful

Customer

- Giving fatigue, NSPCC fatigue
- Suspicion concerning raising the standard of parenting
- Attitudes - scepticism at the charity's ambition to abolish child abuse/cruelty
- Abuse is universally condemned but people feel helpless ... they don't know what to do and they don't think it goes on near them

Stakeholder

Organisations willing to be associated with cause related issues which equate to sponsorship and assistance with fund raising.

Promotional objectives

The aim was to hit every household in the UK.

- Corporate: to end child abuse

- Marketing: to raise £250 million in 12 months - donated or pledged (normal amount £50m)

- Communication: to raise awareness of child cruelty to persuade people to become involved with the cause

Promotional strategy

(a) Strong pull campaign designed to raise awareness of child cruelty. Campaign to be delivered in two main steps. The first to develop awareness and the second step to be action orientated.

(b) In parallel there should be a strategy designed to communicate with businesses in order to generate funds, goodwill and support.

(c) The overall profile of the organisation (NSPCC) shall be raised and communications need to ensure that the integrity of the organisation and those associated with it are maintained. In addition, all communications need to be consistent.

Promotional mix used to create a dialogue with the public

- Public Relations
- TV, Posters
- Field Marketing
- Direct Marketing: Direct Mail, Telemarketing
- Website

First phase

Public relations were used at the initial stages of the campaign to help create awareness. Public address systems at railway stations and airports were used as a reminder mechanism.

A national TV campaign, supported by posters, broke soon after the public relations in order to raise awareness and provoke the question within each individual, 'what can I do?'. The message strategy was very emotional and used strong imagery to create shock and attention.

The heavy TV campaign looked to generate 600 TVRs, 85% coverage at 7.1 OTSs.

The supporting poster campaign used 48 sheets on 3,500 sites designed to deliver 55% coverage with 21 OTSs.

Initial enquiries to this wave of communications were heralded by an automated telemarketing bureau.

Second phase

This initial approach was followed up by a 23 million nationwide doordrop campaign. The aim was to provide the public with an answer to the question that the advertising had provoked, namely, to sign the pledge and/or volunteer as a donor or fundraiser.

The envelope picked up the TV creative treatment, repeating as a subdued background motif the image of nursery wallpaper with a teddy bear covering its eyes with its paws. 'Don't close your eyes to cruelty to children'.

It was thought that the doordrop letter addressed as 'Dear Householder' might offend established donors. To avoid this, 160,000 best donors were sent an early warning letter in advance of the campaign breaking in order to get their support. Another million received personal letters just ahead of the doordrop.

It was anticipated that the bulk of enquiries would come from the doordrop action and these were to be handled through personal telemarketing responses (inbound). The website was also adapted in order that it would be able to accept pledges.

In addition to this the campaign utilised a call-to-action weekend with volunteers staffing 2,000 sites around the country, including most city centres, to remind and raise cash donations.

Promotional mix used to communicate with businesses

- Sponsorship
- Direct Mail/Information Pack
- Internet

Sponsorship deals were made available enabling businesses to align themselves more closely with the campaign. Microsoft have been closely involved with NSPCC for a number of years and they acted as prime movers encouraging other businesses to pledge their support. The advertising for the campaign was sponsored by Microsoft.

Other sponsorship and cause related marketing packages were detailed in a Toolkit distributed to other major organisations.

Direct mail was also used to encourage businesses to make donations and electronic communications were used to promote pledges online.   (Adapted from *Goften* (1999)

This campaign sought to deal with an issue that most people choose to ignore. The ambitious targets needed an extraordinary marketing communications campaign if it was to be successful. The co-ordinated promotional plan enabled a simple yet hard hitting message to be conveyed to a substantial part of the nation.

It should be remembered that without knowing the budgets made available to fund the campaign and the extent of the contribution made by the business-to-business sector, it is doubtful whether a return on the investment will be made known outside of the charity. However, this should not detract from what is a major contribution to the social and moral welfare of the nation, made possible through astute use of an co-ordinated marketing communications campaign.

6 Marketing communications for small businesses

The main feature of marketing communications for **small businesses** is that resources are limited. This will mean that more is done in-house and at a local level, though all the usual promotional tools can still be employed.

Action Programme 4

Devise a marketing communications strategy and programme for a small business of your choice. Describe the advantages and disadvantages of such a low budget campaign.

A glance through the many books on small business management and especially those claiming to reveal the secrets of successful low budget advertising will show that readers are given watered down versions of the conventional promotional principles. This again demonstrates that these principles are of uniform application and this is reassuring.

However, there must be differences between small companies and large companies besides the sizes of the campaign budgets. The overriding differences are of course the limited resources in designing and implementing a communications programme and also the matching limitations in the target audience. The implications of these limitations and other aspects are discussed below.

6.1 Do-it-yourself

The key to saving money is to carry out many of the tasks in-house. This will mean learning about the principles and methods of marketing communications. This in itself is a valuable exercise. Small businesses can use desk top publishing to design advertising material and local media owners will be only too happy to deal directly.

6.2 Small agencies

If a business does need professional help, there are many one-person and small agencies able to offer a package of promotional help on a cost effective basis. Such agencies are keen to help small businesses grow because this is the best way of growing themselves.

6.3 Marketing research

To reduce risks, a business should improve its targeting and get to know customer needs and competition better. It is important here to conduct marketing research. Many small business people rely a great deal on intuition and may be reluctant to conduct research, but it will repay many times the effort devoted to it.

6.4 Personal selling

The owner manager of a small business will also usually be one of the company's main salesmen. This is another way of maintaining a low cost and cost effective marketing budget.

6.5 Public relations

This promotional method does not need substantial sums to get started. Simple press releases can be issued, opening events can be held and even a limited local sponsorship can be done for little expenditure. Again this will often mean doing it in-house or using a small local PR agency.

6.6 Direct marketing

Using direct marketing techniques, either telemarketing or direct mail, can be done cost effectively at local level. The volume of direct marketing activity can be regulated by the amount of time available and by the number of customers a business is trying to reach.

6.7 Door drops

An alternative method of getting to households is to arrange for door to door leaflet distribution in the chosen target area. This can be considerably cheaper than incurring postal charges. It is also accurate in that particular districts and types of houses can be targeted.

6.8 Advertising

With the expansion of local media including free newspapers and local commercial radio stations, it is possible to tailor a campaign to particular locations. Designing advertising and buying media space or airtime, however, can become quite expensive, especially for frequently repeated advertisements.

6.9 Sales promotion

It is possible to devise a whole range of cost effective sales promotions, which will have the benefit of generating immediate sales and improving cash flow.

6.10 Rapid feedback

All these methods can be tried and evaluated at relatively low cost. Rapid feedback of results that will enable an improved campaign to be developed and implemented.

The characteristics specific to low budget campaigns are summarised below.

Feature	Comment
Do it yourself	Planning, implementation and control
Small agencies	Matching your size
Marketing research	Will reduce risk
Personal selling	Likely to be the main method
Public relations	Can be done at low cost
Direct marketing	Cost effective by telephone and mail
Door drops	Very low cost targeting
Advertising	Likely to be more expensive
Sales promotion	Immediate benefits to cash flow
Rapid feedback	Allowing for improvements to be made

Chapter Roundup

- **Industrial marketing communications strategies** can be very different from consumer campaigns. There are differences in such areas as purchase motivation, customer needs, product specifications, level of customer service needed and so on. This calls for different approaches in employing the various promotional tools.

- The marketing of **services** is similar to the marketing of products in many ways, but there can be differences because of such factors as professional and legal constraints, the nature of capacity available, and the buying process itself. Personal selling is more important.

- In **non profit marketing communications** there is likely to be less money available, messages are likely to be subjected to greater scrutiny and the objectives of the communication will be quite different from those applying in consumer marketing. The major categories of non profit communicators are political parties, social causes, the government, religious bodies and professional bodies.

- The main feature of marketing communications for **small businesses** is that resources are limited. This will mean that more is done in-house and at a local level, though all the usual promotional tools can still be employed.

Quick Quiz

1   Ultimately communications are designed to meet three objectives.

A........... Increase brand .... and establish brand ....

T........... Stimulate trial ....

R........... Stimulate and .... brand ....

2   Fill in the gaps in the grid below:

Marketing communications methods	Examples of measurement
Personal selling	
Public relations	
Direct marketing	
Advertising	
Sales promotion	
Exhibitions	

3   When assessing the effectiveness of a communications campaign, why is simplification important?

A   It is more cost-effective
B   It is necessary in view of the avalanche of information faced by customers
C   Less educated customers will pay more attention
D   The message needs to be the same for everybody

4   A recall test is an example of

(a)   Pre testing
(b)   Post testing

5   Why is direct marketing particularly effective for non-profit organisations?

A   The effectiveness of direct marketing can be assessed in terms of behaviour
B   Results are clearly measurable
C   It can be cheap and targeted
D   All of the above

6   How can public relations be undertaken in a low budget campaign?

7   The amount of communication to which people are now being subjected means that it is becoming increasingly difficult to communicate successfully.

True   ☐

False   ☐

8   In non profit marketing communications there is likely to be less money available. What is a possible consequence of this?

Answers to Quick Quiz

1   Awareness   Increase brand awareness and establish brand recognition
     Trial   Stimulate trial purchase
     Reinforcement   Stimulate and reinforce brand loyalty

2

Marketing communications methods	Examples of measurement
Personal selling	Sales targets
Public relations	Editorial coverage
Direct marketing	Enquiries generated
Advertising	Brand awareness
Sales promotion	Coupons redeemed
Exhibitions	Contacts made

3   B

4   Post testing

5   D

6   Simple press releases can be issued, opening events can be held and even a limited local sponsorship can be done for little expenditure. This will often mean 'doing it yourself' or using a small local PR agency.

7   True

8   Proposed media and messages are likely to be subjected to greater scrutiny, as resources are tighter

Action Programme Review

1   (a)   Size of business, market sector, fmcg/business-to-business/service/not for profit.

    (b)   These factors and issues should be based on result of context analysis – business, customer, stakeholder, internal and external.

    (c)   Communications objectives should focus on changes in awareness, attitudes and behaviour. These should relate to marketing and business objectives.

    (d)   Pull, push and profile are the main communications strategies available – what communications tools have you identified for each strategy?

    (e)   If you have identified sales or market share, remember the difficulty of direct association with communications due to other marketing factor effects. You should be measuring the effectiveness against the objectives set.

2   You should have identified integrating factors relating to different levels of strategy – business, marketing and communication – all linked via the objectives set. It is not just a question of using the same strapline or visual image on all of the communication, but also as to how the overall communications activities relate to what the business as a whole is attempting to achieve. Remember that internal communications play an important role in achieving integration and the relevance of push and profile strategies.

3   In theory, as more and more people buy the products and as the website becomes more and more successful, its 'snobbery' appeal will become tarnished by its own popularity. The targeted type of customer is only likely to buy from it once. Someone who is a 'snob' and who doesn't mind what they pay for an item, so long as it comes from the 'right' place, is unlikely to be loyal when the next 'in' thing comes along. The company will have to find new ways to differentiate itself from the competition. Given its product range and the fact that it is much more expensive than other distributors, this could prove extremely difficult.

4   Your answer should have looked at the advantages and disadvantages of different strategic options viz. push, pull and profile. The communications tools should be specific to the strategy or strategies selected. You can identify some of the advantages and disadvantages of a low budget campaign from the table at Paragraph 5.1.

Now try Question 8 at the end of the Study Text

Part C
Marketing channels

Developing and maintaining marketing channels

Syllabus content – knowledge and skill requirements

- How the promotional mix can be suitably configured for use in a range of marketing channels and business-to-business situations (3.1)
- The impact on marketing communications within a relationship context, of the structural concepts: interdependence, independence, disintermediation and reintermediation (3.2)
- The role of trust, commitment and satisfaction when developing marketing communication activities for use in the marketing channel and business-to-business contexts (3.3)
- The causes of conflict in trade channels and how marketing communications can be used to resolve such disagreements (3.4)

Introduction

Business-to-business relationships include **marketing channel relationships** and **supply chain networks**. This chapter looks at the nature of various distribution structures and discusses some of the influences which affect the choice and configuration of the marketing channel.

For many manufacturers, distribution is the 'Cinderella' of the marketing mix, less glamorous and 'creative' than promotion, and less involved in the heart of the company than the product. However some firms use distribution as a means of competitive advantage and retailers, of course, take distribution very seriously. Marketing communicators also need to take account of its importance. Distribution has two aspects, expanded upon in the next paragraph.

- **Tangible** – the physical movement and delivery of goods

- **Intangible** – aspects of channel (or supply chain) management, control and communication. This forms the focus for this chapter.

A firm's **marketing communications** will be strongly influenced by the extent to which the firm is able to obtain wide distribution. Key issues in distribution are these.

(a)   **Coverage and density**, in other words the number of sales outlets.

    (i)   Countries like the UK and US allow large stores.

    (ii)   In Japan, there have been restrictions on store size, to protect the livelihoods of small retailers.

(b)   **Channel length** – the number of intermediaries between producer and consumer.

(c)   **Power and alignment.** The marketer has to realise that distribution channel power is not equal. Different roles are played by retailers, wholesalers and agents. For example, wholesalers are most important where retailing is fragmented. In the UK, where, in groceries, concentration of retail power has gone furthest, the major supermarket chains are powerful.

(d)   **Logistics and physical distribution**

Logistics systems are expensive and can be very damaging to corporate profitability if badly handled. There are several areas which are crucial.

    (i)   Transport and transport management (delivery time and costs)
    (ii)   Inventory control (minimum stock without effective service)
    (iii)   Order processing
    (iv)   Materials handling and warehouse
    (v)   Fixed facilities location management

1 The chain of distribution

Distribution channels provide **transport, stockholding** and **storage, local knowledge, promotion** and **display**.

In order for a product to be distributed a number of basic functions usually need to be fulfilled.

Transport	This function may be provided by the supplier, the distributor or may be sub-contracted to a specialist. For some products, such as perishable goods, transport planning is vital.
Stock holding and storage	For production planning purposes, an uninterrupted flow of production is often essential, so stocks of finished goods accumulate and need to be stored, incurring significant costs and risks. For consumer goods, holding stock at the point of sale is very costly; the overheads for city centre retail locations are prohibitive. A good stock control system is essential, designed to avoid stockouts whilst keeping stockholding costs low.
Local knowledge	As production has tended to become centralised in pursuit of economies of scale, the need to understand local markets has grown, particularly when international marketing takes place. The intricacies and idiosyncrasies of local markets are key marketing information.
Promotion	Major promotional campaigns for national products are likely to be carried out by the supplier.
Display	Presentation of the product is often a function of the local distributor. Specialist help from merchandisers can be bought in.

Action Programme 1

For many goods, producers use retailers as middlemen in getting the product to the customer. Try to think of some of the disadvantages of doing this, from the producer's point of view.

Exam tip

Relationships with intermediaries were examined in December 2003 in the context of L'Oréal's distribution strategies for its various product ranges. Marketing channel relationships were also examined in June 2005, and again in December 2006 where channel *conflict* and conflict management featured in the compulsory question, and the use of digital technology in enhancing channel relationships was worth a further five marks.

1.1 Points in the chain of distribution

An intermediary is someone who 'mediates' or brings about a settlement between two persons: in this case between the original supplier and the ultimate buyer. There are a variety of types of intermediary and several may intervene before a product gets from the original provider and the final buyer: Figure 9.1.

Figure 9.1: Distribution chains

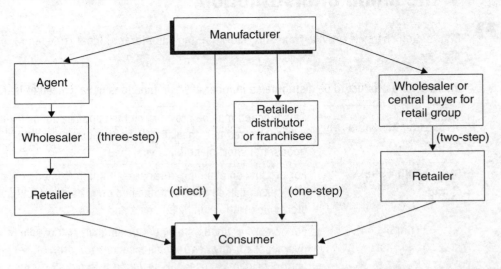

(a)   **Retailers**. These are traders operating outlets which sell directly to households. They may be classified in a number of ways.

   (i)   Type of goods sold (eg hardware, furniture)

   (ii)   Type of service (self-service, counter service)

   (iii)   Size

   (iv)   Location (rural, city-centre, suburban shopping mall, out-of-town shopping centre)

   (v)   **Independent retailers** (including the local corner shop, although independents are not always as small as this)

   (vi)   **Multiple chains**, some of which are associated with one class of product while others are 'variety' chains, holding a wide range of different stocks

   (vii)   Still others are **voluntary groups** of independents, usually grocers.

(b)   **Wholesalers**. These are intermediaries who stock a range of products from competing manufacturers to sell on to other organisations such as retailers. Many wholesalers specialise in particular products. Most deal in consumer goods, but some specialise in industrial goods, such as steel stockholders and builders' merchants.

(c)   **Distributors and dealers**. These are organisations which contract to buy a manufacturer's goods and sell them to customers. Their function is similar to that of wholesalers, but they usually offer a narrower product range, sometimes (as in the case of most car dealers) the products of a single manufacturer. In addition to selling on the manufacturer's product, distributors often promote the products and provide after-sales service.

(d)   **Agents**. Agents differ from distributors.

   (i)   Distributors **buy** the manufacturer's goods and **re-sell** them at a profit.

   (ii)   Agents do not purchase the manufacturer's goods, but earn a commission on whatever sales they make.

(e)   **Franchisees**. These are independent organisations which, in exchange for an initial fee and (usually) a share of sales revenue, are allowed to trade under the name of a parent organisation. Most fast food outlets are franchises.

(f)   **Multiple stores** (eg **supermarkets**) buy goods for retailing direct from the producer, many of them under their 'own label' brand name.

Marketing at Work

Kodak Express Malaysia: on-line information for potential franchisees

As a Kodak Express member, you will enjoy the following benefits.

- **Kodak Express Branding**: the right to use the Kodak Express logo for advertising and promotions in the store.

- **Quality Monitoring Service**: Kodak's engineers will advise and make recommendations on how to maintain our print quality according to international Kodak quality standards. With this support, your store will be able to provide quality prints to consumers.

- **Exclusive Rebates**: Exclusive only to you, these discounts and rebates will provide your business with a leading edge over the rest.

- **Training**: one of the best benefits in the franchise program. Each year, Kodak will organise at least four training sessions to help you improve your business performance.

- **Retail Shop Concept**: A new store concept for the Kodak Express shops is specially designed to project Kodak Express as a young, vibrant and professional retail store to consumers.

- **360-degree Checklist Program**: your Business Support Executive will conduct checks and monitoring exercises in your store regularly. The quality of the photos processed, the visual displays and the quality of staff service will be measured to ensure that your store meets the quality requirements to stay competitive in the market.

- **Best Kodak Express Award**: designed to reward members who provide consistently good service and quality prints to consumers. Every year, the top ten Kodak Express Award winners will receive cash prizes and public recognition in local papers.

- **Newsletter**: one of the ways which you will be kept updated on the latest products, services and trends in the photo-retailing industry.

- **Advertisements**: you will benefit from the advertising plans and strategies initiated by Kodak.

- **Annual Conference**: an annual event where members will not only interact and discuss ways to improve the Kodak Express program, but also gain knowledge.

http://www.kodak.com/my (17th March 2004)

Identify how Kodak uses marketing communications to build relationship with franchisees.

Exam tip

The role of marketing communications in resolving relationship issues experienced by franchisees was the focus of a case study question part in the December 2007 exam.

Do not forget that **direct selling** also occurs.

- Mail order
- Telephone selling
- Door-to-door selling
- Personal selling in the sale of industrial goods
- An organisation which includes both manufacturing and retail outlets
- TV shopping
- E-commerce

1.2 Factors in relationships with distribution channels

FAST FORWARD

Direct distribution occurs when the product goes directly from producer to consumer. **Indirect distribution** happens via an intermediary.

In working with **distributors**, the marketer needs to bear in mind the following points.

(a)   **The independent commercial objectives of the distributor**. Distributors are business organisations with their own requirements for efficiency and profitability. They do not stock products or run promotions as a 'favour' to the supplier!

    (i)   You need to negotiate contract terms.

    (ii)   You need to promote the benefits of the product or collaboration to the distributor.

(b)   **The distributor's relationship with competitors**. Bear in mind that a retailer or wholesaler may well be stocking and promoting competing products. You will need to be discreet to differentiate your product and promotions, and to be aware of opportunities to gain useful market intelligence.

(c)   **The distributor's knowledge of the consumer**. Distributors are in the front line of contact with consumers. Be prepared to seek and respect their research or sense of what will work in terms of product and promotion.

(d)   **The distributor's power in the market.** Major distributors have considerable buying power over suppliers, and good working relationships must be preserved with them, usually at the expense of autonomy and control over promotions. A major distributor may ask for exclusive rights to sell a product, or ask to sell it under an 'own brand' label. It may control all point-of-sale and media promotions regarding its sale of the product, charging a fee for promotional space and collaboration.

(e)   **The mutual benefit of promotional collaboration**

    (i)   If the supplier promotes the product to consumers through PR, advertising and consumer incentives, the distributor selling the product to consumers will benefit.

    (ii)   If the distributor promotes the product to consumers – through advertising its availability through the distributor, or through in-store display and incentives – the supplier will benefit.

Exam tip

> Bear in mind that 'channel relationships' are relationships – not just structural decisions about channels. In June 2007 a question focused on problems caused in relationships with intermediaries by a financial services firm's marketing direct to customers (via its website) – and how trust and commitment could be rebuilt in the channel partners in this scenario.

1.3 Direct and indirect distribution

Choosing distribution channels is important for any organisation, because once a set of channels has been established, subsequent changes are likely to be costly and slow to implement. Distribution channels fall into one of two categories: **direct** and **indirect channels**.

Direct distribution means the product going directly from producer to consumer without the use of a specific intermediary. These methods are often described as **active** since they typically involve the **supplier** making the first approach to a potential customer. Direct distribution methods generally fall into two categories: those using **media** such as the press, leaflets and telephones to invite response and purchase by the consumer and those using a **sales force** to contact consumers face to face.

Indirect distribution is a system of distribution, common among manufactured goods, which makes use of intermediaries; wholesalers, retailers or perhaps both. In contrast to direct distribution, these methods are often thought of as being **passive** in the sense that they rely on consumers to make the first approach by entering the relevant retail outlet.

Exam tip

> Direct and indirect methods of distribution are used by the subject of the case study on the Pilot Paper, Country Style Kitchens.

In building up efficient channels of distribution, a manufacturer must consider several factors.

(a) How many **intermediate stages** should be used and how many dealers at each stage?

(b) What **support** should the manufacturer give to the dealers? It may be necessary to provide an after-sales and repair service, and regular visits to retailers' stores. The manufacturer might need to consider advertising or sales promotion support, including merchandising.

(c) To what extent does the manufacturer wish to **dominate a channel of distribution**? A market leader might wish to ensure that its market share is maintained, so that it could, for example, offer **exclusive distribution contracts** to major retailers.

(d) To what extent does the manufacturer wish to **integrate its marketing effort** up to the point of sale with the consumer? Combined promotions with retailers, for example, would only be possible if the manufacturer dealt directly with the retailer (rather than through a wholesaler).

2 Supply chain management

FAST FORWARD

> Ever-increasing customer demands, together with developments in technology have made **supply chain management** more important. This looks at the whole picture, including the problems of ensuring smooth inflow of raw materials from suppliers so that end products can be available when customers want them.
>
> In marketing channels, organisations have to manage the trade-off between the desire to remain **independent and autonomous**, and the need to be **interdependent and co-operative**.

Many enterprises have been getting larger. Some writers are arguing that the trend will continue – so that for many sectors there will be fewer players of world class dominating the field. We have seen this in the automobile industry for example, with many European companies merging to be able to compete effectively with US giants and the Japanese.

There have been, at the same time, much **closer links** with companies in the supply chain in order to extract best value for money and reduce stockholdings. This has had major consequences on the distribution methods of companies in these supply chains, delivering to their customers on a **just in time** (JIT) basis.

Historically, businesses in the supply chain have operated relatively **independently** of one another to create value for an ultimate customer. **Independence was maintained** through holding buffer stocks, managing capacity and lead-times. This is represented in the 'Traditional' model shown in Figure 9.2. There was very little control over other channel members, and no wider perspective on the system as a whole.

Market and competitive demands are now, however, **compressing lead times** and businesses are reducing inventories and excess capacity. This new condition is shown in the '**Integrated supply chain**' model: Figure 9.2.

Supply chain management has been defined as: 'The integration and management of supply chain organisations and activities through co-operative organisational relationships, effective business processes, and high levels of information sharing to create high-performing value systems that provide member organisations a sustainable competitive advantage' (*Handfield & Nichols*, 2002)

There seems to be increasing recognition that, in the future, it will be **whole supply chains** which will compete and not just individual firms. *Jespersen & Skjøtt-Larsen* (2005) argue that: 'Focus has moved from competition between firms at the same level in the production process to competition between supply chains ... A company's ability to create trust-based and long-term business relationships with customers, suppliers and other strategic partners becomes a crucial competitive parameter'.

Figure 9.2: Supply chain model

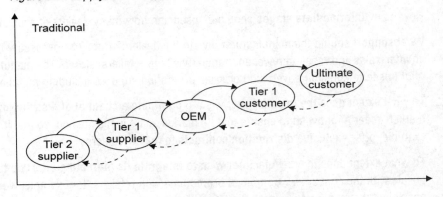
Traditional

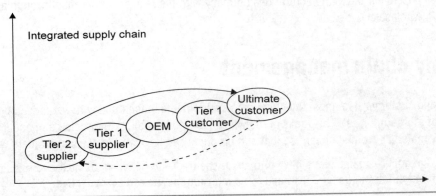
Integrated supply chain

Key concept

> **Supply chain management** is about optimising the activities of companies working together to produce goods and services.

The aim is to co-ordinate the whole chain, from raw material suppliers to end customers. The chain should be considered as a **network** rather than a **pipeline** – a network of vendors support a network of customers, with third parties such as transport firms helping to link the companies. In marketing channels, organisations have to manage the trade-off between the desire to remain **independent and autonomous**, and the need to be **interdependent and cooperative**.

Key concepts

> **Independence**: each channel member operates in isolation and is not affected by others, so maintaining a greater degree of control.
>
> **Interdependence**: each channel member can affect the performance of others in the channel.

Marketing at Work

Li and Fung, the Hong Kong based export trading group (www.lifung.com), co-ordinates the manufacture of goods through a network of 69 offices in 40 countries, which work together to find the best sources. Garments make up a large part of the business, but the business also covers fashion accessories, furnishings, gifts, handicrafts, home products, promotional merchandise, toys, sporting goods and travel goods.

Li and Fung prides itself on being "one of the premier global consumer products export trading companies managing the supply chain for high-volume, time-sensitive consumer goods. Our mission is to deliver the right product at the right price at the right time." Ethical sourcing is also seen as important, and the company is a member of Business for Social Responsibility (www.bsr.org).

If the supplier 'knows' what – its customers want, it does not necessarily have to guess, or wait until the customer places an order. It will be able to plan its own delivery systems better. The potential for using the **Internet** (see Section 5) to allow customers and suppliers to acquire up-to-date information about forecast needs and delivery schedules is a recent development, but one which is being used by an increasing number of companies.

3 Stakeholders

FAST FORWARD

Stakeholders are groups or individuals having a legitimate interest in the activities of an organisation, generally comprising customers, employees, the community, shareholders, suppliers and lenders.

Linked to the idea of networks is the **stakeholder concept**. To quote *Fill* (2002):

> 'The concept of different groups influencing an organisation and in turn being influenced is an important element in the development of integrated marketing communications. The concept enables an organisation to identify all those other organisations and individuals who can be or are influenced by [its] strategies and policies.'

Key concept

> **Stakeholders** are 'those individuals who depend on the organisation to fulfil their own goals and on whom, in turn, the organisation depends' *(Johnson &* Scholes, 2005, p179)

There are three broad types of stakeholder in an organisation, as follows.

- **Internal** stakeholders (employees, management)
- **Connected** stakeholders (shareholders, customers, suppliers, financiers)
- **External** stakeholders (the community, government, pressure groups)

3.1 Internal stakeholders: employees and management

Because **employees and management** are so intimately connected with the company, their objectives are likely to have a strong influence on how it is run. They are interested in the following issues.

(a) The **organisation's continuation and growth**. Management and employees have a special interest in the organisation's continued existence.

(b) Managers and employees have **individual interests** and goals, which can be harnessed to the goals of the organisation.

3.2 Connected stakeholders

Increasing shareholder value usually assumes the core role in the strategic management of an international business. If management performance is measured and rewarded by reference to changes in **shareholder value** then shareholders will be happy, because managers are likely to encourage long-term share price growth.

Customers, suppliers and consumers can increasingly be thought of as 'investing in the company' whenever they buy or sell a particular product or service. They judge the **total value** that the company can offer. This can include:

- **Expertise** (eg support/training offered by manufacturers to retailers)
- **Information** (as offered by retailers to suppliers on market trends)
- **Influence**
- **Infrastructure**   } (use of buying power to source raw materials)
- **Resources**
- **Responsive attitude** (such as alignment of ordering and payment processes between supply chain partners)
- **Social responsibility**

3.3 External stakeholders

External stakeholder groups – the government, local authorities, pressure groups, the community at large, professional bodies – are likely to have quite diverse objectives.

Exam tip

In an exam question, you may have to:

- Identify the stakeholders in the marketing channel
- Identify what their particular interests are

The stakeholder concept is particularly important in relation to Corporate Social Responsibility (discussed in Chapter 2). *Jobber* (2007, p201) defines a stakeholder as 'an individual or group that either is harmed by, or benefits from, the company *or* whose rights can be violated, or have to be respected, by the company'.

3.4 Stakeholder networks and the marketing channel

FAST FORWARD

Within the marketing channel, there are two primary stakeholder roles: **performance** and **support**.

Stakeholder 'maps' indicate the primary relationships and patterns of interdependence within the marketing channel. These networks 'not only constitute those organisations that make up the marketing channel but also seek to integrate all those other organisations that assist the channel members to achieve their objectives of satisfying customer needs' (*Fill*, 2002).

Within the marketing channel, there are two primary stakeholder roles, connected to the idea of internal, connected and external stakeholders described above.

(a) **Performance** – directly involved with adding value in the marketing channel (manufacturer, wholesaler, retailer). These are interdependent.

(b) **Support** – banks, consultancies, government and so on, supporting the 'performing' members. These have no such interdependence.

 Action Programme 2

Identify the 'performance' and 'support' organisations that make up the network in the marketing channel used by your company, or one with which you are familiar.

4 Channel design decisions

4.1 Factors in channel decisions

In setting up a channel of distribution, the supplier must consider five things.

- Customers
- Product characteristics
- Distributor characteristics
- The channel chosen by competitors
- The supplier's own characteristics

4.1.1 Customers

The **number** of potential customers, their **buying habits** and their **geographical locations** are key influences. The use of mail order for those with limited mobility (rural location, illness) is an example of the influence of customers on channel design. Marketing industrial components to the car industry needs to take account of the geographic distribution of the car industry in the UK. The growth of Internet trading, both in consumer and business-to-business markets, has been built on the rapid spread of fast Internet access.

4.1.2 Product characteristics

Some product characteristics have an important effect on the design of the channel of distribution.

(a) **Perishability**

Fresh fruit and newspapers must be distributed very quickly or they become worthless. Speed of delivery is therefore a key factor.

(b) **Customisation**

Customised products tend to be distributed direct. When a wide range of options is available, sales may be made using demonstration units, with customised delivery to follow.

(c) **After-sales service/technical advice**

Extent and cost must be carefully considered, staff training given and quality control systems set up. Training programmes are often provided for distributors by suppliers.

(d) **Franchising**

Franchising has become a popular means of growth both for suppliers and for franchisees who carry the set-up costs and licence fees. The supplier gains additional outlets quickly and exerts more control than is usual in distribution.

4.1.3 Distributor characteristics

The capability of the distributor to take on the distributive functions already discussed above is obviously an important influence on the supplier's choice.

4.1.4 Competitors' channel choice

For many consumer goods, a supplier's brand will sit alongside its competitors' products and there is little the supplier can do about it. For other products, distributors may stock one name brand only (for example, in car distribution) and in return be given an exclusive area. In this case, new suppliers may face difficulties in breaking into a market if all the best distribution outlets have been taken up.

4.1.5 Supplier characteristics

A strong financial base gives the supplier the option of buying and operating their own distribution channel. Boots the Chemist is a prime example. The market position of the supplier is also important: distributors are keen to be associated with the market leader but the third, fourth or fifth brand in a market is likely to find more distribution problems.

4.1.6 Factors favouring the use of direct selling

(a) An expert sales force will be needed to demonstrate products, explain product characteristics and provide after-sales service.

(b) Intermediaries may be unwilling or unable to sell the product.

(c) Existing channels may be linked to other producers or reluctant to carry new product lines.

(d) The intermediaries willing to sell the product may be too costly, or they may not be maximising potential sales.

(e) If specialised transport requirements are involved, intermediaries may not be able to deliver goods to the final customer.

(f) Where potential buyers are geographically concentrated the supplier's own sales force can easily reach them (typically an industrial market). One example is the financial services market centred on the City of London.

4.1.7 Factors favouring the use of intermediaries

(a) There may be insufficient resources to finance a large sales force.

(b) A policy decision to invest in increased productive capacity rather than extra marketing effort may be taken.

(c) The supplier may have insufficient in-house marketing 'know-how' in selling to retail stores.

(d) The assortment of products may be insufficient for a sales force to carry. A wholesaler can complement a limited range and make more efficient use of his sales force.

(e) Intermediaries can market small lots as part of a range of goods. The supplier would incur a heavy sales overhead if its own sales force took small individual orders.

(f) The existence of large numbers of potential buyers spread over a wide geographical area. This is typical of consumer markets.

4.2 Making the channel decision

FAST FORWARD

Different types of market exposure:

- **Intensive** – blanket coverage
- **Exclusive** – appointed agents for exclusive areas
- **Selective** – some but not all in each area

Producers have a number of decisions to make.

(a) What types of distributor are to be used (wholesalers, retailers, agents)?

(b) How many of each type will be used? The answer to this depends on what degree of market exposure will be sought.

    (i) **Intensive** – blanket coverage

    (ii) **Exclusive** – appointed agents for exclusive areas

    (iii) **Selective** – some but not all in each area

(c)   Who will carry out specific marketing tasks?

      (i)   Credit provision
      (ii)   Delivery
      (iii)   After-sales service
      (iv)   Sales and product training
      (v)   Display

Action Programme 3

How might the performance of distributors be evaluated?

To develop a co-ordinated system of distribution, the supplier must consider all the factors influencing distribution combined with a knowledge of the relative merits of the different types of channel available.

4.3 Multi-channel decisions

The distribution channels appropriate for industrial markets may not be suitable for consumer markets. A producer serving both industrial and consumer markets may decide to use the following.

(a)   Intermediaries for his consumer division

(b)   Direct selling for his industrial division. For example, a detergent manufacturer might employ salesmen to sell to wholesalers and large retail groups in their consumer division. It would not be efficient for the sales force to approach small retailers directly.

4.4 Industrial and consumer distribution channels

FAST FORWARD

Different distribution strategies may be adopted for **consumer** and **industrial markets**. Industrial channels tend to be more direct and shorter.

Industrial markets may be characterised as having fewer, larger customers purchasing expensive products which may be custom built. It is due to these characteristics that **industrial distribution channels tend to be more direct and shorter than for consumer markets**. It has to be remembered, however, that the most appropriate distribution channels will depend specifically on the objectives of the company regarding market exposure. There are specialist distributors in the industrial sector, which may be used as well as, or instead of, selling directly to the companies within this sector.

There are fewer direct distribution channels, from the manufacturer to the consumer in the **consumer market**. Examples may be found in small 'cottage' industries or mail order companies. It is more usual for companies in consumer markets to use wholesalers and retailers to move their product to the final consumer.

(a)   **Wholesalers** break down the bulk from manufacturers and pass products on to retailers. They take on some of the supplier's risks by funding stock. Recently in the UK there has been a reduction in importance of this type of intermediary.

(b)   **Retailers** sell to the final consumers. They may give consumers added benefits by providing services such as credit, delivery and a wide variety of goods. In the UK, retailers have increased in power whilst wholesalers have declined. Retailing has also become more concentrated with increased dominance of large multiples.

Exam tip

> Marketing channels in the car industry form the topic of a question in Section B of the Pilot Paper. This is a key example of an industry where distribution patterns are changing away from traditional dealer networks because of:
>
> - Increased price awareness by consumers – driven largely by the Internet
> - Regulations controlling 'price fixing'
> - Direct sales opportunities afforded by the Internet
>
> Car manufacturers also featured on the December 2005 paper.

Marketing at Work

Nestlé

According to Nestlé chief executive Peter Braback, 'Ten years ago we were in a cockfight with the retailers. But we must not forget that they invested in very, very expensive distribution systems that brought prices down and contributed to our volume growth. So now we want to be a partner, not a supplier.'

Mr Braback accepts that concentration in retailing is a fact but argues that relationships with suppliers will not suffer as retailers become bigger. For Mr Braback, the growth of groups such as Wal-Mart, Carrefour or Tesco has helped both sides – as well as consumers – by cutting the complexity of distribution, one of the biggest cost factors in the business.

The company's most senior marketer is deemed central to making such relationships work. That position has three main areas of responsibility, the most basic of which is to be in charge of what he calls 'the function'.

- Consumer insight, communications, promotions, sales
- Channel management
- Retailer relationships

Financial Times, 22 February 2005

4.5 Marketing channel strategy

There are three main strategies.

(a)   **Intensive distribution** involves concentrating on a segment of the total market, such as choosing limited geographical distribution rather than national distribution.

(b)   Using **selective distribution**, the producer selects a group of retail outlets from amongst all retail outlets on grounds of the brand image, or related to the retailers' capacity to provide after-sales service.

(c)   **Exclusive distribution** is an extension of selective distribution. Particular outlets are granted exclusive handling rights within a prescribed geographical area. Sometimes exclusive distribution, or franchise rights, are coupled with making special financial arrangements for land, buildings or equipment, such as petrol station agreements.

4.6 Channel dynamics

Organisations group together when they cannot achieve their objectives independently. If a marketing channel is to function effectively, cooperation is paramount.

(a)   A distribution system with a central core organising and planning marketing throughout the channel is termed a **vertical marketing system (VMS)**. Vertical marketing systems provide channel role specification and co-ordination between members. There is much more **interdependence** than is featured in a conventional system.

(b)   In **corporate marketing systems** the stages in production and distribution are owned by a single corporation in a fairly rigid structure. This common ownership permits close integration and therefore the corporation controls activities along the distribution chain. For example, Laura Ashley shops sell goods produced in Laura Ashley factories.

(c)   **Contractual marketing systems** involve agreement over aspects of distribution marketing. One example of a contractual marketing system that has become popular over the last decade is franchising.

(d)   If a plan is drawn up between channel members to help reduce conflict this is often termed an **administered marketing system**.

4.7 Channel conflict

Channels are subject to **conflicts** between members. This need not be destructive as long as it remains manageable. Manufacturers may have little influence on how their product is presented to the public.

Key concept

> **Conflict** is the breakdown in co-operation between channel partners.

The causes of conflict need to be identified, so that strategies can be formulated to repair any damage. Conflict stems from four main problems (*Fill*, 2002).

- **Failure to do the job** as understood by the rest of the channel
- Disagreement over a **policy issue**, such as territory or margin
- Differing perceptions on **how to get the job done**
- Inadequate **communications**

Exam tip

> Remember that channel conflict can have positive outcomes.
>
> - Avoidance of potential end user problems
> - 'Recharged' relationships
> - Promotion of problem solving
> - Understanding of changed conditions
> - Reduced complacency
> - Opportunity for market, product and customer development

4.8 Interorganisational communication

FAST FORWARD

Conflicts can arise in marketing channels, and the key to managing them is to have good communications.

Communication is key to conflict resolution. The **management of communication** is usually undertaken by a dominant member – the channel 'leader' or 'captain' who holds most of the power in the channel. In industrial markets where channel lengths are generally short, power often lies with manufacturers of products rather than 'middlemen'.

Communication within networks travels not only between levels of dependence (up and down the network) but also across, such as from retailer to retailer. Reflecting its role in the **push** strategy, it has the following roles.

- Provide persuasive **information**
- Foster participative decision making
- Provide for co-ordination
- Allows the exercise of power
- Encourages loyalty and commitment
- Reduces the likelihood of tension and conflict

Trust in and commitment to the network is crucial for success.

Key concepts

> **Trust:** the degree to which partners are confident that each will act in the best interests of the relationship.
>
> **Commitment:** the desire to maintain a valuable relationship.

Exam tip

> "Students will be asked questions regarding marketing channel relationships and the ways in which marketing communications can be used to assist the development and maintenance of such relationships. Conflict, trust and commitment will be examined again." Source: Examiner comments on the December 2005 sitting: channel conflict duly appeared (for 10 compulsory question marks) in December 2005.

Marketing at Work

The use of trade promotions and trade advertising by a company will be designed to keep the channel loyal. Techniques such as offering discounts to wholesalers, in return for extra promotion of the product, or extra shelf space, will help to increase sales as well (if the discount is passed on to the end consumer). Trade advertising in the form of brochures, leaflets and samples should focus on aspects such as margins, turnover, shelf space profitability and the level of manufacturer support.

Exam tip

> Distribution is often not represented and easy to ignore, but is key to issues of communication and profitability, and the syllabus is keen to address it. Each channel has different needs and requirements. The December 2006 exam set an interesting question on *why* and *how* a leading soft drink brand would differentiate its communications mix to its *distributors* from that used for its *customers*. (stop and think about this now …) The December 2007 exam focused on a newly-developed franchise network of ice-cream parlours: you were required to consider the relationship issues from the *franchisees'* perspective, and how marketing communications by the *franchisor* could resolve them.

Action Programme 4

One of the fastest growing forms of selling in the US over the past decade has been via factory outlet centres. Discount factory shops, often situated on factory premises, from which manufacturers sell off overmakes, slight seconds, or retailers' returns are already well-established in the UK, but in the US developers have grouped such outlets together in purpose-built malls.

What would you suggest are the advantages of this method of distribution for customers and manufacturers?

Marketing at Work

OTC Medicines

The supply chain is often a crucial element in the success or failure of a product. In the case of over-the-counter (OTC) medicines, because of the unique features of the product, the situation and the constraints on marketers, the supply chain plays a key role in consumer choice making.

Medicines satisfy a powerful and basic need – relief from pain. As a consequence, products tend to be evaluated in terms of their strict efficacy, and the functions of branding or advertising are far less prominent than usual. This is compounded by regulations and restrictions on the advertising and retail promotion of products. These include:

(a) Strict regulation of claims and impact of advertising

(b) Non-display of items on retailers shelves

(c) Restrictions on merchandising, discounting, the use of personality endorsement, loyalty schemes, cross promotions and free trials

(d) Huge price rises when products transfer from prescription to OTC

(e) Similarity between brand names because of reference to ingredients (for instance, paracetamol based analgesics include Panadeine, Panadol, Panaleve, Panerel, Paracets, and so on)

(f) The influence of the pharmacist who can overcome or counter any promotional effect.

The role of the pharmacist is crucial, and is becoming more ambivalent, as the old semi-medical professional role is combined with one as an employee of commercial and market oriented enterprises. The increasing availability of OTC medicines previously only available on prescription only increases this power. Marketing OTC medicines directly to consumers must involve, to some extent, countering the respect and trust of consumers for pharmacists.

Yet brands can become established in spite of these problems. Nurofen, for example, an ibuprofen based analgesic, has established a powerful presence by building a brand which is distinctive by using advertising which suggests both power and empathy, and also by visualising and emphasising in an imaginative way the experience and relief of pain.

Admap

4.9 International channels

As markets open to international trade, channel decisions become more complex. A company can export using host country middlemen or domestic middlemen. These may or may not take title to the goods. Implications of channel management in the case of exporters include a loss of control over product policies like price, image, packaging and service. A producer may undertake a joint venture or licensing agreement or even manufacture abroad. All will have implications for the power structure and control over the product.

5 Marketing channels and information technology

Technology has brought new methods of displaying wares, new methods of paying for them, and for some goods, new methods of delivering them. The Internet and digital TV will become ever more important as distribution channels.

Exam tip

Relationships with other members of the marketing channel are increasingly being influenced and developed by the Internet. This formed part of the scenario question on the Pilot Paper.

In recent years new technologies have emerged that have changed, and are continuing to change, the way business is conducted. Among the most significant changes are changes relating to the following.

- Mobile communications
- Electronic communications and commerce (eg Electronic Data Interchange (EDI))
- Satellite and cable digital television
- The Internet

The full impact of new technology has only just begun, but already significant changes have occurred in some organisations distribution channels.

Marketing at Work

'BSkyB is to launch a retail marketing channel called 'TV High Street' that will provide companies with half-hour direct-response infomercials to promote their products.

'The channel will broadcast from September 2, offering a 'walled garden' of 12 companies including Argos and Kays, the UK's largest mail-order company.

'Consumers will be able to choose which infomercials to view. As well as encouraging people to go out and shop, mail-order firms can publicise phone order numbers and websites. It is thought retailers will devise exclusive offers for TV High Street.

'As well as appearing on the BSkyB channel, Argos will broadcast its output in-store at its bigger branches.

'Unlike BSkyB's interactive TV service, Sky Active, the channel will not offer e-commerce, but will act purely as a product and brand marketing vehicle. It will reach the **5.7** million UK households that subscribe to BSkyB. Further retailers will be invited to join, although it is understood BSkyB is keen to limit partners to around 20.'

Marketing, 11 July 2002

5.1 Internet distribution

The Internet has **strategic** and **operational** implications, and has contributed towards **disintermediation** in some markets.

5.1.1 Display

Information gathering is still the most common Internet activity, whether it be information about a historical fact, a medical problem or, hopefully, **about your product**. At present the five most common online **purchase** categories are books, CDs, clothing, toys and games, and computer software, but many buyers for other types of product do their initial **'window shopping'** online and then go to a more conventional distribution outlet to actually make their purchase.

The Internet is perfect for the display of many types of product – anything, in fact, that customers don't need to be able handle physically, but which can be adequately shown off in words, still and moving pictures and sound.

A website offers an effortless and impersonal way for customers to find out the details of the products and services that a company provides, and **spend as long as they like** doing so: much longer than they might feel comfortable with if they had a sales person hanging over them.

For businesses the advantage is that it is much cheaper to provide the information in electronic form than it would be to employ staff to man the phones on an enquiry desk or walk the shop floor, and much more effective than sending out mailshots that people would either throw away or forget about.

Exam tip

> This is a key point to think about when reading the case study on the Pilot Paper about 'Country Style Kitchens'.

5.1.2 Transport

The Internet can be used to get certain products **directly** into people's homes. Anything that can be converted into **digital form** can simply be uploaded onto the seller's site and then downloaded onto the customer's PC. The Internet offers huge opportunities to producers of text, graphics/video, and sound-based products. Much computer software is now distributed in this way.

5.2 Disintermediation

Key concepts

> **Disintermediation**: the term referring to the process of 'removing the middleman', giving the consumer direct access to information that would otherwise require an intermediary, such as a salesperson or a retail channel.
>
> **Reintermediation** refers to the replacement of offline intermediaries with online ones.

The new technology of the **Internet** and **e-commerce** gives consumers the power to find product information directly, either removing the need for the salesperson altogether, or at least changing the relationship between buyer and seller.

 Marketing at Work

Online travel sites are a manifestation of disintermediation. Internet-based search agents can now locate flights and fares and book them online. The Internet service may even generate the tickets themselves. Many customers 'surf' these sites without actually making a booking. (Nevertheless, airlines have been moved to lower the fees that they pay to travel agencies, in part because customers can now make purchases without using local agents.) Travellers often do their price research online and then call an agent to make their purchase.

5.3 The impact of the Internet on channel decisions

5.3.1 Strategic ('board level')

- Improve corporate image
- Increase visibility in the market
- Create market growth opportunities
- Lower costs
- Appeal to customers
- Access to the full competitive arena

5.3.2 Operational ('day-to-day' on the factory floor)

Speed of transactions increased
Management of information improved

- Increased service levels
- Removal of time and distance constraints
- Complete transactions electronically
- Opportunity for new revenues
- Cost effectiveness
- Closer relationships with business partners
- Improved understanding of customer requirements

Exam tip

Some of the most important topic areas from this chapter include:

- Identification of different channels of distribution
- Logistical issues
- Exclusive, intensive and selective distribution policies
- Criteria for channel selection
- The increase in direct marketing channels and technology
- The impact of the Internet on channel relationships

Chapter Roundup

- Distribution channels provide **transport, stockholding** and **storage, local knowledge, promotion** and **display**.

- **Direct distribution** occurs when the product goes directly from producer to consumer. **Indirect distribution** happens via an intermediary.

- Ever-increasing customer demands, together with developments in technology have made **supply chain management** ever-more important. This looks at the whole picture, including the problems of ensuring smooth inflow of raw materials from suppliers so that end products can be available when customers want them.

- In marketing channels, organisations have to manage the trade-off between the desire to remain **independent and autonomous**, and the need to be **interdependent and co-operative**.

- **Stakeholders** are groups or individuals having a legitimate interest in the activities of an organisation, generally comprising customers, employees, the community, shareholders, suppliers and lenders.

- Within the marketing channel, there are two primary stakeholder roles: **performance** and **support**.

- In setting up a channel of distribution, the supplier must consider five things.

    - Customers
    - Product characteristics
    - Distributor characteristics
    - The channel chosen by competitors

- The supplier's own characteristics

- Different types of market exposure:

    - **Intensive** – blanket coverage
    - **Exclusive** – appointed agents for exclusive areas
    - **Selective** – some but not all in each area

- Different distribution strategies may be adopted for **consumer** and **industrial markets**. Industrial channels tend to be more direct and shorter.

- **Conflicts** can arise in marketing channels, and the key to managing them is to have good communications.

- **Technology** has brought new methods of displaying wares, new methods of paying for them, and for some goods, new methods of delivering them. The Internet and digital TV will become ever more important as distribution channels.

- The Internet has **strategic** and **operational** implications, and has contributed towards **disintermediation** in some markets.

Quick Quiz

1   Business-to-business relationships include (1).......... relationships and (2).......... networks.

2   What are the two aspects of distribution?

3   An intermediary is:

   A   Someone who 'mediates' or brings about a settlement between two persons
   B   The buyer in the distribution chain
   C   The supplier in the distribution chain
   D   None of the above

4   Why is a distributor's knowledge of customers important?

5   Fill in the gaps using the words from the grid below:

   Direct distribution means the product going directly from producer to consumer without the use of a specific (1)............ Direct distribution methods generally fall into two categories: those using (2).......... such as the press, leaflets and telephones to invite (3).......... by the consumer, and those using a (4).......... to contact consumers face to face.

Sales force	Testing	Media
Interview	Intermediary	Response

6   Supply chain management is about

   A   Getting the goods to the customer in the shortest possible time
   B   Each channel member operating in isolation, so maintaining a greater degree of control
   C   Each channel member affecting the performance of others in the channel
   D   Optimising the activities of companies working together to produce goods and services

7   What are the two primary stakeholder roles in the marketing channel?

8   Why might there be conflict in the marketing channel?

9   What is 'removing the middle man' also known as?

10 A definition of 'trust' says that it is the degree to which (1).......... are confident that each will act in the (2).......... of the relationship.

Answers to Quick Quiz

1 (1) Marketing channel (2) Supply chain

2 Tangible – the physical movement and delivery of goods

Intangible – aspects of supply chain management, control and communication

3 A

4 Distributors are in the front line of contact with consumers. They are likely to have a strong sense of what will work in terms of product and promotion.

5 (1) Intermediary; (2) Media; (3) Response; (4) Sales force

6 D

7 Performance – directly involved with adding value in the marketing channel (manufacturer, wholesaler, retailer).

Support – banks, consultancies, government and so on, supporting the 'performing' members.

8 Failure to do the job as understood by the rest of the channel

- Disagreement over a policy issue, such as territory or margin
- Differing perceptions on how to get the job done
- Inadequate communications

9 Disintermediation

10 (1) Partners (2) Best interests

Action Programme Review

1   Your answers might include some of the following points.

   (a)   The middleman's margin reduces the revenue available to the producer.

   (b)   The producer needs an infrastructure for looking after the retailers – keeping them informed, keeping them well stocked – which might not be necessary in, say, a mail order business.

   (c)   The producer loses some control over the marketing of the product. The power of some retailers (for example, W H Smith in the world of book publishing) is so great that they are able to dictate marketing policy to their suppliers.

2   Your own research

3   Some suggestions:

- In terms of cost
- In terms of sales levels
- According to the degree of control achieved
- By the amount of conflict that arises

4   Prices are up to 50% below conventional retail outlets and shoppers can choose from a wide range of branded goods that they otherwise might not be able to afford. They can also turn a shopping trip into a day out, as factory outlet centres are designed as 'destination' shopping venues, offering facilities such as playgrounds and restaurants.

Manufacturers enjoy the ability to sell surplus stock at a profit in a controlled way that does not damage the brand image. They have also turned the shops into a powerful marketing tool for test-marketing products before their high street launch, and selling avant-garde designs that have not caught on in the main retail market.

Now try Question 9 at the end of the Study Text

10

The use of technology

Syllabus content – knowledge and skill requirements

- How Internet- and digital-based technologies can be used to enhance marketing communication and relationships within channels and between business-to-business partners (3.5)

Introduction

Exam tip

The collapse in the share prices of many 'dot-com' enterprises led some to question the expected impact of the Internet, but, in business-to-business markets especially, the Internet is radically affecting business life. According to De Pelsmacker *et al* (2001) the following communications objectives can be pursued on the Internet.

- Creating **attitudes** and building brand/product **awareness**
- Delivering detailed **information**
- Stimulation of **customer response**, from information request to final purchase
- Facilitation of **transactions**
- **Retention** of customers

The examiner will be very interested in the Internet when setting exams. Possible areas could include:

- General impact of e-commerce

- Does e-commerce turn products into mere commodities? (ie undoing all the carefully designed strategies to target, segment and position?)

- Does the Internet destroy customer loyalty?

- Comparing e-commerce opportunities across different businesses

This topic, therefore, could well arise in almost every exam.

The uses of the Internet already embrace the following.

- Dissemination of information – generally free of charge

- Product/service development – through almost instantaneous test marketing

- Transaction processing – both business-to-business and business-to-consumer

- Relationship enhancement – between various groups of stakeholders, but principally (for our purposes) between consumers and product/service suppliers

- Recruitment and job search – involving organisations worldwide

- Entertainment – including music, humour, art and games

There is agreement on at least one thing, namely, that the Internet is **the greatest force for commoditisation the world has ever seen**. This is because it enables goods (and some services) to be sourced worldwide, easily and cheaply; it also enables them to be promoted worldwide, at relatively low cost. The Internet therefore drives prices downwards, with implications for marketing, margins, infrastructure costs, and customer dynamics.

We have looked at the Internet and digital technologies in Chapters 4 and 6 in the contexts of their specific use in advertising and promoting. This chapter looks more at how the Internet is being used to **enhance communications and relationships**.

1 What is different about the Internet?

FAST FORWARD

The Internet challenges business as it **avoids intermediaries** – small companies can also benefit through 'affiliated programmes'. The Internet is widely used by children, tomorrow's consumers.

There are several features of the Internet which make it radically different from what has gone before.

(a) It **challenges traditional business models** – because, for example, it enables product/service suppliers to interact directly with their customers, instead of using intermediaries (like retail shops, travel agents, insurance brokers, and conventional banks).

(b) Although the Internet is global in its operation, its benefits are not confined to large (or global) organisations. **Small companies** can move instantly into a global marketplace.

(c) It offers a **new economics of information** – because, with the Internet, most information is free. Those with Internet access can view all the world's major newspapers and periodicals without charge.

(d) It supplies an almost incredible **level of velocity** – virtually instant access to organisations, plus the capacity (at least theoretically) to complete purchasing transactions within seconds. This is only truly impressive if it is accompanied by equal speed so far as the delivery of tangible goods is concerned.

(e) It has created **new networks of communication** – between organisations and their customers (either individually or collectively), between customers themselves (through mutual support groups), and between organisations and their suppliers.

(f) It has led to **affiliate programmes** – involving the creation of 'portals' through which small enterprises can gain access to customers on a scale which would have been viewed as impossible a few years ago.

(g) It **promotes transparent pricing** – because potential customers can readily compare prices not only from suppliers within any given country, but also from suppliers across the world.

Marketing at Work

Honing Web 2.0 tools

'Many companies are still grappling with the vast potential offered by Web 2.0 applications and services, keen to figure out just how they can put them to work inside their organisations.

Some of the ways in which Australian companies are already using these tools include:

- **Corporate wikis**. The traditional model of designing and setting up an intranet to capture and present in-house knowledge is fading. Instead companies are establishing wikis into which staff are encouraged to pool their knowledge and ideas. The result is a more dynamic and powerful tool for the entire company.

- **Virtual collaborations**. Staff located in different locations can meet and converse inside a range of games and online worlds. They can discuss projects or problems while sitting in a virtual café or jointly hunting monsters inside a multi-player game. Don't laugh – it's happening.

- **Facebook directories**. Rather than trying to keep contact databases up to date, some companies are building web-based systems using tools such as the popular Facebook service. Members can update their own details and all users can readily search and find the people and information they need.

- **YouTube training**. Instead of distributing training materials on hard media, posting them to sites such as YouTube allows employees to access them when and where they prefer.

- **Hosted applications**. Growing numbers of corporate applications, from email to customer relationship management, are available as hosted services. Lower costs and better flexibility make them attractive.'

Ian Grayson, *The Australian*, July 17, 2007

(h) It facilitates opportunities for very **high levels of (apparent) customer intimacy** between service suppliers and their clients because each client can believe that he or she is receiving personalised attention – even if such attention is actually administered through impersonal yet highly sophisticated IT systems and customer database manipulation.

(i) With **e-commerce**, customer intimacy can be secured without significant cost penalties.

(j) It makes possible **sophisticated market segmentation opportunities**. Visualising and approaching such segments may be one of the few ways in which e-commerce entrepreneurs can truly create competitive advantage.

(k) The web can either be a **separate** or a **complementary** channel. Although much prominence is being given to web-only businesses, in many cases organisations can use the web merely as an additional channel.

(l) A new phenomenon is emerging in the form of **dynamic pricing**, whereby companies can rapidly change their prices to reflect the current state of demand and supply.

FAST FORWARD

Customer service on the web includes website responsiveness, case of navigation, website effectiveness, fulfilment, trust, service level transparency, configuration and customisation, proactive service, and value added service.

 ## Marketing at Work

If you need a bullet-point summary of the differences that the Internet and e-commerce bring to the world of business (and let's not forget, the public sector as well), then it would be useful to memorise the following.

1   **Customers**

- Can buy from any company, anywhere
- Can find best prices and act accordingly
- Can shop when they want

2   **Companies**

- Can compete globally
- Can procure globally
- Can enter new co-operative alliances
- Can achieve immediate access to revenue from sales

3   **Challenges**

- Doubts over the future for retailing
- The achievement of reputations for reliability
- Creation of confidence about security among consumers
- Development of appropriate, cost-effective infrastructures
- Problems with fulfilment (delivery)

1.1 Growth of the Internet

This will be fuelled by the following:

(a) Many households have **multiple Internet access points,** through both parents and children.

(b) Changes in the **telecoms market** are likely to mean that Internet connection time will become much cheaper, if not free.

(c) **Digital TV** will permit the Internet to be accessed without the necessity for purchase of a personal computer. This in turn will widen the market place for the Internet to encompass those in the lower socio-economic categories who are more likely to subscribe to cable or satellite TV companies.

(d) **Web-enabled mobile phones** are already on the market. The emergence of **WAP** (Wireless Application Protocol) is allowing the use of mobile phones for a wide range of interactions with the web.

(e) For many, the preferred Internet interface is not the PC but the **PDA** (Personal Digital Assistant). In the USA and more recently in the UK, there are already several wireless-based PDAs being used to link investors to stock market information.

A critical factor in the long-run expansion of the Internet is its **use today by children**, the adult consumers of tomorrow.

As access to the Internet accelerates, so does the **provision of websites**. Websites are not commercial, have no transaction facilities, and are not truly significant from any marketing viewpoint, yet nonetheless the scale of Internet activity continues to grow at a rate that most observers describe as impressive.

At the same time, the Internet is not expanding at the same rate in every area of business. In reality its growth is very context-dependent, with the significant influencing factors being as follows.

(a) **The degree to which the customer can be persuaded to believe that using the Internet will deliver some added value** – in terms of quickness, simplicity, price, and so forth.

(b) **Whether there are 'costs' that the customer has to bear** – not exclusively 'costs' in the financial sense, but also such psychological 'costs' as the loneliness of single-person shopping.

(c) **The market segment to which the individual belongs** – since the Internet is largely the preserve of younger, more affluent, more technologically competent individuals with above-average amounts of disposable income.

(d) **The frequency of supplier/customer contact required**.

(e) **The availability of incentives which might stimulate Internet acceptance** – for example, interest rates on bank accounts which are higher than those available through conventional banks (Egg), the absence of any charges (Freeserve), the creation of penalties for over-the-counter transactions (Abbey National), and the expectations of important customers (IBM's relationships with its suppliers).

1.2 The B2B e-commerce sector

The major growth so far in the field of e-commerce has concentrated on the **business-to-business (B2B) sector**. Intel claims to be doing more than $1 billion of e-commerce per month. Here are some examples to show the growing significance of the Internet in many business-to-business sectors.

(a) **Major companies** are setting themselves up as e-businesses.

(b) IBM now requires all its suppliers to **quote and invoice electronically** – no paper documentation is permitted.

(c)   Many firms are using the Internet to **exploit the transparency of supplier prices**, and to maximise their purchasing benefits from the availability of world-wide sourcing. Robert Bosch, the German kitchen appliance manufacturer, requires all its suppliers to have web-based catalogues and prices.

(d)   Companies are also **increasing their customer service** through the web. Dell, the computer company, has created extranets for its major business customers, enabling them to receive personalised customer support, their own price lists, and some free value-added services.

1.3 On-line customer service

What constitutes effective and efficient **customer service on the web**? To answer this question we must first disentangle and deconstruct the various elements of customer service from the customer's standpoint. Effective customer service (in any arena of activity, whether Internet-based or not) comprises three levels of perception.

(a)   **The foundation of service: what the customer expects**. Customers now expect that at least minimal levels of functionality will be met by any product or service they purchase; they expect that goods ordered will be delivered within an acceptable time-frame; they expect opportunities for redress if post-purchase problems are experienced. Merely to remain in business, companies must meet these basic customer requirements.

(b)   **Customer-centred service: what differentiates one organisation from another**. This is the point at which customers begin consciously to choose one product/service supplier rather than another, because of perceptions about trust, value and customer focus.

(c)   **Value-added service: what excites the customer**. What Tom Peters calls the "Wow!" sensation happens when the customer receives a level of service which is well beyond the conventional: when response times are almost immediate, when the degree of personal attention if exceptional, when service is proactively connected to customer needs.

Action Programme 1

Select a sample of five websites of customer service organisations and grade them according to how you feel they satisfy these criteria.

1.4 M-commerce

Integration of digital **mobile phone networks** with the Internet has facilitated a range of **m-commerce** (mobile commerce) applications.

(a)   The ability to download data from the Internet. As well as general browsing, this can be used to facilitate conventional commerce: for example, locating stockists of desired products near the current location of the user; accessing maps and directions to meeting venues; accessing stock, product or customer databases for information relevant to meetings and sales visits and so on.

(b)   The ability to order goods and access services directly. As an example, recent trials have enabled mobile phone users to buy soft drinks from vending machines in a cashless transaction: all order and payment details are punched into the phone (not the machine) — but the machine delivers the ordered beverage at the user's location. Interactive SMS text messaging also allows users to respond to offers: for example, by booking event/entertainment tickets.

SMS (Short Message Service) allows 160-character messages, logos and ring-tones to be sent across the mobile telecom networks. It is low-cost, easy-to-use and highly personal and compelling (especially in the youth market). In the UK, SMS has exploded as an advertising medium, with brands including Cadbury, Smirnoff, Avon, BA, Nestlé, Pepsi, Haagen-Dazs and even Liverpool FC using it to offer promotions and motivate responses. SMS is a key interaction tool eg for eliciting entry to competitions, voting in TV game shows, customer feedback and so on.

 Marketing at Work

Mobile phone text messaging (txt or SMS) is a high-growth feature of the marketing communications mix.

One new development was reported in *Ad News* in Australia (June 2007).

Xip Media, a division of Bill Express, has entered into a joint venture with Singapore mobile marketing company BeepCast, to establish Xip Mobile – an SMS information request service that integrates outdoor advertising with one-on-one mobile marketing. (A similar service was trialed in the UK by Txt4).

Xip Mobile's product, Xip Code, allows consumers to request information on an advertiser's product by texting the Xip Code to 19 XIP XIP. Information can be received in the form of a simple text message, email or voice call.

Xip Codes can be included on anything from real estate posters, billboards, trucks and business signage, to newspaper, TV and radio ads.

1.5 The ICT marketing mix

Peppers and Rogers (1997) argue that the traditional 4Ps marketing mix (product, place, price, promotion) is inadequate in the Internet age, and suggest a replacement approach to maximise the potential of ICT: the 5Is.

- **Identification**: learn about the specific preferences of specific customers

- **Individualisation**: tailor products, services and message to develop relationships for lifetime value

- **Interaction**: engage in two-way dialogue to learn about customers' needs

- **Integration**: share knowledge about customers throughout the organisation (internal marketing)

- **Integrity**: develop trust, through non-intrusive use of communication tools (eg persuasive marketing).

As we will see in Chapter 11, these concepts are also high supportive of **relationship marketing**.

2 Creating a strategy for e-commerce

What follows is a set of **guidelines** for organisations which are considering **the addition of an Internet capability** to their sales/marketing repertoire. At the outset, this capability may solely dispense information (operating like a product catalogue), but it may eventually become transactional (so that individuals can place orders) and/or interactive (dealing with queries, complaints and other kinds of customer communications).

The typical questions which have to be asked by entrepreneurs, executives and managers responsible for existing organisations are these:

(a) **How will the Internet impact my industry?** Will it operate only at the periphery, perhaps opening up new market opportunities (for ourselves and our competitors), but no more, or will it fundamentally change our activities?

(b) **Will the Internet imply significant changes to our current business model?** If at present we communicate to our customers through conventional retail outlets, will we be able to approach them directly via a transactional website, thus cutting our costs but imperilling the future for our retailing 'partners'?

(c) **Will the Internet create new channels of distribution, customer contact, supplier relationships, and customer feedback?** If this happens, will these new channels eventually replace the existing ones, or will they remain purely supplementary?

(d) **What new roles will develop?** Will we ourselves become more dependent on IT and our software suppliers?

(e) **What about pricing transparency and the open access to information by customers?** The availability of pricing information, in detail, will undoubtedly facilitate product/service price comparisons – is that a problem for us? How will we (or can we) manage the opportunity created to our customers to contact us 24 hours a day, seven days a week?

(f) **What new markets and customer segment opportunities are now presented to us?** If, at least in theory, we can now gain access to worldwide purchasers, does that make it worthwhile to generate further product/service variations to cater for segments that were hitherto too small to be worthwhile?

(g) **Who will (or could) attack us?** Looking at the situation in other sectors like financial services, competitors can emerge from anywhere: if they did, where would they come from and (more importantly) what might they do in order to take away our customers? How can we pre-empt their activities?

Most observers and experts agree that a successful strategy for e-commerce cannot simply be bolted on to existing processes, systems, delivery routes and business models. Instead, management groups have, in effect, to start again, by asking themselves such **fundamental questions** as:

- What do customers want to buy from us?
- What business should we be in?
- What kind of partners might we need?
- What categories of customer do we want to attract and retain?

FAST FORWARD ▶ Creating a strategy for e-commerce may handily be summarised into ten steps.

2.1 Ten key steps to construct an effective strategy for e-commerce

2.1.1 Step 1: Upgrade customer interaction

The first thing for the organisation to do is to **upgrade the interaction with its existing customers**.

(a) Create **automated responses** for the FAQs (Frequently Asked Questions) posed by customers, so that customers become conditioned to electronic communication. Automated responses, perhaps surprisingly in view of their impersonal nature, can help to improve customer confidence and trust.

(b) Set **fast response standards**, at least to match anything offered by the competition.

(c) Use **email** in order to confirm actions, check understanding, and reassure the customer that their business is being taken forward.

(d)   Establish **ease of navigation** around your website and enhance the site's 'stickiness' so that there is a measurably reduced likelihood that actual or potential customers will migrate elsewhere.

 Marketing at Work

Blackstar, a Belfast-based retailer, specialises in pre-recorded videos and DVDs (**www.blackstar.co.uk**). When sent an email enquiring about product availability, prices and so forth, they normally respond within five minutes with an email along the following lines.

Thanks for emailing blackstar.co.uk.

There are currently 181 e-mails in the queue in front of yours, and our average response time at the minute is 13.2 hours, so hopefully we'll get back to you within that time (if not faster!).

If your request is particularly urgent you can always ring us free on 0800 052 9050 (outside the UK you'll need to ring +44 1232 225 555, but we're afraid you'll have to pay for that call yourself!) between 8am and 8pm weekdays (10am – 4pm weekends).

Don't forget that you can track your order status online at:

http://www.blackstar.co.uk/circle/order_status

Many other common questions are also answered in our help section – click on the big question mark in the header bar or go direct to http://blackstar.co.uk/help/

This shows many elements of very good customer service:

- Fast response
- Automatic response
- Customer communication – length of queue, time to wait before a response
- Choice of phone follow up
- Ability to check status
- Links to Frequently Asked Questions (FAQs)

2.1.2 Step 2: Understand customer segments

Secondly, the organisation preparing its e-commerce strategy should **understand its customer segments** and classify each segment against the likelihood that it will be receptive to an Internet business route.

(a)   Some will be eager to transfer to the new technology, others will do so if persuaded (or incentivised), and residual groups will prefer to remain as they are.

(b)   Once the degree of profitability-per-customer has been established, efforts should be made to **automate the provision of customer service** and **transaction capability** so far as low-value customers are concerned.

(c)   By contrast, the organisation may establish **personalised service relationships** with key (ie high profit-generating) customers, with privileged access to named personnel.

2.1.3 Step 3: Understand service processes

Thirdly, the organisation must **understand its customer service processes** in order to disentangle those processes which can safely be put on to the web and those which have to be delivered in other ways.

(a)   Typically, organisations serving customers may find that there are between five and ten **generic transaction types** which describe their relationships with these customers (eg information query, complaint, and so forth).

(b)   This analysis is essential for addressing such questions as: Which of these processes is appropriate for low-touch automation? Which of these processes will work better, from the customer's standpoint, if put on the web?

(c)   **Transaction costs** also need to be investigated, again from the perspective of the organisation and its overheads, and also taking into account the transaction costs incurred by the customer. These may involve money, but customers are often more conscious about time and timeliness.

(d)   A **short simple transaction** is often better conducted over the telephone.

2.1.4 Step 4: Define the role

Fourth, the organisation needs to **define the role for live interaction with its customers**.

(a)   Live interaction may be very useful if there is scope for cross-selling and the conversion of enquiries into sales.

(b)   The availability of service supplied by **human intervention** can also be appropriate if the organisation needs to build trust (eg it is a new brand which must work hard to establish confidence) and secure diagnostic information from the customer before any product or service can be delivered.

(c)   Email may not be sufficient as a communications route, especially if it involves a delay before replies or acknowledgements are forthcoming.

(d)   Live interaction can be essential for customers who have a strong preference for human contact.

2.1.5 Step 5: Decide technology

Making the key technology decisions, the fifth step, involves some tough choices. Given the pace of change and innovation in this arena, it is difficult to know whether to initiate a pilot programme immediately, with the full IT and people investment scheduled for later, or whether to go for full integration at once. The risk with a pilot programme is that the organisation can be overtaken by pioneering competitors; the risk with full integration is that new systems can be inadequate or may even collapse completely, causing irretrievable havoc with customers.

Marketing at Work

Mobile Internet takes off

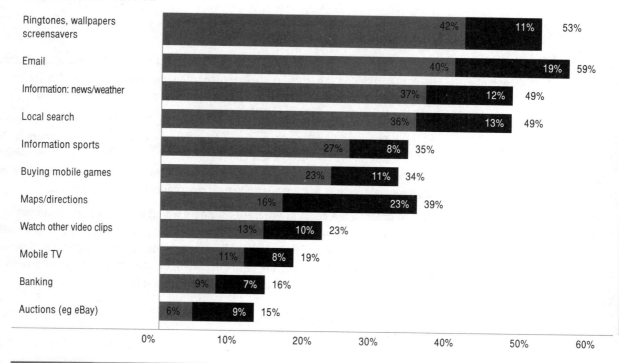

	Current usage
	Use in next 12 months

Source: *Nielsen Online's Australian Internet & Technology report*, February 2008

2.1.6 Step 6: Deal with the tidal wave

There is much evidence that offering an Internet-based service can lead to a major **increase in customer interaction**. This might involve:

- Ensuring **sufficient capacity** is available for worst-case scenarios.
- Using **low-touch technologies** and system design.
- Setting targets for **low-touch interaction**.
- Ensuring facilities are **scaleable** if demand rapidly outstrips supply.

2.1.7 Step 7: Create incentives

Seventh, especially if confronted by customer resistance, the organisation may have to **create incentives for use of the lowest-cost channels**, with savings passed on the customer through discounts, higher interest rates (in the case of bank accounts) or lower interest rates (in the case of credit cards). In the UK, banks have faced this by getting people to use automatic teller machines, and utilities have encouraged customers to use direct debits. In essence, the alternatives are:

(a)   To **create incentives to switch** to the lowest-cost channels, through financial inducements, training, additional benefits, and so forth.

(b)   To **introduce disincentives for continuing to use existing channels**. Thus Abbey has implemented a £5 charge for customers who pursue over-the-counter cash transactions its branches. Such tactics almost invariably generate very hostile reactions from customers themselves and from consumer groups.

2.1.8 Step 8: Decide on channel choices

The eighth consideration involves the decision about **which channel choices to offer**, and whether, for instance, to confine operations to the 'click' route or whether to simultaneously maintain the 'brick' presence through a branch network. There are two crucial questions:

(a)   **Whether to offer the customer a choice of channels**, eg face-to-face, post, phone and Internet. Many banks offer all four; some have single-channel accounts (phone or Internet only), whilst others (like egg) allow constrained choice: egg (the Internet and telephone banking arm of the Prudential Assurance Company) will allow telephone and Internet customer interaction, but only permits new customers to enrol via the web.

(b)   **How to balance the costs of different channels whilst managing the Customer Relationship Management (CRM) database**. In most customer service environments, the quality and scope of the CRM database is central to the successful delivery of service, so it becomes desirable not to operate each customer/communication channel separately, but to integrate existing channels around a single CRM database.

2.1.9 Step 9: Exploit the Internet

The organisation should exploit the Internet in order to **create new relationships** and an experience.

(a)   It is desirable to create **tailor-made service sites** for significant customers.

(b)   **Proactive** product/service offerings should be regularly incorporated into the website architecture.

(c)   **Communities** of users and/or customers (depending on whichever is appropriate) should be facilitated, since these generate additional business through referral and may well undertake a large proportion of the customer-service activity among themselves. Such communities may also stimulate product/service innovation, new uses for existing products and services, and product/service extensions.

(d)   Deliberate mechanisms need to be developed in order **to turn browsers into buyers**, and transform one-off customers into repeat purchasers.

(e)   Any successful e-commerce strategy presupposes the likelihood that the product/service supplier can engage the potential customer **emotionally** despite the technology which surrounds Internet availability.

2.1.10 Step 10: Implement

The concluding and tenth issue concerns the need to **implement the strategy**. No strategy is worth the paper is written on if it simply remains a document, gathering dust: as Peter Drucker once pointed out, 'Strategy is nothing until it degenerates into work.'

Action Programme 2

Does your employer have a strategy for e-commerce? If so, how do you rate it?

3 Customer dynamics and the Internet

> Effective, competent and acceptable customer service through the Internet is a combination of several factors, but it boils down to having a **quick response** to all requests/orders, and **quality delivery**.

It was once believed that potential customers for Internet businesses were relatively relaxed in their expectations about service, but even if this were the case in the first few years of Internet action, it is far from being the reality today. Internet customers are **just as demanding as customers everywhere**.

Effective, competent and acceptable customer service through the Internet is a combination of the following factors.

Factor	Comment
Rapid response time	If the website is not fast, the transient potential shopper will simply click on to another. These 'fickle' visitors to a website will only allow around five to eight seconds: if the site has not captured their attention in that time-frame, they will move elsewhere.
Response quality	The website must be legible, with appropriate graphics and meaningful, relevant information supplied. Generally speaking, website visitors are not interested in the company's history and size: they are much more concerned about what the company can offer them.
Navigability	It is important to create a website that caters for every conceivable customer interest and question. Headings and category-titles should be straightforward and meaningful, not obscure and ambiguous.
Download times	Again, these need to be rapid, given that many Internet shoppers regard themselves (rightly or otherwise) as cash-rich and time-poor.
Security/Trust	One of the biggest barriers to the willingness of potential Internet customers actually to finalise a transaction is their fear that information they provide about themselves (such as credit card details) can be 'stolen' or used as the basis for fraud.
Fulfilment	Customers must believe that if they order goods and services, the items in question will arrive, and will do so within acceptable time limits (which will generally be much faster than the time limits normally associated with conventional mail order). Equally, customers need to be convinced that if there is a subsequent need for service recovery, then speedy and efficient responses can be secured either to rectify the matter or to enable unsatisfactory goods to be returned without penalty.
Up-to-date	Just as window displays need to be constantly refreshed, so do websites require frequent repackaging and redesign.
Availability	Can the user reach the site 24 hours a day, seven days a week? Is the down-time minimal? Can the site always be accessed?
Site effectiveness and functionality	Is the website intuitive and easy to use? Is the content written in a language that will be meaningful even to the first-time browser (ie the potential customer)?

Marketing at Work

When asked, 'What is the core competency for Dell Computers?', Michael Dell replied with a single word: **Relationships**.

We have already seen that Internet customers display little loyalty. Many organisations are busily engaged in mechanisms which will promote **emotional connectivity** (and thus, it is believed, customer retention for reasons which go beyond the purely mechanistic and instrumental arguments of price). Some of these mechanisms involve 'real' people, whilst others call for simulations and 'virtual' people.

4 Digital TV

FAST FORWARD

Digital broadcasting allows viewers greater choice over how and when they watch, eventually allowing them to interact with programmes and select their own programme content.

In the past, television was 'analogue'. The development of digital technologies can be applied to television. Digital TV takes a number of forms.

- Digital terrestrial television delivered via the old 'analogue' aerial
- Digital satellite televisions, in which digital signals are sent via an existing satellite dish (eg Sky digital)
- Digital cable television, in which digital TV is delivered via the cable network.

In outline, transmitting programmes by digital signal rather than by conventional means **dramatically increases the number of services that can be delivered to audiences**: as many as ten digital services will be able to occupy the frequency previously occupied by one conventional 'analogue' service. In addition, digital broadcasting allows viewers greater choice over how and when they watch, eventually allowing them to interact with programmes and select their own programme content. More immediately, the new technology offers many viewers the prospect of improved reception.

The impact was described in depth in a BBC document, *Extending Choice in the Digital Age*, from which much of the following is derived.

Digital technology removes the constraints imposed by conflicting demands within the confines of a few television and radio networks. Viewers and listeners often miss programmes, and it is hard to schedule a range of programmes that suit everyone all the time. At present, programmes can only be scheduled in sequence, with the viewer having to make an appointment with the television to watch a specific programme at a set time. In the digital world, a spectrum can be used to allow networks to have many layers and branches: there is much more flexibility to match services to the viewer's personal timetable.

Using digital flexibility and extra capacity, broadcasters are able to offer additional programmes, information, sound and graphics, to complement what is being shown on the main channel, and to allow viewers to catch up on programmes they have missed. These extra services can be offered alongside (and do not interrupt) the continuing programme schedule. They are there for viewers to activate and explore as they choose.

At the touch of a button, viewers are able to get **supplementary information** on the programmes they are watching. The BBC, for instance, envisaged that viewers could have instant access to the following.

- The musical scores for Young Musician of the Year
- A 'guess the value' game to accompany The Antiques Roadshow
- A summary of the story so far for viewers late to join a film or play

Broadcasters are also able to make use of the improved sound quality available on digital television to offer alternative soundtracks, for example the original language version of foreign films.

A key feature of the technology is the way it allows users to respond to, or interact with, the material they are receiving. Interactive programmes that can be used on computers, or eventually on-demand from the television, will transform on-screen education.

Action Programme 3

If programmers can do this, then so too, of course can advertisers.

See how may applications you can think of for extra information at the touch of a button, alternative soundtracks and matter you can respond to if the viewer is watching advertisements.

5 Impact of interactive systems

FAST FORWARD

The ability to shop and perform other tasks (such as banking) from home and choose items directly with the use of scanners, can be co-ordinated with direct advertising in **interactive systems**.

The **ability to shop from home** and choose items directly with the use of scanners can be co-ordinated with direct advertising. **Infomercials** (which combine information with a commercial) that the consumer has chosen from a databank will be relayed directly to the home down cable links. These may take the form of recipes, DIY hints, car repairs and so on. Consumers will also be able to purchase the necessary ingredients or parts simultaneously, simply by pointing a mouse on a computer screen at the desired goods and clicking its buttons.

It is, however, difficult to predict how successful and how big the market for home shopping will become in the UK.

(a) **Geography**. In the UK and other European countries, distances to retail shopping centres are small. (On the other hand, traffic congestion continues to be an issue.)

(b) However, people are often '**time poor**' and Internet shopping with convenient delivery times is becoming popular for some consumers, for example books, CDs and groceries.

(c) Success depends on consumers' **acceptance** of technology and the reliability of that technology. Technology that is hard to use or unreliable will discourage sales.

5.1 Advantages of interactive systems

- Saving time spent in shopping visits
- Saving use of cars and car parking
- Reduction in congestion and pollution
- Greater variety of products to choose from
- Ability to watch demonstrations from the comfort of one's home
- Ability to browse
- Ability to interrogate, get technical advice
- Getting bank balances immediately
- Transferring funds between accounts
- Paying bankers' orders
- Access to directories of suppliers
- It may be possible to closely segment markets
- The specific needs of individual customers could be met
- The costs of stockholding could be reduced

Australian Airline **Jetstar** will introduce *interactive Internet check-in and airport kiosks* from next month, while looking at ways to automate luggage drop-off.

The airline has signed a $3 million agreement with IBM to introduce check-in kiosks at Melbourne, Sydney, Brisbane and Avalon airports and says it could extend the system to other airports.

Kiosks at the other three airports are expected to be operating before the end of the year.

While the airline says the roll-out will not mean the loss of existing jobs, it will allow it to cope with the big increases in passenger load, while keeping costs low by significantly reducing the number of additional people it needs to hire.

"Overseas, web check-in at low-cost airlines is between 40 per cent and 70 per cent (of all check-ins). Australians are very tech-savvy and the vast majority have access to high-speed Internet either at work or at home. We think it will be a very appealing product."

The airline is also looking at other ways it can use technology to streamline the check-in process, including simplifying the process of dropping off luggage.

Steve Creedy, *The Australian*, 2 October 2007 p23

Home shopping in America is a £1 billion business and is growing at the rate of 20% per annum. These shopping channels are increasingly being used by professionals without time to wander around department stores. The amount of broad band multimedia will accelerate the process, firstly, by increasing the number of channels available, and secondly, by increasing the interactivity. Instead of having to ring up to order, viewers will be able to punch in a code on their handset and pay by swiping their credit card through a slot in the set top box.

What might be some of the limitations of interactive systems? Why do you think such limitations exist?

5.2 Interactive catalogues and newsletters

Product information can be conveyed with added interactivity by various means.

- **Interactive catalogues** can be downloaded or viewed online, with web-based links to more information on specific products; links to 'shopping trolley' and 'checkout' pages for placing orders and so on.

- Print-based catalogues sent to customer's homes can be combined with other **interactive technologies**, such as voice-response computers: the client's queries about price, availability and delivery can be communicated and answered by telephone. Postma notes that 'the strong points of each medium are tapped to full potential, while the weaker points of one (minimal interactivity; minimal stimulation of the senses) are offset by the other.'

- **Interactive newsletters** can similarly be e-mailed, downloaded or viewed online, to convey information to customers on topics of interest (new products, industry developments, exhibitions, sales promotions and so on), with web-based links to related pages if customers want to follow up on particular items.

These approaches allow complex data to be made available to customers, with the element of choice reinforcing their interest and motivation at the follow-up stage. Instant gratification of curiosity/desire to act can be offered through interactivity. Meanwhile, the 'mechanics' of enquiry/ordering can be separated from the sensory stimulation and relationship marketing aspects of product pictures, news/information and so on, so that they retain their full impact.

Interactive kiosks are a relatively new development, currently under trial by some banks and travel marketers to provide information about financial services, potential holiday destinations and so on. In bank kiosks, access can be controlled by customer recognition using retinal image ('eye print'), avoiding the need for cards which can be lost or stolen. These kiosks will 'speak' to the customer and understand spoken commands, making a wider range of services available without human intervention.

Interactive information displays are increasingly being used in museums and art galleries, to allow visitors to explore artefacts and related databases.

There are limitations to such interactive systems, which may be related to the state of the technology or to ingrained social and cultural habits.

- There are inevitably high set up costs.
- There is a lack of knowledge of the system.
- Some people suffer from technophobia.
- There is a lack of personal contact.
- Expectations of quality may not be realised.
- It is necessary to touch, feel, smell or taste some products.
- Shopping for some people has social benefits.
- Existing shopping centres may be destabilised.

Exam tip

This may seem like a rther 'minority-interest' syllabus topic, but the December 2007 exam made 10 marks available for discussing how interactive media could be used by a railway operator, as part of its campaign to encourage car drivers to commute by rail. (Think of interactive journey planners, timetables, alerts about schedule delays, and so on.)

6 Measuring the effectiveness of online marketing

FAST FORWARD

Key **measures of online advertising success** can be grouped under the following headings:

- Channel satisfaction
- Channel buyer behaviour
- Channel promotion
- Channel outcomes
- Channel profitability

We first looked at this briefly in Chapter 6. Many e-commerce enterprises are equipped with little more than guesswork when designing their initiatives and assessing their commercial value. As the e-commerce environment matures, so the necessity for objective and dispassionate measurement of performance accelerates. Here are some of the key issues.

First, the success of a commercial website has to be evaluated against the overall product/service offer from the company.

(a)   In the words of www.emystery.shopper.com 'An e-commerce site has to be a complete customer service fulfilment picture; it can't just be one bit working online that is not supported offline'.

(b)   Thus website usability + email + telephone contact + product fulfilment + customer interaction = the customer experience; it is not website usability on its own.

Channel satisfaction is typically scored through online focus groups or online questionnaires, or both.

(a)   Online focus groups are cheap but hard to moderate dispassionately.

(b)   Online questionnaires are also cheap, but present problems with sample bias, since those most likely to respond are either committed advocates or deeply-hostile aliens (ie customers and ex-customers who are too alienated to be objective or constructive).

(c)   For samples of online questionnaires, see www.epson.lco.uk.

Channel buyer behaviour is measured by the extent to which the customer interacts with on-site marketing communications. Website registration usually provides information about the prospective purchaser's lifestyle and can therefore contribute to segmented behaviour profiles. Techniques for quantifying customer reactions include log file analysis (see www.webtrends.com) and key ratios (eg page impressions per website visit).

Channel promotion. Significant criteria in this arena include volume (number of 'hits' or views of the website's home page) and quality (the degree to which visitors are appropriate to the target market and whether they have a propensity to purchase the products or services being offered). Log files can produce basic data about 'hits' but no more, so there are important data gaps here.

Channel outcomes. The traditional marketing objectives apply: sales, leads, conversion rates, repeat purchases, and so forth. Problems can occur (so far as website effectiveness is concerned) if customers obtain product information from the Internet, and then make their purchases through conventional retailing outlets.

 Marketing at Work

As an example of an attempt at least partially to overcome this, Dell records on-site sales plus telephone orders received after web visits (the website supplies a special telephone number not accessible elsewhere, thus enabling close correlations to be established).

Channel profitability. The key index here is achievement of a targeted proportion of sales via the Internet channel. In 1998, EasyJet (the low-cost airline based in the UK) set out to achieve a contribution target of 30% of ticket sales via the Internet by the year 2000 – and this was achieved within twelve months.

Chapter Roundup

- The Internet challenges business as it **avoids intermediaries** – small companies can also benefit through 'affiliated programmes'. The Internet is widely used by children, tomorrow's consumers.

- **Customer service** on the web includes website responsiveness, case of navigation, website effectiveness, fulfilment, trust, service level transparency, configuration and customisation, proactive service, and value added service.

- Creating a strategy for **e-commerce** can be defined in ten steps.
    - Upgrade interaction with customers
    - Understand customer segments
    - Understand service processes
    - Define the role for live interaction
    - Decide the technology
    - Deal with the 'tidal wave' of new business
    - Create incentives to use the cheapest channel
    - Decide on channel options
    - Exploit the Internet
    - Implement the strategy

- Effective, competent and acceptable customer service through the Internet is a combination of several factors, but it boils down to having a **quick response** to all requests/orders, and **quality delivery**.

- **Digital broadcasting** allows viewers greater choice over how and when they watch, eventually allowing them to interact with programmes and select their own programme content.

- The ability to shop and perform other tasks (such as banking) from home and choose items directly with the use of scanners, can be co-ordinated with direct advertising in **interactive systems**.

- Key **measures of online advertising success** can be grouped under the following headings:
    - Channel satisfaction
    - Channel buyer behaviour
    - Channel promotion
    - Channel outcomes
    - Channel profitability

Quick Quiz

1   What are the communication objectives that can be fulfilled by the Internet?

C...

R...

A...

I...

T...

2   Which is the following is true of the Internet?

A   It is currently most significant in the business-to-consumer market

B   It can enhance communications and relationships

C   For an SME with limited resources, the Internet is not appropriate

D   Enhanced customer service via the Internet is unlikely to occur

3   What is the 'tidal wave' referred to in Section 2 of this chapter?

4   Why should download times be as quick as possible?

A   All customers who use the Internet are inherently impatient

B   It saves money for the company

C   Customers in the modern age regard themselves as increasingly 'time-poor', and expect to be able to view website contents quickly

D   The quicker the download time, the clearer the pictures on the website

5   Fill in the gaps using the words in the grid below:

(1)   .... takes a number of forms.

- Digital (2).......... television delivered via the old 'analogue' aerial

- Digital (3).......... television, in which digital signals are sent via an existing (4)...........

- Digital (5)........... television, in which digital TV is delivered via the (6)...........

Cable network	Digital TV	Terrestrial
Satellite dish	Cable	Satellite

6   Digital television technology allows users to respond to, or interact with, the material they are receiving.

True   ☐

False   ☐

7   Give some advantages of interactive systems.

8   From the following grid, how can buyer behaviour on the Internet be measured?

Examining the extent to which the customer interacts with online communications	Log file analysis and key ratios (such as page impressions per website visit)
Examining conversion rates and repeat purchases	The use of online focus groups and questionnaires

Answers to Quick Quiz

1   Customer response stimulation
Retention of customers
Attitude and awareness building
Information delivery
Transactions facilitated

2   B

3   A dramatic increase in the level of customer interaction

4   C

5   (1) Digital TV; (2) Terrestrial; (3) Satellite; (4) Satellite dish; (5) Cable; (6) Cable network

6   True

7   Check your answer against the list in Paragraph 5.0.1

8   All of these could be used!

Action Programme Review

1   Do try to gain access to the Internet and complete this activity. Refer to the 'website links' section at the front of this Text if you require further ideas.

2   If your employer doesn't have a strategy for e-commerce (or at lest a website), they probably soon will have!

3   The following extract from an American article on Interactive TV (ITV) may give you some ideas.

'When it comes to peddling high-ticket items, Paula George Tompkins, CEO of The SoftAd Group, a Mill Valley (Calif.) creator of interactive marketing materials, says the most effective efforts aren't 'full-motion video and razzle-dazzle ads.' They're the information-laden programs that help buyers make complex decisions such as choosing a car or an industrial-products supplier.

Consider the flow chart for a typical car purchase: talk to friends, buy (and read) consumer reports, spend weekends checking out local dealerships and weekdays checking out other cars on the freeway, test drive a few cars, decide on a model, make arrangements with a lender, and – whew! – buy the car.

Now, eliminate a significant portion of that legwork. Using a mouse and TV screen, the consumer would be able to flip through manufacturers' catalogues – complete with backup data related to performance and pricing – 'trying on' the various models in terms of size and color. The shopper could then request a test drive via his or her TV. Later, the dealer brings a car over and, if the buyer is ready, goes online with a laptop to check inventory, leasing vs. financing options, and even fill out the paperwork. Voila!'

4   • There are high set up costs
    • There is a lack of knowledge of the system
    • Some people suffer from technophobia
    • There is a lack of personal contact
    • Expectations of quality may not be realised
    • It is necessary to touch, feel, smell or taste some products
    • Shopping for some people has social benefits

Such limitations may be related to the current state of the technology, and also to ingrained social and cultural habits.

Now try Question 10 at the end of the Study Text

Part D
Relationship management

Developing relationship marketing

11

Syllabus content – knowledge and skill requirements

- The main characteristics of key accounts and the stages and issues associated with key account management (2.10)
- How co-ordinated marketing communications can be used to develop key account relationships (2.11)
- How marketing communications can be used to launch new products, support brands, maintain market share, develop retention levels, encourage customer loyalty, and support internal marketing within the organisation (2.12)
- Comparison of the principles of transaction and relationship marketing (4.1)
- The characteristics of relationship marketing including the features, types, levels, development and implementation steps and communication issues (4.2)
- How marketing communications can be used to develop relationships with a range of stakeholders, based on an understanding of source credibility, trust and commitment (4.3)

257

Introduction

The syllabus emphasises the **wider relationships marketers must nurture** if they are to succeed. This chapter deals with the management of some of those relationships. Section 1 explores the concept of relationship marketing and how relationships with customers and other stakeholders can be exploited for competitive advantage and profitability. Section 2 deals with internal marketing, a phrase which has a range of meanings.

The remainder of the chapter is concerned with the organisation's **use of outside resources**. Section 3 illustrates the wide range available and offers some ideas on their applicability. Where external services are used, it is important that control is not abdicated; the client organisation must ensure that the contractor performs properly. Section 4 is about the management of external suppliers.

1 Relationship marketing

1.1 What is Relationship Marketing (RM)?

Key concept

Relationship marketing has been variously defined as:

- 'The process of creating, maintaining and enhancing strong, value-laden relationships with customers and other stakeholders' (*Kotler et al*, 1999, p11)

- 'Marketing based on interaction within networks of relationships' (Gummesson, 2002, p3)

- 'All marketing activities directed towards establishing, developing and maintaining successful relational exchanges' (*Morgan & Hunt*, 1994, p22)

There are different schools of thought on the exact scope and nature of relationship marketing, and the term tends to be used to express a wide range of 'relationship-type' strategies. However, it is possible to distinguish a number of distinctive features of Relationship Marketing as a broad philosophy and strategic approach.

- A shift from marketing activities which emphasise customer acquisition to those which emphasise **customer retention (in addition to acquisition)**, with an intentional balance between the two – based on the economics of customer retention (discussed further below).

- The development of **on-going (and, if possible, constantly deepening and improving) relationships**, as opposed to one-off transactions. A key principle is to extend the duration, or lifetime, of a customer's purchasing relationship with the firm, and therefore to maximise their 'lifetime value': that is, the future flow of net profit arising from the relationship.

- Recognition of the potential for customer/supplier **co-operation, collaboration or partnership**, borrowed from industrial and service marketing. Traditional marketing could be seen as adversarial, with firms battling customer bargaining power. Relationship marketing is co-operative: by working together, customer and supplier can create, share and exchange more value, to mutual benefit (*Gummesson*, 2002; *Grönroos*, 1996).

- The aim of **long-term customer profitability**, or maximum lifetime value. Not all customers are equally profitable: the firm must identify and prioritise potentially profitable customers – and avoid over-investing in unprofitable customers. Marketers may need to communicate in different ways with customers and potential customers, depending on their status and worth to the firm.

- Emphasis on providing **sustained and complex value** to the customer, over and above the short-term satisfaction of product features and quality. High levels of service quality, in particular, are required at every touch point with the customer.

- A move from functionally-based marketing to **cross-functionally-based marketing**: customer value and quality are the responsibility of all employees, not just those who work in the marketing department: internal marketing is recognised as critical in achieving external marketing success. (One co-founder of Hewlett-Packard is said to have remarked that 'marketing is too important to be left to the marketing department'!)

- The development of **supportive network relationships** with other internal and external stakeholders, rather than a focus on the customer-supplier dyad. Relationship marketing principles are extended to a range of diverse market domains, not just customer markets. We will examine this point next.

1.2 The six markets model

The six markets model offers a helpful overview of the key categories of relationships for any given firm (sometimes called the 'core' or 'focal' firm, because we are looking at relationships from its point of view). It presents six role-related market domains or 'markets', each involving relationships with a number of parties – organisations or individuals – who can potentially contribute, directly or indirectly, to an organisation's marketplace effectiveness (*Peck et al*, 1999, p 5): Figure 11.1.

Figure 11.1: The six markets model

- **Customer markets**. The concept of relationship marketing is based on the belief that firms must invest in building relationships with customers, in order to enhance profitability through customer retention and loyalty. For consumer goods or services, the customer market domain represents **end customers**, users and consumers. For business-to-business marketing, it also embraces channel **intermediaries**, including agents, retailers and distributors who are effectively 'customers' of the organisation, but operate between them and the end users.

- **Referral markets**. Referrals, recommendations and endorsements by existing customers are an important source of new business. Potential sources of referrals must be cultivated and motivated. 'Given that satisfied customers will happily endorse the products or services of the supplier if prompted, relationships with existing customers are an unrecognised or underutilised facility for many organisations' (*Peck et al, op cit*, p7).

- **Internal markets**. The internal market comprises all employees, and other functions, divisions and strategic business units (SBUs) of the firm. The concept of 'internal marketing' (discussed in Section 2), argues that employees and units throughout an organisation can contribute to the effectiveness of marketing to customers: most notably, through value-adding customer service and communications.

- **Recruitment markets**. The recruitment market comprises the **external labour pool** and **third parties**, such as colleges, universities, recruitment agencies and other employers, who can give the firm access to quality potential employees. Relationships with these markets must be cultivated in order for the firm to be able to compete with other employers to attract the best people, particularly in times, regions and disciplines in which there are acute skill shortages.

- **Influence markets**. Key influencers of consumer decisions (and organisational activity) include governments and government agencies, the press/media, investors and interest/pressure groups. Relationships with these markets can be exploited to generate positive PR (and/or minimise negative PR); influence public opinion in the organisation's favour; gain access to markets (eg through cause-related marketing); and enhance or replace other marketing activities (as in The Body Shop's exploitation of referral, media and pressure group relationships in place of advertising).

- **Supplier and alliance markets**. The **supplier market** refers to the relationships that the firm must cultivate with its supply chain or network, in order to enable reliable, flexible, value-adding, cost-effective flows of supplies into and through the firm to the end customer. The **alliance market** recognises a wide range of opportunities to add value through collaborative relationships between the core firm and other partners: in joint promotions, strategic alliances, joint ventures, knowledge-sharing networks and so on.

 Marketing at Work

Shareholder Communications: HBOS plc

With this form we are asking you to choose how you would like us to communicate with you in the future

We are committed to reducing the impact our business has on the environment. Our Climate Change Action Plan sets out clear objectives, including our commitment to reduce the amount of resources we consume.

The good news is, it's working. Our UK business has already achieved carbon neutral status. However, there's still some way to go. In 2006, for example, we used an estimated 14,950 tonnes of paper and we are aiming to reduce this.

At the AGM we will be asking shareholders to adopt New Articles of Association that enable us to communicate with you through our website – by supporting this you will help us to reduce our paper usage significantly, and lessen our impact on the environment.

Of course, this will save us money too, which is why we are donating £150,000 to the HBOS Foundation in support of the HBOS 2008 Charity of the Year – CLIC Sargent. In addition, the HBOS Foundation will match our figure, to make a total donation of £300,000 through this initiative.

HBOS Shareholder Communication, April 2008

1.3 Transaction marketing and relationship marketing

Transactions are single exchanges between an organisation and a customer: a single market exchange in the form of a purchase (goods exchanged for money), or an exchange of information or influence (such as an offer and a response).

The focus of **transactional marketing (TM)** is to look to each transaction or encounter as an opportunity to maximise short-term gains, without necessarily considering future contacts, or the effect of *this* transaction on the potential for future contacts.

The focus is therefore on **winning customers** (either creating new customers or attracting dissatisfied customers away from competitors), through techniques such as market research and targeting, customer satisfaction through product features and product quality, and the use of mass media advertising, promotion and short-term sales incentives to stimulate purchase. There is little emphasis on customer service or customer contacts, over and above what is necessary to process each transaction.

At its worst, transactional marketing can be seen as a manipulative or exploitative approach (*Egan*, 2004). More generally, it has been recognised that:

- Transaction marketing is **inadequate to cope with today's business environment**. A focus on customer acquisition works where populations and markets are growing, and competition is relatively stable – but in many markets, those conditions no longer exist. In the face of global competition and overcapacity (or market saturation), the focus has to switch:

    - From volume growth to **profit growth**, based on building and leveraging longer-lasting relationships with more profitable customers

    - From short-term customer satisfaction based on product quality (easily emulated by competitors) to **long-term customer satisfaction** through a wider and more sustained value and service proposition.

- It is more **expensive** to continually win new customers (especially if you later lose them 'out the back door') than it is to keep existing customers happy, thereby encouraging them to make repeat and extended purchases.

- A focus on single transactions fails to **leverage the potential** inherent in the customer base, and other relationships, to add value for the organisation and for the customer. For example, it fails to gather on-going customer feedback which could be used to refine marketing strategy.

These arguments, and others, have brought about 'a shift in the nature of marketplace transactions from **discrete to relational exchanges**, from exchanges between parties with no past history and no future to interactions between parties with a history and plans for future interaction' (*Weitz & Jap*, 2000, cited in *Egan*, *op cit*, p 25).

The differences between transactional marketing and relationship marketing can be directly compared as follows (*Egan*, *op cit*, p26; *Peck et al*, *op cit*, p44).

Transaction marketing	Relationship marketing
Focus on obtaining new customers: single sales and sales volume	Focus on retaining existing (profitable) customers: repeat purchases and loyalty
Short timescale	Longer-term timescale
Customer satisfaction through product features	Customer satisfaction through (sustained) value delivery
Quality as the concern of production	Quality as the concern of all staff
Primary concern with product quality	Concern with relationship quality (including supportive network relationships)
Little emphasis on customer service	High emphasis on customer service
Limited, discontinuous customer contact	High, continuous customer contact
Limited commitment to meeting customer expectations	High commitment to meeting customer expectations

Exam tip

The distinction between transactional and relationship marketing was examined in December 2003 and again in June 2007. In December 2006, you were asked to discuss how the change from transactional to relationship marketing would be reflected in the communication mix (of a ferry operator).

1.4 The relationship marketing ladder of loyalty

FAST FORWARD

The ladder of loyalty (*Kotler*, 1997; *Peck et al*, 1999) is designed to illustrate how relationship marketing seeks to increase the loyalty of customer groups: Figure 11.2.

It can be applied in many relational settings: for example, charities and pressure groups use it to gauge the loyalty of donors, volunteers and members.

Figure 11.2: Ladder of loyalty

PARTNERS	Those who have become an active part of the value-creating process, closely linked in a long-term relationship of trust and collaboration (most common in B2B buyer-supplier relationships).
ADVOCATES	Those who actively support your marketing through word-of-mouth endorsement, recommendations and referrals.
SUPPORTERS	Those who like you, but only support you passively by responding to your marketing.
CLIENTS	Those who do business with you repeatedly, but may nevertheless be neutral (or even negative) towards the organisation.
CUSTOMERS (or Purchasers)	Those who have done business with you once: a first-time or one-off purchaser of your product/service.
PROSPECTS	Potential customers: people who might be persuaded to do business with you. (Better quality if profiled, qualified, referred to you – or active enquirers.)

Finding **prospects** and converting them into **customers** (ie securing purchase) is the preoccupation of traditional or transactional marketing. Relationship marketing emphasises the conversion of new or one-off customers into repeat customers – followed by progressive conversion to each higher rung of the ladder, which represents a strengthening of the relationship over time.

Getting customers to **advocate** level is a particularly helpful source of leverage, as recommendations and referrals by existing customers are an easy and cost-effective way of both getting new prospects and converting them into customers and clients.

Few consumer relationships go beyond the advocate level to **partnership** (which is mainly a feature of B2B buyer-supplier relationships). However, some ladder models include an intermediate stage called 'membership', which implies genuine affiliation of some sort. This has long been a feature of voluntary sector relationships: membership of political parties and charities, for example, requires commitment and cost/effort, and offers corresponding opportunities for active involvement in fund-raising and policy development. In the consumer sector, some organisations have introduced tactics to create or simulate membership-type relationships.

Action Programme 1

How does your work organisation, or another organisation that you know well, go about:

- Finding prospects?
- Converting prospects to customers?
- Converting customers to clients?
- Creating advocates?

If it has a defined relationship 'scale' or 'ladder' of involvement, status or membership for its customers or members, draw this and add explanatory notes where necessary.

1.5 Customer retention and loyalty

FAST FORWARD

Relationship marketing intentionally aims to retain customers (keep them purchasing repeatedly over time) and foster customer loyalty (create a favourable attitude or bias which drives repeat purchase).

1.5.1 Why focus on customer retention?

People trade repeatedly in some goods or services over a lifetime (eg purchasing cars or banking and insurance services) – and it makes sense for the marketing organisation to secure as large a share of the value of that lifetime expenditure as possible (where this can be done profitably).

Research by Frederick Reichheld, a management consultant at Bain & Co, found a high correlation between customer retention and company profitability: retained customers are more profitable than new customers for several reasons.

- Retaining customers **costs less** than winning new ones.

- Retained customers are amenable to **cross-selling** (selling other products of the firm) and **up-selling** (selling higher-value products of the firm), so their spending increases over time.

- Retained customers **cost less to serve**, as they place frequent, consistent orders (allowing better inventory planning and capacity forecasting, say).

- Retained customers may become less sensitive to price over time, and may be willing to pay **price premiums** for products which they know and trust.

- Retained customers are a cost-effective source of word-of-mouth **referrals and recommendations** to potential new customers

Reichheld (1996, p39) argues that the profit potential of a customer relationship increases, the longer the relationship continues, because of revenue growth over time, cost savings over time, the addition of referral income and the potential for price premiums.

1.5.1.1 Strategies for customer retention

Customers give loyalty in exchange for their expectation that value will flow to them from a relationship with a supplier. Relationship marketing methods for contributing to short- and long-term customer retention include the following.

- **Service quality**: a high, consistent and competitive level of customer service is a key to customer satisfaction and loyalty – and therefore to long-term relationships of mutual advantage – in many industries. It is also one of the main ways in which an organisation can add customer value.

- **Loyalty programmes**: The purpose of loyalty programmes, for an organisation or brand, is to establish a higher level of customer retention in profitable segments, by providing increased satisfaction and value to certain customers. We discuss loyalty programmes further below.

- **Brand engagement**: In addition to forming relationships through engagement with the supplier *organisation* (through interactions, dialogue and developing contacts), marketers can attempt to foster a bias, preference or commitment towards a *brand*, by creating powerful brand symbols, characteristics and values that attract customer loyalty: the Apple i-Pod is one example.

 Marketing at Work

The Flying Dutchman' program

'Customer rewards are essential to the success of an airline and one of 2004's most innovative schemes was from the Dutch airline **KLM** which created a 'customer lifetime experience' through a **personalised customer loyalty program** that was strategically different from those being offered by its competitors...

KLM vice-president of marketing and services, Simone Wickenhagne, says good and clear **communication** of the benefits and services to the customer is essential.

A major part of KLM's strategy has been integrating the program **online as well as offline** and **improving the online proposition** to make it the more attractive service channel for customers to use. This has been done by giving a **discount** on award tickets ordered online or by giving **extra miles** when using a service online, such as Internet check-in.

'The aim is to offer certain services exclusively online, not offering these services via the offline channels any more. The goal is to make things easier and more convenient for the client and less costly for KLM.'

As a result of the scheme, benchmarking research has shown that KLM's customer loyalty program scores position KLM above its competitors for those in the scheme and online members are now responsible for approximately 40% of KLM passenger revenues.'

(*Professional Marketing*, February 2005)

Think about how KLM has used this programme to establish loyalty among its *most profitable* customers, and how it has used the most *cost-effective channels* available, and how it has therefore added value both for itself and for its customers.

1.6 Database marketing

Key concept

> **Database marketing** is an interactive approach which builds a database of all communications and interactions with customers and then uses individually addressable marketing media and channels to further contact with them (for promotional messages, help and support, and relationship-building contacts).

Database marketing techniques may be used for a range of relationship marketing projects (*Allen et al*, 2001) including:

- Identifying the most profitable customers, using RFM analysis (recency of the latest purchase, frequency of purchases and monetary value of all purchases)

- Developing new customers (eg by collecting data on prospects, leads and referrals)

- Tailoring messages and offerings, based on customers' purchase profiles. (Actual customer buying preferences and patterns are a much more reliable guide to their future behaviour than market research, which gathers their 'stated' preferences...)

- Personalising customer service, by providing service staff with relevant customer details

- Eliminating conflicting or confusing communications: presenting a coherent image over time to individual customers – however different the message to different customer groups. (For example, don't keep sending 'dear first-time customer' messages to long-standing customers!)

1.7 Customer Relationship Management (CRM)

Key concept

> **Customer Relationship Management** (CRM) is an umbrella term describing the methodologies and ICT systems that help an enterprise to manage its customer information and customer relationships in an organised and profitable way.

CRM is a more comprehensive approach to the use of database technology, designed to:

- Enable marketers to predict and manage customer behaviour, by allowing them to learn and analyse what customers value

- Segment customers based on their relative profitability or lifetime value to the organisation

- Enhance customer satisfaction and retention by facilitating seamless, coherent and consistent customer service across the full range of communication channels and multiple points of contact between the customer and the organisation.

A CRM system involves a comprehensive database that can be accessed from any of the points of contact with the customer, including website contacts, field sales teams, call centres and order processing functions. Information can be accessed and updated from any point, so that participants in customer-facing processes – sales, customer service, marketing, maintenance, accounts and so on – can co-ordinate their efforts and give consistent, coherent messages to the customer. Information can also be analysed (through a process called 'data-mining') to determine profitability, purchasing trends, web browsing patterns and so on.

Each time a customer contacts a company with an effective CRM system – whether by telephone, in a retail outlet or online – the customer should be recognised and should receive appropriate information and attention on that basis. CRM software also provides advanced personalisation and customised solutions to customer demands, giving customer care staff a range of information about each customer which can be applied to the contact or transaction.

Marketing at Work

Customer relationship management at a UK local government authority

The first challenge that **Hull Council** residents faced was finding the right phone number to call. The authority ran no less than 250 separate lines, each connected to a different department with its own team of receptionists dealing with requests in their own way. Once callers found the right number to ring, there was still, on average, only a 50:50 chance that somebody would pick up the phone.

That was how things stood until 2002, when the authority decided to run its services through a single call centre built on customer relationship management technology from the world's second-biggest software company, Oracle.

Twelve months on, [residents] suddenly found that all council services could be accessed through a single, easy-to-remember number. The effect on the housing benefit department was dramatic. The back office staff, freed from their responsibility of occasionally answering the phone, cut their time to process housing benefits queries by two thirds – from 60 days to the department's target of 20 days.

The specially-trained front office call centre staff were able to answer more than 96 per cent of the 850,000 calls Hull received every year, most of them within 15 seconds, a far cry from the bad old days of the one-in-ten answer rate.

"One of the key things we've learned is that a CRM application won't do much good if you haven't got good data behind it," says Harrison.

Hull's call centre staff are backed up by an interactive map that can help them track down the exact location of each call. They can also call on an A-Z database of council services, developed in-house and updated directly by every council department, to give the receptionists accurate procedures to cover any request.

The other key lesson was to keep council employees on side while making huge changes to established processes. "We still have a few departments reluctant to make the change," admits Harrison. "Those are the departments where people are not getting good service. If the most up-to-date service is not backed up with current information – and engaged people – it will still remain shoddy."

(Heavens, 2004)

Exam tip

A question in June 2007 exam focused on the use of CRM systems by an manufacturer of industrial oil-based products, and the communications problems it might experience in implementing CRM. These aspects are highlighted by the Marketing at Work example above. Note the interdependency of *customer* relationship marketing and management and *internal* relationship marketing and management: that is, the need for excellent internal relationships and service orientation before you can create excellent *external* relationships and service…

1.8 Key Account Management

FAST FORWARD

Customers can be analysed for their **value to the business**. **Key account management** allows the most valuable customers to be given an enhanced service.

We have already looked briefly at this topic in Chapter 5 in the context of marketing communications strategy. So far in this chapter we have considered the retention of customers as an unquestionably desirable objective. **However, for many businesses a degree of discretion will be advisable**. 'Key' does not mean large.

Action Programme 2

If not 'large', what *does* 'key' mean in this context?

Customer analysis will almost certainly conform to a Pareto distribution and show, for instance, that 80% of profit comes from 20% of the customers, while a different 20% generate most of the credit control or administrative problems. Some businesses will be very aggressive about getting rid of their problem customers, but a more positive technique would be to concentrate effort on the most desirable ones. These are the **key accounts** and the company's relationship with them can be built up by appointing **key account managers**.

Key account management is often seen as a high level selling task, but should in fact be a business-wide team effort about relationships and customer retention. It can be seen as a form of co-operation with the customer's supply chain management function.

The key account manager's role is to:

- **Integrate** the efforts of the organisation in order to deliver an enhanced service
- **Maintain communication** with the customer
- Note any **developments in his circumstances**
- Deal with any **problems** arising in the relationship
- Develop the **long-term** business relationship

(a) The key account relationship may progress through several stages, leading ultimately to **trust and commitment**.

(b) At first, there may be a typical **adversarial** sales-purchasing relationship with emphasis on price, delivery and so on. Attempts to widen contact with the customer organisation will be seen as a **threat** by its purchasing staff.

(c) Later, the sales staff may be able to foster a mutual desire to increase understanding by wider contacts. **Trust** may increase.

(d) A mature **partnership** stage may be reached in which there are contacts at all levels and information is shared. The key account manager becomes responsible for integrating the partnership business processes and contributing to the customer's supply chain management. High 'vendor ratings', stable quality, continuous improvement and fair pricing are taken for granted.

Exam tip

> Relationship marketing in the context of the relationship between advertising agency and client was examined on the Specimen Paper and again in December 2006. The tasks of key account management and its role in customer relationship management were the specific focus of questions in June 2006, June 2007 and December 2007, all in the context of B2B personal selling relationships.

1.9 Loyalty programmes

Some loyalty programmes focus on securing **multiple on-going purchases**, usually with the incentive of earning points for each purchase, which can be redeemed for rewards, discounts or Fly-Buys. Reward cards memorise the redeemable points, and generate information on the holder's purchasing behaviour for the provider. Such cards lend themselves to co-branding and other forms of alliance: consortia of retail, financial services and other providers have been formed to pool resources and share information in joint loyalty schemes (eg the Nectar Loyalty Card Scheme).

Some schemes are based on receiving **added value benefits** once you reach a higher category of status/value (eg frequent flyer clubs, or 'patrons' of arts organisations).

Others use affinity marketing, by linking purchases with donations to a charity or other cause (eg building up points towards donation of books or computers to local schools). **Affinity cards**, which link a business with a charity or cause, have become a popular way for consumers to identify with a cause and donate to charity from their spending. Such schemes have been exploited for fundraising by the RSPCA, Save the Children and some commercial football clubs.

Most loyalty programmes have some kind of 'club' aspect to them, and offer a variety of **member benefits**. The Waterstones Card, for example, offers points which build towards cash discounts on further purchases; email newsletters (with book reviews, offers and competitions); a free copy of the quarterly magazine; and invitations to exclusive shopping events.

The intention of a loyalty scheme for the organisation is that:

- A brand preference or habit will develop from repeat purchase and familiarity, which creates psychological barriers to switching

- A sense of belonging to a community or club (even if 'virtual') will reinforce the relationship

- The brand will be differentiated from similar competing brands and/or defended against the effect of competitors' loyalty programmes

- The incentives and their accessories (VIP cards and so on) add economic and social benefits, which will be valued and desired by customers – creating further barriers to switching (if similar benefits are not available elsewhere)

- Customer data gathered from the scheme (details provided by the customer or point of sale data) can be used to fine-tune the marketing mix – which in turn may create a genuine bias or commitment to the brand.

- Additional revenue can be raised through repeat purchases, cross-selling and up-selling, on the back of customer loyalty. Incentives can also be added for short-term sales promotions (eg 'double points' on selected purchases).

 Marketing at Work

American Express (Australia)

'Being quick to move with the times is essential for any good rewards scheme and **American Express** has received plenty of good press recently for its help in the tsunami relief effort.

'American Express is encouraging card holders to redeem reward points to donate cash to the tsunami appeal by matching donations dollar for dollar (in January/February 2005).'

Professional Marketing, February 2005

1.10 Relational marketing communications

Relationship marketing communications place a high emphasis on frequency, quality and personalisation of contact with customers and other stakeholders.

- **Multiple on-going customer contacts**, using multiple touch points within the marketing organisation: eg sales or direct marketing, customer research and feedback-seeking, customer service, after-sales service/maintenance, the website, loyalty programmes, newsletters, product up-dates, maintenance reminders, invitations to launches and other events, notification of special offers – and so on.

Designated account managers or customer contacts may be used to focus initial contact on an individual touch point, to create personal familiarity and add value by having a single 'gatekeeper' to direct customer queries to other parts of the organisation.

- **Two-way dialogue** with customers: not just marketing messages (business-to-customer or B2C) but **customer-to-business (C2B)** communication, through mechanisms such as feedback and suggestion seeking, the creation of customer communities, customer-generated web and advertising content, and so on.

  This may be augmented by encouraging **customer-to-customer (C2C)** communication via discussion boards, user groups, customer networking events and so on. C2C happens anyway, so it makes sense for the organisation to monitor the exchanges (to gather information on customers' perceptions and interests); create a sense of belonging or affiliation (adding a social benefit to the total product/service offering); and offer social/entertainment value which draws people repeatedly to the website and other mechanisms (where they can be targeted with promotional messages).

- **Personalised and customised contacts**: making customers feel recognised and valued, and that their individual needs are being catered for. Examples include: customer 'recognition' by customer service staff (enabled by computer-telephony integration); the use of customer data to send birthday cards or service reminders (such as you might get from a dentist or car dealership); the personalisation of mailings, e-mail and web pages; and the customisation of offers on the basis of customers' previous purchases.

 Marketing at Work

'This week **Dell** computers responded to customer complains on various blogs regarding excessive packaging for one of its products.

While, in this instance the problem was reasonably small, Dell has demonstrated it sees massive value to its business and brand by *engaging its audience on product and service improvements*.

It has been actively driving people to its site ideastorm.com where it has a section specifically encouraging ideas to improve its environmental performance.

Each idea is peer reviewed, commented on and promoted by registered site users based on its merits. Winning ideas are then put on review by Dell to be considered for implementation.

Obviously we cannot expect every last lolly manufacturer and insurance company to ask its customers to get involved in all aspects of NPD. Yet there is something very compelling about brands encouraging shared thinking to solve shared problems.

After all, the old adage that the customer is always right, has never been more true. Today, a disgruntled customer can recruit a virtual army of others to 'prove' they are right.

On the flip side, what better way for companies to build equity in their brand while getting invaluable input into tricky problems with little investment.'

Matt Perry, 'Bright Green', *Ad News* (Australia), 16 May 2008, p19

2 Internal marketing

Internal marketing has a range of meanings but the most useful relates to the promotion of a high level of customer awareness throughout the organisation using marketing communication techniques to change culture and deliver training.

Key concept

Internal marketing may be defined as a variety of approaches and techniques by which an organisation acquires, motivates, equips and retains customer-conscious employees (*Grönroos*, 1989)

Internal marketing has been well summarised by Peck *et al* (*op cit*, p 313):

'Internal marketing is concerned with creating, developing and maintaining an **internal service culture and orientation**, which in turn assists and supports the organisation in the achievement of its goals. The internal service culture has a vital impact on how service-oriented and customer-oriented employees are, and, thus, how well they perform their tasks... The development and maintenance of a customer-oriented culture is a critical determinant of long-term success in relationship marketing...

'The basic premise behind the development of internal marketing is the acknowledgement of the **impact of employee behaviour and attitudes** on the relationship between staff and external customers. This is particularly true where employees occupy boundary-spanning positions in the organisation... The skills and customer orientation of these employees are, therefore, critical to the customers' perception of the organisation and their future loyalty to the organisation.'

In other words, it is through internal marketing that all employees can develop an understanding of how their tasks, and the way they perform them, create and deliver customer value and build relationship.

The achievement of such a widespread marketing orientation may involve **major changes in working practices and organisational culture**. The successful management of organisational change depends to a great extent upon successful communication and communication is a major marketing activity. 'Internal marketing' has therefore also come to mean the communication aspect of any programme of change and, even more simply, **the presentation by management to staff of any information at all**.

2.1 Internal marketing as part of marketing management

If we concentrate on the use of the term to mean the use of marketing approaches and techniques to gain the support and co-operation of other departments and managers for the marketing plan, we will see that a number of challenges may exist. The first is that we may well be looking at a **major cultural shift**. Even in businesses that have highly skilled and motivated sales teams, **there may be areas of the organisation whose culture, aims and practices have nothing to do with customer satisfaction**.

 Marketing at Work

The old nationalised industries like British Railways and Post Office Telecommunications saw engineering effectiveness as their major goal, with customer service nowhere. A business that takes this view is unlikely to succeed, but achieving a change of orientation can be a long, difficult and painful process. It will involve a major change in culture and probably entail significant changes to the shape of the organisation, as departments that contribute little to customer service lose influence and shrink or even disappear as the cost base is cut.

2.1.1 Organisational change

(a) Measuring activities against contribution to customer satisfaction means that some areas of the organisation are likely to shrink. The process of **delayering** may be necessary. This utilises modern information technology systems to replace the chiefly 'communications' role of middle management. The result is a much reduced requirement for general managers and an increased span of control.

(b) At the same time as these changes are being made, front line sales and marketing capability will probably have to be enhanced. This is likely to involve more than just an increase in numbers. New methods of working will be introduced, including working in cross-functional teams. In particular, the natural partner of delayering is **empowerment**. Front line staff will take greater responsibility for delivering customer satisfaction and will be given the necessary authority to do so. Relationship marketing databases and staff will be installed and key account managers appointed.

Such restructuring of the organisation has important **human resources (HR)** implications.

(a) There are likely to be **redundancies**. Staff who cannot adjust to the new methods must be released, with proper attention to both the legal requirements relating to redundancy and the organisation's policies on social responsibility.

(b) **Recruitment** will continue, because of natural wastage, but it will probably be necessary to adjust recruitment policy and practice to reflect the new requirements. Recruits must be selected who will be able to absorb the new approach and respond to the necessary training.

(c) **Training** will become a major feature of the change management programme. As well as new recruits, existing staff must be educated in the new methods and approach. The marketing department may have an input here, or the task of inculcating the marketing orientation and ideal of customer service may be contracted out to consultants.

Research suggests that although the principles involved may be acknowledged by a large number of companies, **formalised internal marketing programmes in the UK are still fairly uncommon**. Initial findings make several other suggestions.

(a) Internal marketing is **implicit in other strategies** such as quality programmes and customer care initiatives, rather than standing alone as an explicit policy in its own right.

(b) Where it is practised, internal marketing tends to involve a **core of structured activities** surrounded by less rigorously defined *ad hoc* practices.

(c) To operate successfully, internal marketing relies heavily on **good communication** networks.

(d) Internal marketing is a key factor in **competitive differentiation**.

(e) **Conflicts** between functional areas are significantly **reduced** by internal marketing.

(f) Internal marketing depends heavily on **commitment at the highest level of management, co-operation,** and on the presence of **an open management style**.

Scandinavian Airlines Systems

Companies using this approach to great effect include SAS (Scandinavian Airline Systems), which has increased the involvement of employees in the decision-making process to achieve the highest levels of satisfaction, empowered them to make decisions appropriate to the requirements of particular customers, and trained them to feel a responsibility towards customers of all kinds. As a consequence, the company culture fosters a caring relationship internally and externally.

2.2 The marketing mix for internal marketing

Product under the internal marketing concept is the changing nature of the job. **Price** is the balance of psychological costs and benefits involved in adopting the new orientation, plus those things which have to be given up in order to carry out the new tasks. Difficulties here relate to the problem of arriving at an accurate and adequate evaluation of psychological costs.

Many of the methods used for communication and **promotion** in external marketing may be employed to motivate employees and influence attitudes and behaviour. HRM practice is beginning to employ techniques such as multi-media presentations and in-house publications. Presentational skills are borrowed from personal selling techniques, while incentive schemes are being employed to generate changes in employee behaviour.

Advertising is increasingly used to generate a favourable corporate image amongst employees as well as external customers. Federal Express has the largest corporate television network in the world, with 1,200 sites.

Distribution for internal marketing means emails, meetings, conferences and physical means like noticeboards which can be used to announce policies and deliver policies and training programmes.

Physical evidence refers to tangible items which facilitate delivery or communication of the product. Quality standards such as BS 5750/ISO 9000, for instance, place great emphasis on documentation. Other tangible elements might involve training sessions, which would constitute a manifestation of commitment to standards or policies.

Process, which refers to how a 'customer' actually receives a product, is linked to communication and the medium of training which may be used to promote customer consciousness.

Participants are the people involved in producing and delivering the product. Those receiving the product, who may influence the customer's perceptions, are clearly important within the internal marketing process. Communications must be delivered by someone of the right level of authority in order to achieve their aims. The way in which employees act is strongly influenced by fellow employees, particularly their immediate superiors. Inter-departmental or interfunctional communications are likely to be least effective, because they have equal status or lack the authority to ensure compliance.

Segmentation and marketing research can also be used in internal marketing. Employees may be grouped according to their service characteristics, needs, wants or tasks in order to organise the dissemination of a service orientation. Research will monitor the needs and wants of employees, and identify the impact of corporate policies.

2.2.1 Problems with the internal marketing concept

Even effective use of inwardly directed marketing techniques cannot solve all employee related quality and customer satisfaction problems. **Research clearly shows that actions by the personnel department, or effective programmes of personnel selection and training, are likely to be more effective than marketing based activities.**

 Marketing at Work

In the UK retail sector, for example, while many large scale operations now operate Sunday trading, there has been significant resistance from employee organisations. Internal marketing would argue that employees should be persuaded by means of a well-executed communications campaign and by the offer of proper incentives. Although these strategies have been tried, they have met with little success, or, in the case of incentives, have been too expensive. Employers have solved the problem by specifically recruiting employees who are required to work on Sunday, and who may be paid slightly higher wage rates for the time in question. Rather than internal marketing, external recruitment proved to be the solution.

Claims that marketing can replace or fulfil the objectives of some other functions are clearly overstated. However, the internal marketing concept has a major role to play in making employees customer conscious.

Exam tip

> Do not marginalise this topic. Internal marketing is mentioned specifically in the syllabus. It came up in an exam in June 2002 under the old *Integrated Marketing Communications* syllabus when candidates were asked why internal marketing communications could be an important aspect of a low cost airline's marketing communications.

3 Types of outside resources

FAST FORWARD

> Almost any activity can be **outsourced**. Typical areas for outsourcing activities are manufacture, distribution, finance and marketing. Marketing activities that can be outsourced include consultancy, marketing research, promotion and 'full service'.
>
> As a general rule, the use of **outside resources** can be considered whenever external suppliers can provide better services at the same cost or equivalent services at a lower cost.

In the modern world, it is possible to outsource everything. There are a great many management and marketing consultants in the UK. The CIM, for example, provides a comprehensive service. Some consultants specialise in design, research or promotion.

3.1 Marketing research agencies

Not many organisations have all the in-house facilities needed to cater for their total information requirements. Nearly all organisations find it necessary from time-to-time to outsource surveys to specialists.

3.2 Promotional agencies

There is a great variety of **promotional agencies** including advertising agencies and agencies specialising in sales promotion, in PR, and in telesales/telemarketing. Within sales promotion there is a range of specialists in such areas as packaging design, POS display material, exhibition services, and mail-order.

3.2.1 Full-service agencies

Full service agencies supply the full range of marketing services.

In smaller companies, many of the functions associated with marketing may actually be sourced from outside the company. Obvious examples would be market research services, advertising, design of packaging, and specialist aspects of product testing (for example, sensory testing of new food products, or safety tests on new electrical goods). When promotional campaigns are being mounted, 'leafleting' is typically the province of small subcontractors as are teams who dispense free samples during in-store promotional exercises.

Employing **advertising agencies** not only gives access to their expertise but may also improve the finances of a media campaign because of the commission which the media pay to *bona fide* agents only.

The use of outside resources can add a great deal of flexibility to an organisation. It reduces the need for investment and offers the possibility of greater profits.

Outsourcing also reduces the strain on the organisation's **limited human resources** and frees marketing management to concentrate on the more important strategic rather than tactical aspects of its marketing plans.

Action Programme 3

What are the main advantages of outsourcing?

4 Management of external suppliers

FAST FORWARD   **Good briefing** provides a solid foundation for a successful working relationship.

Exam tip

> The CIM syllabus document for this module emphasises how trust and commitment can be developed. This applies to relationships with suppliers as well as customers. Services upon which organisations depend to function properly must be well managed, so that the outside suppliers who are called upon to carry out these tasks are a key aspect of the overall functioning of the organisation.

4.1 Briefing

Good briefing ensures good working relationships. Bad briefing will lead to misunderstandings between client and supplier to the detriment of the ultimate customer. In the event of a dispute, a full brief will leave less room for doubt as to the requirements of the contract. There must be basic ground rules for briefing outside suppliers.

- To what extent do we take outside suppliers into our confidence?
- What do they need to know?
- Who will draw up the briefs?
- How often should the brief be reviewed?

4.2 Management of externally sourced factors

4.2.1 Control and review

Direct supervision of externally sourced staff and equipment will normally be the responsibility of the contractor, but the hiring company must maintain its own management input into the relationship. Costs, benefits and risks must be considered during the life of the contract as well as before it is let. **The company must be clear about what it wants to achieve from outsourcing and set quantifiable standards against which the contractor's performance can be reviewed**.

One or more managers should be charged with oversight of every important aspect of every contract. These managers should also maintain communication with the contractors and promote good relations between the parties. If performance is unsatisfactory, the contractor must be informed directly rather than via the operational staff so that effective corrective action is taken.

Costs, risks and performance should be reviewed regularly and the results reported to the senior managers responsible for outsourcing policy. A framework for review is given below. The supervising manager should be particularly alert to developments that may affect the relationship, such as new legislation and changes in labour relations. For instance, minimum wage legislation will undoubtedly affect the profitability of many contractors, and some will be tempted to evade it. No company conscious of its image would wish to be associated with such evasion.

One of the main potential problems is lack of response to client input. There are some mechanisms, such as staged payments and incentive structure, which attempt to address this issue by making the outsourced function responsible for meeting particular targets, and holding back payment. There is a tendency for this to be seen as somewhat excessive in smaller contracts. Control rests, ultimately, upon the **market power of the client**, and on the **quality of the management control system** operated within the client organisation.

Control might be applied selectively. Should a supplier who involves small or spasmodic expenditure be subjected to the same degree of control as a supplier the organisation uses regularly or extensively? The answer cannot depend on expenditure alone. The organisation could, for example, be making a relatively small spend with an agency on concept testing a proposed new product. However, this proposed new product could be vital to the organisation's future and therefore the agency could require stricter control than a dependable supplier of raw materials.

The nature of the control should perhaps be different **according to the nature of the product or service being bought**. For raw material suppliers, an organisation might have scientific tests on quality and maintain records of deliveries late/on time/before time. However, for an advertising agency, control might be more informal and based on frequent personal meetings.

4.2.2 A framework for review

- Supplier's name, address, telephone number
- Names and positions of contacts
- Description of types of goods and services supplied
- Total annual spend for last three years
- Splits of annual spends by types of product/service where relevant
- Number of years we have been trading with this supplier
- Perceived strengths and weaknesses of supplier
- Record of improvements made by supplier during trading period
- Record of growth of supplier: turnover, staff, number of branches
- List of alternative suppliers
- Perceived strengths and weaknesses of top three alternative suppliers
- Date of last review of this supplier
- Name/position of person conducting this last review
- Recommended date of next review

Chapter Roundup

- **Customers are stakeholders**. This means that they should be valued and not taken for granted. They differ in their characteristics and can be analysed or segmented to increase profitability.

- **Intermediaries** such as agents and franchisees are also customers. They have their own different needs, which must be considered.

- **Customer retention** is an important contribution to profitability since each customer can represent a lifetime's cash flow and creating a new customer requires far more promotional and administrative effort than retaining an existing one. The vital factor in customer retention is the skill and approach of the front line staff.

- **Relationship marketing** is more than customer retention. It is the fostering of a mutually beneficial relationship by precision in meeting the needs of individual customers. It uses powerful computer database systems.

- The focus of **transactional marketing (TM)** is to look to each transaction or encounter as an opportunity to maximise short-term gains, without necessarily considering future contacts, or the effect of *this* transaction on the potential for future contacts.

- The ladder of loyalty (*Kotler*, 1997; *Peck et al*, 1999) is designed to illustrate how relationship marketing seeks to increase the loyalty of customer groups: Figure 11.2.

- Relationship marketing intentionally aims to retain customers (keep them purchasing repeatedly over time) and foster customer loyalty (create a favourable attitude or bias which drives repeat purchase).

- Customers can be analysed for their **value to the business**. **Key account management** allows the most valuable customers to be given an enhanced service.

- **Internal marketing** has a range of meanings but the most useful relates to the promotion of a high level of customer awareness throughout the organisation using marketing communication techniques to change culture and deliver training.

- Almost any activity can be **outsourced**. Typical areas for outsourcing activities are manufacture, distribution, finance and marketing. Marketing activities that can be outsourced include consultancy, marketing research, promotion and 'full service'.

- As a general rule, the use of **outside resources** can be considered whenever external suppliers can provide better services at the same cost or equivalent services at a lower cost.

- **Good briefing** provides a solid foundation for a successful working relationship.

Quick Quiz

1   Customers make up one of the groups of stakeholders whose interests marketing management should address.

    True   ☐

    False   ☐

2   Why is 'word of mouth' communication so powerful?

    A   People tend not to write things down these days
    B   It always happens when the customer is happy
    C   The company does not have to pay for it
    D   An unhappy customer may advise many others of his discontent

3   Even within a particular business, customers will vary. What are some of these variable factors influencing their purchasing decisions?

4   An intermediary is not a type of customer

    True   ☐

    False   ☐

5   Give a simple definition of 'relationship marketing'.

6   Classify these characteristics as features of either 'transactional' (T) or 'relationship' (R) marketing:

Importance of single sale	T/R	Importance of customer relationship	T/R
Importance of customer benefits	T/R	Competitive commitment	T/R
Short time scale	T/R	Less emphasis on service	T/R
Longer time scale	T/R	High customer service	T/R
Quality is concern of production	T/R	Quality is concern of all	T/R
High customer commitment	T/R	Importance of product features	T/R
Persuasive communication	T/R	Regular communication	T/R

7   Fill in the gaps using words from the grid below.

    The key account relationship may progress through several stages. At first, there may be a typical (1)………. sales-purchasing relationship. Later, the sales staff may be able to foster a mutual desire to increase (2)………..A mature (3)………. stage may be reached in which there are contacts at all levels and (4)………. is shared.

Information	Trust	Management
Conflict	Adversarial	Partnership

8   Advertising can be used to generate a favourable corporate image amongst employees (internal marketing) as well as external customers.

    True   ☐

    False   ☐

Answers to Quick Quiz

1 True

2 D (although there is some merit in option C as well)

3 Check your answer against Section 1

4 False

5 The management of a firm's market relationships

6

Importance of single sale	T	Importance of customer relationship	R
Importance of customer benefits	R	Competitive commitment	T
Short time scale	T	Less emphasis on service	T
Longer time scale	R	High customer service	R
Quality is concern of production	T	Quality is concern of all	R
High customer commitment	R	Importance of product features	T
Persuasive communication	T	Regular communication	R

7 (1) Adversarial; (2) Trust; (3) Partnership; (4) Information

8 True

Action Programme Review

1 Your own research.

2 The definition of a key account depends on the circumstances, but a customer's **potential** is very important. In addition, customers might be assessed for desirability according to the following criteria.

- **Profitability** of their accounts
- **Prestige** they confer
- Amount of **non-value adding administrative work** they generate
- **Cost of the selling effort** they absorb
- **Rate of growth** of their accounts
- **Turnover** of their own businesses
- Willingness to **adopt new products**
- **Credit history**

3 (a) Cost savings

   (b) Specialism of the company

   (c) Accountability is tied to specific performance

   (d) Introduction of desirable outside qualities such as imagination and fresh ideas into particular sorts of activities

Now try Question 11 at the end of the Study Text

The marketing communications industry

Syllabus content – knowledge and skill requirements

- The nature, structure, ownership and any key issues facing the marketing communications industry in any single country or region (4.4)

- How agencies manage their operations in order to meet client needs: pitching, briefing, structure, review, the role of account planners and managers, relationship management (4.5)

- How advertising agencies and marketing communication agencies use resources to meet the needs of clients with international and global requirements (4.6)

- In broad terms, the regulatory and voluntary arrangements that are used to manage relationships between the public, customers, clients and agencies (4.7)

Introduction

External agencies exist to provide services that a client does not retain **in-house**. Indeed, the argument that communication activity should be kept in-house is discredited, as the **communications techniques available are now so varied** that it makes no commercial sense to retain in-house the entire range, when each specialism is only likely to be called upon infrequently. Agencies are generally dealing with a number of clients and will be more in touch with the latest techniques and developments. Competitive deals on **media buying**, for example, are far more likely to be achieved by a large agency than by a single staff member in a relatively small marketing department.

So, in the last few decades marketing techniques have increased dramatically in range and complexity. The marketing communications industry has had to evolve as technology and business realities contribute to both **audience** and **media fragmentation**.

Standard '**above-the-line**' marketing (where media space is paid for), handled by large advertising agencies, has been increasingly replaced by '**below-the-line**' (promotional) and '**through-the-line**' activities, as we saw in Chapter 4. Agencies specialising in sales promotion, direct marketing and PR have sprung up as independent operations and divisions of large advertising agencies. Many companies now use more than one agency to handle a **portfolio** of techniques above-, below-and through-the-line, or to cover **local and on-going** work as well as **national strategic** campaign. As a result, many larger, integrated agencies now have divisions specialising in various areas.

- Sales promotion
- Direct marketing
- Public relations
- 'New' media (Internet, CD-ROM)
- Design

According to *Fill* (2002), the marketing communications industry consists of four principal groups.

- **Media**
- **Clients**
- **Agencies**
- **Support organisations** (such as production companies and research agencies)

There is a certain level of **interdependence** between these organisations, so co-operative working relationships between them are required.

Exam tip

We will discuss relationships with advertising agencies in detail in section 6 below. The CIM syllabus document for this module discusses the importance of what it terms 'the agency dimension', and the relationships that develop between client and agency. The marketing communication industry in general was examined on the December 2003 paper and again in both 2006 sittings, where you were invited to discuss its structure and key issues in any country/region of your choice. In June 2005, the Part A question was all about the client/agency relationship.

Broadly speaking there are only two types of agency that a marketing communicator will deal with: **creative advertising agencies** and **research agencies**.

Advertising agencies are still the most commonly used marketing service. Agencies come in a range of sizes and specialisms to reflect the increasingly fragmented and diverse range of media.

Key concepts

(a) '**Media only**' service: the agency selects schedules and books advertising space at a discount, which is in part passed onto the client.

(b) '**Full service**': the agency creates the whole campaign from concept through production to press/air.

1 Research agencies

FAST FORWARD

Marketing communicators need to be fully aware of the range of **qualitative and quantitative research data** that is available or obtainable and also of the limitations of research.

It is essential that a marketing communicator has a thorough understanding of the role, scope, and reliability of both **quantitative** and **qualitative** research. Thus equipped he can develop a healthy distrust of data that is presented in the form of research. Unless the research proves itself to be both relevant and valid for the intended purpose it should not be trusted.

1.1 The cost of research

Cost is a major problem in securing accurate **primary research**. Budget constraints sometimes reduce a sample size to a very low level and however impressively they may be presented, the results can be misleading. **Secondary sources**, such as syndicated surveys, tend to carry a high price, and value must therefore be the criteria of purchase.

Action Programme 1

Wait for the next publication of ABC audit figures and examine how each major newspaper presents the results. What conclusions can you draw from what you observe?

1.2 Research decision sequence

Prior to commissioning research the decision sequence should be this.

Step 1	Do we need research?
Step 2	If so, what for?
Step 3	By when is it needed?
Step 4	How much can we afford?
Step 5	Can we locate a quality researcher who is free at the time needed?
Step 6	Is our budget (cost and time) sufficient?
Step 7	Do we go ahead and commission the research?

When deciding on sources of research it is essential to consider what is really needed in terms of sample reliability rather then to choose on the basis of availability or cheapness. It is essential to check the credentials of any research organisation: can it deliver what you want at the time that you want it? Most will say they can, but what is their record?

All advertising agencies have links with the other specialists that are needed. Clients should therefore remember that the benefit of engaging specialists who are used to working together could be outweighed by the specialists' natural desire to continue working together whether or not it is appropriate to the client's needs to do so.

1.3 Retail audits (eg A C Nielsen)

(a) These measure stocks moving through retail outlets. However, Nielsen have been denied access to certain major stores such as Marks & Spencer so their data has to be adjusted. Their data shows sales in any two-month period, but does not show usage.

(b)   Such research can be self-fulfilling, however. When Nielsen declare the market shares for each segment shops tend to adjust their shelf-space allocation so that the market share percentage is given to each brand stocked.

Consumer panels comprise shoppers who complete diaries showing purchases in detail. Alternatively, researchers are sent into the home to carry out 'pantry checks' in similar fashion to retail audit. They have not made inroads into Nielsen's supremacy, but provide very useful data that helps in the marketing communications task.

Omnibus surveys are vehicles provided by a research organisation that carries out a regular survey on a syndicated basis.

(a)   Client companies are invited to buy questions at a fixed price. Discounts are usually available for several questions and/or for repeating the questions in a series of surveys.

(b)   The research is carried out at a far lower cost than could be achieved by individual commission. They are particularly suitable for those who want to ask a limited number of questions of a large, representative sample of the population. The largest is the ICD Survey.

(c)   There are many general omnibus surveys available and each claims to offer unique benefits. Potential clients should consider not only the sample size, but also its quality in terms of structure and method of data collection.

(d)   There are a wide variety of specialist omnibus surveys working to niche markets such as motorists or mothers with children under two.

1.3.1 The Target Group Index

The TGI is a national product and media survey which collects information from 24,000 adults each year. The TGI is a 'single source' measurement and all elements of the survey can be cross-referenced, for example media usage to product usage; brand usage to demographics.

Action Programme 2

Here are two small ads from a recent edition of *Marketing Week*. (The names have been omitted.) What sort of companies/products might use these services?

<table>
<tr><td>

Market Research Limited

Trade Research Specialists

- Retail audits
- Product availability surveys
- Mystery shopping
- Shop testing
- Trade interviews
- Tailor made studies
- Overnight pricing checks
- Customer interviews
- Consumer research

</td><td>

CHILDREN AND YOUTH

BRITAIN AND CONTINENT

GB *Core Sample:* 1200 7 – 19 year olds with bi-monthly extensions to include ages 3 to 6 and 20-24. Any age range within these limits.

Field dates: every 2 – 4 weeks.

Rates: from £290 per question according to age range covered.

Continent: Five country child and youth surveys

</td></tr>
</table>

2 Other marketing communications agencies

Before we look at creative agencies in detail in the next section, here is an outline of some other agencies available for the marketing communicator.

2.1 Promotion agencies

Promotional activities – collaborations between brands, competitions and incentives – have been a huge growth area in marketing. Some agencies specialise in these areas.

- Sourcing promotional incentive products and merchandise
- Devising links and negotiating deals between brands
- Organising competitions
- Designing and producing promotional packaging and information material

PR consultancies handle several areas.

(a) **Media or press relations** (keeping the media informed, in order to manage the company's portrayal and secure 'free' coverage of product/service information)

(b) **Corporate relations** (promoting a corporate image to the public, market and business world, through a range of PR techniques)

(c) **Marketing support** (promoting specific products or services via publicity, events, press coverage and so on)

(d) **Government relations** (lobbying on behalf of the company's interests)

(e) **Community relations** (targeted at the general public or local residents, via communication and social programmes, community involvement, sponsorship etc)

(f) **Financial relations** (communicating with shareholders, financial media, the Stock Market)

(g) **Employee relations** (communicating with staff)

PR agencies are less easy to manage than advertising agencies, because their activity and output is often less tangible. The major cost is their time plus expenses. In order to make cost effective use of their services you need to consider the following.

- Set clear **objectives** for the on-going PR plan or specific project
- Set a project **fee** where possible
- **Brief** comprehensively
- **Monitor activity** perhaps via an independent cuttings or media monitoring agency
- **Monitor expenditure**

2.2 Direct marketing services

Direct marketing agencies (and separate specialists) offer a range of services from database and mailing list development, analysis and segmentation to telemarketing, direct mail package design, copy writing, mailing and fulfilment. This area of marketing has grown with Internet usage , as many of the 'dotcoms' have used direct mail to drive visitors to their websites.

2.3 Brand identity

There are specialist agencies that perform specific brand-related services.

- Design and produce product **packaging** and display
- Orchestrate the updating of **brand identity** and style
- Research, devise, market-test and register **brand names**

2.4 Sponsorship

Agencies undertake negotiations:

- **Sponsorship agreements**
- **Product endorsements** by celebrities
- **Product placement** (the inclusion of branded products in films or TV programmes)

3 Creative agencies

3.1 Types of agency

Full service agency	This is an agency that provides a complete advertising service encompassing creative work, production, media planning and buying. The full service agency may also provide or sub-contract research services for a client. Some large advertising agencies will provide other communications services, for example direct marketing, public relations or sales promotion. There has been some concern that such large agencies may not always be able to provide a full quality service in all the areas that they cover. Some creative teams left large agencies to set up their own **creative shops** (or **'HotShops'**) to provide an alternative.
Media independents	Media independents provide media services (such as planning and buying) only.
A la carte	A client may decide to share out his communication tasks, choosing to cherry pick services *à la carte* from the different providers available. Responsibility for controlling and co-ordinating the activities of these service providers rests with the client, usually in the form of the brand or marketing Manager.
New media	This area has grown hugely in recent years. The main area of work is the provision of Internet facilities. Agencies tend to fall along a spectrum of expertise and be either marketing orientated, or technology specialists.

4 Agency selection

FAST FORWARD

The **process of selecting a new agency** involves initial search; credentials presentation and shortlist; competitive pitch; and final selection. The client will gauge competing agencies against set criteria such as expertise in the client's field of business, previous work handled, resources provided and costs. The final selection decision will involve a judgement about how well the agency has answered the client brief.

The pages of the trade magazine *Campaign* regularly carry news of client accounts on the move from one agency to another. There are a number of reasons why clients may change agencies. The client may feel the agency is lacking in new ideas, or is overcharging. Alternatively, a new client won by the agency may result in a conflict of interests between new and old clients. Often, a change in personnel on either the client or the agency side can result in an account moving on.

A whole 25-mark question was set in the December 2007 exam around the need for a luxury watchmaker to change its lead advertising agency. The question included a range of issues, including: the sequence of activities required to appoint a new agency; the criteria for agency selection; the role and content of a client brief; the tasks of an account manager, creative team and media planner' *and* ways of developing client/agency relationships! Obviously, not much detail was required on each aspect – but you certainly needed a good grasp of the whole topic ....

4.1 Search

Sources of information include the following.

(a)   Publications such as *Campaign Portfolio* provide a listing of agencies and the types of business they handle, alongside addresses and contact numbers.

(b)   The Advertising Agency Register (AAR) is a specialist intermediary type service that clients can use to help them with their search. For a fee, AAR will provide a list of candidate agencies and a selection of their work.

(c)   Many agencies engage in self promotion via advertising, direct mail or even cold calling.

(d)   Personal recommendation may bring some agency names to light.

(e)   Some agencies now produce CD-ROMs containing case studies, examples of work and background information about them and their offices.

4.2 Shortlist

From the initial search, a shortlist of perhaps six to eight agencies will be drawn up, usually on the basis of their current work and past track record. The prospective client will then visit those agencies for a series of what are known as credentials presentations. A preliminary evaluation of the agencies may be carried out using the criteria below.

(a)   Previous work handled

(b)   Experience in relevant fields of business (for example, do they handle other clients with similar target audiences to mine? Have they carried out work in the fmcg/industrial/ business-to-business market before?)

(c)   Agency costs/terms of business

(d)   Resources in-house as opposed to bought in

(e)   Staff expertise

(f)   Personalities

4.3 Agency pitch

Following these initial visits, it is likely that a smaller number of agencies will be formally invited to **pitch** for the client's business. There is some controversy regarding whether an agency should be reimbursed for a pitch. Some agencies will only carry out pitches if they can claim some of the expense back again from the potential client. Other agencies will only carry out an ideas pitch as opposed to presenting creative work.

Normally, three or four agencies will be invited to compete for the client's business. All will receive a standard brief and will be given a set period in which to reply to the brief.

4.4 Detailed selection process

It is essential that each agency is judged by the same criteria. The criteria should be established by the client in advance, and they must be understood and agreed by all who will be part of the selection team.

4.4.1 Criteria for assessing an agency

Item	Comment
Present work	• Is it exciting/interesting? • Is it effective? What proof is there? • It is allied to our marketplace?
Present clients	• Are there any clashes that will worry us or the agency or the other client(s)? • Do previous clients come back for more or are agency/client relationships short-lived?
Chemistry	• Is the chemistry between us good? • Will we feel able to trust the agency all the way? • Will the trust be reciprocated?
Staffing	• Will the people who worked on the pitch work on the account? • How stable will our account team be? • What depth of experience can the account team offer?
Evidence	• Have we seen evidence of creativity, of production, of media planning, of management, of the particular skills we need?
The pitch	• Is it a package or tailored specially? • Does it arouse us to buy?
The agency	• Is its size, age and structure suitable? • Does it have to have international capacity? • Is it a full service agency or a specialist? • What is its workload? Does it have time for us? • Does it possess the necessary business skills? (For example, has it negotiated a fee for specialised work necessary to meet the requirements of our invitation to pitch for the account?)
Specialised knowledge	• Has it demonstrated realistic and satisfactory understanding of our organisation and market?
Price	• Does the asking fee represent value for money when the above points are taken into account? • Does the agency know its value to us?
Judgement	• Is this the agency for us?

4.5 Final selection

The final selection will involve a judgement about how well the client believes the agency has responded to the brief in terms of the strategic thinking involved, the creative work (if presented) and the agency's all round understanding of the client's industry. Courtesy dictates that the client should inform both the successful agency and the unsuccessful ones in a prompt manner.

4.6 Criticism of the formal selection process

The formalised process is now being questioned, especially because with the arrival of new media and Internet technology, campaigns are having to be resolved in days rather than weeks. The **pitching process** can lead to tensions, especially on the part of unsuccessful agencies who may have invested a great amount of time and effort for no reward. Perhaps most significantly for them, they will have shared their ideas, over which they will have no subsequent control .

The pitching process also gives little insight into **subsequent working relationships**.

 Marketing at Work

An example solution to this particular problem (cited by *Fill*, 2002) is that adopted by *Iceland* and *Dyson*. They invite agencies to discuss and work with client staff on 'mini-briefs' for a day. Such briefs are more like discussion topics for the agency to think about, as opposed to the traditional 'outline your proposed campaign for Product X and we'll tell you if we like it' approach. Most importantly, it gives senior management the chance to see agency and client staff working together on a task, and the agencies are spared weeks of costly preparation work.

Exam tip

The Pilot Paper features a question on the ways in which **trust** between clients and agencies may be improved, and this formed a question again in December 2006.

5 Briefing the agency

FAST FORWARD

It is the responsibility of the client to provide a **full campaign briefing** for any new piece of advertising work. An oral brief is usually backed up by a written document. The account executive in turn will provide a creative briefing for the specific use of the creative team.

The **agency brief** is the initial and most important stage of any project undertaken. The planning and creative teams of the agency need initially to get to know the client, its products, brands, market and customers, and its culture, style, self-image and designed image.

Key concept

A **brief** (in advertising agency terms) is an interpretation of a given market in relation to the product, plus every usable detail about the features and benefits of that product.

A comprehensive brief will include the following details.

(a) **The product**, including its design and marketing history, and current 'life cycle' stage, its technical specifications, pack sizes, shelf-life, packaging/distribution arrangements and associated after-sales services.

(b) **The market**: who uses the product, how, when and why, how it is distributed (via wholesale, retail or direct selling), the product's current and desired market share, pricing and discount/margin policies for the product, and sales strategies.

(c) **Previous advertising**: the previous advertising budget (if any), competitors' advertising spend, breakdown of spend above– and below-the-line.

(d) **Current advertising policy**: budget available, desired image for the product and company, objectives of advertising.

The brief may also contain the company's current ideas about the theme for advertising: what it believes is the key concept or **unique selling proposition (USP)** of the product or brand.

The brief is usually given to the agency account executive who relays it to the relevant agency personnel.

A **proforma for a creative brief** is set out below.

CREATIVE BRIEF

Agency

Briefing date

Company

Contact name

Project name

Project description

Budget

Key deadlines

Company background

Business objectives

Background to the brief

Communications objectives

Target audience

Proposition

 Action Programme 3

Explain the significance of each of these elements of the creative brief.

6 Managing the relationship

FAST FORWARD

> Managing the relationship requires **trust**, a free flow of **information**, proper allocation of **responsibilities** and careful **control**.

The specialist agencies providing support services (advertising, public relations, sales promotion, research) usually all work to much the same principles. There will be an **account director** directly responsible for the client's account and working directly with the client **brand manager**. Thus all contact between client and agency is via the conduit established by these two individuals.

6.1 Who's who in the agency?

The simplest form of **agency structure** is as follows: Figure 12.1.

Figure 12.1: Simple agency structure

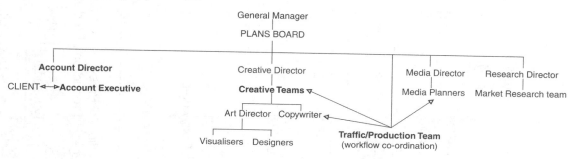

- The **account executives** service the clients on a day-to-day basis
- The **account director** monitors work on given accounts
- The **creative team** 'produces' the ad
- The **traffic/production team** plans and schedules agency workflow, monitors progress against deadlines and 'chases' work

FAST FORWARD

> A variety of agency staff will handle the **workflow** on a client's account. The account executive acts as the key intermediary between agency and client.

The account director/manager is vitally important because a full service agency will provide the services of not fewer than 20 departments, and these need to be co-ordinated around a client focus. The departments commonly found in a full service agency are as follows.

• Creative	• TV and radio production	• Marketing
• Typography	• Press production	• Media planning
• Presentation	• Press buying	• Market intelligence
• Studio	• Print buying	• Personnel
• Account management	• Art buying	• Finance
• Economic forecasting	• TV and radio buying	• Administration
• Research	• Sales promotion	• Management

A large full service agency might look more like Figure 12.2.

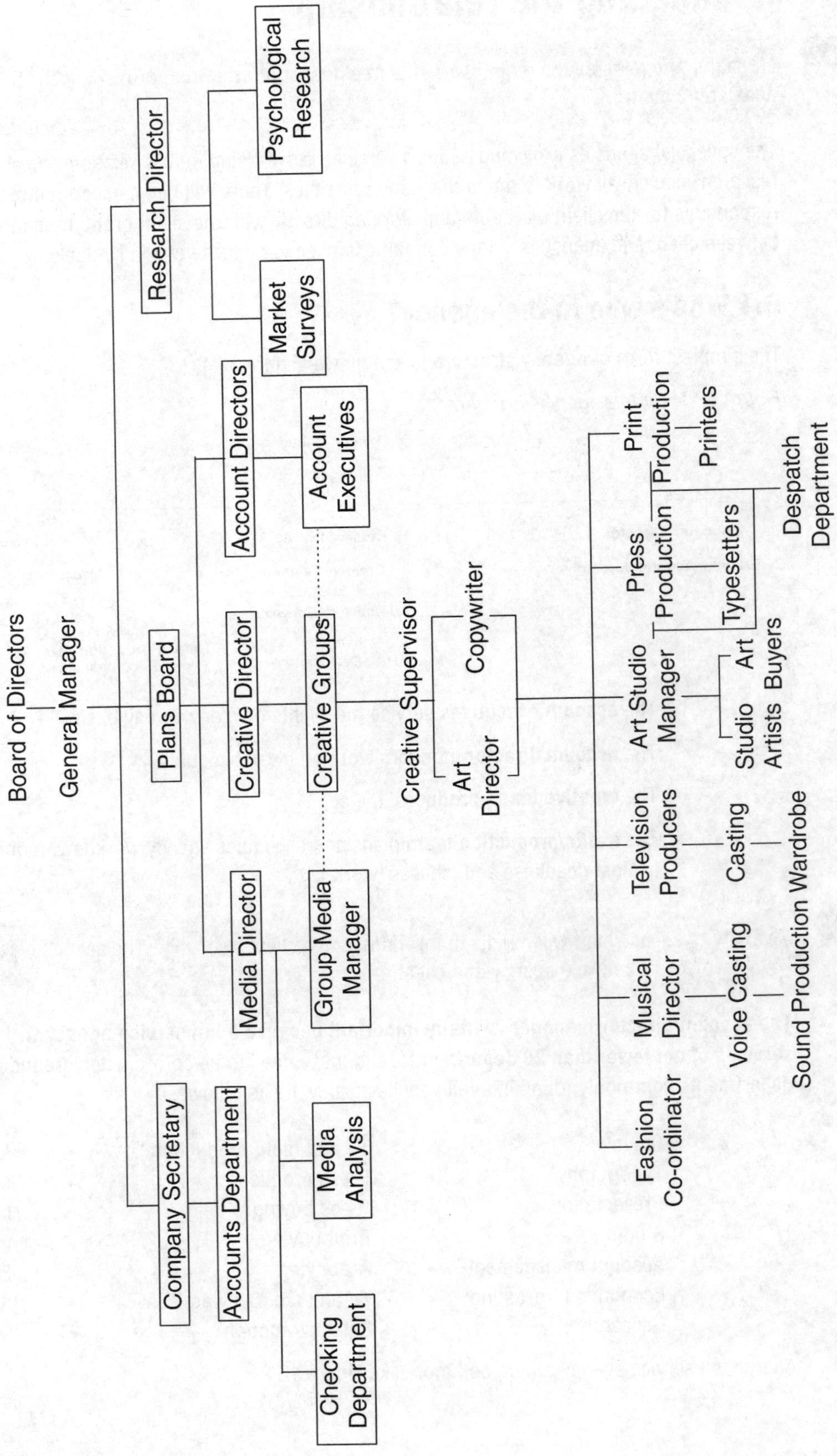

Figure 12.2: Large agency organisation chart

The flow of work through the agency can be depicted as follows: Figure 12.3.

Figure 12.3: Agency work flow

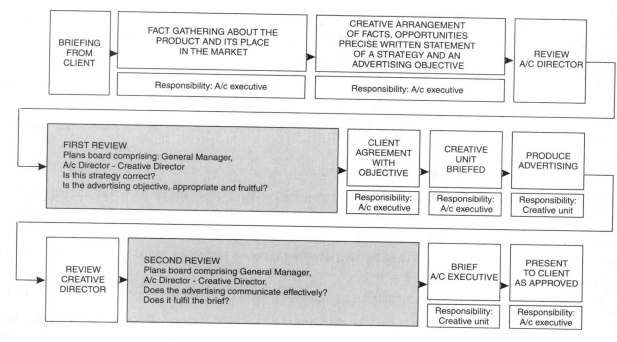

Source: *Hearne* (1987)

Note the **client's responsibilities**.

(a)   The advertising co-ordinator (or marketing department head) briefs the agency.

(b)   The marketing department head approves the agency's assessment of the advertising objective, strategy, schedule and cost estimates.

(c)   The advertising co-ordinator provides the agency with all available materials and information to help the creative team to produce effective ads.

(d)   The advertising co-ordinator is the first one to see work that comes back from the agency at each stage of production (copy, story boards, sketches), and will probably check, correct and recommend any necessary changes before the ad is finally approved by the marketing department head.

(e)   The ad is returned to the agency for typesetting, final art, filming and sound production.

(f)   The advertising co-ordinator carries out final checks, and gets final approval before giving the agency clearance to release the ad to the media.

Establishing a relationship with a creative agency takes time. The end result has to be an on-going relationship based upon mutual understanding and respect. Therefore both the selection process and the day-to-day relationships have to receive very careful attention.

A creative agency should be a full member of the client's marketing team. As such, members of the agency have to be trusted with market information and, to some extent, with profit information as well. If they are not, then information will be withheld and the relationship will suffer. The creative work will suffer too, and sales and profitability will fall. If an agency understands the costing of a package it is less likely to spend time devising a promotion that the client will not be able to afford, and so keeping working data from an agency is counter-productive, morale sapping and expensive.

The only reason an agency is engaged is because it can do a job or provide a service better (and more quickly) than the client can do it for himself. It follows that the client should not meddle with their work. If the client does not like it, of course, he must say so, but **the test must be** 'will it work with the target audience?'.

6.1.1 Key principles for managing the relationship

1	Management is by the client.
2	The agency team must work closely within the client's marketing department.
3	Briefings must be specific and unambiguous.
4	All research data and management control information available to the brand manager must be provided to the agency.
5	The agency should sit in on the client's strategic planning meetings as an equal member, and as of right.
6	Time and cost requirements must be reasonable and must be accepted by the agency.
7	The client should not meddle in the creative process and the agency should not interfere with the production of the package, although both may make an input, as appropriate, as part of the strategic planning process.
8	Full credit must be given when the agency is successful, and shared responsibility must be accepted as appropriate.
9	Fees and commissions should be agreed in advance and accounts should be paid promptly.
10	Copy should never be changed once it has been approved. It should be fully checked before it is signed off. Changes after that stage are not only expensive but, more importantly, they are damaging to the brand manager's personal credibility with the agency.

Given that the agency is accepted as part of the marketing communications team it should take full responsibility for the production of cost-effective work that meets the brief and hits time targets.

6.2 Payment of creative agencies

Historically, agencies have earned their money through commission on media space purchased for their clients. The practice arises from the time when the advertising agent was a media broker who also provided other services. This method of payment also highlights the agency's legal standing. The agency is liable for bills to the media if the client defaults on payment. Nearly 50% of agency income still comes from commission, according to a recent survey.

6.3 Agency commission

Fifteen per cent used to be the standard rate of agency commission. This is now no longer the case. Some large clients have argued that they should pay the agency a discounted rate of commission, because of the volume of media throughput that the agency handles. Other clients, themselves under pressure to make advertising money work harder, have argued for commission rates of 10% or 13%.

6.4 Fee payment

Some advertisers and their agencies prefer to work on a project by project fee system. This ensures the agency earns money, whether or not the work is media based. About 40% of agency income is earned in this way.

Marketing at Work

David Ogilvy is on record as saying 'I pioneered the fee system but I no longer care how I get paid, providing I make a reasonable profit. With a fee system the advertiser pays only for the services he wants, no more and no less. Every fee account pays its own way. Large profitable accounts do not subsidise small, unprofitable ones. Cuts in clients' budgets do not oblige you to cut staff. When you advise a client to increase his advertising he does not suspect your motive.'

It is essential for the agency to have an efficient system to capture accurately and promptly all data relating to the allocation of staff time, and the utilisation of other resources. It is reasonable for a client to expect to be shown the control method in use, but not to have access to the agency's detailed profitability. A typical fee calculation is shown below.

Advertising agency: typical fee calculation

	Actual hours	Amount £
Direct time cost*		
Account management	1,000	40,000
Creative	1,500	60,000
Media	300	12,000
Production	400	16,000
Research and planning	750	30,000
		158,000
Overheads at 110% (including secretarial, managerial, accounting and administration payroll; also establishment and general costs)	–	174,000
Direct expenses (including directly attributable travel and presentation costs)	–	14,000
Total hours/cost	3,950	346,000
Gross profit at 25%	–	86,500
Total (£109.50 per hour)	3,950	432,500

* Includes direct and indirect payroll costs of all staff who allocate their time.

The sums charged per hour will obviously vary from agency to agency and over time. The hours needed, however, should remain constant. It will be seen that a new product development can occupy many hours. Even more hours will be used within the client, but they are unlikely to be controlled as rigorously. There is therefore considerable unquantified investment in any new creative development. The only party able to account for its involvement accurately is the agency. (Unfortunately for the agency, its efficiency in this respect means that is likely to be the first target in any cost-cutting exercise!)

6.5 Payment by results

Payment by results schemes have been used mainly in the USA, although they are becoming more common in the UK. With performance-related payment, the agency is judged on the effect its advertising has on client company sales. Different rates of commission then come into force, depending on performance to target, over-achievement or under-achievement. The major drawback to this method of remuneration is that it pre-supposes a direct correlation between advertising effort and sales.

Marketing at Work

Every year *Campaign* conducts a survey on choosing an agency. The results shed some further light on the best approach to managing the relationship – or not managing it, as the case may be.

Marketing directors were asked a series of questions and given suggested answers. The questions and the percentages agreeing with the answers are as follows.

(a)   *Why do you change agency?*

(i)	It is not devoting enough time/resources to your account	87
(ii)	It has lost its enthusiasm for working on your product/service	85
(iii)	It is working on a conflicting account	61
(iv)	There is a personality clash	44
(v)	It lacks *co-ordinated* communication skills	32
(vi)	It lacks the technology to service your account	15
(vii)	You change agency regularly as a matter of course	2

(b)   *How do you go about drawing up a shortlist?*

(i)	You take into consideration advertising you admire	86
(ii)	You ask acquaintances for recommendations	77
(iii)	You read the marketing press	59
(iv)	You read *Campaign*	45
(v)	You take into consideration creative/effectiveness ad awards	44
(vi)	You use the Advertising Agency Register	38
(vii)	You use *Campaign Portfolio*	36
(viii)	You appoint a selection consultant	5

(c)   *What do you look for at the pitch?*

(i)	Evidence the agency understands and can enhance your brand	95
(ii)	Quality of thinking	94
(iii)	Good chemistry between both parties	90
(iv)	Presence of senior agency staff who will stay on your account	81
(v)	Evidence of sound business/management skills	75
(vi)	Strategy that offers value for money	73
(vii)	A powerful creative idea	68
(viii)	An agency culture that fits your own	64

(d)   *What do you look for in a new agency?*

(i)	It is fundamentally committed to creative excellence	74
(ii)	It has previous experience working in your market sector	46
(iii)	It offers a remuneration system based on fees not commissions	41
(iv)	It has embraced new technology and uses it	38
(v)	It offers a fully *co-ordinated* service, including below-the-line	35
(vi)	It is able to advise you on the information superhighway	22
(vii)	It offers international resources	16

(e)   *How could your agency improve its service to you?*

(i)	Unprompted original ideas	78
(ii)	Cut costs	66
(iii)	Not be afraid to challenge your viewpoint	56
(iv)	Devote more time/resources to your account	49
(v)	Embrace new technology and use it to your advantage	44
(vi)	Offer a more through-the-line approach	41
(vii)	Spend less time wining and dining and more time working	21

(f)   *In which of the following areas could your agency improve its skills?*

(i)	Creativity	55
(ii)	Strategy	50
(iii)	Research	42
(iv)	Planning	36
(v)	Below-the-line	27
(vi)	Media	23

Perhaps not surprisingly *quality* seemed to be main issue in each case. Notable trends were the interest of a sizeable minority in *co-ordinated* communications and in the possibilities of information technology.

Exam tip

Agency remuneration has featured in the December 2004, December 2005 and June 2006 exams. Note that it may be referred to as remuneration as reward (and in June 2006, the examiner even clarified by adding 'how it is paid'!)

6.6 Agency structures

Within the agency, a variety of personnel will be involved in handling the client's business. The account executive or account manager is the lynchpin between the numerous agency personnel and their client. His role is to liaise with client staff and to brief, supervise and co-ordinate the appropriate agency staff at appropriate times.

Exam tip

The role of the account manager is examined on the Pilot Paper. The examiner has specifically commented that issues concerning new media techniques and agency operations will feature in future sittings.

The internal structure of an agency can best be explained by considering how the agency handles a piece of client work.

(a)   **The client problem**

A client and agency who have been together for some time will have built up a good working relationship. The agency will understand the client's business, and the motivations and decision-making processes of end consumers. A new product or service, new situation or changing market conditions may provide the starting point for a new role to be performed by advertising. The client needs to brief the account executive on the task in hand.

(b)   **The internal briefing**

The account executive will brief the members of the account team who work on the client's business. These members are:

(i)   An **account planner**, responsible for using market research to develop advertising strategy for the clients.

(ii)   A **creative team** or duo of art director and copywriter, responsible for conceiving a creative idea which meets the advertising brief and working that idea up into visual form and written copy.

(iii) A **media planner/buyer**, responsible for recommending an appropriate media strategy and ensuring media is bought cost effectively.

(c)   **The client presentation**

The account executive will present back to the client. He will show examples of how the final advertising execution will look, using rough visuals or storyboards and will explain the rationale for the ideas presented. Depending on the client's reaction to the team's interpretation of the brief, the team will either be asked to go ahead in developing the work, or will be asked to rework their ideas.

The go-ahead stage may include a decision to test the advertising in research prior to full production of the advert.

(d)   **Production of advert(s)**

Some simple advertising executions will be carried out almost entirely in-house by the advertising agency. For more complex executions, the agency will buy in specialist functions on behalf of the client.

Whilst production is ongoing, the media department will be involved in the actual commitment of the media budget. Dates, times and positions will be agreed with media owners.

During this stage, there will be continuous liaison between the account executive and the client. The client is likely to attend some of the key production stages such as filming or photography of the commercial.

If time allows, further research may take place to identify the need for any additional changes.

(e)   **The campaign appears**

The time span between the briefing of the account executive by the client and the campaign appearing can be as little as six or eight weeks for a simple photographic newspaper execution, to 20 weeks plus for an animated TV commercial. Once the campaign has appeared, it is important that it is properly evaluated against the objectives initially set.

Members of the account team who work directly on the client's business in creating a campaign, are those the client is most likely to come into contact with, although the main point of contact will of course be the account executive. There are other behind the scenes staff with whom the account executive must liaise but who will not have direct client contact.

(i)   **Accounts department**, responsible for billing the client and paying agency invoices
(ii)   **Vouchers department** checks that press adverts appear
(iii) **Traffic department** ensures that jobs are taken through their different stages on time

A large agency may additionally have an **information** or **library service**, and **legal department**.

Marketing at Work

An IPA (*Institute for Practitioners in Advertising*) booklet 'Getting the most out of the client – agency partnership' suggests the following checklist of questions.

1   Are the client's **corporate objectives**, and the **marketing objectives** that derive from them, entirely clear to both parties? Have the marketing and communications tasks been quantified, together with their financial and profit implications?

2   Are the marketing and communications planners fully informed about **relevant factors in the commercial environment**, particularly:

- Actual and potential customers
- Product advantages and limitations
- Competitors
- Current or predictable marketing problems
- Product and marketing development plans?

3   Has sufficient **lead-time** been allowed for planning purposes?

4   Has the agency's **creative policy** been fully thought through and discussed in relation to the defined communications tasks?

5   Do the various creative manifestations (whether advertisements in paid media, explanatory literature, direct mail shots, audio-visual and other sales aids, exhibition stands or press publicity) **express the policy** effectively?

6   Have the **media plan and budget** been fully thought through and discussed? Are both agency and client convinced that they are as cost-effective as available information will permit?

7   If **results** in one area or another have not come up to expectations, has there been a serious effort to find out *why*, instead of shrugging it off or explaining it away?

8   Is there sufficient readiness not just to change for change's sake, but progressively to **improve performance** within an agreed long-term policy?

9   Is the level of **financial and administrative control** satisfactory on both sides?

10   Is the level of **client-agency communications** – in both directions – as good as it should be?

11   Is there **mutual understanding and respect** between the individuals working on the account, on the client and on the agency side?

7 International agency selection and management

FAST FORWARD

Clients and their **agencies** can choose to handle **international advertising campaigns** in a number of ways. Although a variety of factors will influence the management of any particular campaign, the organisational structure of the client company will play an important role.

Some agencies have **expanded abroad** by setting up their own overseas subsidiaries. Others have established alliances with local agencies already in existence.

There are arguments both for and against using the services of an **international advertising agency**. The current preference amongst large clients is to centralise advertising with an internationally based agency.

7.1 International agencies

Over the last forty years, as companies have expanded their operations internationally, so too have advertising agencies. Many of the large agencies have developed internationally, either by setting up branch offices in foreign countries or by merging with or acquiring local agencies.

Some agencies expanding abroad prefer to establish international networks or alliances where local offices are not wholly controlled. The argument is that local partners with a stake in the agency will be motivated to produce superior work.

Media independents have mirrored the pattern of agency development and many belong to international media planning and buying groups.

The trend amongst clients is towards the centralisation of advertising. Many large companies believe **international brands** are best served by an agency operating internationally.

7.2 Selection

Selecting an international advertising agency will follow a series of well defined stages. Locating suitable agency candidates is the first step in the process.

(a) **Initial search**. Prospective clients will probably be aware of the large multinational agencies based within their own country.

(b) A **shortlist** of agencies will then be drawn up, usually on the basis of their current work and past track record.

(c) The **client will then visit** the local offices of those agencies for a series of credentials presentations. These initial visits will help to form an opinion about which candidates should be requested to formally pitch for the client's business. All agencies involved in the pitch should be given the same written brief to follow.

(d) The **agency's response to the brief** will usually involve a formal presentation backed by a written proposal document with several important features.

  (i) The agency's interpretation of the client's advertising problem
  (ii) The creative and media strategy which will ensure objectives are met
  (iii) Control mechanisms to be used
  (iv) Timing schedules
  (v) Allocation of responsibilities
  (vi) Costings
  (vii) Terms and conditions of business

(e) The **final selection decision** will have to take into account many client side factors such as the client's organisational structure and management style, the number of brands to be advertised and the degree to which brands penetrate different markets.

Other criteria for selection would include the following.

(a) The **types of advertising** and other communications services offered

(b) Level of **expertise** in the client's field of work

(c) The agency's **international creative track record**

(d) The **balance** within the agency of campaigns handled for local clients and those handled for international ones

(e) Whether the agency has **strong local offices** in the client's home and other key markets

(f)   The extent to which the agency's **culture and management** style fits with that of the prospective client

(g)   The **potential conflict** with existing business handled within the agency network

(h)   The **control and co-ordination** procedures in place

Action Programme 4

Your company is about to launch a group of new consumer toiletries products in the Middle East. What sorts of assurance would you want from an advertising agency pitching for this account?

The **advantages** of using an **international agency**

- Less duplication and dilution of effort on the part of agency and client
- Centralised control of all advertising effort
- Speedy response across markets
- Pooling of talent and ideas from the entire agency network
- Specialised resources available
- Standardised working methods by the agency
- Reduced costs due to economies of scale

Possible **criticisms of international agencies**

- They provide an uneven quality of service in their different branches
- They produce bland campaigns
- Quality control suffers due to handling hundreds of campaigns simultaneously
- Clients have to tailor their campaigns to suit the conventions of the agency
- Small or medium sized clients suffer a lack of attention from senior staff
- High staff turnover rates exist amongst creative employees

7.3 Local or international?

Despite the increasing presence and power of international advertising and media networks, **independent local agencies** exist in the markets of most countries. Some companies prefer to retain country by country agency arrangements, believing local agencies to be **creatively closer** to their own markets.

Cherry picking **local agencies** is an appropriate strategy for the client who has only a small portfolio of products to be advertised in a limited number of markets.

7.4 Management issues

External factors, such as **market diversity,** segmentation and competition affect the type of co-ordination chosen. **Internal factors,** unrelated to the market, can also dictate the management and co-ordination of international promotions.

(a)   **Organisation structure**

(i)   **Local autonomy**. Each subsidiary of an international agency may act as a separate profit centre, attracting its own clients in the home market. Upon appointment, the subsidiary which has brought in the client takes the role of lead agency office, with overall supervision of the client's account.

(ii)   **Central control**. Alternatively, an agency may exert strong central control on regional offices from its headquarters base.

(b) **Organisation culture**. Managers may have different assumptions as to how advertising ought to be done, and it might be a basic hidden assumption that decisions are taken at the top or, on the other hand, by giving local managers their head.

(c) The need for **co-ordinated marketing communications**; firms with worldwide exposure may need central control of marketing communications to ensure they are, in fact, co-ordinated.

7.5 Control

7.5.1 The advertiser

A number of management and control problems need attention.

(a) **Budgets**. If advertising budgets will be split among the different units, the money might be spent less effectively than if control is centralised.

(b) **Timing**. The local advertising campaigns might need to be co-ordinated so that the production side can cope with demand. This is especially true if the firm is an exporter, with a number of local sales offices and warehouses. Local advertisers may generate demands that cannot be met.

(c) Some central review is necessary so that good ideas can be passed around within the group.

(d) **Expertise**. The person responsible for advertising in a 'small' subsidiary may not have a great deal of expertise and may rely too much on local advertising agencies for ideas, rather than controlling the output directly.

(e) Finally, all advertising campaigns need to be **evaluated** for effectiveness.

  (i) Local campaigns may have different objectives, and so appropriate effectiveness measures need to be outlined.

  (ii) It is easier to measure message recall and media buyer efficiency in advanced economies, and there may not be the facilities in less developed countries, even if these promise high growth.

7.5.2 Between client and agency

Relationships with agencies need to be managed. In many agencies, there will be an 'account manager' responsible for overall liaisons with client. It is in the agency's interests to establish a long-term relationship with the client.

The agency's account executive is a lynchpin, in communicating the client's needs to the creative team. The agency must also be able to liaise, where necessary, lower down the chain of command, and to communicate to the units of the business, in clear terms, the objectives of the promotion campaign.

7.5.3 Within the agency

Within the agency, there are the following issues of management and control.

(a) A general problem of **central direction vs local freedom**. This we have already discussed, in terms of tailoring local advertising campaigns or adopting a standard approach.

(b) **Conflicts of interest**: how free are local offices to tout for business, if this involves offending a major client?

(c) How do you co-ordinate the activities of **different creative teams**?

(d) There may exist problems of corporate culture, particularly if an agency grows up as the result of a takeover.

(e)   **Performance appraisal** and culture.

(f)   Many human resources issues are relevant (eg corporate culture, details of organisation structure).

7.6 Current client/agency issues

As markets expand, clients are likely to forsake traditional, vertical organisational structures where brands are managed on a country by country basis, in favour of a horizontal structure which cuts across country divides. This implies **brand and product management at a centralised level** and may result in a preference for centralised agencies. Consequences might be as follows.

(a)   **Clients** are likely to become more demanding of their agencies, as clients strive to ensure that their advertising is accountable and effective. In America, the trend is already towards payment by results. Clients are also likely to demand a larger base of expertise in terms of communications and research services provided.

(b)   **Agencies** will continue to expand internationally to meet the needs of their clients. This may lead to a concentration in advertising agency ownership as the large agencies seek to expand still further by way of acquisition and merger.

(c)   Agency expansion will also mean that an increasing number of local agency offices will be established in new markets (eg Russia, Eastern Europe, China). Agencies may need to take a **long-term perspective** on emerging markets. Initial resource requirements will be high.

Media buying and selling power continues to concentrate. On the one hand, large international media independents hold consolidated buying power and have the ability to level volume or other discounts. On the other hand there is increasing concentration in global media ownership.

Exam tip

> An interesting angle on this topic was taken in the December 2006 exam, where (in the role of a communications agency executive) you were asked to discuss the advantages and disadvantages (to the client) of moving from a local to a global MC strategy *and* identify what the impact on the *agency* would be from such a change.

8 Controlling the marketing communications industry

There are two types of control in the marketing communications industry in the UK, and they are specifically mentioned in the syllabus.

- **Voluntary**. This provides self regulation to promote high standards of practice, often in areas that are difficult to judge in law.

- **Statutory** protection afforded to consumers by the legal framework.

8.1 Self regulation

The self regulatory system of advertising control consists of the following bodies, between them covering non-broadcast and broadcast media.

(a)   **The Advertising Standards Authority (ASA)**

(i)   This covers the **non-broadcast media** (press, posters, cinema, direct mail, sales promotion, lists and databases), and ensures that the **British Code of Advertising Practice** functions in the public interest. This is the body to which the public and industry complain about advertisements that are not '**legal, decent, honest and truthful**'.

(ii)   It **scrutinises advertisements** in order to anticipate potential complaints and problems

(iii)   It provides a **copywriting advice service** to advertisers

(b)   The **Committee of Advertising Practice (CAP)** runs in parallel with the ASA and co-ordinates the trade and professional organisations that comprise the advertising business. Together, the ASA and the CAP ensure that the British Code of Advertising Practice (as put together by CAP) is followed.

(c)   The **Independent Television Commission (ITC)** governs television advertising with its own code of Advertising Standards and Practice, which has the force of law.

(d)   Radio advertising is regulated by the **Radio Authority (RA)**, which also has its own code with statutory force.

(e)   Bodies representing particular sectors in the industry, such as the **Institute of Sales Promotion** and the **Direct Selling Association**, also have their own codes of practice.

8.2 Statutory regulation

This system of self regulation (which is not punishable by the courts) is designed to operate alongside the **legal protection** that is now afforded to the consumer by statute, via government departments including the Office of Fair Trading. Criminal and civil prosecution could be expected by those who break the laws contained within the following (in the UK):

- Trade Descriptions Act 1968
- Fair Trading Act 1973
- Unfair Contract Terms Act 1977 and Unfair Terms in Consumer Contracts Regulations 1999
- Food Act 1984
- Weights and Measures Act 1985
- Consumer Protection Act 1987
- Privacy and Electronic Communications Regulations 2003

Chapter Roundup

- Marketing communicators need to be fully aware of the range of **qualitative and quantitative research data** that is available or obtainable and also of the limitations of research.

- Clients can choose to handle their advertising function in a number of ways. Very large advertisers may keep the function internal to the company. Alternatively, a client can buy in expertise from a **full service advertising agency**, or combine services from a **creative shop** and a **media independent**.

- It is the responsibility of the client to provide a **full campaign briefing** for any new piece of advertising work. An oral brief is usually backed up by a written document. The account executive in turn will provide a creative briefing for the specific use of the creative team.

- A variety of agency staff will handle the **workflow** on a client's account. The account executive acts as the key intermediary between agency and client.

- The **process of selecting a new agency** involves initial search; credentials presentation and shortlist; competitive pitch and final selection. The client will gauge competing agencies against set criteria such as expertise in the client's field of business, previous work handled, resources provided and costs. The final selection decision will involve a judgement about how well the agency has answered the client brief.

- Managing the relationship requires **trust**, a free flow of **information**, proper allocation of **responsibilities** and careful **control**.

- Clients and their **agencies** can choose to handle **international advertising campaigns** in a number of ways. Although a variety of factors will influence the management of any particular campaign, the organisational structure of the client company will play an important role.

- Some agencies have **expanded abroad** by setting up their own overseas subsidiaries. Others have established alliances with local agencies already in existence.

- There are arguments both for and against using the services of an **international advertising agency**. The current preference amongst large clients is to centralise advertising with an internationally based agency.

- The **standardisation versus adaptation** debate has implications for agency management. If campaigns are totally standardised across markets, the lead market agency office will take the major role in designing and implementing the global campaign.

Quick Quiz

1   Most companies use one agency to handle a portfolio of techniques.

    True   ☐

    False   ☐

2   Why does it often make no commercial sense to retain in-house the full range of marketing expertise?

    A   Agencies deal with a number of clients and so have relevant up-to-date experience
    B   Each marketing specialism is likely to be only called upon infrequently
    C   Competitive deals on media buying are difficult to achieve for small marketing departments
    D   All of the above

3   The marketing communications industry consists of four principal groups.

    M..........
    A..........
    C..........
    S..........

4   What services can direct marketing agencies offer?

5   How does a full service agency differ from a media independent?

6   What influence has the development of the Internet had on the formal agency selection process?

7   List the elements in the creative brief.

    N..........   B..........
    D..........   B..........
    B..........   C..........
    K..........   T..........
    C..........   P..........

8   What role does the Advertising Standards Authority (ASA) play?

Answers to Quick Quiz

1   False

2   D

3   **M**edia
   Agencies
   Clients
   Support organisations

4   Check your answer against Section 2.2

5   A full service agency provides a complete advertising service encompassing creative work, production, media planning and buying. A media independent provides media services (such as planning and buying) only.

6   With the arrival of new media and Internet technology, campaigns are having to be resolved in days rather than weeks, so a long drawn out selection process is inappropriate.

7   **N**ame   **B**usiness objectives
   Description   **B**ackground to the brief
   Budget   **C**ommunication objectives
   Key deadlines   **T**arget market
   Company background **P**roposition

8   It covers the non-broadcast media and ensures that the British Code of Advertising Practice functions in the public interest. This is the body that receives complaints about advertisements that are not 'legal, decent, honest and truthful'.

Action Programme Review

1   Each newspaper will have presented the aspects of the data which showed itself in the best light. The *Sunday Times* may have increased overall circulation, and increased the percentage of AB readers. The *Sunday Telegraph* may have lost circulation (you will know from the *Sunday Times*), but have increased its colour magazine readership. The *Guardian* may show a large *percentage* gain in readership, and an increasing number of ABC1 readers. Only by researching back to the original ABC report will you be able to ascertain the truth, but you can come close by cross-referencing the data provided by each, and filling in the gaps from the rivals and by inference. Beware the switch from real numbers to percentages!

2   Market Research Limited will provide retailers of different kinds of products with useful information as well as the product manufacturers, most likely consumer goods given this description. Children and Youth – companies producing goods and services aimed at the youth markets who want to conduct research but may not have the resources to undertake surveys independently.

3   (a)   *Project name and description*

The project needs a meaningful name to refer to. The specifics of the product along with the style are needed.

(b)   *Budget*

Client and agency needs to be clear about what the budget covers. For example, how many new photographs need to be shot? This will have a bearing on the production costs. The budget for media will determine the choice for media selection. The agency can alter the resources according to the job.

(c)   *Key deadlines*

Important key deadlines must be listed. The agency should draw up a timetable for presentation of design concepts, proofs, final proofs and so on.

(d)   *Company background*

A brief description of the company will assist the agency in getting a 'feel' for an appropriate design.

(e)   *Business objectives*

This will help the agency position the campaign (or whatever the project involves).

(f)   *Background to the brief*

For example, is this a complete redesign, or just a freshen up?

(g)   *Communications objectives*

The primary objective may be to increase sales. This can be incorporated in the design.

(h)   *Target audience*

The agency needs a full description of the characteristics of the audience. This will enable them to design the campaign with them in mind.

(i)   *Proposition*

Be clear what the USP is. For example, you cannot have high quality, cheap products, top brands and commodity goods all in the same catalogue. With a clear picture, the agency will be able to focus on producing what is required without constantly referring back to the client.

4   Ideally, the agency should be able to assure the client of experience in both consumer market generally and the toiletries market in particular. The agency should have local offices in a number of the Middle East states in which the client does business and be used to handling local and international campaigns in those countries.

The agency must demonstrate knowledge concerning cultural, legal, and media difficulties which may be encountered and be able to propose solutions for overcoming these problems. Proof of successful campaign outcomes for other British based clients advertising in related markets would also be reassuring.

Now try Questions 12 and 13 at the end of the Study Text

Question and Answer bank

1 Opinion leaders

Many marketing communication campaigns make use of opinion leaders and opinion formers. Using examples to illustrate your points, explain how and why these personal influencers might be used.

(25 marks)

2 Different sectors

Using consumer and business-to-business marketing communication campaigns to illustrate your answer, explain the differences in the purpose and use of marketing communications in these two different sectors.

(25 marks)

3 Marketing communications strategy

Prepare an outline of a talk you are to give to a group of Marketing Managers on the subject of Marketing Communications Strategy. Describe the key elements of the communications planning process, showing how marketing communications strategy is distinguishable from, though part of, overall marketing strategy. Plan to illustrate your talk with examples of strategy drawn from your experience. **(25 marks)**

4 Promotional mix

In your capacity as an entrepreneur who has established a successful regional marketing communications agency you have been asked to make a presentation to an audience of local business people.

Prepare notes for this presentation entitled 'The Strategic Significance of the Promotional Mix'. You aim to cover each of the main tools of the promotional mix and provide brief examples to illustrate each point.

(25 marks)

5 Push and pull

An office furniture manufacturing company is about to launch a new range of products.

(a)   Explain what is meant by a push communication strategy and contrast this with a pull communication strategy.

(13 marks)

(b)   Briefly outline the main characteristics of the marketing communications mix used to reach members of the marketing channel.

(12 marks)

(Total = 25 marks)

6 Internet based communications

For many organisations, business-to-business marketing communications have been transformed by the development of the Internet and related digital technologies. Prepare notes for a meeting at which you are expected to argue the case for the development of Internet based marketing communications for a business or company of your choice.

(25 marks)

7 Managing global communications

Determine and explain the key issues that an international advertising agency might advise a client about when discussing the development of an co-ordinated marketing communications strategy for consumer products across several countries. **(25 marks)**

8 Measuring success

As manager of a small/medium sized direct marketing business, producing and distributing toiletries for a number of niche markets, prepare a short report for your managing director evaluating the methods available to measure the success of your promotional strategy. **(25 marks)**

9 Distribution channels

As the Marketing Operations Manager of a tour operations business that targets package holidays at the 55 and over age group, you have been asked by your Marketing Director to review your distribution strategy.

(a)   Outline the various channels of distribution available. **(7 marks)**
(b)   Identify a set of criteria for their evaluation. **(8 marks)**
(c)   Recommend an appropriate strategy for your target market. **(10 marks)**

(Total = 25 marks)

10 Internet

Evaluate the ways in which the rapid growth of the Internet is changing the way businesses communicate with their customers, suppliers and within their own organisations. **(25 marks)**

11 Managing outside suppliers

You have been asked to write an article for *Marketing Business* that describes the types of outside resources that various Marketing Directors use, suggests how outside suppliers should be briefed, and indicates how the relationship with such suppliers might be managed and controlled. You should use examples throughout the article to illustrate the points you raise. **(25 marks)**

12 Agency restructuring

It has been noted that many advertising agencies have failed to adapt and restructure themselves in order to keep pace with the increasing demands and international communications strategies of their clients. What are the reasons for this apparent incompatibility and suggest how agencies might adjust to better meet their client needs. **(25 marks)**

13 AP Engineering

AP Engineering (AP) is a privately owned civil engineering company, employing approximately 4,200 people in the Asia Pacific region. The company designs and manages the building of major civil engineering projects in a variety of vertical market sectors.

The company wins contracts by bidding for client-specified projects and offering the best (perceived) value for money. The problem with this approach is that the appointed civil engineering company has limited input to the original requirements/specification and, as soon as the project is completed, its involvement is normally terminated. Perhaps even more importantly, the margins earned on such projects are notoriously slim, so in order to grow the business, higher margins need to be generated.

Following a review of the business, AP's new strategy is based upon a total engineering service, one that centres on client needs and their total project requirements, rather than the previous engineering/product focus. In other words, the company now adopts a relationship marketing approach. The emphasis is upon providing added value by shifting the offering both upstream and downstream. Therefore, AP Engineering now provides three connected offerings.

(a)   The front-end work, which involves undertaking the planning and risk analysis work for its clients
(b)   The core work, which is about the design and build aspect of the project
(c)   The tail-end work, which is essentially Facilities Management

Among the many advantages this strategic approach presents, there are two significant benefits. The first lies in the substantially higher margins that the front-and tail-end work attracts. The second concerns the reduced 'resource' wastage by being able to help accurately define the client problem at the earliest possible stage in the project life cycle.

In order to develop and implement this strategy, AP has had to evolve a new skills mix, namely Asset Management and Facilities Management skills. AP chose to purchase a number of small consultancies and formed alliances with other targeted companies specialising in these particular skill areas.

Whilst this might sound reasonably straightforward, AP has had to address further issues concerning the development of a suitable commercial culture for the established employees and those new to the enlarged organisation. The company now views each project as a commercial activity and all employees must adopt increased levels of commercial awareness (eg project risk assessment, the importance of working within budget and invoicing on time). In addition, the employees of the newly acquired organisations have to be incorporated into the values and corporate philosophy of the new company culture. A further issue concerns the way the company presents itself to clients and other key stakeholders.

The organisation is deliberately seeking to develop closer client relationships based upon trust and empathy. It has done this by improving understanding of its clients' business, by getting involved right from the start of a new project, by completing projects on time and within budget, and by a willingness to share sensitive information. It also helps that the AP Engineering brand is highly visible and has developed a credible reputation based upon clients' perceived value.

The level of communication frequency between client and AP Engineering varies across the life of a project. There is a great deal of communication at the outset of a project as the brief is determined by all parties. As the project moves to the design phase, the level of communication tends to fall. However, projects often run tight on their deadlines; hence interorganisational, and even intraorganisational communication levels intensify in an attempt to resolve on-site problems as quickly as possible.

The company realises that personal contact is the most significant communication tool used in the development and maintenance of client relationships but the company is undecided about its communication strategy, and has asked you, in your capacity as Marketing Communications Consultant, for your advice.

Required

As a Marketing Communications Consultant, advise AP with regard to the following questions:

(a)   Identify a communication strategy that AP should pursue in the next year.   **(8 marks)**

(b)   What is the justification for your strategy?   **(12 marks)**

(c)   Which tools of the promotional mix might best be used to implement this strategy? Why?
                                                                                                     (12 marks)

(d)   What might be the core message that needs to be delivered over the next year?   **(6 marks)**

(e)   Make a list of the issues that AP might consider before implementing a co-ordinated marketing
        communications policy.   **(12 marks)**

                                                                                        (Total = 50 marks)

1 Opinion leaders

> **Tutorial note**. You must understand the difference between an opinion leader and former, which could form the start of your answer. The use of diffusion of innovation models can help, providing a link with the marketing communications strategy, but this is not the only issue to be considered. Word-of-mouth campaigns could also be discussed.
>
> This response to this question will be based around an understanding of communication flows, and then an appraisal of the opinion former and opinion leader concepts.

Multi-step Flows of Communication

The flow of communication in a campaign was first considered to be linear, in that information flowed from a **source** through a **channel** to a **receiver**, who then provided **feedback**. This interpretation proved to be inaccurate in that it failed to account for the many variables that can impact on the communication process. One of the main variables is the **influence of other people** as they shape and redirect the **flow, content and intended meaning** of messages.

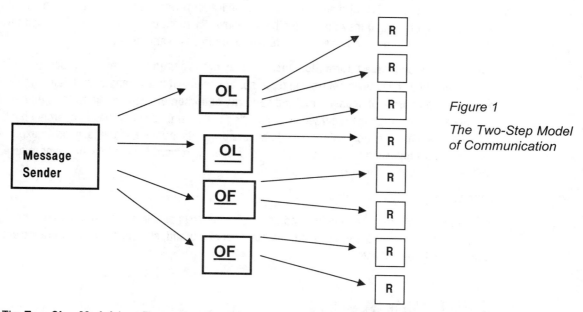

Figure 1

The Two-Step Model of Communication

The **Two-Step Model** (see Figure 1) and multi-step flow models of communication reflect the potential impact that these individuals might have on communications.

Types of Influencers

There are two main types of influencer, **opinion leaders** and **opinion formers**. The first are usually members of a peer group who have a particular interest and knowledge about a product category or area of interest. They may be friends, family or work colleagues to whom others (**opinion followers**) turn for advice and reassurance when contemplating a particularly significant purchase. They believe the information they receive is both **credible and unbiased** when considered in the light of many commercial messages.

Opinion formers on the other hand are people who are designated as expert and knowledgeable about a particular topic or subject. Very often these people are public figures and it is the nature of their work that bestows the perceived expertise. Opinion formers therefore help shape the thoughts of others by providing information and advice that opinion followers value and believe is credible. Pharmacists, motoring journalists and qualified accountants, for example, can provide **credible information** about medicines, cars and taxation issues respectively for those active in the decision making process. This information may be **communicated person to person**, or through broadcast or print **media**.

In a marketing context this is an important factor because if it is possible to identify and **direct marketing communication messages to those people who are capable of influencing** other people, then the implications for the efficiency and effectiveness of marketing communications activities is enormous. A popular advertising format is to use a 'slice of life' approach, where typical members of the target market are observed discussing issues, and one of the characters uses the sponsor's product to resolve the difficulty (eg soap powders and shampoo).

Opinion leaders provide information for a number of reasons. People like to talk about their product purchases because it can relieve post purchase tension, bestow status on them and provide a means of advising and showing care for others (in this case those considering a similar purchase).

Whilst it is difficult to isolate opinion leaders and target them directly, many are known to be **innovators** or part of the **early adopters** group within the **process of diffusion**. These people are actively interested in their topic/area and seek out information in advance of the general population. Identification therefore is helped because they are more likely to attend exhibitions, access specific websites and read the specialist press. For example, when Sony launched the mini disc it targeted specialist music equipment retailers and held premium prices. The hi-fi enthusiasts (opinion leaders) were keen to buy the latest technology (regardless of price) and they then told others (followers) about their discovery, which fed further demand and then allowed Sony to release the product through mainstream outlets.

Opinion formers provide information because they are required to do so, either because it is part of the job, because they have been contracted to do so, or because it is a means of maintaining their own position. Some forms of **sponsorship and celebrity endorsement** can be regarded as opinion forming, if only because they might be regarded as supporting the central object of the sponsorship itself. David Ginola may act as an endorser for L'Oreal haircare products, but he is not known as an expert in haircare. He is seen as supporting the brand in return for a specific reward (which may however induce cynicism in some of the target audience!).

Conclusion

Recognition of the role that opinion leaders and formers can play in assisting the marketing communication process is important if the potential of a brand, and especially new brands and product launches, is to be fulfilled.

2 Different sectors

Tutorial note. This question requires you to explain how the purpose and use of marketing communications differs, not just explain what the differences are between the two sectors. A good answer discusses marketing communications by exploring what the tasks are in the two sectors, how the sector characteristics demand a different approach, and how strategy and tactics can be accommodated through different approaches and the deployment of marketing communication tools.

Introduction

This essay sets out to identify the main differences between **business-to-business** and **business-to-consumer** sectors, and highlights the **impact of these differences on the marketing communications strategies**. It offers examples of each sector and concludes that the differences are perhaps becoming less pronounced, as companies from both sectors are using a variety of promotional tools and pay considerable attention to the role of **branding**.

	Consumer Markets	Business Markets	Impact on Marketing Communications
No of buyers	Many	Few	Personal selling more relevant in b-t-b markets. Mass communication methods like advertising more often used in consumer markets
Decision making unit	The family	Gatekeepers Influencers Deciders Buyers	Targeting is easier for the consumer markets. Many different types of media and message may be necessary to reach the different members of the DMUs in b-t-b markets
Buyer Behaviour	Influenced by intangible and tangible differences	Rational, based on benefits	Branding important in consumer markets. May also be important in business markets if the buyer is a risk avoider and where there are not many perceived functional differences
	Impulse purchase	Likely to be extended decision making	Sales promotion less relevant in b-t-b markets
	Price may be more important	Functional benefits more important	Impact on marketing communications messages

Main Differences

The main difference between business-to-business communications can be seen in the choice of marketing communications methods and messages. This becomes clear when we consider the communications strategies for the following companies.

Siebel – selling customer relationship management (CRM) systems

This company will rely largely on **personal selling**, with a sales team made up of a number of different experts. Each expert will communicate with his or her opposite number in the client company.

They may do some **trade advertising** but in different magazines – the marketing manager will hear about the benefits of data mining systems in a direct marketing magazine, whereas the IT manager will hear about the technicalities of the system in the IT trade press.

Public relations activity will concentrate on press releases, using a case study approach to reduce perceived risk.

Direct marketing methods will be used alongside **exhibitions and road shows**.

The buying of a full CRM system is extremely expensive, and so the amount spent prior to and post purchase will be high. As the **distribution chain** is likely to be short, the **push strategy** will concentrate on personal selling, allowing control of message and methods.

The message will vary, depending on the role in the decision-making unit, but is likely to be technical. **Profile strategies** are becoming increasingly important here since by having a good profile (and hence brand name) the initial approach to a new customer will be eased.

Thomson Holidays

Much **above-the-line** activity and **sales promotion** activity will be used, to stimulate interest and get a booking from the decision making unit. The whole family is involved and Thomson has recognised this by providing special videotapes for the youngsters showing them what the holiday will be like.

Branding is very important, and as this is a **service**, trust must be established at the beginning. **Membership of trade bodies** will help. Exhibitions are less likely to be used although they may attend lifestyle shows at relevant times. Communications with the marketing channel and a **push strategy** is important here, along with possibly some **direct marketing** activity.

It is important to note, especially in the context of the travel industry, that the adoption of new methods of promotion and booking via the **Internet** has removed some of the reliance on distributors and agents. Public relations is important, and sponsorship of popular television shows like 'Wish you were here?' develop the profile of the company and keeps it in the memory of the target audience.

Conclusion

It can be seen that there are differences between the two sectors, but these differences are becoming blurred as business-to-business markets realise the importance of branding and profiling and consumer markets start to adopt CRM techniques through the opportunities offered by new technologies, especially the Internet.

3 Marketing communications strategy

Tutorial note. This challenging question requires a well structured answer. Students are required to have a thorough knowledge of:

(a) the business and marketing planning processes

(b) the marketing communications planning process

(c) how to co-ordinate the two processes

(d) examples of practical and successful communication strategies derived from such an co-ordinated process

REPORT

To: Marketing Managers
From: Marketing Communications Manager
Date: June 20XX
Ref: Presentation on the subject of marketing communication strategy

1   Audience/objectives

The audience consists of marketing managers. We can assume therefore that they are reasonably well versed in the actual **marketing planning process**.

Although they will be knowledgeable about the planning process their involvement in the detail will vary from person to person. Some will have a close working knowledge; others will only have limited experience of planning directly themselves.

The objectives of the talk can therefore be defined as follows.

(a) To show how **marketing communication planning is an integral part of the overall company planning process**.

(b) To demonstrate that **without this link communications planning would be less effective**.

(c) To illustrate the talk with **practical examples** of strategy.

The strategic marketing and tactical communications planning process within the overall marketing planning process

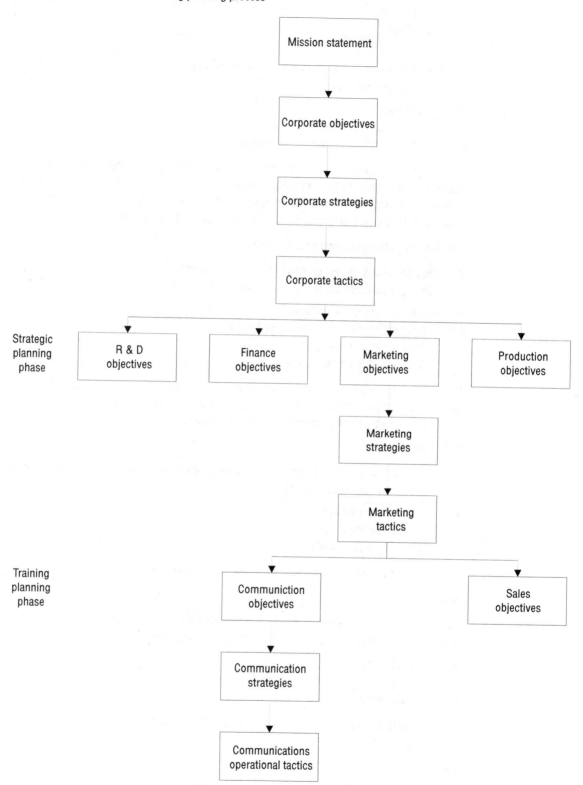

2 The total planning process

It is vital that marketing managers understand the corporate planning process and the role of marketing planning within it. Furthermore, because marketing communications accounts for a significant share of the marketing mix, it is important also to understand the co-ordination of the marketing communications planning process.

Each level of the organisation has a **hierarchy** of:

- Objectives
- Strategy
- Tactics

The tactics of the upper level then become the objectives of the next level down in the organisation. The levels we can consider usually are:

- Corporate
- Functional (including marketing)
- Activity (including marketing communications)

Clearly the actual situation will vary from company to company according to size, nature of business, and experience of planning. In some predominantly marketing organisations, the link between corporate and marketing objectives will be a very close one. The following diagram shows **how marketing objectives will fit with overall company objectives**.

3   **The details of the planning process itself**

The **situation analysis**, which starts the process, can be seen as part of the overall corporate and marketing analysis and audit process. Four areas of analysis are carried out.

- Internal company analysis
- Analysis of the market and customers
- Analysis of competitors
- Analysis of the external environment

In the case of marketing communications planning in particular, note is made of any strengths, weaknesses, opportunities or threats which have a direct bearing on possible communication solutions. The stages of planning are then as follows.

Objectives

Objectives can be developed under the following headings, depending upon the goals of the campaign for the product in question.

- **Market penetration** or
- **Market development or**
- **Product development**

Each of these broad areas will require a different communications objective.

Strategy

Strategy in communication terms is then best developed by reference to particular target audiences. The most useful approach to this is to work through the steps of:

- **Segmentation**
- **Targeting**
- **Positioning**

Positioning is achieved by a judicious choice of the marketing mix, including promotions or marketing communications.

Tactics

To help to remember a systematic approach to the tactics of marketing communications we can use 3Ms.

- Which **methods**?
- Which **media**?
- Which **messages**?

Implementation

Before the plan can be implemented, the following elements need to be defined.

- **Responsibilities**
- **Timescales**
- **Budgets**

Control

Finally it is necessary to control the effectiveness of the marketing communications process by measuring the achievement of the objectives against the original planned measures and budget.

4 Examples of strategies

The most powerful examples of marketing communications strategies are those linked directly to the corporate and marketing strategies. A number of such examples are given below.

(a) *Boddington's beer*

Whitbread's marketing objective was to launch the beer nationally in a controlled manner. The communication strategy was to promote the brand as an authentic regional beer brewed in Manchester using the slogan 'The Cream of Manchester'. This reflected the creamy full head obtained from this cask conditioned beer. The media strategy was to use the rear covers of colour magazines to promote the golden colour of the product. Television was not used initially in part because of limited brewing capacity.

(b) *PPP Healthcare*

PPP were facing increasing competition in the health insurance market, especially from the commercial insurance companies such as Norwich Union. The PPP management decided to plan for an increase in market share, to distinguish themselves from their rivals and to rebrand. Marketing communications obviously had an important role to play in this. To increase the awareness of the new company name (PPP Healthcare) and to reposition itself as a healthcare rather than an insurance company, PPP chose to use a television and national press campaign which stressed the support it provides to customers.

(c) *BMW cars*

BMW cars were exported to the UK mainly as performance cars. BMW (GB) was established in 1979 with the ambitious aim of tripling UK sales by 1990, whilst maintaining high profit-margins. The 'Ultimate Driving Machine' campaign was developed and is still running 17 years later. The marketing communications objectives were:

(i) To enrich the image of the vehicle
(ii) To build positive aspects of the image
(iii) To raise the brand's image

These objectives have been met over a prolonged period in spite of the sales targets meaning that there would be more models on the road, making them ultimately less exclusive. An advertising strategy was developed partly through TV, but mainly through quality colour magazines.

5 Conclusions

These are examples of successful marketing communications strategies which have produced outstanding business results. This has only been possible because the management of those companies have had clear business and marketing objectives which in turn have provided the drive for clear marketing communications plans.

The marketing communications planning process has therefore to be a close and integrated component of the overall planning process. One way of achieving this is to use the SOSTAC planning framework which is memorable, easy to apply and powerful in its effect.

4 Promotional mix

'The Strategic Significance of the Promotional Mix'

by

CIM Student

Slide 1 – Introduction and Welcome

May I take this opportunity to thank you for inviting me to talk to you about marketing communications and in particular the strategic impact of the various elements of the promotional mix.

Slide 2 – Agenda

As you can see, my plan for this session is to first consider the elements of the promotional mix before examining the strategic significance and benefits of an co-ordinated approach to marketing communications practice.

The promotional plan
Strategic significance
Integration
Benefits and difficulties
Conclusions
Questions

I shall be using a few examples to illustrate my points and, of course, I welcome questions at any time, although there will be some time at the end to discuss points of interest.

Slide 3 – The Promotional Mix

Marketing communications is just a part of the total marketing plan or marketing mix. These two elements are often confused, but for clarity the marketing mix is composed of a number of different elements such as price, product, distribution, people and promotional activities. It is these elements in combination that provide the overall marketing plan.

One of these elements, promotion, provides a powerful means by which a marketing mix is presented to its target audience. **The successful communication of the marketing mix is paramount if target markets are to understand the offer being made to them**.

In order to effect this communication, there are a number of **promotional tools** that are used or 'mixed' together. These are:

- Advertising
- Sales promotion
- Public relations
- Personal selling
- Direct marketing

By mixing the tools together in different ways to meet the needs of the marketing plan, it is possible to achieve one of a number of **goals**. These are to:

Create awareness
To persuade
To remind/reassure
To differentiate

The first of these is to **make an audience aware of an offering**, existence or benefits. Before anyone can form an opinion or attitude, it is necessary to be informed of a product's existence.

Alternatively, awareness levels may already be adequate, so the task becomes that of **persuading an audience to try a product**, or to resist defecting to a competitive product offering.

A third requirement may be to **remind and/or reassure** an audience of a product or of the experiences associated with a previous purchase.

Finally, communications can be used to **differentiate a product offering** and set it aside from the competition.

Slide 4 – Strategic Significance

Plans are the articulation of strategy, a means of bringing together the various means by which a strategy is implemented and goals achieved.

Promotional strategy is about the overall direction and focus of communications. There are three main options: a pull strategy, a push strategy and a profile strategy.

A **pull strategy** is concerned with communications directed at end users or customers.

A **push strategy** concerns those channel partnerships formed to deliver products and services to end users, commonly referred to as the trade or distributors.

A **profile strategy** concerns the way an organisation is presented to a range of stakeholder audiences and is essentially about corporate image and reputation management.

These three strategies (3Ps) are not used independently of each other. They need to work together, and management need to make a judgement about the appropriate balance.

Please remember that this balance need not be static, but must be expected to shift as the context within which **each communication campaign changes and evolves**, as the environment inside and outside an organisation reshapes itself.

Slide 5 – Co-ordination

If this is to be achieved, then understanding and setting the strategic balance of an organisation's communications is very important.

For successful implementation of each of the 3Ps it is necessary to utilise a different promotional mix. The tools have different properties and enable different goals to be achieved.

For example, when launching a new consumer product such as Sunny Delight, it is first **necessary to create distribution (push)** through the major grocery multiples. This involves **personal selling and direct marketing**.

Once distribution is secured, **awareness needs to be established in the target audience**. This strategy (pull) may require the use of **mass communications**, which involves the use of television, poster and print advertising. This can be supported with **public relations activities** designed to create credible third party comment, and **endorsement** of the brand.

Procter & Gamble does not use a profile strategy to any greater degree partly because of its multi-brand policy. However, other companies, such as the AA or British Airways, focus a great deal of their communications on raising and sustaining their corporate brands. The **corporate brand** can act as an umbrella, under which **product brands** can be infused with the corporate ideal and values, saving investment and human resources.

Slide 6 – Benefits and Difficulties

The promotional mix should be co-ordinated if a consistent message is to be conveyed to each of the various audiences with which a brand and its parent organisation interacts. By adopting a strategic approach, promotional activities can be targeted, streamlined, made efficient and effective.

If the goal is to **differentiate through positioning**, then by using the different tools of the promotional mix and by delivering clear messages positioning can be used as a form of sustainable competitive advantage and thus be difficult for a competitor to replicate.

Communications used by Procter & Gamble enabled Sunny Delight to be positioned as a distinct new refreshing drink for kids. The communications also informed people where to find it in supermarkets (chiller cabinets) and where it should be stored at home (in refrigerators).

Slide 7 – Conclusions

The promotional mix consists of different tools which are each capable of undertaking different tasks. By setting a communication strategy and then by using the right mix of tools in the right way, it is possible to create awareness, persuade, remind/reassure and differentiate a product brand or a corporate brand.

Slide 8 – Questions

Have you any questions?

5 Push and pull

> **Tutorial note.** A contrast between push and pull should be made in part (a), and part (b) should emphasise the importance of key account management and long-term support.

(a) There are three strategies that can be used by this company when launching a new range. They can be used independently, or together, depending upon the resources available, the target audiences, the objectives set, the competition and the present reputation of the company.

  (i) **Push**– to influence the distributor to stock the new range and develop our relationship. They, in turn, will encourage the end user to buy our range at point of sale.

  (ii) **Pull**– Communications aimed at the end consumer so that they be aware of the range and wish to buy.

  (iii) **Profile**– aimed at all relevant stakeholders, including internal audiences, to build company reputation.

  Our company has an established reputation amongst office retailers, but the new range is also appropriate for home office use. Therefore a mix of push and pull strategies should be used.

  Firstly, distributors will be encouraged to take the full range and display it well, and include it in their catalogues and own promotions (push).

  Secondly, a pull strategy aimed at end users (both purchasing managers and home customers) will create awareness, generating demand and store traffic. This will in turn encourage distributors to support the launch.

(b)   **Suggested mix to reach channel members**

    (i)   **Personal selling** is important in business-to-business relationships since it builds trust. The sales force can demonstrate the product benefits and negotiate discounts and local promotional support. They will also advise on **merchandising** displays and give training.

    (ii)   **Point of purchase** material will be made available, stressing the quality of the product, along with literature that can be used by the distributor to mail out to their customers or distribute in store.

    (iii)   **Non personal direct marketing**. This might include a secure **extranet** site, so that distributors can get information on stock availability, order status and product specifications. **Direct mail** to launch the range may be used to pre-warn distributors, or initially to tell new retailers about the range, and the special benefits of stocking the range.

    (iv)   **CD ROMs** could be mailed out to distributors with room design software included, so that distributors can offer this benefit to their customers when selling the new range. The disk will carry the catalogue.

    (v)   **Sales promotions.** Special discounts for large orders or pre launch discounts will encourage sales into the distributor. Incentives and competitions for distributor sales teams will encourage their support at the point of sale.

    (vi)   **Exhibitions** supported by corporate hospitality will create interest in the new range and facilitate dialogue between the company and its distribution network.

    (vii)   **Advertising** in trade journals will create awareness and may encourage opportunities for PR support.

    (viii)   **Public relations** will feature the new range and tell of the support that will be offered to the distributors on taking the new range.

Conclusion

Support from members of the supply chain is extremely important for a furniture manufacturer such as ours. **Push strategies must be undertaken to encourage dialogue with channel members**, and ensure that they have the right tools to sell on the products. The mix will be used to create awareness, persuade distributors to take stock, develop relationships and create sales. The push strategies must be integrated with pull techniques to ensure long-term success for the new range.

6 Internet based communications

Tutorial note. This is a straightforward question with an easy format. Facts about the Internet need to be related to the context of the question. Better answers will recognise the development of relationships as an important factor, and address the strategic aspects.

In business-to-business (B2B) markets, organisational **buying behaviour** is more complex than that observed in consumer markets. This is because of the increased number of people involved in the **decision making process** and the nature of the relationships between organisations.

As a result of this and other factors, marketing communications in the **B2B** market is traditionally characterised by the predominance of **personal selling**, and relatively little use of advertising. In fact it is the complete reversal of business-to-consumer based promotional activity (**B2C**) where **mass media communications** have tended to be the most important route to the target audience.

The development of the **Internet and related digital technologies** has introduced new ways in which audiences in both sectors can be reached. There are many other ways in which organisations can benefit from these developments but these notes will concentrate on communications in the B2B sector.

Very briefly, the Internet and digital technologies can lead to:

- Faster communication
- More information
- Lower costs
- More effective transactions
- A reduction in sales force personnel costs
- Improved relationships with intermediaries
- The development of new/revised types of intermediary
- Potential for improved levels of customer satisfaction
- Speedier problem resolution
- Greater accuracy and less noise in the communication system
- Provision of exit barriers for intermediaries
- Improved use of the communication mix

I will not go into these in detail but will highlight some of the points made.

In the B2B sector, the development and maintenance of **profitable relationships** is important. Part of marketing communications' role is to develop these relationships by **reducing perceived risk and uncertainty**. It also needs to provide **clarity** and provide fast, pertinent and timely **information** in order that decisions can be made.

Loyalty

Loyalty between organisations can be improved by **targeting information and customised messages** at the right people within the partner organisation. **Speed of response** to customer questions, and the **clarity of the information** provided, is important for the development of trust and loyalty.

Productivity

Productivity should be increased as electronic communication not only saves time, but also **shortens the time between order and delivery**.

Reputation

The reputation of our organisation should be enhanced considerably, not only through our website but also through the way we are perceived to meet the needs of our customers. Subject to the actions of our competitors in this area, we may also have a competitive advantage.

Costs

The costs of our communications can also be considerably reduced. Just as sales literature and demonstration packs take time to prepare, change and update, and are quite expensive with a great deal of wastage, **brochureware on the website** is fast, easily accessible and adaptable.

Further website development will enable us to collect names and addresses, respond to **email** questions and provide **data** for our sales force. If we develop the website still further, then **e-commerce transactions** will enable routine orders to be completed quickly and at a lower cost.

This frees up the sales force to visit established customers more often, and gives them the opportunity to open new accounts and attentively manage those accounts that are strategically important. This is referred to as **key account management**.

Marketing communications mix

Digital technologies enable the **collection of data** for use through online and offline sources. So our **direct marketing** activities can be improved, and our **sales promotions** targeted to provide real and valued incentives. Even our **public relations** activities can benefit by placing suitable material on our web pages.

Effectiveness

Finally, digitally-based communications can improve the **accuracy of the information** we provide and also enable us to measure the **effectiveness** of our marketing communication activities. However, we must not forget that **offline communications** will still be important, and these new communication formats should be considered as an addition to rather than a substitution for our current marketing communications.

Now, whilst I have set out the advantages we must be aware of some of the drawbacks.

Traditional customers

Internet access for some of our smaller business partners may be restricted and they may prefer to continue having **face-to-face contact** with our sales force. This must be respected. We need to deploy our new marketing communications mix carefully and not impose it on unwilling organisations.

Investment/set up costs

The set-up costs will be expensive, and an **appropriate investment approach** needs to be adopted. Some parts of this technology can also lock us into relationships which might be difficult to get out of, should conditions change. In effect, these are barriers to exit for each party.

Legal and security

There will also be some **legal and information security issues** that we need to address in order to **reduce any risk** our partners might perceive.

End notes

To conclude and summarise, our marketing communications with business partners will improve through improved efficiency and effectiveness, which in turn will be reflected in the nature and **quality of the relationships** we hold. This will ultimately be reflected in our overall performance in meeting our corporate goals.

Improved trust, commitment and a higher propensity to share information must lead to increased business performance. The development of Internet based communications is a strategic decision that needs to be thought through in terms of the impact it will have on the way we and our partners do business.

7 Managing global communications

Tutorial note. This question requires a detailed look at the effect on marketing communications strategy of the issues of globalisation. It is often tempting to repeat the typical International marketing theory without considering the impact of these on the management of the campaign. This answer takes the form of a presentation, although you may have chosen to do a standard essay. Either approach is fine, given the question wording.

Presentation to Client, 'Happy Foods'
By
'Global Advertising'
Going Global– the Pitfalls and Opportunities

Introduction

Our agency has been helping to develop the advertising for your UK business for several years. Now we would like you to consider us as you expand your operations further into international markets. Today we would like to present to you some of the issues that you might wish to consider when developing your international marketing communications strategies. Our presentation this morning will cover the following.

- Strategic issues in international marketing communications
- Pitfalls and opportunities
- How 'Global Advertising' can help

Strategic Issues

Branding

Although your brand is extremely well established in UK markets, it is relatively unknown in the new regions. A decision must be made on the **branding strategy** – should the brand be **positioned** in a different way in the new markets? As an imported brand there may be an opportunity to position the product as a luxury, which will command a much higher price than the cheaper home brands. This will affect the promotional **mix**, **media** (target markets will be exposed to a different media) and **message**.

Your **marketing communications objectives** will tend to focus on **creating awareness**, rather than developing brand values to maintain market share. This will require a potentially large **share of voice**.

Push or pull?

As a new entrant to the market, a **push strategy** will need to be considered, particularly in markets with **strong distribution networks**. However, shelf space is not necessarily the only challenge, and **local custom and legislation** must be considered. For example:

- Would **sampling** by door drop be allowed?
- Could **coupons** be offered to allow a trial of the product?
- What **merchandising** is possible?

Standardisation or adaptation?

The marketing communications debate needs to reflect whether a **standardised global strategy** is acceptable, or whether an **adapted campaign** is more suitable to reflect tastes, culture, and market trends.

A standardised approach offers benefits in terms of global **synergy** and **economies of scale**, and allows a corporate **branding** approach, but there is the danger that the brand message becomes bland, and irrelevant to local markets. The communications must take account of the **political, legal, economic, social and technological differences** in the new markets.

The following must be considered before a solution to this question is found.

Pitfalls and opportunities

1   Market differences
2   Internal organisation
3   Message
4   Media
5   Measurement and research

1 **Market differences**

(a) **Social and cultural aspects**

As you operate in the food industry, your products may be culturally bound, and so may not be eaten in the same context as in domestic markets. The **message** will therefore be affected, along with **packaging**.

(b) **Language**

Checks will be needed to ensure that your **brand names and labelling** do not offend local tastes, and to see if promotional material needs to be accurately **translated** in full. Messages using **music and non-verbal content** are often considered better if a global standardised approach is going to be taken.

(c) **Competition**

The level and nature of competition may well affect the best tactics to use in the promotional mix. If **sales promotion** is the norm for this type of product then some use of this may be necessary to enter distribution channels and consumer **awareness sets**.

(d) **Economic aspects**

This may affect the positioning of the brand – if a **premium position** is to be taken then the **message and media must be consistent** with this, even if the actual price is lower than may be expected in home markets.

(e) **Legal aspects**

As referred to above, we must ensure that no laws are broken. **Knocking copy** is not tolerated in some countries.

(f) **Technology**

The **use of and access to technology** does vary across the world. Although the website in the UK has been extremely effective at gaining involvement from children, this may not be the case in all countries. The address of the website needs to be considered to suit local conditions.

2 **Internal organisation**

Your company is not manufacturing overseas at the present time, but there will be **local sales and marketing** people on the ground. It is important that you use an **agency** which has local offices and contacts in the countries in which you operate. They will be able to advise on the above issues, and also **feedback** information on how the campaign is being received.

It will be important not to alienate the local managers, and so one way to **manage the campaign** would be to **circulate the strategy in advance** to gain approval and allow them an opportunity to **brief local agencies** on their own needs. There will be some aspects of the Happy Foods brand position that you will wish to keep constant, and the use of a **brand manual** showing what can and cannot be altered will be essential.

3 **Message**

This should be appropriate to the local market needs, method and media used, but reflect **consistent brand values**.

4 **Media**

Availability of media for advertising varies from country to country. Cinema advertising and the use of radio may be more appropriate in rural India, but the use of press advertising may be significant elsewhere.

The availability of **media research** to help with media selection is potentially less sophisticated. Local guidance about the best space to buy will be necessary. Although there are many more **global media** available (e.g. satellite stations like MTV) these may not be appropriate for all audiences. **Local advertising opportunities** might exist and should be used. **Set an objective in terms of share of voice expected**, and then allow local representatives to buy media, taking account of last minute opportunities, within pre-determined **budget constraints**.

5   **Measurement and research**

Access to relevant measurement methods and market research could be sketchy, and so decisions may need to be based on less scientific methods. It remains the case that progress towards the achievement of objectives must be measured appropriately.

How can we help?

Global Advertising has offices or associates in the first countries that you will be investigating, with skilled local personnel to handle your business. Although they will liaise with your own local staff, you will have access to what is going on through our own **account directors** who will be able to **consolidate all local activity** on your behalf.

We can advise on **local legal, economic and cultural differences** and we understand **local media buying** conditions. In addition, our **full service capabilities** extend to overseas markets, through our creative and other associates. This will save costs in the long term, since a single contact ensures that **communication is more direct** and less likely to be distorted.

Most importantly, because of our existing relationship with you we feel that we understand your brands and can ensure an integrated brand strategy, albeit with local differences.

8   Measuring success

Tutorial note. The key in this question is the term 'direct marketing'. Do not fall into the trap of discussing evaluation for any type of mass communication campaign.

How successful is our direct Marketing?

To: Managing Director

From: Manager
Bubbles Aromatherapy Ltd

June 20XX

Contents

1 Introduction and background
2 Direct marketing methods
3 Evaluation methods
4 Appraisal of methods
5 Conclusions

Introduction

Since our launch last year it is now time to formalise the **effectiveness of our direct marketing techniques**. This will enable us to review our plans for the next few years and also provide a benchmark for measuring subsequent activity. The report will look at each method in turn, and **evaluate** each one to see if a better method could be used.

Background

Bubbles Aromatherapy is a relatively small company offering a range of upmarket aromatherapy toiletries. **Direct marketing** has been the main method of distribution and communication since the launch.

(a) The **target market** consists of a relatively small niche of prosperous buyers who are involved in alternative products, seeing aromatherapy as an important part of their **lifestyle**.

(b) Distribution via chemists and supermarkets would require heavy investment in **mainstream advertising**. This would negate our positioning as 'real' aromatherapy products.

(c) The launch has been supported by some fairly successful **public relations** activity.

Direct marketing methods

The following direct marketing methods have been utilised at various stages throughout the year. The method used to evaluate the campaign is stated in each section.

(a) **Direct response advertising**, offering a free catalogue, to stimulate interest and contribute towards a database, in a number of different publications including female titles, some specialist alternative therapy magazines and small classifieds in more mainstream titles like *The Guardian*.

These have been evaluated using the number of catalogue **enquiries**, and **subsequent sales**. Analysis has been undertaken on an ad-by-ad and title-by-title basis.

(b) **Direct mailing** of catalogue twice a year to British Association of Retail Therapists list, subscribers to *Alternative Today* and own list of previous buyers.

Evaluated through number of orders, value of orders and cost of order.

(c) **Internet banner advertising** on websites of similarly minded manufacturers. Orders not taken online, but number of 'hits' established and also 'click throughs' on the site monitored.

(d) **Telemarketing** – customer rings order through, and telemarketing team is charged with order administration and **customer satisfaction surveys**.

Evaluated through **sales conversions**, length of call, **survey results**.

(e) **Personal selling – product demonstrations** are held each year at Women's Institute meetings.

(f) **Evaluation methods**

Evaluated by **sales** per event and per number of attendees.

Method appraisal

It would appear that much of our direct marketing activity is wasted, since the evaluation suggests that much of our activity yields little in the way of sales. This may be due to a flaw in the evaluation methods used, which are largely **quantitative**. The following suggestions are made, which may complement our existing evaluation methods.

(a) **Customer lifetime value** might be a more strategic measurement method.

(b) **Conversion rates** and **cost per sale** would demonstrate where effort is wasted.

(c) **Measurement must be related to objectives**. Only direct methods have been used so far, based on sales, which is a fairly crude measure.

(d) Measurement on **qualitative issues** should be undertaken. This would give some understanding on why customers bought (or did not buy).

(e) **Methods should be tested** before they are rolled out. Testing of lists, media used, message, promotional offer and all elements of our direct marketing is possible as we now have some history of what has been successful in the past.

(f)   Direct marketing is just one aspect of our **overall marketing communications strategy**. The other communications strategies that we use (such as public relations) must also be evaluated.

(g)   More use could be made of our **online** presence, and it is also hoped that this method can be used to pre-and post-test our strategies through online surveys.

(h)   Our **direct selling activity** is an ideal basis for **focus groups** to evaluate our own and competitors' marketing communications strategy.

Conclusions

Evaluation of direct marketing activity is crucial and many methods can be used to complement our existing methods of evaluation. However as a small company we should not be too sophisticated, and should ideally use evaluation to help identify the best possible future strategies and keep us from wasting money on the worst ones.

9 Distribution channels

Review to: The Marketing Director
From: The Marketing Operations Manager
Date: June 20XX
Subject: DISTRIBUTION STRATEGY

Introduction and outline of the various channels available to our company

Distribution is increasingly important for effective marketing operations in the modern context. Innovative distribution can create competitive advantage, as evidenced by Amazon.com's use of the Internet. **Alternative distribution channels** today include the following.

* Manufacturer to agent/factor/broker to wholesaler to retailer to consumer/user
* Manufacturer to wholesaler to retailer to consumer/user
* Manufacturer to retailer to consumer/user
* Manufacturer to franchisor to consumer/user
* Manufacturer to consumer/user

In the latter case, manufacturers can use **mail order** or a **call centre**, perhaps **outsourced**. Companies increasingly use a multiplicity of channels to reach different target market segments.

In our company's case there are two alternative channels.

* Wholesaler (tour operator) to retailer (travel agent) to consumer/user
* Tour operator to consumer/user

The use of travel agents entails the payment of a **commission**, which raises the question of whether we should market **direct to consumers** via the **Internet, direct mail brochures, or telemarketing** (or all three). Another option would be to **vertically integrate** downwards, by setting up our own travel agencies. Furthermore, we could offer **exclusive distribution** to retail chains (Co-op Travel), perhaps in the form of own-brand or label. We have to recognise that distribution channels are changing and look for opportunities to increase business by seeking new outlets.

Criteria for the evaluation of alternative channels

Overall distribution strategy, whether **intensive, selective or exclusive**, needs to be **consistent with brand strategy**. If we want to develop an up-market brand image, then we should pursue an exclusive distribution strategy.

Equally, there should be **strategic fit** between distribution and company objectives. The right **channel mix** is also dependent on:

- Market size
- Market dispersion
- Buying behaviour and complexity
- Product characteristics
- Technology
- Competition
- Regulations

When **evaluating individual channel choices**, the following evaluation criteria apply.

- Access to and coverage of target market segments
- Cost of operation and margins
- Expected return
- Amount of control over brand
- Reputation/image
- Compatibility of culture
- Creditworthiness
- Degree of promotional support needed
- Staff knowledge/expertise
- Power-dependency relationships

The acid test when deciding whether to market direct to consumer is – can we do a better job than the travel agents at an equivalent cost, or can we do an equivalent job at a lower cost?

Recommendation of an appropriate strategy for our target market

Since we address **a number of target markets** with a **range of products**, a **multiplicity of channels** is appropriate.

For our exclusive **luxury** cruises, a **direct channel** is the most appropriate since this affords us maximum control over the quality of the service. Advertising the cruises can be targeted more accurately by choosing media used by people with particular characteristics, who would not appreciate having to consult a down-market travel agent catering for the mass market.

Equally, our new range of **special interest** tours is best suited to a direct channel using the **Internet**, which can be backed up by a dedicated chat-room and help-line.

For our **standard packages**, we should continue to use the travel agents who provide a service meeting the needs of our target customers for this product, and who have the necessary presence in the population conurbations.

10 Internet

Tutorial note. To produce a good answer, you need to stick closely to the question asked – ways in which the Internet is being used (and will be used) by suppliers, customers and internally. Do not be tempted to reproduce general lists of advantages and disadvantages of the Internet.

What is the Internet?

The Internet is a worldwide network of computers. These are linked together so that users can search for and access data and information provided by others.

The World Wide Web is the element that provides facilities such as full-colour, graphics, sound and video. **websites** are points within the network created by members who wish to provide an information point for searchers to visit and benefit by the provision of **information** and/or by entering into a **transaction**.

Current uses and development issues

There are an increasing number of interactive uses that the Internet can be used for:

- Communication (information provision)
- Product development
- Facilitating transactions
- Fostering dialogue and relationships with different stakeholders

The attributes of the Internet that allow for these uses also need to be considered.

- High speed of interaction
- Low cost provision and maintenance
- Ability to provide mass customisation
- Global reach and wide search facilities
- Instant dialogue
- Multi-directional communications (eg: to suppliers, customers and regulators)
- High level of user control
- Customer (visitor) driven
- Moderate level of credibility

Use with customers

The use of the Internet by organisations with their customers has generally to date been focussed upon the **business-to-business sector** rather than consumer end users. Those customers that have used the Internet do so primarily in search of entertainment and information. Web sites have become increasingly sophisticated and are a useful means of meeting the needs of customers and organisations.

Businesses can communicate more **cost-effectively** with their customers and provide a wide range of facilities. The **volume of customer traffic** that can be handled is far larger and quicker than through traditional means. Sales literature, product designs and innovations, ideas, price lists, complaints, sales promotions such as competitions, and orders and sales can all be undertaken over the Internet.

The objectives are essentially two-fold. The first is to **generate the first steps of a relationship** (or maintain one already established). The second is the collection of **customer profile information** to be added to the database. Names, addresses and other demographic and psychographic data can be collected without any human intervention or the associated costs.

The execution of financial transactions over the Internet has been a stumbling block, due to the fear of fraud. More **secure systems** and protection devices are now becoming available and this will spur the growth of purchasing activities.

A further development is to **integrate the Internet with other elements of the marketing and promotional mix**. For example, the Tesco and Sainsbury's initiatives to develop home shopping have met with great success in influencing shopping patterns.

Use with suppliers

The use of the Internet with suppliers will provide a more **dynamic form of communication exchange** via:

- Problem identification
- Formation of solutions, including tailored product modifications
- Constant dialogue opportunities

These factors will enable suppliers to forge **closer relationships in the marketing channel**.

Marketing communications opportunities will arise where, for example, **new products** can be presented to suppliers much more quickly, **sales literature and product specification data can be relayed instantly** and advertising materials presented more effectively.

Use within organisations: intranets

Internally the greatest advance is the development of intranets. The provision of internal, password-protected communication networks allows for the **rapid dissemination of corporate and marketing information**. For global organisations this represents a tremendous step forward, as an intranet can overcome time barriers and allow for the transmission of materials to all parts of a company.

The development of and interest in **internal marketing** has been assisted by this new form of communication. The involvement of staff, and the motivational opportunities afforded by intranet technology, enable employees and management to work more closely together.

Future of the Internet

The future of the Internet is bounded only by imagination and technological advances. Essentially there will be greater **interactive opportunities**, which will enable a **range of stakeholders** to interact with organisations for information, education, entertainment, products, services and financial transactions quickly and efficiently.

11 Managing outside suppliers

Article (Marketing Business): 'Getting to grips with outsourcing'

From: A Marketing Director

1   **Introduction**

In this world of increasing globalisation and faster change, organisations need to continually **review their core competences** and to consider which marketing activities might be better **outsourced**.

Generally speaking, if an outside supplier can do a better job than your own company at an equivalent cost, or an equivalent job at a lower cost, then a switch should be made.

When reviewing the possibilities, the process should cover

- The types of outside marketing resources the company could use
- How contenders for these services should be briefed
- How the selected suppliers should be managed and controlled

2   **Types of outside marketing resources we could use**

2.1   **Consultants**

There are a great many management and marketing consultants in the UK. The CIM, for example, provides a comprehensive service. Some consultants specialise in design, research or promotion.

2.2   **Marketing research agencies**

Not many organisations have all the in-house facilities needed to cater for their total information requirements. Nearly all organisations find it necessary to outsource surveys to specialists.

2.3   **Promotional agencies**

There are a great variety of promotional agencies, ranging from advertising agencies to agencies specialising in sales promotion, PR and telesales/telemarketing. With sales promotion there is a range of specialists in packaging design, POS display material, exhibition services, mail order and so on. The opportunities provided by the Internet have given rise to a number of agencies specialising in website design.

2.4 Marketing training organisations

Universities and professional bodies can be used to improve the skills of marketing departments and provide specialist courses.

2.5 Full-service agencies

These endeavour to supply the full range of marketing services from consultancy to marketing research and promotion and are particularly suitable for smaller organisations.

2.6 New product development

This is a controversial issue and covers a very wide field, but pharmaceutical companies, for example, will often subcontract at least part of their extremely costly and risky laboratory research to a number of selected specialists, such as biotechnology companies.

3 How outside suppliers should be briefed

3.1 The **briefing** of outside suppliers is of paramount importance, since an inadequate brief will lead to misunderstandings.

3.2 We need to adopt a position of mutual **trust** with our suppliers. Being able to trust them should be the most important criterion for doing business. We can then provide them with a full statement of our requirements.

3.3 Our detailed requirements should include a full **specification** of the services we are seeking, the standards we expect and any special conditions of contract such as penalty clauses.

3.4 We should make suppliers aware that competitive tenders will be sought.

3.5 Suppliers should be given the right to query the detail of our requirements, and to make suggestions for any amendments.

3.6 An indication of the **budget** and any other limitations should be provided where appropriate.

3.7 Suppliers should be made fully aware of the **timescales**.

3.8 Finally, all suppliers should be made aware that their performance will be **appraised**.

4 How suppliers might be controlled and measured

A decision has to be made whether to **apply controls selectively**. A supplier we use irregularly or for small amounts should not be subjected to the same degree of control as a supplier whose goods/services are a major item of expenditure.

However, the answer cannot depend on spend alone. We could, for example, be spending relatively little on an agency on concept testing for a proposed new product. However, this proposed new product could be vital to our future and therefore the agency could require stricter control than a supplier of high cost materials who has proved to be highly dependable for a number of years.

The nature of the control should perhaps be different according to the nature of the product/service being bought. For some materials suppliers we would, for example, have scientific tests on quality and maintain records of deliveries late/on time/before time. However, for our advertising agency, control might be more informal and based on frequent personal meetings.

Bearing in mind the above difficulties in setting standards and the rating of performance, I would recommend the following controls.

- Supplier's name
- Type of goods/services supplied

- Estimated annual expenditure

- Record of complaints made by us

- Record of actions taken by supplier

- Performance standard   *Rating (scale 0 to 10)*   *Notes*
  - Quality of product/service
  - Reliability
  - Prices relative to competitors
  - Working relationships
  - Overall

- Special terms and conditions relative to this supplier

- Recommended special controls, if any

- Recommended frequency of review

- Person responsible for review, position/department

There should, following the initial review, be a **rolling system of reviewing** outside suppliers, on the recommended frequencies and against the agreed standards. **Formal ratings are preferred to informal measures**. The frequency of the reviews and the nature of the standards set should be changed in accordance with circumstances.

All suppliers should be informed about our review system and invited to comment/co-operate.

5   **Conclusion**

There are of course a number of implications for other business functions in the decision to extend the number of subcontracted marketing activities. Not the least of these are the implications for staffing and finance. It will be necessary for me to meet with co-directors before taking any further action on this organisational issue.

12 Agency restructuring

Introduction

Advertising agencies have been subjected to a number of significant external pressures in the last ten to fifteen years. Their response to these pressures has been mixed and in many cases cautious, perhaps mindful of the need to monitor and avoid fashion swings and management fads.

Reasons for possible incompatibility

The reasons why some of these organisations have failed to keep pace with their clients' needs are as follows.

1   Hierarchical structures
2   Market complexity
3   Reliance on the commission payment scheme
4   Failure to implement integrated marketing communications
5   The plethora of new media and subsequent fragmentation
6   Audience fragmentation
7   The variable quality of overseas support
8   Poor positioning
9   Agency complacency

335

Many of these points are interrelated and the causality factor often hard to determine. Time does not permit a full examination of all these issues, so I shall select a few and consider some of the points in more detail.

The structure adopted by many advertising agencies is **hierarchical** and in many ways ill-suited to flexibility and the necessary **speed of reaction** required by many clients. These structures have strong historical roots, and in that sense are hard to change.

International operations demand consideration and preferably experience of **cross cultural issues**, **networking** and, in many cases, **delegation** to country agencies, some of whom may require more support and guidance than others. Hierarchies require authority and control in order that they function appropriately. Such conditions may not always exist overseas, may be incompatible with client structures and may hinder the decision making process.

Developing international and global brands is a complex activity which requires special skills, from both a client and agency perspective. These may be hard to secure. When looked at in terms of the level of investment associated with **international brand support**, the issue becomes increasingly more complex and difficult.

Management consultancies have taken a lot of strategic work away from many advertising agencies. This has had a knock-on effect in terms of international brand support. Poor positioning therefore has been a contributory factor to this problem of incompatibility.

The plethora of **new media and subsequent fragmentation** of both audiences and media have proved problematic. Some traditional full service agencies have developed central **media buying** units in order to provide added value for clients, but the issue of media planning and scheduling has become more complex. When an international dimension is superimposed, so the degree of complexity increases.

Complacency and a lack of drive to change is a contributory factor in many cases. A predilection to preserve the status quo regarding their relationships with clients suggests that some agencies lack strategic vision and may also not be fully aware of their **clients' goals**. The fault may, perhaps, lie with clients not communicating their marketing communication strategies effectively. Matters are certainly not helped by the willingness of many clients to change agencies mid term.

How might agencies adjust?

There are therefore, many potential gaps between the expectation of clients and their respective agencies. One of the choices agencies need to make is whether to anticipate client needs internationally or whether to remain orientated to the domestic arena and make ad hoc arrangements to support any client who develops an overseas requirement.

How integrated does the agency need to be?

Full integration for all agencies is obviously not practical or strategically viable. However, in terms of meeting client needs, restructuring and adaptation to the new environment with a view to establishing differing levels of integration, and in this case international support, may be useful. Agencies need to establish the right balance to suit their client needs.

At the heart of this problem about incompatibility there seem to lie three main issues. These are about **structure, strategy and relationships**. Agencies and clients need direction and knowledge in order that they can manage these three variables and in doing so reduce or at least minimise any gap in expectations and support.

13 AP Engineering

> **Tutorial note.** Under this syllabus, the intention in the mini-case is to direct candidates to specific parts of the scenario, and not use a marketing communications plan. The question is essentially about corporate branding and marketing communications strategy. Parts (c) and (e) are the most challenging. Part (c) requires some acknowledgement and understanding of the differences between emotional and rational messages for low and high involvement scenarios.
>
> Implementation issues for marketing communications planning are different from development issues, and should include aspects on budgeting, timetabling, managing, controlling and evaluating. Target audience choice and strategy development are not relevant at the implementation stage.

To: Board of Directors
From: Marketing Communications Consultant

Date: June 20X0

Communications Strategies: AP Engineering 20X6 and Beyond

This report assesses **suitable marketing communications strategies** that will enable AP Engineering (AP) to move forward with its new approach of total engineering solutions. The report is presented in six main sections, each addressing a specific aspect as follows.

(a)   Communications strategy for 20X6/20X7
(b)   Justification and explanation for strategy
(c)   Suggested promotional tools
(d)   Core messages
(e)   Issues of implementation and integration
(f)   Conclusions

(a)   **Communications strategy for 20X6/20X7**

Cultural and **organisational changes** at the company suggest that one of the first jobs that will be required of the communications is to pull together all areas of the business. This will enable an **integrated approach** and offering to be made, and suggests the importance of **internal communications**. In addition our company will need to tell its existing customers and other **stakeholders** about the new one-stop service now on offer.

The strategy that we should propose is initially one of **profile**. This is relevant when a number of different stakeholders need to be addressed, and the main aim of this strategy is to develop our corporate **brand** and **reputation** for providing a full solution for all engineering needs. A **pull** strategy, aimed at existing customers and new business, will then be used to **raise awareness** of specific services.

(b)   **Justification and explanation for strategy**

The reasons for the suggestion of a profile strategy can be summarised as follows.

1   The reorganisation has pulled together **new staff** from a number of acquisitions and new alliances. Profile strategies cover **internal marketing** and this will be vital to ensure that all staff and associates work together, uniting to offer an integrated service.

       Our **mission** and **vision** need to filter through the organisation, and a dialogue set up to ensure that any issues affecting **strategy implementation** are understood. Front line staff need to feel valued, particularly when they are new to AP – they may be feeling vulnerable and unsure of new roles in the enlarged organisation. It can be seen that internal marketing provides an essential role during this time of **change management**.

2   **External audiences** such as **customers** need to be told about our new services, and reassured that the changes will make things easier for them. **Suppliers** may also be an important audience. The combined approach of profile and push will ensure that our **corporate brand** is **repositioned** as an integrated service provider. The existing **core values** of credibility and value for money will be retained, but the **service** element will now be highlighted (generally higher margins for us).

3   **Profile strategies** are particularly important in service industries, where **people** are key to delivering the offering.

4   AP needs to maintain its **external visibility** to ensure that it is considered as a supplier by other influential audiences, such as specifiers and architects.

5   Profile strategies concentrate on building **reputation** and corporate **image**, to allow a later pull strategy to concentrate on specific markets with specific products.

6   Margins have been tight, and a profile strategy can be more **cost effective** in generating awareness.

(c)   **Suggested promotional tools**

The primary tools that should be used for implementation of the strategy are as follows.

1   **Internal marketing communication** to include training, staff conferences, intranet facilities and newsletters. The flow of communication needs to be two-way. Employees should be encouraged, and even incentivised, to make suggestions, get involved with writing press releases about projects they have worked on and take part in external events.

2   **Video conference facilities** to bring relevant experts into the team when required for internal and external communication.

3   Corporate **website development** with areas for clients, suppliers, staff and other influential professionals, including the press. This should offer a range of useful information to help customers with their projects.

4   **Direct marketing** to existing customers will explain the changes. This will be highly **targeted**, and explain the impact that our new services will have upon ongoing business.

5   **Personal selling** and **key account management**. As a service industry, the new structure and vision can best be explained through personal contact. Key accounts might be invited to a road show.

6   **Key account management system**. Computer systems should be organised around customers, so that all aspects of the business focus on the customer and **integrate** all activity.

7   **Public relations**. This venture is newsworthy, and AP should encourage editorial coverage to get its corporate message out to customers, suppliers and influencers. AP may wish to set up a **reference programme** which encourages joint PR between the client and AP, using civil engineering and building **journals** and the client's **trade press**. Site visits and speaking on the conference circuit may boost AP's reputation as 'one stop' experts, and ensure that it is the first company that comes to mind when a business project is being considered.

8   **Trade shows** and **advertising** may be considered towards the end of the profile strategy.

A combination of the above tools will implement both profile and pull strategies and build the new corporate brand.

(d)   **Core messages**

Although communicating with a number of different stakeholders, a single and **consistent message** will be required to show the simplicity of the new vision and the **benefits** that the integrated service will bring.

As the decision to use AP's service will tend to be **high involvement**, **rational product appeals** will often work best. This requires longer copy and complex messages. Some symbolism of the **brand** may be useful, to present the new ethos in an easy to remember way. This will be followed by more detailed message content, outlining the **features** and **benefits** of AP's combined services for different stakeholders.

An **example** might be:

"AP – the best specialised staff, coming together for a total solution to engineering problems."

This will give a sense of belonging to staff, and functional benefits can be elaborated on in terms of features and benefits for customers. A new logo, showing parts of a jigsaw coming together, could be used to show this visually. This **branding instrument** could then be used on all marketing communications activity.

(e)   **Issues of implementation and integration**

Before implanting an integrated marketing communications policy several key issues need to be addressed.

1   **Budgets** – without sufficient resource put behind the strategy, it cannot be implemented. The size of budget will depend on the availability of funds, and the attitude of top management towards seeing this as an **investment** rather than a cost. **Internal markets** must be dealt with first when **allocating** the budget, because we have already seen that the change management must be effective to make the service deliverable. Money spent on communicating the service to the customer and other stakeholders will be wasted if the internal processes are not capable of delivering what is promised.

2   **Cultural differences** and methods of working between new and existing staff will need to be addressed. Training and development will be needed, as well as consultation with staff at all levels.

3   **Management of communications** – should this be undertaken **in house** or via an **agency**? Internal marketing communications is a specialised area and consultants could advise on implementation. A senior manager should be empowered with introducing the internal marketing communications changes necessary.

4   **Measurement and evaluation**. A decision needs to be made on how and when to measure the effectiveness of the campaign. A number of techniques will be used e.g. internal **focus groups** amongst staff to judge whether the change of culture is working, staff satisfaction **surveys**, editorial coverage assessed to judge whether favourable or not. The measurement will depend on the **objectives** set.

5   **Timing issues** – the project will start with internal marketing communications, and then follow through with the external strategies. Budgets will need to be spread, and therefore actions will need to be **prioritised.**

6   Identification of **key influencers** that will need to be brought on board to implement the change strategy eg unions, professional membership bodies.

7   Are **computer** and other **systems** capable of the necessary reorganisation around key account management?

8   Are all **managers and staff** behind the new changes? Are they **capable of delivering** the marketing communications strategy? What will we do if they will not or cannot implement the changes needed?

9   What is the **procedure** for ensuring that all aspects of the plan are **integrated**? Should a **corporate identity manual** be issued, to guide all areas of the business on the new approach? Are messages to all stakeholders **consistent**?

10   Does the plan **complement** and help achieve corporate and marketing **objectives**?

(f)   **Conclusions**

AP Engineering is entering an exciting new period in its evolution. The company has grown and we will need to become more participative in our approach, so that we can offer our customers a complete engineering service.

This requires a culture change and a mix of internal and external communications. Initially a profile strategy will be required, and this report has suggested several tools that might be used to implement this. This will be followed with a more specific pull strategy. A simple message has been suggested to portray the new service and, finally, a list of issues that will need to be considered before we implement the strategy. The future for AP Engineering is looking good, and now the role of marketing communications comes to the fore to achieve corporate goals.

Pilot paper and answer plans

A plan of attack

If this were the actual exam paper in front of you right now, how would you react? Having read all the questions, would you be panicking, or feeling relieved because a favourite topic had come up? Would you be dreading all the work ahead of you over the next three hours?

What you should really do is spend a good **5 minutes looking through the paper**, working out which questions to do and the order in which to attempt them. A plan of attack for the whole paper is now needed. We'll consider two options.

Option 1 (if you're thinking, 'Help!)

If you are a bit worried about the paper, do the questions in the order of how well you think you can answer them.

Question 1 must be attempted if you are going to pass this paper. However daunting it seems, take a calm look at it and break down the requirements. It concerns a relatively small domestic company. Read through the scenario and identify the key issues arising. Perhaps you would like to annotate the paragraphs of the scenario to help to focus your thoughts, as the question is quite broken up and you need to think carefully about each part. There is a lot to think about. Here are some potential areas for consideration.

- CSK's market share/profitability
- Privately owned
- Medium quality product
- Self assembly – cost conscious
- Direct and indirect channels
- High staff loyalty
- Old processes and systems
- Competition increasing
- Budget constraints

- Marketing plan targeting growth
- Needs a marketing communications plan
- Promotional ideas need development
- Conversion rates to be maintained
- Press ads / brochures used
- Sales team works on commission
- Word of mouth important
- Customer contact and trust is vital
- Use of Internet and websites

Part (a) of the question deals with the current and future roles of promotional activity – what does CSK use now, and what could / should it use for the future, given its objectives? Part (b) brings in the concept of perceived risk – the customers of CSK are likely to attach a lot of importance to their choice of kitchen. Think about the types of perceived risk and how it can be alleviated. For example, performance risk leads the customer to ask questions like: "Will the kitchen be the one I really want, and will it work well for me, given the price that I can pay?" Communications need to specifically address this concern.

Part (c) concerns the use of the Internet and specifically its effect on relationships with distributors – CSK should think about the effect it could have on the timely supply of its products to distributors, dealing with queries, sending out product information etc. It is likely that the big budget competition will have Internet capabilities already, and distributors may even come to expect Internet capability as a standard facility offered by manufacturers. In part (d), you need to make your recommendations based on your previous analysis. Think about the primary tools:

- Personal selling
- Advertising
- Sales promotion
- Sponsorship

Publicity
Point of purchase
Direct mail

Exhibitions
Events
E-marketing

Which ones are best? Do not forget the budget constraints that CSK operates with.

Question 2 is a question about the promotional mix that also brings in some aspects of the agency / client relationship. In part (a) you are asked to discuss sales promotion and public relations, and then to apply your knowledge of the product life cycle concept in part (b). If you are familiar with the issues here (introduction, growth, maturity, decline) then this part is straightforward, but do not forget that it is only worth 5 marks. Remember too, that your answer must be set in the context of the food manufacturing industry and in briefing document format. Part (c) on improving trust between client and agencies calls on common sense to an extent, but do not overlook the importance of setting clear objectives and consistent communications.

Question 3 is again a dual aspect question. When choosing media opportunities to compare in part (a), make them appropriate choices for your report to an international electrical appliances manufacturer. Internet advertising and national newspapers are more likely to be used than the small ads. Part (b) represents an easy 8 marks – define, explain and provide an example for each. For part (c), refer to the headings identified by the syllabus when thinking about international markets – media availability, culture, religion, education and literacy.

Question 4 is a fairly challenging one on marketing channels in the car industry. The definitions in part (a) for 5 marks should cause few problems. Sources of conflict (part b) can usually come down to communication issues. As we saw in Chapter 9 of this text, Fill (2002) quotes the main reasons as follows:

- Failure to carry out the job as understood by all channel members
- Particular specific issues arising that cause disagreement, such as territories / margins
- Different ways of reaching the same objectives
- Inadequate communications

Part (c) calls upon your knowledge of differences between B2B and B2C markets – fundamentally, these derive from differences in the buying decision process (influenced by factors such as motivations and risk). Such differences will affect the choice of marketing communications.

Question 5 is a nice question about the agency relationship. Part (b) is more difficult than the straightforward definitions and explanations in part (a). The relationship marketing approach (using concepts such as trust, loyalty and commitment) is well documented, however, so it should not be too difficult to discuss its importance in the context of this particular agency / client partnership. The fact that the client has international operations adds to the complications in, as well as the importance of, developing a potentially lucrative relationship. Your documentation pack should reflect this.

Option 2 (if you are thinking, 'No problem!')

Try not to be overconfident, but if you are feeling fairly comfortable, and relieved that the paper is not the nightmare that you were anticipating, then **turn straight to the Section A compulsory question**. It has to be done, and you need 90 minutes in which to have a good go at it, so why not tackle it while you are still relatively fresh, and at the height of your powers?

Once you've done the compulsory question, choose two of the questions from Section B.

Questions 2 and **3** are a mix of easy definitions and applied analysis. To make your answers relevant, it is supremely important that you constantly refer to the specific context of the organisations described in the question wording.

Question 4 on marketing channels draws heavily on the syllabus content. It is probably the most challenging question on the paper, but should present few problems if you have studied business-to-business marketing channels. The car industry is a key example of an industry where distribution channels have been subject to revision and regulation in the face of market pressures.

Question 5 on the agency relationship is another mixture of definitions and evaluation. The main challenge is to keep your answer relevant to the circumstances of the client, PEN, given that you are preparing specific documents for presentation to its staff.

No matter how may times we remind you...

Always, always allocate your time according to the marks for the question in total and then according to the parts of the question. And **always, always follow the question requirements exactly.**

You've got spare time at the end of the exam... ?

If you have allocated your time properly then you shouldn't have time on your hands, but if you do find yourself with a spare ten minutes, go back over the paper and check your work.

Finally...

Do not worry if you found the paper difficult. Others will have too. Forget about it and think about the next one!

PART A

Country Style Kitchens

The general kitchen furniture market in the UK is worth over £900 million per annum. Country Style Kitchens (CSK) is a privately owned company located in a small west country town. The company makes medium quality kitchen furniture which has a strong country styling and design. The units are available in both finished and self-assembly format, and unit sales reflect a 35% and 65% split respectively. The move into the self-assembly market proved successful as it enabled the company to reach customers in a wider geographic area. An installation facility is available for the finished units but the trend appears to be in favour of self-assembly products.

CSK's sales have grown steadily over their 45 years of trading and currently stand at £13.7 million per annum with net profit at 8.2%. Products are sold through both direct and indirect marketing channels. The indirect channels consist of a small number of appointed distributors who sell a range of kitchen and bathroom products from many different manufacturers. They hold limited stock but work from brochures and their own showrooms.

Staff are very supportive of the company and appear to have a strong identification with the country style positioning. Over 50% have been with the company in excess of 15 years. It should be noted that many of the internal systems and procedures are old, slow and in need of updating, perhaps a reflection of the slower, rural culture that identifies the Country Style Kitchens company.

In addition to these internal challenges the company has begun to experience increased competition from major national kitchen furniture manufacturers. These companies either buy in prefabricated panels and apply a (rural) design template, or import them direct from overseas manufacturers. In addition, they have sufficient resources to use broadcast media and offer lower prices.

In recognition of some of these problems facing the company, management have developed a marketing plan which seeks growth of 15% per annum achieved by market penetration and in particular the attraction of new customers. It now needs a marketing communication programme to deliver the marketing strategy.

Annotations (margin notes):

- Scope here for quality improvements?
- Stakeholder analysis – no shareholders
- Large market
- Is s subject to fashion trends?
- Cost conscious customers
- % market share?
- How does CSK make sure its products are properly promoted?
- Old fashioned – how to attract younger customers?
- How easy/expensive will this be? Internal marketing likely to be needed to get staff support
- Biggest challenge faced by CSK
- CSK at a big disadvantage here
- Can this be achieved with current range?
- Make sure that you understand the terms 'marketing plan', 'marketing communications programme' and 'marketing strategy'

Refer to theories of customer buying behaviour

An area for development

CSK cannot afford to do this

Need to find best way to use available resources

How much effort is wasted having to do this vetting process?

Are these lists sufficiently targeted at likely customers, or are they too general?

This could also be done via the Internet

How can this be developed?

The competition, as Country Style Kitchens sees it, have huge resources which can be used to invest in promotional campaigns to drive awareness and action. For example, these companies have authentic websites, unlike Country Style Kitchens' website which is little more than an online brochure. Many of the large, national standardised companies can produce promotional literature in large production runs and are happy to ignore wastage. Using expert photography of pretend kitchens the quality and impact of the literature is high. Country Style Kitchens' smaller budgets dictate that photographs of real customers' kitchens are used, which seldom look perfect and can appear amateurish. It costs £5 to produce each of the CSK brochures, so the vetting of each request for literature is important to avoid those people merely intent on collecting brochures. A high conversion rate is necessary, and although 50% of quotations are converted into sales, this figure cannot afford to be lowered.

Unlikely to attract significant numbers of new customers

A risk area, with price based competition and competitor promotion

Unlikely to be eye catching

Current promotional activities centre on small space advertising in the supplements of weekend newspapers to generate leads, and the use of brochures distributed via direct mail using bought in lists. In addition to this, a small number of largely commission-based sales consultants work in the geographic areas not covered by the distributors. This sales team is supported by a few office staff, who advise clients by telephone should they have any product assembly related problems. They also liaise with the distributors. Sales promotions are used seasonally to promote sales and to reduce any excess stock. Word of mouth is important although little is undertaken to manage or develop it.

This could be improved using an 'FAQ' section on a website

Seems there is little scope for price increases

Do customers trust their advice?

Does this affect brand image?

Country Style Kitchens' customers want self-assembly country style kitchen units, but at mid to low range prices. Because they are bought direct there is little opportunity to inspect the quality before purchasing, so it is important that all customer contact is reassuring. For many price is a key issue and a high degree of trust is necessary in order that a sale is completed.

Performance risk

Might not be able to rely on using the Internet for some customers

PART A

Question 1

You are a newly qualified Marketing Executive, and as a friend of one of the Directors, have agreed to advise CSK on their marketing communications. Prepare a report in response to the following:

(a)   Evaluate the current and future roles of marketing communications at Country Style Kitchens.

What has happened to date?

What needs to happen now?

Define this. Why is it important?

(15 marks)

(b)   Consider the importance of perceived risk to end user customers of CSK, and in the light of this

knowledge make recommendations about how marketing communications might best be used.

Don't sit on the fence

Think about the effects, not necessarily whether it is currently feasible for CSK

(10 marks)

(c)   How might the development of Internet and digital-based technologies influence relationships with

the distributors?   **(5 marks)**

Not customers

(d)   Recommend and justify a suitable co-ordinated marketing communications mix.   **(20 marks)**

(Total = 50 marks)

Must be suitable for CSK's budget

Select the most suitable elements

BPP

LEARNING MEDIA

PART B – Answer TWO questions only

Question 2

> Keep your answer in this context

As a newly appointed Marketing Assistant at a branded food manufacturing organisation, your Marketing Manager has asked you to prepare a briefing document for her use at a forthcoming meeting with your current advertising agency. She is concerned that there is too much above-the-line activity and would like to see greater use of other promotional tools. Prepare your briefing document answering the following questions:

> Qualitative and quantitative

> What is this? Why might it not be appropriate?

(a) Using appropriate criteria, compare and contrast the effectiveness of the following two promotional tools: sales promotion and public relations.

> Key to the question

(10 marks)

> ust these, no more

(b) Explain how the tools of the promotional mix might be best used over the life of a product.

> Apply the product life cycle phases

(5 marks)

> This is a key syllabus term. Feel free to state the obvious, but it comes down to clear communication

(b) Recommend ways in which trust between clients and agencies might be improved.   **(10 marks)**

(Total = 25 marks)

Question 3

> Keep this context in your answer

You are a Media Planner/Buyer working for a large media independent in a country of your choice. One of your clients, a consumer electrical appliances manufacturer, operating across a number of international markets, has asked you to provide a short report explaining key media concepts and the media opportunities that exist to support its promotional activities over the next five years. Write a short report setting out your response to the following questions:

> Large resource

> Emphasis on the future

(a) Discuss the advantages and disadvantages of any two media that you would recommend to your client.

> Easy marks

> Select two that are appropriate to this company

(10 marks)

(b) Explain the media concepts reach, frequency and opportunities-to-see.   **(8 marks)**

(c) Describe the key factors that might influence the choice of media in (the client's) international markets.

> Might be limited in certain countries

(7 marks)

> Issues such as literacy, culture, education

(Total = 25 marks)

Question 4

A question on marketing channels

Car manufacturers have traditionally used dealer networks to distribute their cars to end-user consumers.

Context analysis

Recent changes to EU regulations and developments in information technology have encouraged

manufacturers to review their channels of distribution. For example, some have reduced the number of

Why?

independently owned franchises, and some have introduced a direct sales operation via the Internet. Both

How does this benefit both manufacturer and customer?

initiatives have caused some dealer-based conflict and unrest.

Why would dealers be unhappy with these developments?

As a Passenger Car Marketing Executive you have been requested to advise your colleagues about

particular aspects of channel marketing. In anticipation of the meeting, you should prepare notes with

Easy marks for definitions

regard to the following questions and the car market in a country of your choice.

Important instruction re the context of your answer

(a)   What is the meaning of 'independence' and 'interdependence' when referring to the relationships

between members of marketing channels?   **(5 marks)**

(b)   Appraise the main sources of conflict that can appear between members of marketing channels.

Which ones are the most significant?

(10 marks)

(c)   Explain how marketing communications in marketing channels (B2B) are fundamentally different to

those used in consumer markets.   **(10 marks)**

Characterised by different risks – very personal communications often used

(Total = 25 marks)

Question 5

> Answer the question from an agency perspective, not the client

The PEN company, an established manufacturer and distributor of personal electronic products, seeks an agency to help launch their new personal organiser. The advertising agency for whom you work has just been invited to pitch for PEN's international account following a successful credentials visit. As the potential Account Manager for this client you are required to organise a documentation pack that will be given to the client at the pitch. You are required to prepare the following:

(a)   An explanation of the role of the Account Manager and the nature and characteristics of the Client Brief.

> Define and apply

(15 marks)

(b)   An evaluation of the importance of adopting a relationship marketing approach with clients.

(10 marks)

(Total = 25 marks)

Answer plans

PART A

Question 1

(a)

Current role (5-6 marks)	*Future role* (9-10 marks)
Maintain market share	Grow market share by 15%
Maintain conversion rate	Increase conversion rate
Traditional media – small ads	Internet/website/word of mouth
Poor quality literature	Need to 'show off' the kitchens
Use of distributors	Increased use of direct selling?
Old processes	Coping with sophisticated competition
Budget constraints	Budget constraints
Little done to enhance brand	Promote brand more widely
Holding the customer's hand	Some customer contact to be maintained
Considerable staff loyalty	Use internal marketing to 'sell' changes

(b) Define perceived risk – why it is important and how each type of risk can be addressed? (for 2 marks each):

- Performance
- Financial
- Physical
- Social
- Ego

(c) How might CSK develop its Internet capability to help its relationships with distributors? Examples for 1 – 2 marks each:

- A website could facilitate online ordering of stock by distributors
- Instant information on CSK's latest products
- Relationships would be improved by instant communication
- Saves having to employ dedicated office telephone staff

Make the point (for another mark) that this would need investment and CSK may need to analyse whether it is worthwhile – although it is highly likely that the competition will have Internet capability, and distributors may even come to expect it as a standard way of doing business for the future.

(d) Present the list of available tools and make recommendations as to which is suitable, given what you have already concluded re CSK's objectives and its limited budget. Divide answer into direct and indirect channels (as a guide, aim for 10 marks per channel for a total of 20 marks). Which of these would be appropriate in each?

• Personal selling	Publicity	Exhibitions
• Advertising	Point of purchase	Events
• Sales promotion	Direct mail	E-marketing
• Sponsorship		

PART B

Question 2

(a) Directly compare sales promotion and public relations on measures such as (2 marks each):

    (i)   Cost
    (ii)   Awareness building
    (iii)   Conversion to sales
    (iv)   Suitability for the market/target customer
    (v)   Suitability for the chosen distribution channel

(Measures need to be relevant for a food manufacturer)

(b) Examine each stage of the product life cycle (PLC) – introduction, growth, maturity, decline – give example of relevant tool at each stage, and why, for 1-2 marks each:

Introduction	Intense TV campaign/direct mailings for awareness building
Growth	Continued press and TV coverage, over longer period. Stands at suitable events and shows
Maturity	Promotional coupons/POS to keep product in customer's mind
Decline	Decline in spend, maybe some limited in-store promotion

(c) Why trust is important – unlikely to have a long term relationship without it. Five ways, for 10 marks:

    (i)   Communicate via regular briefings and updates
    (ii)   Budget constraints made clear at outset
    (iii)   Staff relationships fostered
    (iv)   Share important market information/any concerns
    (v)   Appoint a team leader to co-ordinate

Question 3

(a) The chosen media must represent future opportunities that are appropriate for an electrical appliance manufacturer – it is likely to have large resources as it is international. 5 marks available for each one chosen, listing 2 or 3 advantages and disadvantages for each. Suggest use TV and Internet advertising.

(b) 2/3 marks each – define/explain/example (see Chapter 6) up to a total of 8 marks.

(c) Key factors are set out by the syllabus – media availability, culture, religion, education and literacy in local area – describe each one for 1 – 2 marks per factor up to a total of 7 marks (answer will consider the likely market for a consumer electrical appliances manufacturer, and therefore which factors will be more relevant than others).

Question 4

(a) *Independence* – maintain own role and do own job and fulfil objectives in the marketing channel

Interdependence – activities impinge on others in the marketing channel.

(Apply both of these to the car market, for 2 – 3 marks each)

(b) 4 main sources of conflict per Chapter 9. 2 or 3 marks for each one up to a total of 10 marks, again as relevant to the car market. Explain why such conflict exist – ie why the dealers are not happy with the changes.

(c) Set out key differences, for 10 marks. Explain each one, and why communications are affected. Possible inclusions:

(i) Buyer motivation
(ii) Usually use rational appeals
(iii) Technical/complex products
(iv) Seeking information and reassurance
(v) Use of personal selling/demonstrations

Question 5

(a) Role of account manager for 7 marks:

(i) 'Go between' for agency / client relationship
(ii) Leads the team
(iii) Co-ordinator
(iv) Communicator
(v) Takes overall responsibility for agency work
(vi) Seeks input from client to keep agency informed

Nature/characteristics of the client brief for 8 marks. Make it relevant to PEN, using the proforma from Chapter 12:

(i) Budget   Background to the brief
(ii) Key deadlines   Communications objectives
(iii) Company background   Target market and proposition
(iv) Business objectives

(b) Relationship marketing:

(i) What it is (definition) for 2 marks
(ii) How it applies in an advertising agency for 3 marks
(iii) Why it is important in today's advertising industry for 3 marks
(iv) Possible consequences of non-adoption of such an approach for 2 marks

List of Key Concepts, Index and References

A/S ratio, 85
Above-the-line promotion, 92
Adoption, 10
Adstock effect, 64
Advertising, 97
Affectivity, 19
Attitude, 19

Banner advertisement, 155
Belief, 19
Below-the-line promotion, 92
Brand, 121
Brief, 287

Cognition, 19
Commitment, 224
Conation, 19
Conflict, 223
Consumer buying behaviour, 13
Corporate strategy, 61
Culture, 14

Decision making unit, 32
Diffusion, 10
Direct marketing, 105
Disintermediation, 227

E-commerce, 111
Ethical issues, 38
Exchange, 5

Frequency, 150, 162
Full service agency, 280

Globalisation, 166

Independence, 216
Innovation, 9
Interdependence, 216
Internet marketing, 111

Key accounts, 128

Lifestyle, 15

Market segmentation, 68
Marketing positioning, 76
Media only, 280
Motivation, 16
Multinational corporations, 166

Noise, 7

Offline promotion, 155
Online promotion, 155
Opinion formers, 8
Opinion leaders, 8
Organisational (or industrial) buying, 30

Perception, 18
Personal selling, 98
Positioning, 76
Post testing, 182
PR, 102
Pre-testing, 182
Profile strategy, 129
Psychological positioning, 77
Public relations, 102
Pull strategy, 120
Push strategy, 128

Ratings, 150
Reach, 150, 162
Reintermediation, 227
Risk, 24

Sales promotion, 101
Share of voice, 85
Source credibility, 23
Stakeholder, 217
Successful brand, 121
Supply chain management, 216
Sustainability, 48

Target Marketing Process (TMP), 68
Trust, 224

Word of mouth, 23

References

The following are the key publications cited in the text.

Allen C, Kania D & Yaeckel B (2001) *One to One Web Marketing*. 2nd edition. New York: Wiley & Sons

Cowell, D (1989) *The Marketing of Services* Oxford: Butterworth Heinemann

De Pelsmacker P, Geuens M & Van den Bergh J (2000) *Marketing Communications: A European Perspective*. Harlow, Essex: FT Prentice Hall

Dib S, Simkin L, Price WM & Ferrell OC (2001) *Marketing: Concepts and Strategies*. Houghton Mifflin

Egan, J (2004) *Relationship Marketing: Exploring Relational Strategies in Marketing* (2nd edition). Harlow, Essex: Pearson Education

Fill, C (2002) *Marketing Communications: Contexts, Strategies and Applications*. Harlow, Essex: FT Prentice Hall

George, WR & Grönroos, C (1989) 'Developing customer-conscious employees at every level – internal marketing' in Congram, CA & Friedman, ML (eds) *Handbook of Services Marketing*. New York: AMACOM

Goften, K (1999) 'NSPCC aims to convert abuse anger into cash' in *Marketing*

Grönroos, C (2000) *Service Management and Marketing* Chichester: Wiley

Grunig, JE & Hunt TT (1983) *Managing Public Relations*. Thomson

Gummesson, E (2002) *Total Relationship Marketing*. (2nd edition). Oxford: Elsevier Butterworth-Heinemann

Hainsworth, B & Meng, M (1988) 'How corporations define issues management' in Public Relations Review 14 (4) pp 18-30

Handfield, RB & Nichols, EL (2002) *Supply Chain Re-design*. Englewood Cliffs, New Jersey: Prentice Hall

Heavens, A (2004) 'Call to Action', Times Online, business.timesonline.co.uk, February 12

Herzberg, FW (1966) *Work and the Nature of Man*. New York: Staples

Jespersen, B & Skjøtt-Larsen, T (2005) *Supply Chain Management in Theory and Practice*. Copenhagen: Copenhagen Business School Press.

Jobber, D (2007) *Principles and Practice of Marketing* (5th edition). Maidenhead, Berks: McGraw Hill Education

Johnson, G & Scholes, K *Exploring Corporate Strategy* (6th edition). Harlow, Essex: FT Prentice Hall

Keegan, WJ (2002) *Global Marketing Management*. Englewood Cliffs, New Jersey: Prentice Hall

Kotler, P (1991) *Principles of Marketing*. Englewood Cliffs, New Jersey: Prentice Hall

Kotler P (1997) 'Method for the millennium' in *Marketing Business* February pp 26-27

Kotler P, Armstrong G, Meggs D, Bradbury E & Grech J (1999) *Marketing: An Introduction*. Sydney: Prentice Hall Australia

Lancaster, G & Withey, F (2005) *Marketing Fundamentals*. Oxford: Elsevier Butterworth-Heinemann

Majaro, S (1993) *Creative Marketer*. Oxford: Butterworth Heinemann

Maslow, A (1954) *Motivation and Personality*. New York: Harper & Row

Mintzberg, H (1983) *Power in and Around Organisations*. New Jersey: Prentice Hall

Morgan, RM & Hunt, SD (1994) 'The commitment-trust theory of relationship marketing' in *Journal of Marketing*. 58(3) pp 20-38

Ohmae, K (1993) *The Mind of the Strategist.* Harmondsworth, Essex: Penguin

Peattie, K (1992) *Green Marketing.* Harlow, Essex: Longman

Peck HL, Payne A, Christopher M & Clark M (1999) *Relationship Marketing: Strategy & Implementation.* Oxford: Elsevier Butterworth-Heinemann

Peppers, D & Rogers, M (1997) *The One to One Future: Building Relationships One Customer at a Time.* New York: Doubleday

Reichheld, F (1996) *The Loyalty Effect.* Boston, Mass: Harvard Business School Press

Smithson, R (2005) 'Sowing the seeds for success', in AdNews (Australia), March

Swaminath, V & Reddy, SK (2000) 'Affinity Partnering' in Sheth, JN & Parvatiyar, A (eds) *Handbook of Relationship Marketing.* Thousand Oaks, California: Sage

Varey, RJ (2002) *Marketing Communications: Principles & Practice.* Abingdon, Oxford: Routledge

Webster, RMS & Wind, Y (1972). *Organisational Buying Behaviour.* Englewod Cliffs, New Jersey: Prentice Hall

Weitz, BA & Jap SD (2000) 'Relationship marketing and distribution channels', in Sheth, JN & Parvatiyar, A (eds) *Handbook of Relationship Marketing.* Thousand Oaks, CA: Sage

Wells, WD & Gubar, G (1966): 'Lifecycle concept in marketing research' in *Journal of Marketing Research,* November p355-363

Wilson, RMS & Gilligan, C (1997) *Strategic Marketing Management: Planning, Implementation and Control* Oxford: Butterworth Heinemann

Worthington, I & Britton, C (2006) *The Business Environment* (5th edition). Harlow, Essex: Pearson Education

REVIEW FORM & FREE PRIZE DRAW

All original review forms from the entire BPP range, completed with genuine comments, will be entered into one of two draws on 31 January 2009 and 30 July 2009. The names on the first four forms picked out on each occasion will be sent a cheque for £50.

Name: _____ Address: _____

_____

_____

How have you used this Text?
(Tick one box only)

☐ Self study (book only)

☐ On a course: college_____

☐ With BPP Home Study package

☐ Other _____

Why did you decide to purchase this Text?
(Tick one box only)

☐ Have used companion Kit

☐ Have used BPP Texts in the past

☐ Recommendation by friend/colleague

☐ Recommendation by a lecturer at college

☐ Saw advertising in journals

☐ Saw website

☐ Other _____

During the past six months do you recall seeing/receiving any of the following?
(Tick as many boxes as are relevant)

☐ Our advertisement in *Marketing Success*

☐ Our advertisement in *Marketing Business*

☐ Our brochure with a letter through the post

☐ Our brochure with *Marketing Business*

☐ Saw website

Which (if any) aspects of our advertising do you find useful?
(Tick as many boxes as are relevant)

☐ Prices and publication dates of new editions

☐ Information on product content

☐ Facility to order books off-the-page

☐ None of the above

Have you used the companion Practice & Revision Kit for this subject?   ☐ Yes   ☐ No

Your ratings, comments and suggestions would be appreciated on the following areas.

	Very useful	Useful	Not useful
Introductory section (How to use this text, study checklist, etc)	☐	☐	☐
Chapter introduction	☐	☐	☐
Syllabus coverage	☐	☐	☐
Action Programmes and Marketing at Work examples	☐	☐	☐
Chapter roundups	☐	☐	☐
Quick quizzes	☐	☐	☐
Illustrative questions	☐	☐	☐
Content of suggested answers	☐	☐	☐
Index	☐	☐	☐
Structure and presentation	☐	☐	☐

	Excellent	Good	Adequate	Poor
Overall opinion of this Text	☐	☐	☐	☐

Do you intend to continue using BPP Study Texts/Kits/Passcards?   ☐ Yes   ☐ No

Please note any further comments and suggestions/errors on the reverse of this page.

Please return to: Kellie Vincent, BPP Learning Media, FREEPOST, London, W12 8BR

REVIEW FORM & FREE PRIZE DRAW (continued)

Please note any further comments and suggestions/errors below.

FREE PRIZE DRAW RULES

1 Closing date for 31 January 2009 draw is 31 December 2008. Closing date for 31 July 2009 draw is 30 June 2009.

2 Restricted to entries with UK and Eire addresses only. BPP employees, their families and business associates are excluded.

3 No purchase necessary. Entry forms are available upon request from BPP Learning Media. No more than one entry per title, per person. Draw restricted to persons aged sixteen and over.

4 Winners will be notified by post and receive their cheques not later than six weeks after the relevant draw date. List of winners will be supplied on request.

5 The decision of the promoter in all matters is final and binding. No correspondence will be entered into.